SETTLING THE FRONTIER

JOSEPH P. ALESSI

SETTLING THE FRONTIER

URBAN DEVELOPMENT IN AMERICA'S BORDERLANDS, 1600–1830

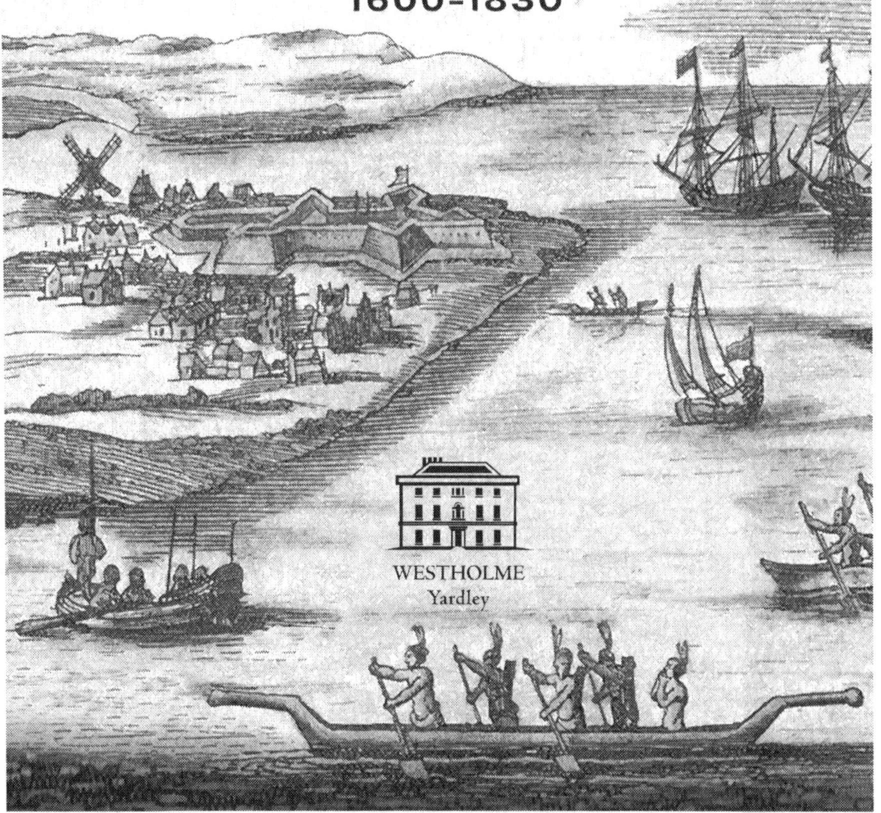

WESTHOLME
Yardley

Westholme Publishing, LLC
904 Edgewood Road
Yardley, Pennsylvania 19067
Visit our Web site at www.westholmepublishing.com

ISBN: 978-1-59416-333-3
Also available as an eBook.

Printed in the United States of America.

CONTENTS

PART 2. RESETTLING THE AMERICAN FRONTIER

MAPS

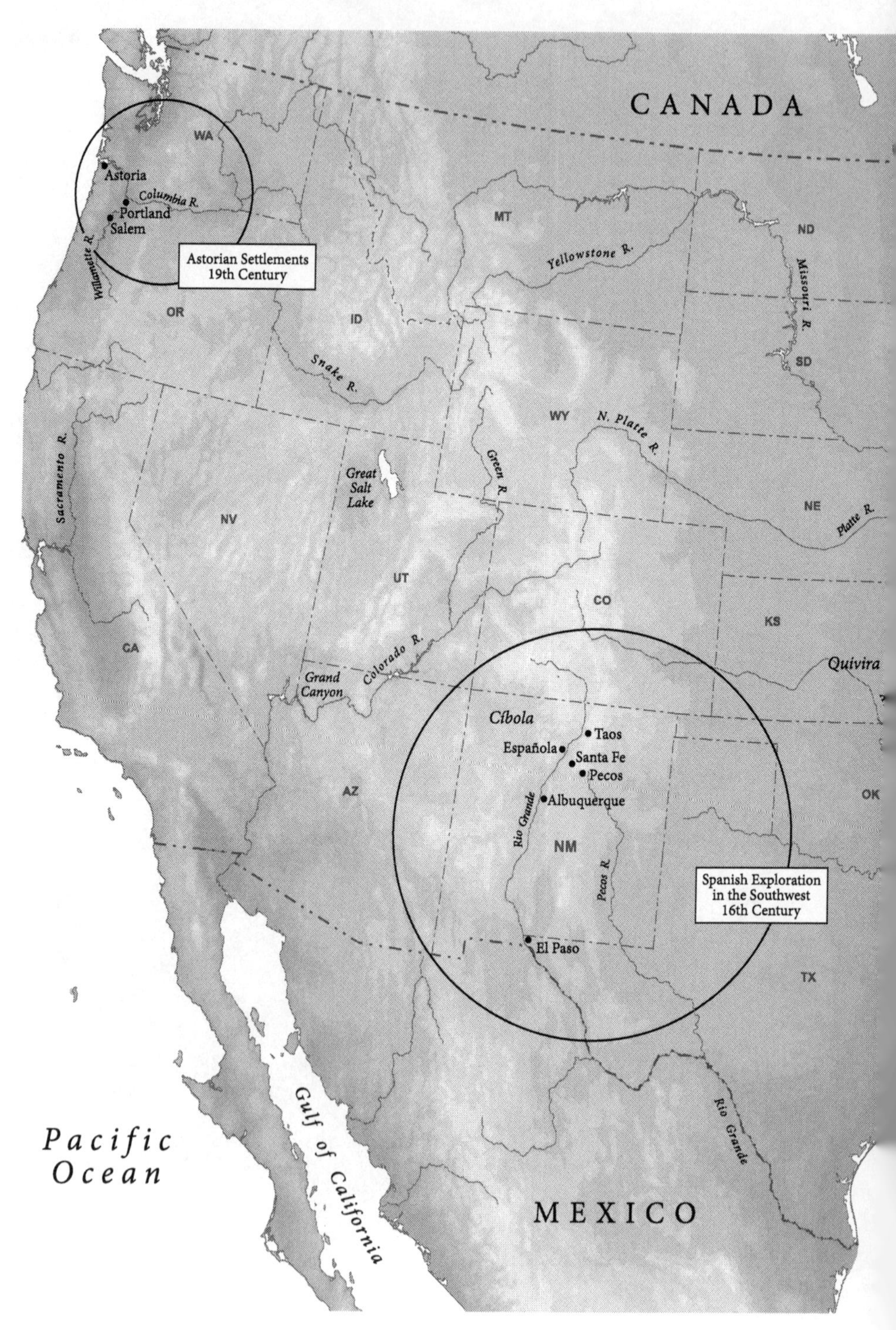

CANADA
WA
Astoria
Columbia R.
Portland
Salem
Willamette R.
Astorian Settlements
19th Century
OR
ID
MT
ND
Yellowstone R.
Missouri R.
SD
Snake R.
WY
N. Platte R.
Sacramento R.
Great
Salt
Lake
Green R.
NV
NE
Platte R.
UT
CO
KS
CA
Colorado R.
Quivira
Grand
Canyon
Cíbola
Taos
Española
Santa Fe
Pecos
AZ
Albuquerque
OK
Rio Grande
NM
Pecos R.
Spanish Exploration
in the Southwest
16th Century
El Paso
TX
Rio Grande
Gulf of California
Pacific
Ocean
MEXICO

N
E
S
W
Quebec
ME
Lake Superior
Lake Champlain
VT
NH
MN
Lake Huron
Lake Ontario
NY
WI
Mississippi R.
Schenectady
Fort Orange
MA
Lake Michigan
MI
Hudson R.
RI
Lake Erie
Hackensack
CT
New Netherland 17th Century
Poughkeepsie
IA
Fort Augusta
PA
New Amsterdam (New York)
Logstown
Ohio Valley 18th Century
Fort Duquesne (Fort Pitt)
NJ
Ohio R.
Monongahela R.
Fort Necessity
MD
IL
IN
OH
DE
Missouri R.
WV
VA
MO
Ohio R.
KY
Roanoke R.
NC
TN
AR
Tenn. R.
SC
Savannah R.
Mississippi R.
AL
MS
GA
Alabama R.
Atlantic Ocean
LA
FL
Gulf of Mexico
0
100
200
300
400
500
MILES

Introduction

The Urban Frontier Revisited

"NEW" IS THE TREND IN NEARLY EVERY FACET OF LIFE TODAY—NEW technology, new style, new ideas, and new history, for example. The incessant quest for fresh interpretations and improvements often leads many to ignore the old, yet it is in the old that one may find the path to the new. Thus, this study examines the work of past scholars, many of whom have long passed from this world, to create a "new" perspective of the role Native Americans played in the Euroamerican development of the present-day United States of America.

Over the past forty years, historians have depicted Indians in a more positive light. Unlike their predecessors, who portrayed Indian resistance through violence and warfare, historians now present another form of resistance through accommodation and the preservation of cultural institutions.[1] No longer viewed as being the pawns of colonial empires, Indians are described by scholars as shrewd politicians who successfully negotiated for the preservation of their culture. Yet all Indian scholars must concede that Indians lost the struggle to retain their traditional ways and lands regardless of how they attempted to resist. Hence, Indian history remains the story of an indigenous people's fight against the onslaught of European and American cultures.

Despite being first published in 1991, Richard White's work *The Middle Ground: Indians, Empires, and Republics in the Great Lakes Region, 1650–1815* exemplifies the newer Indian history. Likening the chronicle of Indian-Euroamerican relations to a narrative that resembled the sea pounding on a rock, historians, White noted, portrayed the Euroamericans as the sea that either completely dissolved or eroded the rock, which was the Indians. Recognizing this as being a simple and "linear narrative" of what really transpired, White sought to, and successfully did, explain Indian-Euroamerican relations as a creative process of accommodation where the two broadly defined groups first "met and regarded each other as alien" but, over two centuries, "constructed a common, mutually comprehensible world . . . [where] peoples adjust[ed] their differences" and created a middle ground, a "place in between cultures, peoples . . . empires, and the nonstate world of villages." Though often a place of turbulent relationships that erupted into violence, the middle ground developed because of the Euroamericans' inability to dictate to or ignore the Indians. Euroamericans "needed Indians as allies, as partners in exchange, as sexual partners, as friendly neighbors." Yet, despite their initial need, Euroamericans, primarily through their weight in numbers, eventually possessed the ability and power to dismantle the middle ground and to re-create the Indians as "alien, as exotic, as other." And once the middle ground dissolved, the importance of Indians "faded."[2]

While White and other scholars cast Indians in a more impressive and positive light, few historians attempted to explain how Indians influenced or played a larger role in the development of America. In 1997, historian Donald Fixico raised this issue in *Rethinking American Indian History*, a work comprising seven essays from two conferences held in 1994 and 1995 that focused on the study of North American Indians. The conferences resulted from concerns of scholars about the enormous complexity of Indian life and the various cultures and languages of the more than five hundred Indian nations that "challenged" their interpretations. This complexity, Fixico explained, caused scholars dealing with the subject to rethink their work, theories, and methodologies.[3] From this collection of articles, Fixico deduced that Indian history is following a trend that focuses heavily on cultural and ethnographic studies, approaches that some historians, such as Eugene Genovese, argue fail to answer the more weighty issues of American history.[4] While it is not the intention of Genovese and his supporters to convince Indian historians to abandon their cultural and ethnographic research, it is their summation that scholars using these new approaches fail at best and refuse at worst to attempt to answer the more profound questions of history.[5] Despite this revelation more than twenty years ago, Genovese's call remains virtually unaddressed.

In an attempt to answer the weightier question of how Indians influenced the development of America, this study examines the role Indians played in the development of the American frontier. Though all scholars must concede that Indians eventually succumbed to the pressures of Euroamerican settlement, the American Indian significantly contributed to the growth and development of North America. As active participants in a multitude of middle grounds that expanded beyond time, geographical space, and groups, Indians laid the very foundation for America's frontier development by actively and intentionally facilitating the Euroamerican establishment of frontier settlements. Euroamericans needed Indians as "friendly neighbors" because they lacked the resources, protection, companionship, and knowledge needed to survive the rigors of North America's various frontier environments. On the frontier, Indian settlements existed as the hubs for logistical resources, military support, companionship, and diplomacy that Euroamericans needed to survive. Consequently, until the political dynamics of the various frontier regions changed and made Indian assistance unnecessary, Euroamerican settlement patterns mirrored Indian settlement patterns on the frontier, and Euroamerican settlers relied on and negotiated for Indian diplomatic, military, informational, and logistical support to survive and to establish permanent settlements. With the aid of Indians, Euroamericans battled starvation, fought off hostile neighbors, expanded their empires, created economically viable markets, and successfully planted the seeds of America's first frontier settlements at places like Fort Pitt, Fort Orange, Santa Fe, Fort Astoria, and New Amsterdam. Once established, these early frontier posts enabled Euroamericans to ignore the dynamics of middle ground relationships by supplanting Indian settlements as the resource and political centers for America's frontier development. However, before they faded from the scene, Indians left behind North America's first towns, the spearheads for the subsequent colonization and development of the continent.

To advance this thesis, this work is divided into two parts and uses a model of frontier development as an analytical framework to examine the establishment of five American towns. The areas and groups studied are the Spanish and Pecos Indian development of Santa Fe in sixteenth- and seventeenth-century New Mexico; the Mohawk, Mahican, and Dutch development of Fort Orange (Albany) and New Amsterdam (New York City) in the seventeenth-century Hudson River Valley; the Ohio Indians (located primarily at Logstown and Kuskuski), French, and English development of Fort Pitt (Pittsburgh) in the eighteenth-century Ohio Valley; and the Chinook (mainly from Comcommoley), American, and English development of Forts Astoria and Vancouver (Portland) in nineteenth-century Oregon. The model used in this study expands and synthesizes Richard C. Wade's work *The Urban Frontier*, Kenneth Lewis's *The American Frontier*, Richard White's *The Middle Ground*, and Francis Jennings's *The Invasion of America* and offers a six-stage model of frontier development that illustrates how Indians, regardless of place, time, or group, assisted Euroamericans in establishing America's first towns.

The conceptual basis of this work is derived from Wade's 1959 publication *The Urban Frontier* that challenged Frederick Jackson Turner's romantic portrayal of the steadily advancing wave of the lone frontiersman, trader, and pioneer "striking" his way "into the woods with his family . . . a horse, cow and one or two breeders of swine" to become "the founder of a new country."[6] In contrast, Wade introduced the idea that urban settlements existed on the frontier prior to the migration of pioneer farmers and were therefore the spearheads in the development of the frontier.[7] Wade studied five towns west of the Appalachian Mountains—Pittsburgh, Saint Louis, Cincinnati, Louisville, and Lexington—and showed how these settlements provided the economic resources and physical security essential for homesteaders to settle and survive on the frontier. Long before the frontier fell to the pioneer's plow, Wade noted that towns existed as "centers of economic activity for the whole region, the focuses of cultural life . . . the scenes of great social change . . . and gave a stimulus and sophistication to a young, raw society." Yet, despite its contribution to the field of history, Wade's work offered no process or model to explain frontier development and neglected to consider the role that Indians played in the development of the frontier. As Wade indicated, the frontier existed as nothing more than the "mere haunt of Indian and animal" prior to Euroamerican settlement.[8] Towns like Pittsburgh simply sprang up in the wilderness through the trials, tribulations, and triumphs of Euroamericans.

Nearly twenty-five years after Wade produced his study, Lewis, in his work *The American Frontier*, generated the base model for this manuscript. Building on Wade's work, Lewis identified a process of Euroamerican frontier development that occurred in five stages beginning with the establishment of primary settlements such as trading posts like Fort Orange (Albany) in 1624 and ending with the creation of secondary settlements like Schenectady, New York, in 1662. Primary settlement areas, Lewis explained, consisted of those communities established at the de facto limit of a state's authority, while secondary settlement areas consisted of those regions passed over during initial expansion and settled later. Lewis noted that in most instances, primary development areas initially consisted of economically oriented activity settlements such as trading posts that arose in frontier areas to extract specialized resources such as furs as part of the world economy.[9]

Lewis divided primary frontiers into six subtypes: trading, ranching, exploitative plantations, transportation, military, and industrial. While he offered a more explanatory model of frontier development, Lewis, like Wade, believed that Indians contributed little to the development of the American frontier and reduced them to insignificant members of the frontier ecology. However, "because trade involved a reciprocal arrangement," Lewis claimed that "resident aboriginal groups . . . may be included as part of the . . . trading frontier."[10] In the case of the North American fur trade, Lewis indicated that traders primarily involved themselves in an interaction with the frontier environment. According to Lewis, trading frontiers involved forms of settlement oriented toward the task of extracting a marketable product from the environment and required only the traders and their stock, a transportation system, and a marketable product native to the trade region. As long as the extractable commodity existed, the trading frontier continued to expand and develop the area by encouraging both Euroamerican and Indian settlement of the region.[11] By viewing them and the settlement process in this fashion, Lewis disregarded Indians as active contributors to the development of the frontier and reduced them to a mere economic factor that contributed equally with several other elements in the development of the trade frontier.

Unlike Lewis's other primary frontier settlements, military and transportation frontiers developed as specialized activity areas that arose to meet the particular needs of the intrusive Euroamerican society: protection, political control, communication, and travel. While they were not the primary motives for the colonization process, military activities and transportation systems supported the expansion efforts of the trading, ranching, and exploitative plantation frontiers they accompanied. Military facilities, placed in locations with strategic value such as trading posts, transportation routes, lakes, and the confluence of rivers, Lewis noted, overlapped with the other types of primary settlements. In most instances, Euroamericans built nonmilitary settlements adjacent to forts, camps, and other sites of frontier military activity. More importantly, however, Lewis claimed that "forts established in areas that later became insular frontiers were often the nuclei of . . . settlements that retained the names of their military predecessors."

While military activities provided primary frontiers with protection and political control over the region, transportation frontiers provided Euroamericans with a means to travel and communicate. Governments established settlements to facilitate the flow of information, goods, and people into and out of frontier areas they claimed. Since the routes of travel were usually linear in form, Euroamericans often situated transportation settlements along roads, rivers, or trails. Unlike with other forms of frontier settlement, governments or interest groups initiated the development of military and transportation settlements and not individual settlers. Once established, however, primary settlements acted as Wade's urban spearheads and provided the resources necessary for permanent secondary farming communities to be built.[12]

Though he offers more detail on frontier settlement, Lewis, like Wade, tells only half the story. His shortfall comes with his failure to answer or pose several questions in regard to frontier settlement, such as: Where did the traders go, and why did they go there? Who established the routes of travel for the early traders? Why did traders and military personnel build trading posts, stockades, and forts in certain areas? Why were soldiers and forts needed? And where did Euroamerican and American settlements emerge? Ironically, the people Lewis and Wade overlooked as settlers and developers of the frontier provided a destination for traders and a means to efficiently exploit many of the frontier's resources, and they significantly influenced Euroamerican and American frontier settlement. Lewis overlooked the fact that Indians had much to gain with the presence of Euroamericans at their doorsteps. Indians did not merely settle for beads and baubles but traded for significant items that augmented their elaborate gift economies and enabled them to maintain the stratification of their societies. Additionally, Indians allied themselves with Euroamericans to control the middle ground political dynamics of the various frontier regions they occupied. While his model offers a viable way to examine frontier development, Lewis recognized only the Euroamerican elements required to establish primary settlements and failed to consider the role of Indians in the process.

To correct this inaccurate narrative of frontier development, Wade and Lewis's Eurocentric view of frontier settlement must be infused with the new scholarship depicting the frontier as a multidimensional meeting place of peoples in which geographic and cultural borders were not clearly defined, a place where "interaction of diverse peoples . . . created new cultural forms."[13] No longer viewed as the pounding wave of civilizing pioneers progressing through the unoccupied wilderness in a never-ending file of trader, trapper, rancher, and farmer, the frontier zones were areas of diverse Indian and Euroamerican groups that interacted with one another through a process of accommodation that brought a change to each group's political, economic, social, cultural, and religious institutions. Areas where the land, Jennings wrote, "was more like a widow than a virgin" and where "Europeans did not find a wilderness . . . [but] involuntarily . . . made one." Places such as "Jamestown, Plymouth, Salem, Boston, Providence, New Amsterdam, [and] Philadelphia... grew upon sites previously occupied by Indian communities."[14] Places where, Turner himself noted, "the Indian trade pioneered the way to civilization . . . [and] . . . the trading posts . . . were on the sites of

Indian villages."[15] Hence, "the so-called settlement of America," as Jennings so aptly put it, "was a resettlement, a reoccupation," or more accurately, a settlement near, Indian communities.[16] Therefore, the spearheads of Wade and Lewis's urban frontiers were Indian and not Euroamerican settlements.

By synthesizing Lewis's, Wade's, Jennings's, and White's works, this study introduces a six- rather than a five-stage process that explains the role that Indians and their settlements played in the development of the American frontier. Similar to Wade's spearheads, Indian settlements provided Euroamerican and Indian migrants with the security and resources necessary to settle and economically exploit the frontier. This first stage of frontier development involved Indians only and dealt primarily with their development of a settled frontier environment. Stage two began with Euroamericans' efforts to make inroads into the frontier to exploit its resources with the assistance of Indian patrons and ended only when they successfully established primary settlements in, around, or adjacent to Indian communities that became the foci of frontier settlement activity. The next stage began when Euroamerican settlers migrated to the established settlements and began building secondary farming communities, bringing them in direct competition with their Indian neighbors for possession and use of the land. Eventually, the Euroamerican population growth outpaced that of the Indian community, forcing the latter to either leave their land and migrate west, actively and passively resist their former friends and allies, or remain in the area as a marginalized group, leaving the region to be settled and developed primarily by Euroamericans. From these early frontier settlements, towns grew and initiated the further development and settlement of the region. Hence, the process of frontier development began with Indian settlements acting as the foci of frontier development and ended with the emergence of frontier towns that hastened the settlement of America. Because various discussions concerning the Euroamerican development of Santa Fe, Albany, New York, Pittsburgh, and Portland have been completed by previous scholars, this study focuses on the first two stages of the settlement process to better illustrate how Indians, based out of their settlements, first helped Euroamericans to survive the rigors of the frontier and then aided them with their establishment of permanent posts.

Using this analytical model, the first part of this work, "The Frontier's First Settlements," focuses on the initial stage of frontier development by describing the cultural features that existed in Indian frontier settlements. Amending Wade's and Lewis's shortfalls, part 1 utilizes an interdisciplinary approach drawing on primary sources and the secondary works of historians, anthropologists, and sociologists to show how various Indian groups developed and settled the frontier. Though many in-depth studies exist on North American Indians, this work offers a broader way of viewing Indians by placing them within a sociological framework of civilizations that classifies them as being preindustrial peoples who built settlements with complex political, economic, and social institutions that were more developed than, or on par with, the early settlements of their Euroamerican counterparts in North America. Part 1 shows that in place of a widowed, savage, and untamed American wilderness that scholars portrayed, Indians created vibrant and dynamic settlements on the American frontier that possessed the economic, political, military, and subsistence technology capable of supporting and inspiring Euroamerican settlement.

Part 2, "Resettling the American Frontier," focuses on stage two of the model and presents the four studies that describe the interaction between Indians and Euroamericans on the frontier that resulted in the establishment of Euroamerican frontier settlements. It illustrates how Indian subsistence kept Euroamericans from starving during their first few years on the frontier, as well as how Indian military, political, and economic objectives motivated Euroamericans to venture to the frontier, aided them with the establishment and protection of their frontier posts, and made many of their colonial enterprises economically feasible. Moreover, part 2 exposes the fragility of Euroamericans on the frontier without Indian assistance.

To view things with an eighteenth-century perspective, several terms used in this work need to be more clearly defined. First, due to the multicultural nature of this study, the way it refers to broader ethnic and political groups needs explaining. Though this is a politically charged issue among some groups, for literary purposes only, this work uses the terms *Indians*, *North American Indians*, and specific group or regional names such as *Mohawk*, *Chinook*, *Pecos*, and *Ohio Indians* to represent America's first peoples in lieu of the more cumbersome phrase *Native Americans*. Likewise, this work uses terms like *Euroamerican*, *Dutch*, *Spanish*, *French*, *American*, and *English* to represent non-Indian groups.

Second, due primarily to the lack of census data, contemporary writers and later historians failed to establish an accepted numerical or cultural determinant to classify the size and type of settlements built in North America during the colonial period. In other words, they never established that a settlement with *x* number of individuals is a hamlet while a settlement with *y* number of individuals is a town, or a settlement with a local government is a city while a settlement without an established system of laws is a village. In 1900, Henry Gannett, director of the United States Census, established the only criteria to determine if a settlement qualified as an urban area. According to Gannett and the Census Bureau, "the Census generally regards as the urban element that portion of the population living in cities of 8,000 inhabitants or more."[17] At the time of the first census in 1790, only five out of the nearly two thousand settlements regarded as towns in North America contained populations of over eight thousand inhabitants.[18] Rather, the majority of colonial towns contained populations of less than two thousand inhabitants.[19] For the purposes of this study, the term *urban* refers to an area of the frontier dotted with fixed settlements where a network of sophisticated and firmly established political, economic, social, and military relationships existed. Therefore, this work uses the term *settlement*, or the label given by contemporary observers when dealing with the various Indian "towns" being discussed, instead of using adjectives such as *urban*.

Finally, similar to the term *urban*, the word *frontier* means different things to different people. As defined by *Webster's Dictionary*, a frontier is a border of a country or an undeveloped area of a country.[20] According to Frederick Jackson Turner, "the frontier is the outer edge of the wave—the meeting point between savagery and civilization."[21] More specifically, Turner noted that the American frontier is the region that lies at the hither edge of free land, while European frontiers are fortified boundary lines running through dense populations.[22] In most instances, when the term *frontier* is applied to the American West, Turner's definition of the meeting point between "savagery" and "civilization" is usually the assumed or implied meaning. However, as Jennings indicated, the American landscape was not devoid of civilization. In reality, North America consisted of a variety of Indian peoples who were as diverse and socially advanced as the nations of Europe. The outer edge of Turner's frontier existed as a meeting point between two civilizations, or as the historian Jack D. Forbes more poignantly stated, "the frontier, in the sociopolitical sense, is a region where two or more ethnic groups or nationalities enter into relations or confront each other . . . the very essence of a frontier is the interaction of two or more people."[23] "The concept frontier," Forbes noted, "refers to a meeting point where two forces come up against each other . . . a contact point" where the boundary line "is seldom clear-cut."[24] For the purpose of this work, the term *frontier* does not refer to an uncivilized or savage region but to a borderline, the meeting point between Euroamericans and Indians.

In his work *It's Your Misfortune and None of My Own,* Richard White noted that "from the villages of Texas and New Mexico . . . [to] the villages of the Missouri, it [is] impossible not to find a social world in which Indians did not play intimate and essential roles. Indians might often be abused and oppressed, but Indians mattered."[25] The goal of this study is twofold. First and foremost, by explaining how Indians helped Euroamericans successfully plant primary settlements in hostile frontier environments, this manuscript poses and answers a weightier question of American history focused on showing how Indians "mattered." Second, by showing how Indians contributed to the Euroamerican development of the frontier, this work recasts Indians in yet an even newer light, not as the stereotypical victims, barriers, and resisters, whether active or passive, to Euroamerican progress, or as the "unique others," but as contributors to the growth and development of America.

PART 1

The Frontier's First Settlements

"THE FIRST WHITE VISITORS," historian Roderick Nash suggested, "regarded wilderness as a moral and physical wasteland fit only for conquest and fructification in the name of progress, civilization, and Christianity."[1] Unfortunately for Indians, the Euroamerican image of the part of the North American continent that would become the United States as being a wilderness remains an enduring constant throughout America's history. In reality, the first traces of human civilization on the continent proved to be those of Indians. As early as the twelfth century, Indians created large and small settlements that housed complex societies with sophisticated subsistence technologies, political institutions, and economic systems that were as well developed as those of Euroamericans of the seventeenth, eighteenth, and early nineteenth centuries.[2] Indian settlements existed as the centers of activity in North America and functioned as the hubs of cultural contact and exchange. In this capacity, Indian settlements played host to virtually all of the major events and decisions that took place in America's early development and provided the resources and security Euroamericans needed to settle the frontier.

To correct this inaccurate image of the American landscape at the time of European contact, the first part of this work takes a perspective that faces outward from Indian country and looks at human societies through a generic lens. In lieu of automatically assuming Euroamericans possessed civilizations superior to various Indian groups, the first three chapters of this study examine the complexity of the Pecos, Mohawk, Ohio Indian, and Chinook political and economic systems by using sociologist Gideon Sjoberg's morphological hierarchy of societies as a tool of comparison to illustrate how America's landscape was neither a wild nor widowed land as scholars like Francis Jennings and others suggest, but a country inhabited by preindustrial societies with the resources and cultural institutions capable of supporting Euroamerican settlement.[3]

A HIERARCHY OF CIVILIZATION

In his work *The Preindustrial City*, Sjoberg developed a framework to categorize and compare the sophistication of human societies that existed prior to the Industrial Revolution. In this, perhaps his most influential and controversial work, Sjoberg intended to create a constructed type of preindustrial city that generalized the nature of the cultural institutions that developed within such communities.[4] Sjoberg recognized that differences existed between groups, noting that "preindustrial societies everywhere display strikingly similar," not identical, "social and ecological structures . . . certainly in basic form."[5] The value of Sjoberg's work lies not in the development of a constructed type of nonindustrial city but in his creation of a framework to compare societies.

Sjoberg submitted that three types of societies existed in the world: folk, preindustrial, and industrial. Although many forces influenced the development of human societies, technology, Sjoberg suggested, associated with distinctive types of social structures, was the key independent variable for differentiating between the three.[6] He explained that technology consisted of three basic elements: sources of energy, tools, and the intelligence necessary to utilize and create resources and instruments.[7] Although he omitted North American Indians from his study, Sjoberg's treatment of preindustrial societies allows scholars to compare divergent civilizations.

Sjoberg explained that folk societies were primarily small, homogeneous, self-sufficient, isolated, preliterate groups of people with a low degree of technology who lacked a staple food surplus. In these societies, the people limited themselves primarily to subsistence-oriented activities. Although a modicum of labor specialization existed, work varied little between women and men. Furthermore, the lack of a division of labor inhibited the development of a tiered society or of substantial technological innovations that denoted more-advanced civilizations.[8] Examples of these societies exist today in the remote forests of South America and New Guinea. The Siriono of eastern Bolivia provide an excellent example of a folk society where the men and women are engaged in the fundamental duties of the society: food collection, cooking, and basket making.[9]

Unlike folk societies, preindustrial groups developed an agricultural technology that produced sufficient food surpluses for a large nonagricultural population, enabling the creation of complex social, political, economic, and cultural institutions. "In all instances," Sjoberg noted, "this technology includes the cultivation of grains . . . embraces (except in ancient Meso-America) animal husbandry, large-scale irrigation works, the plow, metallurgy, the wheel, and . . . is almost entirely dependent upon animate, i.e., human and animal, sources of energy."[10] As a result of an advanced subsistence technology, preindustrial peoples developed tiered societies based on age, sex, labor, and occupation; consolidated their populations in urban settlements that existed as part of the environment and were void of the concept of city limits; and developed well-structured political and economic systems.[11]

Industrial societies, Sjoberg explained, utilize inanimate sources of energy such as electricity, steam, nuclear fission; a complex set of tools; and specialized scientific know-how in the production of goods and services. Moreover, the populations of these societies reside primarily in large, well-developed settlements with complex infrastructures that possess highly fluid class systems and diffused social-power structures.[12]

While at first glance North American Indians fail to meet all the criteria Sjoberg established for preindustrial societies, his treatment of ancient Mesoamerica lends proof that many North American Indian groups existed as preindustrial societies. According to Sjoberg, in addition to possessing the three elements of technology, a society's settlements needed to contain further prerequisites to be considered preindustrial. These prerequisites consisted of a favorable ecological base, advanced forms of technology, and a complex social organization. Sjoberg noted that although they lacked some of the technological advances found in most preindustrial societies, Mesoamericans cultivated a superior crop that did not demand large-scale irrigation, metal tools, or domesticated animals for its cultivation.[13] Consequently, due to a superior form of subsistence, maize, that required little effort to cultivate, Mesoamericans possessed the time and food surplus needed to create settlements and social institutions complex enough to be considered preindustrial.

Though North American Indians lacked several features present in preindustrial societies, the Pecos, Mohawk, Ohio Indians, and Chinook created complex social institutions and possessed efficient forms of subsistence that enabled them to develop into preindustrial societies. Part 1 of this book consists of three chapters that describe those forms of subsistence, economic structures, and political systems. While no one chapter deals solely with the structure and form of Indian societies, each chapter explains how subsistence, economics, and politics shaped and were influenced by social relations, gender roles, and cultural belief systems. By creating these preindustrial institutions and the subsistence technology to support and develop them, the Pecos, Mohawk, Ohio Indians, and Chinook built some of America's earliest settlements. These Indian peoples, and many others like them, manicured the environment to meet their subsistence needs; created the political boundaries that determined the limits, procedures, and forums for frontier diplomacy; and established the framework and conditions for economic exchange and societal relations in North America. Thus, Euroamericans found neither a wilderness nor a widowed land when they arrived but a preindustrial frontier with clear political boundaries dotted with settlements inhabited with the people, resources, and societal structures capable of supporting their exploration and colonization of North America.

CHAPTER 1

American Indian Subsistence Technologies

THE ROMANTIC IMAGE OF THE LONE PIONEER TRAVERSING THE PEAKS of America's mountains and breaking the brush to unlock the secrets and resources of the land is an image embedded in the American mind. However, these pioneers did not make their romantic journey without facing the many physical hazards of the frontier. For many Euroamericans, starvation was the most significant obstacle they faced. Whether they came from Europe, New Spain, the English colonies, or the Eastern Seaboard of the United States, the logistical supply lines that connected Euroamerican settlers to their host nations stretched for hundreds, and sometimes thousands, of miles when they attempted to settle the frontier. What they brought with them in the hulls of their ships, in their wagons, and on the backs of their pack animals were the only resources they had to settle the frontier. While the continent teemed with foodstuffs and building materials, Euroamericans lacked the knowledge, tools, technologies, and skills required to initially benefit from them. Besieged by such conditions, the first settlers occupied nearly all their time trying to fulfill their basic needs of food, shelter, and clothing—the physical things they needed to simply survive. Despite their best efforts and planning, Euroamerican settlers more often than not found themselves on the brink of starvation. Fortunately for them, they found two things on the frontier that relieved their logistical problems: the Indians and their settlements.

Indian settlements existed as the resource centers that produced the surplus foodstuffs necessary for groups like the Pecos, Mohawk, Ohio Indians, and Chinook to develop into preindustrial societies and to support the Euroamerican settlement of the North American frontier between the late sixteenth and mid-nineteenth centuries. To become preindustrial societies, Indians needed to possess an efficient form of subsistence technology capable of producing the surplus foodstuffs necessary to support and influence their construction of communal settlements, the stratification of their societies, and their creation of sophisticated social, economic, and political systems.[1] Thus, the key feature, that is, the cornerstone, of North American Indian preindustrial development and Euroamerican frontier settlement was an efficient form of subsistence technology that influenced the development of Indian political and economic systems as well as Euroamerican frontier settlement.

DESERT FARMERS: THE PECOS

Over the course of six hundred years, the Pecos developed a highly efficient subsistence system that enabled them to create a settlement that numbered over two thousand inhabitants and generated enough surplus foodstuffs in one year to support its population for three.[2] As a result of this efficient technology, the Pecos stratified their settlement along age and gender lines, developed sophisticated economic and political systems, and slowly evolved into a complex and well-established preindustrial society. In so doing, Pecos and neighboring pueblos existed as the logistical oases for the Spanish settlement of New Mexico between the sixteenth and seventeenth centuries.

Located on a plateau seven thousand feet above sea level and averaging only fifteen inches of rainfall each year, the Pecos designed a subsistence technology to counter the effects of the arid New Mexico environment.[3] While the subsistence system they used involved fishing, hunting, and gathering, farming corn, squash, and beans existed as the bedrock of the Pecos diet. Challenged by the shortened growing seasons that were caused by the high altitude they lived in, the Pecos farmed only from May to August. Though their planting season was short, Pecos farmers produced enough food from a single year's crop to support their settlement for several years. To produce these high yields, the Pecos planted several fields throughout the spring and designed a system of farming that combined irrigation and lowland planting to compensate for the unpredictability and harshness of the New Mexico environment. The success of their system rested on their ability to maximize the use of all the available land around their pueblo. To do this, they planted their fields in essentially two places, the high mesas and the low river valleys. On the mesas, the Pecos irrigated some of their fields by simply digging and flooding ditches adjacent to them.[4] However, due to water shortages, the Pecos lacked the ability to irrigate all their fields, which forced them to leave some of their success up to the whims of nature.[5] In the lowlands, the farmers planted fields in the sandy washes of the rivers and relied on flash floods and rainfall to irrigate these crops.[6] The Pecos developed such an efficient system of farming that "one fanega [the equivalent of a bushel-and-a-half, or 96 pounds], of . . . seed produced thirty-five to forty fanegas," essentially four thousand pounds, of corn.[7] Blessed with hundreds of acres of flat land for farming, the Pecos could produce over three hundred thousand pounds of corn annually.[8]

The Pecos divided their farming duties according to gender and age. However, unlike many Indian societies, the men, and not the women, performed the majority of tasks associated with farming. While the men and boys performed the farming duties, the women and girls focused their attention on preparing the food for storage and consumption. Perhaps the most important aspect of farming fell on the male leader of the Pecos, who had to choose the locations and times for planting. If the Pecos sowed the crops too soon, or late, and placed them in poor locations, the survival of the entire settlement might be in question.[9] Because of this division of labor, the Pecos created a stratified society where men dominated the political, economic, and religious institutions and women significantly influenced all of the social relations behind these cultural organizations.

While corn existed as the staple of their subsistence cycle, the Pecos augmented their diet with fish, meat, and wild plants. Located near several streams and rivers, the Pecos collected an assortment of herbs and grasses, caught a "variety of fish such as bagre, eel, and trout . . . [and] hunted venison, hare, rabbits, and sheep." When they conducted a collective hunt, the person leading the excursion went "through the pueblo, calling like a town crier" acquiring able-bodied men to accompany him. Following the hunt, the men distributed the meat equally, and those who actually killed the game kept the animal's hide.[10] Coupled with the food they hunted, grew, caught, and gathered, the Pecos traded for buffalo and turkey with their Pueblo and Plains Indian neighbors. Combined, this highly efficient subsistence cycle enabled the Pecos to produce enough foodstuffs in a single year to develop the political, social, and cultural features found in preindustrial societies.

Because of the unforgiving and unpredictable nature of New Mexico's environment, the Pecos developed a system of storage that enabled them to keep food for over three years. The Pecos stored unused corn, as well as other items such as beans and wheat, in their houses. When the Spaniards first encountered the Pecos, they marveled at the quantity of the foodstuffs stored. "There were those who maintained that the total must amount to more than thirty thousand fanegas," the explorer Gaspar Castaño de Sosa wrote, "since each house had two or three rooms full of it, all excellent quality . . . [along with] a good supply of beans . . . herbs, chili, and calabashes."[11] With this excess food on hand, the Pecos could survive the cycles of drought that routinely hit the southwestern desert, and when the Spanish arrived in New Mexico in 1598, it was this surplus stock of corn that they used to avoid starving to death during the first few years of their occupation.[12]

As fate would have it, the gold that the Spanish found when they arrived in New Mexico was not in the form of rock or dust as they had hoped, but in the shape of an ear of corn. Because of the existence of Pecos, the Spanish had a logistical supply depot in an inhospitable and arid land. Able to produce over three hundred thousand pounds of corn in a single year, the Pecos built a preindustrial settlement on the New Mexico frontier that stood like an oasis in the harsh desert and possessed the food and people that the Spanish needed, but lacked, to settle New Mexico.

WOODLAND FARMERS OF THE EAST: THE MOHAWK AND OHIO INDIANS

As with the Pecos, corn proved to be the efficient form of subsistence that enabled the Mohawk and Ohio Indians to develop into preindustrial societies and to support Euroamerican frontier development. Like those of many Eastern Woodland groups, the Mohawk and Ohio Indians subsistence cycles followed a seasonal pattern that roughly focused on the growing of corn, squashes, beans, and sunflowers between March and September and on hunting, trapping, and fishing between October and February.[13] Because of this highly efficient subsistence cycle, both the Mohawk and Ohio Indians created large settlements; stratified their societies along gender, age, and social lines; developed sophisticated political, economic, and social institutions; and produced enough excess foodstuffs to support the Dutch, English, and French development of the New York and Ohio Valley frontiers during the seventeenth and eighteenth centuries.

While they hunted and trapped, agricultural produce existed as the mainstay of the Mohawk and Ohio Indian diets. The women and children usually worked the fields, while the men hunted and fished in the immediate vicinity of the settlement.[14] The major crops produced by the two groups were the "three sisters": corn, beans, and squash. Of the three, corn was the "the principal one."[15]

To maximize the effectiveness of their land, the Mohawk and Ohio Indians relied primarily on the agricultural practice known as horticulture. They began preparing for the growing season by clearing their lands of vegetation using a process of deforestation known as the slash-and-burn technique.[16] This enabled the groups to clear large areas of forest surrounding their settlements in a controlled, fast, and efficient manner. To clear the vegetation, the men first removed all the large trees by either chopping them down or girdling them. They girdled the largest trees by removing a strip of bark around the trunk to create an unprotected band that exposed them to insects and the elements.[17] Over time, the exposure caused the tree to die.

Once they removed the large trees from the area, the men cleared the underbrush by chopping it out and piling it up to dry.[18] After it dried, the men burned the underbrush and the fallen trees together. The women then used the wood ash from the fire as fertilizer for the soil. This process of fertilization coupled with others used by the two groups enabled them to replenish the soil of its nutrients and allowed Indian settlements to flourish for decades, and in some cases centuries, in one place.[19] During the clearing of the fields, the men usually performed most of the arduous tasks associated with the slash-and-burn technique. However, once they cleared the fields, the men yielded the responsibilities of producing the crops to the women and children.

The growing and tending of crops acted as social and economic functions for women. During this process, women seldom worked their fields alone. Often, the women assisted each other to hasten the planting process. However, while the planting became a communal effort, each woman dictated the type of crops planted in her field and held sole right to its yield.[20] Generally, women planted an area of about two acres. Oliver Spencer, a captive of the Shawnee, described this activity, noting: "The low rich bottom, about three-quarters of a mile in width, was one entire field covered with corn. . . . [T]he Indian women inhabiting large villages wherever it was practicable cultivated portions of the same field, separated from each other only by spaces of a few feet, and varying in size according to the number and strength of their families."[21]

On average, one woman raised between twenty-five and sixty bushels—approximately four thousand pounds—of corn by working only one or two acres and provided nearly half or more of the annual caloric requirements for a family of five.[22] In a single field of one-hundred acres at Logstown, for instance, the trader James Kenny explained that the women produced between 2,500 and 6,000 bushels of corn per season, enough to provide over 150,000 pounds of food for a population of upwards of five hundred people from just one field.[23]

Digging sticks were the primary tool women used for planting. When the corn grew to about a foot high, the women planted other crops among the corn—such as squashes, beans, sunflowers, and pumpkins—to augment their diets and to prevent the growth of weeds.[24] With the planting completed, the women tended the fields by hoeing the corn and weeding the soil. The women constructed their hoes using shells, stones, or shoulder blades from large game animals such as deer, elk, and bear and attached them to wooden handles with rawhide. After European contact, the women traded for gardening tools to assist them with the cultivation process. In a letter to a merchant in 1628, Isaack de Rasieres, the chief commercial agent of New Netherland, noted:

> At the end of March, [the Lenape and Mohawk] begin to break up the earth with mattocks. . . . They make heaps like molehills, each about two and a half feet from the others, which they sow or plant in April with maize, in each heap five or six grains; in the middle of May, when the maize is the height of a finger or more, they plant in each heap three or four Turkish beans, which then grow up with and against the maize, which serves for props. It is a grain to which much labor must be given, with weeding and earthing-up, or it does not thrive; and to this the women must attend very closely.[25]

The Mohawk and Ohio Indians planted several types of corn to include "white, red, blue, flesh-colored, brown, yellow, and spotted ears."[26] The four types they planted most, however, were the flint corn, used to make hominy; a soft white corn, used to make bread; a medium hard grain, used for corn meal; and a small-eared corn, used to roast or make succotash.[27] The women prepared the corn for consumption in a variety of manners. They used corn to make *wes-ku-pi-mi*, a mixture of sun dried corn kernels, peas, salt, and grease or boiled meat; *nee peeh-dub-wah*, a corn oatmeal; *tak-wha-ne-pii*, a fermented corn drink made with water; *osah-saw-bo*, also a fermented drink; blue bread or biscuits, made from corn meal and the ashes of burnt pea hulls; corn bread; sour bread; and hominy.[28] Colonel James Smith, a Shawnee captive in the eighteenth century, explained the importance of corn to the Indians' daily diet. Smith wrote, "At this time homony plentifully mixed with bears' oil and sugar; is what they offer to every one who comes in any time of the day; and so they go on until their sugar, bears oil and venison is all gone, and then they have to eat homony by itself, without bread, salt or any thing else."[29]

Because corn was so important to their societies' survival, the women kept the best corn to provide the seeds for the following year's planting. To ensure the success of those crops, the women coated the kernels with grease or dipped them in water with fish bones to protect the seeds through the winter.[30] Additionally, they stored the kernels in ground pits and other facilities throughout the winter to further protect them from the harsh elements. When spring arrived, the women uncovered their winter stores and used the seeds to plant that year's crops.

While farming served as the primary means of subsistence during the summer months, the Mohawk and Ohio Indians hunted and trapped essentially all year to supplement their diet with meat. Additionally, hunting and trapping provided them with the furs necessary to clothe and shelter themselves. During the summer months, they seldom engaged in extensive hunting trips. Often, the men hunted within the immediate vicinity of their settlements, while the women assumed the primary role of provider with their production of corn.[31] However, during the winter, the men provided their families with the majority of their food.

As with farming, the entire family involved themselves in the hunt. At the beginning of the season, many Indian families practically abandoned their settlements and traveled to their winter hunting camps, though some remained in the settlements throughout the winter and hunted from there.[32] While many scholars may perceive them as being seminomadic because of this, the Mohawk and Ohio Indians maintained permanent populations in their settlements throughout the year and in the winter occupied hunting camps less than a day away. The Indians regarded their larger settlements as their primary homes and moved to their winter camps not because of a scarcity of food but because of seasonal shortages of wood for fuel due to the construction of their houses.

Once settled into their hunting camps, the males began collecting game and furs. They primarily sought deer, buffalo, elk, bear, and turkey on their hunts.[33] Though furs such as beaver and otter eventually brought them more European trade goods, the hunters sought animals such as deer, elk, and bear because they provided not only trade goods but meat and clothing as well.[34]

When they arrived at their winter quarters, the hunters left their camps for several days tracking, killing, and stockpiling game. As they killed their game, the hunters hung it up in trees to prevent animals from disturbing the catch.[35] When storing game in this fashion, only buzzards and tree-climbing vermin were a problem for the hunters. Other Indians seldom if ever disturbed or removed game properly marked by a fellow hunter.[36]

After collecting a modest amount of game, the hunters returned to their camps to supply their families with meat and to rest. Once rested, the males set out and gathered the remainder of their stored meat and brought it back to camp. Along with being a source of food for the Indians, the meat eventually became a major trade item. On more than one occasion, a starving Euroamerican settler willingly traded away shot, powder, cloth, and in some cases firearms for Indian-procured meat.[37]

As in many preindustrial societies, the Mohawk and Ohio Indians organized their division of labor according to gender and age. While the men hunted, the women and children prepared the catch. To prepare the meat and furs for trade, the women dried the venison hams by fire and then treated and tanned the hides with the brains of the animals.[38] The families repeated this cycle of hunting throughout the winter and then returned to their settlements near the end of February to begin their planting.[39]

To augment their hunting during the winter months, some males trapped. Trapping season began when the frogs started to awake from their hibernation. This marked the start of the season because frogs were a favorite food source of the animal the Indians trapped most, raccoons.[40] Along with raccoons, the Indians trapped beavers, muskrats, foxes, wild cats, and opossums. They used various types of traps to capture their quarry, the most effective being snares and deadfalls.[41] The etiquette of trapping mirrored that of hunting. If a trapper happened upon a sprung trap of another individual, he simply reset it and hung the game in a tree.[42] As with hunting, trapping was a male-dominated activity in which the women and children played minor roles.

Scholars continue to debate the impact that European trade had on Indian subsistence hunting and trapping. While hunting proved the primary means to obtain prized furs, historian Richard White explained the link between Indian subsistence and economics in the Ohio Valley. White noted that "in the local economies where trade goods satisfied limited *besoins* [needs], the fur trade involved relatively little disruption of native subsistence systems. Production for the fur trade came from the hunt not yet separated from the larger subsistence cycle." White concluded his argument by noting that "when the distance of beaver from villages and the scarcity of other game in the region did create a conflict, the demands of subsistence took priority."[43]

Anthropologist Herbert Kraft strengthens White's argument regarding the Indians' preference for subsistence game over economic game through the examination of Lenape archeological sites. Kraft noted that while the pelts of beavers, otters, martens, and fishers were the desired furs of the Dutch, French, and English traders, the most abundant animal archeological remains found in the refuse pits of many Eastern Woodland cultures were those of deer, elks, black bears, raccoons, turkeys, geese, and turtles.[44] C. C.

Trowbridge, a nineteenth-century historian who lived among the Shawnee, supports Kraft's observation in his work "Shawnese Traditions." Trowbridge observed that in the daily life of the Shawnee: "They never eat the wolf unless they are in a state of starvation. The reason given is that the meat is very strong & disagreeable. Otters, fishers & minks are not used, for the same reason."[45]

Though beaver and martens remained prized trade items among Euroamericans, the Indians' need for survival outweighed their need for European trade items, which caused them to focus a majority of their time on procuring large game animals for subsistence. Eventually, the Euroamerican need for food made Indian subsistence hunting and trapping as profitable as "cash" hunting.

Along with hunting, trapping, and farming, the Ohio Indians and Mohawk also gathered a variety of foodstuffs from the environment. The women and children gathered plants in the spring and fall. In the spring, the gatherers collected fruits such as blackberries and strawberries as well as vegetables like wild onions and cabbages, while in the fall they gathered a variety of nuts, including hickory nuts, walnuts, acorns, and beechnuts.[46] Amazingly, while gathering was not a major subsistence activity, the Mohawk and Ohio Indians, like many Indian groups living around the Great Lakes area, used 558 different types of plants, including 275 for medicinal purposes, 130 for food, and 27 for smoking.[47] In addition to these wild fruits and vegetables, the Indians also collected maple sugar and salt, which they used to trade and flavor their foods.[48]

Because of their efficient system of farming, hunting, trapping, and gathering, the Mohawk and Ohio Indians produced enough surplus resources to build preindustrial settlements that housed populations in excess of one thousand people in some cases. Residing in these settlements, the two groups stratified their societies according to age and sex and developed the complex political, economic, and social institutions that governed their daily lives and connected them to the world outside their communities. Subsequently, when the Dutch, English, and French began to settle New York and the Ohio Valley, they found neither an unoccupied nor undeveloped wilderness, but places like Logstown and Ossernenon (also known as Caughnawaga) with the surplus foodstuffs they needed to settle the American frontier.

FISHERMEN OF THE NORTHWEST COAST: THE CHINOOK

"Corn-growing," anthropologist Alfred Kidder stated, "was without any question the factor which made possible the development of all the higher American civilizations."[49] However, in the case of the Chinook, fish from the

Columbia River was the form of subsistence that enabled them to develop into a preindustrial people. Or as anthropologist George Woodcock more poignantly explained, the abundance of fish freed the Chinook from the "unceasing daily pursuit of food that is the fate of so many hunting and gathering cultures." Subsequently, the Chinook divided their year into three functional seasons—subsistence, trading, and communal improvement—which afforded them the time and resources to develop into a preindustrial society and to support the American and English settlement of present-day Oregon during the first half of the nineteenth century.[50]

Like the Pecos, Mohawk, and Ohio Indians, the Chinook nutritional and economic subsistence practices followed a seasonal pattern. In the summer months, the Chinook fished and hunted, and in the autumn and winter they concentrated on nonsubsistence-oriented tasks such as trading, carving, canoe building, and weaving.[51] Because of the abundance of spawning salmon that populated the coastal waters from spring to autumn, the Chinook obtained the majority of their food for an entire year in only a few months. Gabriel Franchere, one of the builders of Fort Astoria, described the Chinook's seasonal fishing patterns. "The principal food of the natives of the Columbia is fish," Franchere wrote:

> The salmon-fishery begins in July: that fish is here of an exquisite flavor. . . . The months of August and September furnish excellent sturgeon. This fish varies exceedingly in size; I have seen some eleven foot long; and we took one that weighed, after the removal of the eggs and intestines, three hundred and ninety pounds. We took nine gallons of roe. In October and November we had salmon, too, but of a quite different species. . . . February brings a small fish about the size of a sardine. It has an exquisite flavor and is taken in immense quantities . . . but the season is short, not even lasting two weeks.[52]

Alexander Ross, another of the first Astorian settlers, echoed Franchere's assessment of the Chinook's ability to live solely off of fishing, explaining:

> The greater part of their food is derived from the waters. The Columbia salmon of which there are two species, are perhaps as fine as any in the world, and are caught in the utmost abundance during the summer season: so that were a foreign market to present itself, the natives alone might furnish 1,000 tons annually. The largest caught in my time weighed forty-seven pounds. Sturgeon also are very abundant and of uncommon size . . . weighing upwards of 700 pounds, and one caught and brought to us measured thirteen feet nine inches in length, and weighed 1,130 pounds.[53]

As George Simpson surmised in a letter to his Hudson Bay superiors in 1825, "the Chinooks among whom we are resident do not exert themselves in hunting and rarely employ their Slaves in that same way . . . the waters afford ample Provision, the earth yields spontaneously nutricious Roots and Fruits, and all descriptions of Game are abundant" in their land.[54]

Because of their superior localized subsistence system, the Chinook had the time to build and reside in permanent, well-constructed settlements along the banks of the Columbia River and its tributaries from the rapids known as The Dalles to the sea. Ross estimated that collectively, the Indians living on the Columbia numbered about two thousand warriors.[55] Using historian Gregory Dowd's ratio of five family members for every male counted in order to estimate the size of Indian populations, the settlements along the Columbia probably numbered around ten thousand people[56]

As with agrarian-based Indian societies, the abundance of fish along the Columbia River enabled the Chinook to build permanent settlements and to consolidate a large number of people into a relatively small geographic region, the first two steps to developing into a preindustrial society. Because of predictable spawning patterns of salmon, sturgeon, and sardines, the Chinook successfully caught an estimated two hundred thousand pounds of fish in just one season, which enabled them to focus only a third of their time on subsistence-oriented activities. With so much time to spare, the Chinook mastered their skills at canoe building and basket making while they created preindustrial political and economic systems. Subsequently, when the American and British fur traders arrived at Astoria in 1811, they found a civilized people occupying the Columbia River in "European style" settlements with the foodstuffs and resources they needed to settle the Oregon country.[57]

Gideon Sjoberg contended that an efficient subsistence technology, much like other forms of advanced technology, enabled people to come together, remain together for long periods of time, and develop into preindustrial societies. In his book *Changes in the Land*, historian William Cronon supports this hypothesis with statistical data and found that population sizes differed greatly between nonagricultural and agricultural Indians occupying similar-size territories. In Maine for instance, Cronon discovered that "nonagricultural Indians . . . sustained population densities, on average of perhaps 41 persons per hundred square miles, [while] crop-raising Indians . . . maintained 287 persons on an identical amount of land, a sevenfold difference."[58] Unlike smaller, more-nomadic societies, the Pecos, Mohawk, Ohio Indians, and Chinook possessed highly efficient forms of subsistence technologies that enabled them to produce over three hundred thousand pounds of corn and two hundred thousand pounds of fish in just one year. However, their knowledge and ability to produce these large yields did not simply develop overnight. For centuries, Indians learned the most-effective techniques and efficient technologies to maximize the yields from their subsistence systems, thereby enabling them to create settlement-oriented preindustrial societies. When Euroamericans arrived on the frontier, in lieu of a wilderness they found well-established preindustrial Indian settlements with the excess foodstuffs and people capable and knowledgeable enough to provide them with the logistical support they needed to settle the American frontier.

CHAPTER 2

The Socioeconomic World of the American Indian Frontier

THE FIRST EUROPEANS WHO BROKE THE BRUSH OF THE FRONTIER DID so with economic interests in mind. They went not to farm or to create permanent settlements but to extract marketable and profitable resources from the frontier environment. Long before Euroamericans entered the American woods, the future frontier existed, not as a wilderness but as a region with economically oriented, often interconnected enclaves of Indian settlements dotting the landscape. Indian economies fulfilled more than just the simple subsistence needs of their communities. Their economic motives helped to shape the intricacies and structure of Indian societies, led to the creation of elaborate trade networks with neighboring native peoples, and fostered the development and thrifty management of the frontier environment. Euroamericans did not hack their way out of an unsettled wilderness; rather, they fell in upon, used, and exploited Indian socioeconomic systems that existed for centuries, systems that, while they were different from those on the European continent, greatly enhanced and motivated Euroamerican efforts to develop and settle the American frontier.

THE COMPONENTS OF AMERICAN INDIAN PREINDUSTRIAL ECONOMIES

Gideon Sjoberg established several determinants to distinguish how economic factors caused different levels of societal stratification to develop in folk and preindustrial groups. Folk economies, Sjoberg noted, caused people to develop societies that lacked any real division of labor or class system, while preindustrial economies enabled individuals to create societies based on an efficient form of subsistence technology where a clear division of labor existed between age and gender groups.[1] Sjoberg further explained that preindustrial economies directly affected kinship ties, group relations, and the way communities ordered themselves, which led to the creation of societies with little fragmentation or specialization of work where individuals relied on bartering and haggling in lieu of fixed prices and standardized production to regulate the flow of goods.[2] Because they developed these types of economic features, Indians inadvertently created the commodities of exchange Euroamericans desired and needed such as furs and wampum, generated a high demand for European goods, and established far-reaching and well-established networks of trade throughout the frontier.

Like most societies, the Pecos, Mohawk, Ohio Indians, and Chinook divided their labor according to age and gender. In the simplest of descriptions, men hunted, fished, and farmed; women planted and gathered; children assisted their mothers in the tending of crops; and grandparents provided wisdom, insight, and leadership to their families and communities while performing less physically demanding tasks such as sewing, scrimshawing, and educating the young. In short, the Pecos, Mohawk, Ohio Indians, and Chinook possessed clear and well-defined systems of labor dependent on human work. All individuals knew their responsibilities and performed them according to societal norms.[3] However, while the four groups meet the requirements for preindustrial economies, Sjoberg's broad criteria leave much to the scholar's interpretation and, therefore, much to debate. A major flaw of Sjoberg's argument is that he never explained or put forth criteria to determine distinctions in the divisions of labor that separated folk from preindustrial economies, or mentioned how the economy affected the way preindustrial societies organized themselves in regard to rank and structure. At first glance, one could easily argue that hunters and gatherers developed a clear division of labor based on gender and age. Using this simple argument, scholars could claim that the Pecos, Mohawk, Ohio Indians, and Chinook, and the archaic hunters and gatherers of the Late Woodland period, for example, all developed similar preindustrial economies. By using Sjoberg's simple economic criteria, it is easy to reduce agrarian or more advanced Indian groups to folk societies or promote hunters and gatherers to preindustrial societies. To avoid this pitfall, the degree of the division of labor between folk and preindustrial societies needs explaining.

Though he failed to elaborate on the degree of difference, Sjoberg did explain that preindustrial economies influenced the structuring of their societies into classes, something folk economies failed, or lacked the means, to do. Therefore, the feature that separates folk from preindustrial economies is the existence of a stratified society. The stratification of North American Indian preindustrial societies occurred because of the presence of a gift economy that enabled kinship groups and individuals to perpetuate their preeminence through the acquisition of prestige.[4] Individuals gained rank, prestige, prominence, or an influential status in their respective societies through success, renown, or wealth. By attaining prestige, an individual generally achieved rank and commanded the admiration and respect of society.[5]

Anthropologist Marshall Sahlins indicated that people fulfill their need for social advancement in two ways: accumulation of capital and satisfaction of wants. The Pecos, Mohawk, Ohio Indians, and Chinook developed gift economies to fulfill their desire for prestige and social advancement (i.e., their wants) while their subsistence economy provided them with their necessities of life. Those necessities consisted of items Indians needed to remain alive, such as food, while wants, which could be satisfied through "producing much or desiring little," comprised those things individuals desired to make their lives more comfortable or to improve their station in society.[6] The wants of the Pecos, Mohawk, Ohio Indians, and Chinook (i.e., those things they as individuals essentially desired most) consisted of luxury goods, the items that enabled them as individuals to increase their prestige and to advance socially through the practice of reciprocal gift exchange.[7] The four groups created elaborate gift economies based on the exchange of goods that not only stratified their societies but also laid the foundation for the Euroamerican economic interest in and exploitation of the American frontier.

AGE, OBLIGATION, PRESTIGE, AND POSITION IN PECOS SOCIETY

The stratification of Pecos society resulted from the socioeconomic relationships established by the people of the pueblo to address their five major concerns: the weather, illness, warfare, environmental control, and harmony.[8] While some Pueblo groups addressed these issues by employing magical practices or by engaging in elaborate religious ceremonies, the Pecos addressed these concerns through more-secular means, such as undertaking community irrigation projects to counter the effects of droughts in lieu of relying on supernatural involvement. Secular authority, control, and position in society rested on kinship ties, both real and fictive, that followed bilateral extended descent lines according to both parents and moiety ceremonial associations that created formal relationships and bonds between members inside and outside of one's family unit.[9] While membership in a certain kinship group, moiety, or clan granted some individuals access to positions of authority and determined what positions or roles an individual might assume in society, the concept of obligation, or *compadrazgo*, based on the reciprocity of gift exchange, determined the structure and rank of Pecos society.[10]

The Pecos marked each phase of an individual's life from birth to death with ceremonies and rites of passage. Gifts, presented on behalf of a newborn child or initiated by the child's guardian or sponsor, were a major component of these rites and ceremonies. Since these young people lacked the ability to repay their guardian and sponsors with gifts, they became indebted to them and were obligated to behave in an obedient and respectful manner when dealing with these individuals.[11] Gift exchange created dyadic status relationships between individuals. "A gift properly reciprocated with a counter-gift established the exchanging parties as equals . . . [b]ut if only one side gave and the other could not reciprocate, the receiver out of gratitude had to give the presenter unending obedience and respect."[12] Thus, obligation to one's family and parents began at birth and to one's moiety or ceremonial association at selection into the group, thereby creating the basis for the stratification of Pecos society. However, obligation through gift exchange was only one of two major ways Pecos society was stratified; age was the other.

The family was the basic social and economic unit where age rather than sex determined an individual's role and position in the Pecos. As individuals progressed through life, married, became members in moieties, emerged as the male and female heads of households, and eventually rose to the rank of elder, their prestige, power, influence, and subsequently their ability to control the affairs of the Pecos grew. [13] While age granted to the individual the opportunity to advance in society, one's rise depended on the ability to grant gifts in order to indebt others. As with many societies, some individuals in the Pecos proved more successful than others, and those less-fortunate members of society often sought the patronage of those whom fortune favored. Since ceremonies required gifts, if individuals lacked the ability to provide gifts for their children's or initiates' rites and ceremonies of passage, they often approached the more successful members of society for the gifts, thereby creating a relationship of obligation between the requester and giver. The more individuals one could indebt, the more powerful and influential one became. However, people's positions lasted only as long as they could create obligation. Once they lost this ability, they eventually dropped from their positions of power and influence.[14]

The ability to create obligation and patronage through gift exchange relied on an individual's ability to acquire luxury goods and foodstuffs by manipulating and participating in the Pecos's subsistence and trade economies. To supply the settlement with many of the commodities for gift exchange that the immediate surroundings lacked—such as flint, salt, obsidian, and buffalo hides—the Pecos economy, and subsequently the sociopolitical stratification, relied heavily on trading. Located in the Glorieta-Pecos pass, Pecos occupied a strategic position that stood as a gateway between the worlds of the Pueblos in the Upper Rio Grande Valley and that of the Great Plains Indians. Centuries before the Spanish arrived in New Mexico, the Pecos helped to develop and participated in an elaborate trade network that stretched from present-day New Mexico to Colorado and Texas. In this network, Pecos stood as a major marketplace where a wide variety of items such as shells, slaves, pottery, turquoise, cloths, and food were exchanged between the Pecos and their Indian neighbors the Apache, Comanche, Kiowa, Arapaho, and Ute.[15] As intermediaries, the Pecos moved goods such as cotton, acquired from the Pueblo Indians of the Upper Rio Grande, to the Plains Indians for items such as buffalo robes. In addition to these items, the Pecos trafficked their own goods, in particular, corn and pottery, the latter being a trademark item made of a fine, shiny-glazed, polychromeware that many coveted.[16] So important was the settlement to the economy of the area that hundreds of Plains Indians journeyed to Pecos each winter and remained there for several months to live and trade.[17]

While not much historical information exists on certain key individuals in Pecos due to the destruction of Spanish records following the 1680 Pueblo Revolt, some explorers mention the personal characteristics of some individuals in their chronicling that suggests their position in society and how they may have obtained it. Bigotes, one of the first Pecos Indians whom the Coronado expedition encountered in 1540, provides an excellent example of an individual who may have used the trade and gift exchange network to advance socially. Bigotes, so named by the Spanish because of his unusually long mustache, first met the Spanish at Cibola Pueblo while acting as an emissary for the Pecos. Aware that the Spanish were moving through New Mexico toward Pecos, Bigotes; Cacique (mayor), an elderly statesman so named by the Spanish because of his apparent position of importance; and a delegation of Pecos Indians met and treated with the Europeans. Impressed with the younger Pecos leader, the Spanish reckoned that he was a war captain, based on his demeanor and appearance. They described him as a "captain . . . tall, well-built, young-fellow, with a fine figure."[18] However, Bigotes's appearance suggests he may have been a well-traveled trader. The mustache indicates an air of individuality that many Pueblo Indians chose not to display in the interest of maintaining harmony within their respective communities. Not only is the mustache an indicator of his worldliness, but many scholars, such as John Kessell, suggest he may have spoken Nahuatl, a Central Mexico dialect that the Spanish used to communicate with the New Mexican Indians.[19] As a trader, Bigotes could traffic luxury items from Mexico through Pecos to the Plains, bringing his neighbors some of the items essential in creating obligation and advancing socially. Moreover, Bigotes probably could provide gifts to other members of Pecos, creating obligation and promoting himself to the rank of an influential member of society, so much so that they chose him to be one of their first representatives to meet the Spanish.

For five hundred years, the Pecos socioeconomic system evolved into an elaborate network of blood and fictive kin-based relationships founded on the concept of obligation through gifting. So important was the concept of obligation and gifting to the makeup of the community that the Pecos economy became the building block for the social structure of the pueblo. As a result, the Pecos created a well-developed economy that consisted of an effective subsistence base and an elaborate trade network that stretched from the northern reaches of Mexico and the Texas Panhandle to the vast Plains of North America, a network that by the time the Spanish arrived had existed for several hundred years and shaped the southwestern frontier.

THE ESTABLISHMENT OF RANK IN MOHAWK AND OHIO INDIAN SOCIETIES

In Mohawk, Ohio Indian, and many Eastern Woodland societies of the seventeenth and eighteenth centuries, gift economies provided the basis for rank and leadership. Prior to European contact, the ancestral people of the Mohawk and Ohio Indians followed formalized and well-established kinship lines to structure their respective societies. In the Mohawk and multiethnic settlements of the Ohio Indians, lineage, composed of an extended family, was the core social, economic, and political element in the community. In the case of the Shawnee, Lenape, Mingo (Ohio Iroquois)—the three most prevalent Ohio groups—and Mohawk, each followed essentially matrilineal lines of descent. Lineages, or *ohwachira*, consisted of several nuclear families related by blood who were further associated with larger fictive kin-based clans that established a person's relations inside and outside the frontier settlement. In these complex societies, personal and group relationships revolved around the family matriarchs and were governed by the principals of reciprocity, obligation, collection, and redistribution of wealth through gift giving.[20]

In this kin-based system, women, through the fruits of their labor, "owned" the yields of their crops and the homes, and controlled the day-to-day affairs of the community.[21] If crops needed planting or new fields sowing, for example, the women made the decision.[22] Subsequently, the matriarch, the most prestigious and often the oldest woman in the family, held the greatest economic, political, and social sway over the *ohwachira*. Because of their important positions, family matriarchs selected and promoted the prestigious headmen or sachems, those individuals the Euroamericans mistakenly labeled kings and half-kings, to represent their *ohwachiras*, clans, and communities based on their abilities to display patience, benevolence, and selflessness in regard to gifting and sharing or by way of their prowess as warriors.[23] As Cadwallader Colden, lieutenant governor of New York, observed, the authority of "Sachems or Old Men . . . is gain'd by and consists wholly in the Opinion the rest of the Nation have of their Wisdom and Integrity."[24] So rank in Mohawk and Ohio Indian societies depended on the acquisition of prestige through benevolent gifting and action.

While women's economic roles made them the masters of settlement life, men's economic roles made them the masters of external affairs, or as historian Daniel Richter so aptly put it, "the 'clearing' was the woman's domain; the 'forest' belonged to the men."[25] As dealings between Indians and Euroamericans intensified, Euroamerican traders and statesmen chose to deal solely with the "kings," which increased the prestige of these individuals. In dealing with the Lenape, William Penn, the founder of Pennsylvania, wrote:

> Their Government is by Kings, which they call Sachema, and those by Succession, but always of the Mothers side. . . . Every King hath his council, and that consists of all the Old and Wise men of his Nation . . . nothing of Moment is undertaken, be it War, Peace, Selling of Land, or Traffick, without advising with them. . . . 'Tis admirable to consider, how Powerful the Kings are, and yet how they move by the Breath of their People.[26]

While he mistakenly believed the sachems to be all-powerful kings, Penn correctly assessed that these leaders "move by the breath of their people." Unlike in European society, the Mohawk and Ohio Indian leaders, whose position and influence rested on their prestige, acted in accordance with the consensus of the people and not by their own wills or those of a few select individuals, for they, according to a Mohawk leader, possessed "no forcing rules or laws."[27]

While prestige and position could be gained through a variety of ways, the Mohawk and Ohio Indians increased their status primarily by fulfilling the needs of their neighbors, families, and friends through the selfless presentation of gifts. A gift, sociologist Aafke E. Komter suggested, "may be a vehicle for exercising power . . . to gain security and to fortify . . . against risks incurred through alliances and rivalry."[28] Gift giving enabled the Mohawk and Ohio Indians to create obligation and establish status between themselves and others inside and outside their communities.[29] As William Penn described:

> In Liberality they excell, nothing is too good for their friend; give them a fine Gun, Coat, or other thing, it may pass twenty hands, before it sticks; light of Heart, strong Affections, but soon spent; the most merry Creatures that live, Feast and Dance perpetually; they never have much, or want much: Wealth circulateth like the Blood, all parts partake; and though none shall want what another hath, yet exact Observers of Property. Some Kings have sold, others presented me with several parcels of Land; the Pay or Presents I made them, were not hoarded by the particular Owners.[30]

Though Indian gift giving may be perceived as a social act rather than an economic one, sociologist Claude Levi-Strauss noted that while individuals accumulate riches in order to rise in the social hierarchy, "even when pigs are exchanged for pigs, and food for food, the transactions do not lose all economic significance for they encourage work and stimulate a need for cooperation."[31] As a result, in Logstown, Ossernenon, and other Indian settlements, gift giving remained both an economic and social act.

Because of the interconnectedness of their social and economic institutions, the Mohawk and Ohio Indians developed economic systems that consisted of subsistence, gift, and moral elements. While farming and hunting were the subsistence elements of the economy and fulfilled their needs for survival, the gift and moral economies fulfilled their need for prestige and position. Dependent on the exchange of luxury goods and foodstuffs, the gift and moral economies revolved around the principle of redundancy and served to create rank and obligation in Mohawk and Ohio Indian societies.[32] In this system, the gifting of goods acted as the tool to create obligation, and the moral element essentially made one committed to reciprocate the benevolent action or to become beholden and subordinate to the individual who provided the gift. To ensure the success of this system, the Mohawk and Ohio Indians managed their economic resources (i.e., their environments), and therefore their gift and moral economies, through their subsistence cycle and a vibrant trade network established with fellow Indians and, after contact, Europeans.

The prehistoric ancestors of the Mohawk and Ohio Indians, such as the Hopewell, Adena, and Mississippian cultures, first created this network of trade that stretched from Ontario to the Gulf of Mexico and from the Atlantic Coast to the Rocky Mountains.[33] At various prehistoric sites such as Fort Ancient, Ohio, archeologists found artifacts that included Black Hills obsidian, Great Lakes copper, Atlantic and Gulf Coast shells, mica and crystal from the Appalachians, gold and silver from Canada, conch shells and alligator teeth from the Gulf of Mexico, and salt and lead from southern and northern Illinois.[34] While the majority of these cultures disappeared prior to European contact, many scholars believe their descendants formed the various groups of Woodland Indians such as the Shawnee and Twightwee (Miami) who occupied the multiethnic settlements of the Ohio Valley. Though the Hopewell, Adena, and Mississippian cultures disappeared, their descendants preserved, to some degree, their economic ties with one another and continued to trade traditional commodities such as surplus corn, beans, and squash to their neighbors and migrating bands of hunters and gatherers for meat, furs, and hides up to and after European contact.[35]

The Mohawk and Ohio Indians used and presented these commodities as gifts at births, deaths, marriages, peace treaties, and a host of other events to strengthen or improve their status or to influence the specific action of a person or group. This being a reciprocal transaction, the receiver either immediately gave the presenter an equivalent gift or accepted the present with the understanding that on a subsequent occasion, he or she would give a gift that exceeded that of the first. Furthermore, the receiver understood that the counter gift obligated the original giver to receive it or refuse it and end the reciprocal exchange, thereby ceasing any obligatory ties creating parity between the two parties, or to give another item that would surpass those previously given in value. In the case of a funeral, for example, a settlement divided into essentially two groups, those who were related to the dead person and grieved and those who had an obligation to host the ceremony. For hosting the ceremony, the family knew and expected that in the future when one of its own should pass on, the now-grieving family would reciprocate the obligation and arrange and resource a funeral on its behalf.[36]

An activity that permeated all their social institutions, the exchange of gifts was not only a means to transfer goods and receive an economic advantage or profit but also as a way to attain a level of prestige in society. Because in some societies, Levi-Strauss noted: "There is something else in what we call a 'commodity' than that which renders it commodious to its owner or its merchant. Goods are not only economic commodities but vehicles and instruments for realities of another order: influence, power, sympathy, status, emotion; and the skillful game of exchange consists of a complex totality of maneuvers, conscious or unconscious, in order to gain security."[37]

In Ohio Valley towns like Logstown, Kuskuski, and the three Mohawk settlements that Dutch explorers called "castles"—Ossernenon, Kanagaro (also known as Canajoharie), and Tionnontoguen—the exchange of items such as wampum, furs, foodstuffs, and luxury goods in the form of gifts enabled individuals to obtain prestige and status in their community.

Theyanoguin (also known as Hendrick), perhaps the most influential Mohawk leader between 1701 and 1755, is an excellent example of how individuals rose to and held positions of prestige and influence in Iroquois society. Born sometime between 1675 and 1680 near Westfield, Massachusetts, to a Mohegan father and Mohawk mother, Theyanoguin moved to the Mohawk Valley at a young age to live with his mother's family and was adopted into her clan. A member of the Wolf Clan, Theyanoguin, a charismatic, independent, and "bold artfull intriguing fellow" who stood well over six feet tall, proved himself through personal bravery in battle and skillful oration. Because of these attributes and skills, he ascended to the position of a headman and assumed the honorary name of Sharenhowaneh.[38] Like many other headmen, war captains, and Pine Tree chiefs who rose to levels of leadership despite not belonging to clan segments that held rights to titles, Theyanoguin established himself first through deed and then through gifting. Early in his days as a headman, Theyanoguin allied himself with a noted English trader and frontier diplomat, William Johnson. Together, Theyanoguin and Johnson secured the interests of the Mohawk and English all along the Hudson and Mohawk Valleys. Through his position, diplomatic skill, and relationship with Johnson, Theyanoguin continually received state gifts that he immediately transferred to those of his lineage, clan, and settlement.[39] As Colden explained, "Their Great Men, both Sachems and Captains, are generally poorer than the common People, for they affect to give away and distribute all the Presents or Plunder they get in their Treaties or War, so as to leave nothing to themselves. If they should once be suspected of Selfishness, they . . . would consequently loose their Authority."[40] Though the Mohawk fell on hard times during his tenure, Theyanoguin's influence continued to rise until his death in 1755 due to his diplomatic ability to tap into the flow of trade goods coming out of Montreal, Boston, New York City, and Philadelphia and redirecting them toward his settlement of Kanagaro.[41] Through gifting, deed, and his ability to maintain a steady flow of luxury goods into his settlement, Theyanoguin rose to and remained in power, and in so doing enabled himself to rise above his peers and assume and achieve a higher position and greater degree of influence and prestige in his community despite his birth.

Individuals such as Theyanoguin rose to these new positions of leadership because of the middle ground identified by Richard White. According to White, the middle ground emerged from the socioeconomic exchange between Indians and Euroamericans. In other words, the middle ground arose from the Indian and Euroamerican participants' needs to find a nonforceful way to solicit the cooperation and consent of all involved to attain their various necessities. Through these exchanges and interactions, Indians and Europeans adjusted their differences "through a creative, and often expedient, process of misunderstandings," thus resulting in the middle ground.[42] In the middle ground, gift exchange was the primary tool to solicit cooperation in a nonforceful way and to create obligation among and between Indian and Euroamerican partners. The Mohawk and Ohio Indians engaged Euroamericans, formed relationships with them, and sought their goods to fulfill their needs for prestige and position by leveraging their gift and moral economies.[43]

As Theyanoguin's experience indicates, among the Mohawk and Ohio Indians, trade transcended economic boundaries and became a social conduit between peoples of varying groups.[44] So the Mohawk and Ohio Indians, as well as many other Indian groups in America's northeastern frontier, exchanged trade goods as gifts to solidify relations between members of the same or differing settlements. By exchanging traditional and European made gifts, individuals gained prestige, honor, and influence in and outside their settlements. Subsequently, European trade goods became an important part of the Mohawk and Ohio Indian gift economies, augmenting traditional commodities such as furs and foodstuffs. Indians initially desired European trade goods more for the prestige they brought than for the technological advantage they offered.[45] The Mohawk and Ohio Indians readily infused Dutch, English, and French trade goods into their gift economies and trade networks.

In addition to fulfilling their own individual needs for prestige, Mohawk and Ohio Indian leaders sought to use the newly forged Euroamerican-Indian gift economy to satisfy the political and economic needs of their communities. By engaging in this new, broader gift economy, the Mohawk and Ohio Indians wrapped themselves into the much larger world of European mercantilism, thereby directly affecting and slightly altering the gift and moral aspects of their economies and the way individuals gained rank and prestige. By desiring Euroamerican trade goods, Ohio Indians and Mohawks created what social scientists term political economies, systems that develop when a political state or leader forges political bonds by "acquir[ing] goods to provide for the prosperity of their members."[46] Social scientist Karl Polanyi noted that "man's economy, as a rule, is submerged in his social relationships. He does not act so as to safeguard his individual interest in the possession of material goods; he acts so as to safeguard his social standing, his social claims, his social assets [and] values material goods only insofar as they serve this end."[47] In settlements such as Ossernenon and Logstown, the political economy reshaped the gift and moral economies of the Mohawk and Ohio Indians and tied them more closely to Euroamerican trade and political affairs, thereby influencing the way some individuals achieved rank and prestige in society.

Because of this broadening of the gift and moral economies, Indian sachems and their female counterparts outside the hereditary clan leadership rose to positions of prestige in their societies as disease and warfare ravaged the Mohawk and Ohio Indians during the late seventeenth and the eighteenth centuries. Traditional kinship lines became blurred and caused the absorption of large numbers of adopted peoples through military actions to capture individuals known as "mourning wars" and the disintegration of refugees into Ohio Valley settlements.[48] Over time, the absence of clear kinship lines coupled with the ever-growing multiethnicity of the frontier settlements opened the public forum to all individuals desiring to attain prestige and influence in their communities, thereby creating a fierce competition between individuals to promote themselves through benevolent actions such as gifting.[49] In a society where a majority of the people ruled, the individual prestige of a person directly affected his or her influence over peers. The more prestige an individual could amass, the more influence that person had within the settlement, and thus, the more esteemed and important positions the individual held. In Mohawk and Ohio Indian societies, prestige was the inherent character trait that created social division.[50]

Shingas, a noted warrior who helped engineer the western migration of the Lenape from the Susquehanna Valley to the Ohio Valley during the eighteenth century, is an example of an individual who was not from the traditional kinship line and clan associated with Lenape leadership but attained an important position in the Ohio Valley nevertheless. According to tradition, the leaders of the three Lenape groups came from the Turtle Clan. However, Shingas came from the Turkey Clan.[51] In 1747, the representative of the Lenape, Olumapies, died without a son or appointing a successor.[52] Desiring to continue its newly established trade with the Ohio Indians, the Pennsylvania government requested that the Ohio Indians appoint a leader in

Olumapies' place who, according to George Croghan, "so chosen by [the Lenape] shall be looked upon by us as your King, with whom Publick Business shall be transacted."[53] At the Virginia treaty at Logstown in 1752, the Mingo leader Tanacharison, a resident of Logstown, fulfilled the request of the Pennsylvania government and, on behalf of the Ohio Indians, bestowed on Shingas the title King of the Delaware.[54] A noted warrior and leader, Shingas earned enough prestige and influence through successful deeds that the leaders and people of Logstown and Kuskuski appointed and accepted him as the Lenape king, despite his affiliation with the Turkey Clan.

The key component to the greater political economy of the Ohio Valley and America's northeastern frontier rested on the Indian-Euroamerican gift exchange economy. While some scholars suggest that the ruin of the "noble savage" was the introduction of European trade goods—items that offered Indians such an overwhelming technological advantage or caused them to become so intoxicated with rum that within time they abandoned or forgot their traditional ways of subsisting—the Mohawk and Ohio Indians used European trade goods to "invent new appearances, new ceremonies, and a new visual language" to achieve their personal and political ends.[55] While European trade goods were highly sought after by Indians for their technological advantages and augmented their abilities to attain prestige, the limited number of these items did little to alter traditional Indian socioeconomic practices. For example, firearms, perhaps the most coveted European trade goods, were scarce among Indian populations until the advent of the French and Indian War. An estimated twenty thousand Indians resided in the Ohio Valley's major settlements at the dawn of the eighteenth century, however, despite this large number of Indians, Europeans only traded or gave away approximately 1,300 firearms, meaning a mere 7 percent of the known population possessed guns.[56] Though Indians eventually became more reliant on manufactured goods following the eighteenth century, the majority of Indians continued to engage in the same economic practices that yielded them their necessities of life prior to European contact and continued to use them for the same purposes—survival and social advancement. Though many came to desire European-made goods, the Mohawk and Ohio Indians continued to rely heavily on traditional commodities to fulfill their need for prestige and rank.

In the ranked settlements of the Mohawk and Ohio Indians, people gained prestige by improving their relations with individuals inside and outside their communities through the benevolent presentation of gifts acquired through a stable subsistence and elaborate trade economy. Thus the gift economy was the key element in the Mohawk and Ohio Indians' moral economies, their systems of socially desirable transactions that enabled individuals within a community to maintain, improve, and balance their social relationships. Consequently, the redistribution of resources to others in the form of gifts was an economically rational act when it was essential to build, improve, maintain, or restore social relations among members of the various Mohawk and Ohio Indian communities.[57] Prestige, gained through an elaborate gift economy, was the inherent character trait in the community that enabled individuals to rise above one another and to create the preindustrial economies able to support Euroamerican settlement.

When Dutch, English, and French traders entered the Hudson and Ohio Valleys, they found preindustrial Indian settlements with well-developed economies with the ability and desire to support the Euroamericans' physical presence on the frontier while also fulfilling their economic and political objectives. Subsequently, European traders did not blaze trails through the wilderness; rather, they followed those already established by Indians. "We were very fortunate," George Croghan wrote on his first trip to the Ohio country, "in finding a good road all the way and particularly thro the Allegheny Hills Considering how Mountainous this Country is."[58] That road, and others like it, incorporated Euroamericans into an elaborate gift economy and led them to the sociopolitical hubs of frontier exchange, Indian settlements.

THE CHINOOK

The Chinook belonged to the cultural group known as the Northwest Coast Indians who occupied the region that stretched two thousand miles south from the Alaskan Panhandle to northern California and east from the Pacific Ocean to the Coast and Cascade Mountains. The Chinook lived along the banks of the Columbia River and its tributaries in present-day Washington from the rapids known as The Dalles to the sea in their five settlements that the American explorer William Clark named Stockhome, Comcommoley (Chinookville), Shilarlawit, Norcarte, and Chinnini.[59] While several groups related by language occupied the Northwest Coast region, each frontier settlement was a politically autonomous unit that served as the socioeconomic center for its population much like the ancient Greek city-states. Because of the political nature of this densely populated region, the Chinook created an elaborate gift economy and trade network based on the acquisition of prestige through wealth and heredity to organize their lives.

Living in these frontier settlements for literally generations, the Chinook created a graduated society based on prestige, wealth, and at times birth.[60] For the sake of simplicity, some scholars described the Chinook social structure as a caste system composed of chiefs, nobles, commoners, and slaves. However, in reality, Chinook society consisted of essentially two broad groupings of people, freemen and slaves.[61] Freemen rose through the ranks of society and validated their positions through the acquisition and distribution of wealth in the form of luxury goods and foodstuffs.[62] Slaves, who were usually in a state of temporary bondage because of indebtedness or captivity, possessed no rights save those granted by their masters and merely existed as property, often having to eat their food from the floor.[63] However, from the lowliest slave to the highest ranking individual, each person had a specific place in the Chinook's "unbroken series of graduated statuses," a ranking differentiated more so by degrees than by kind.[64] Evidence of this gradational structure appears in the way the Chinook designated their leadership, constructed their homes, and practiced the art of head flattening.

The Chinook designated the leadership of their society based on the rule of hereditary chiefs and patrilineal kinship ties. In Chinook settlements, each extended family resided in a single house that had its own family head or chief. Several families made up a clan, with the most influential and prestigious family chief acting also as the clan head. The settlement, which consisted of usually thirty or more family houses and several clans, selected the most prestigious of the clan heads to act as the village chief.[65] While the wealthiest males held the highest and most prestigious positions in their society, the Chinook leadership lacked complete autonomy. Though leadership generally passed from father to son, the people approved the hereditary descent of the chiefdom.[66] Moreover, if the community deemed the heir apparent unworthy to become chief, the people bestowed the position on the next adult male in the ruling family or in some instances on a high-ranking female in the hereditary kinship group.[67] As American explorer Meriwether Lewis described in 1806, "the creation of a chief depends upon the upright deportment of the individual & his ability and disposition to render service to the community; and his authority or the deference paid him is in exact equilibrio with the popularity or voluntary esteem he has acquired among the individuals of his band or nation."[68] Gabriel Franchere, one of the first Astorians, supports Lewis's observations, noting that "the politics of the natives of the Columbia are a simple affair: each village has its chief, but the chief does not seem to exercise a great authority over his fellow citizens.... The chiefs are considered in proportion to their riches: such a chief has a great many wives, slaves and strings of beads—he is accounted a great chief."[69]

Due to their positions in society, the chiefs held certain privileges that freeborn individuals and slaves lacked. In addition to portions of the community's and group's various industries, the chief held rights to "the surplus of . . . the economy and received special remuneration such as the first measure of blubber from whales stranded on the beach and of game brought in by hunters."[70] Additionally, though all property remained sacred in the eye of the law, the chief stood "above the law, or rather posses[sed] arbitrary power without any positive check, so that if he conceive[d] a liking to anything belonging to his subjects," he had the right to take any object a person owned without violating the law by merely offering an appropriate payment.[71] However, the key to an individual's success lay in the ability to present gifts and distribute personal and family wealth, not confiscate it.

Chinook individuals accumulated wealth to eventually redistribute it in the form of gifts to improve their stature in society.[72] Wealth consisted of family and personal possessions. Of all the chief's privileges, the ability to grant individuals the right to use family and clan property was perhaps the greatest benefit of being a chief. Over the course of centuries, each settlement divided the land—in particular prime fishing waters, clam beaches, and hunting grounds—into clan and family plots, and each family possessed the right to grant or deny its usage to nonfamily members. In each family and clan, land passed through the hands of the chiefs, giving that individual the right to use family and clan property to promote the social advancement of himself and his group.[73] However, while chiefs held certain privileges, freemen could gain prestige and improve their social standing through an elaborate gift-giving ceremony known as the potlatch.

The potlatch was the venue for individuals and families to exchange gifts and to improve their social standing by distributing personal wealth. Held for a number of reasons, such as weddings, funerals, and to resolve disputes, the potlatch involved an individual or family distributing gifts such as slaves, canoes, carved objects, and eventually Euroamerican trade goods to the community to demonstrate their wealth, power, and prestige.[74] The greater display of wealth an individual or group showed, the more prestige they garnered.[75] More importantly, the ceremony enabled individuals and families to assemble and impress audiences outside their localized kinship groups; establish a sense of obligation to themselves and their group; reinforce and promote claims to certain distinctions and privileges to include land rights outside their communities; and to express, recognize, and reinforce the status of all individuals involved in the ceremony through an unequal distribution of wealth that favored the more-esteemed and worthy members of society.[76] Though less formalized than that of some other Northwest Coast groups, the Chinook potlatch consisted of feasting and gift presentation that led to and reinforced the creation of a gradational society based on wealth and heredity.[77] As historians Merwyn S. Garbarino and Robert F. Sasso explained, "potlatches helped integrate social groups by making kinfolk more dependent on each other, and were investments that would be returned, often with interest, in the future."[78]

The gradation caused by and the prestige earned from the potlatch system permeated Chinook society and governed many aspects of their daily lives to include the way they built their homes and lived with one another. Whether they were residing in their summer fishing homes or main family houses in the five major settlements, the Chinook lived in homes that were, as the trader Alexander Ross described, on the outside "something in the European style" very similar to the Euroamerican frontier log cabin.[79] Built of broad, split-cedar planks connected by an ingenious system of overlapping jointing, Chinook homes measured about one hundred feet long by thirty or forty feet wide.[80]

The Chinook designed their homes to reflect the social gradation of their settlements. They were rectangular in design and partially underground, and one door ornately carved and painted with effigies of animals and other designs was the only means to exit and enter the dwellings. Upon entering the oftentimes smoked-filled house, an individual found essentially three levels to the home: on the lowest level lay the recessed communal fire pit; at mid-level, the sitting area; and on the third level, the bedroom compartments. The chief's compartment stood at the head of the dwelling farthest from the door and was the largest. As an individual moved from the door toward the chief's compartment, he or she passed the family compartments, usually organized in rank order and each with its own fire pits—from the lowliest and poorest nuclear family to the highest—until they reached the far side. Thus, the home reflected the community.[81]

Like their homes, the Chinook practice of head flattening also depicted the social gradation of their society. Soon after a child was born, the Chinook placed the infant's head into a press to mold its forehead. Alexander Ross described the art of head flattening and the appearance of the Chinook, noting:

> No sooner . . . is a child born . . . than its head is put into a press or mould of boards in order to flatten it . . . giving the head the form of a wedge, and the more acute the angle, the greater the beauty. The flatness of the head is considered the distinguishing mark of being free born. All slaves are forbidden to bear this aristocratic distinction. Yet, I have seen one or two instances . . . where a favorite slave was permitted to flatten the head of a first-born child.[82]

Gabriel Franchere also commented on the Chinook practice of head flattening among the freeborn, stating "it is an indispensable ornament: and when we signified to them how much this mode of flattening the forehead appeared to us to violate nature and good taste, they answered that it was only slaves who had not their heads flattened. The slaves, in fact, have the usual rounded head, and they are not permitted to flatten the foreheads of their children, destined to bear the chains of their sires."[83] The Chinook reinforced and promoted the gradation of their society through cultural practices to regulate social mobility and to ensure that "no two individuals were of precisely the same status."[84]

Because the acquisition of wealth was so important to the makeup of their society, the Chinook attempted to acquire goods by becoming the middlemen, and monopolizing the elaborate trade network, of the Columbia River.[85] Located in such an ideal and strategic position, the five Chinook settlements, especially Comcommoley, became the hubs of trade in the region. As early as 1812, Astorian traders recognized the Chinook as "the intermediate traders between the whites and inland Tribes, particularly those to the northward."[86] The Chinook played such a central role in the regional trading that Indian and Euroamerican traders adopted their language as the accepted trade jargon.[87] More importantly however, the trade enabled the Chinook to become one of the most, if not the most, influential groups and the major exporters and importers of goods along the river.

Since subsistence activities only occupied a third of their year, the Chinook had the freedom to become proficient traders, artisans, weavers, pseudoshipwrights, basket makers, and potters. They divided these occupational skills according to sex and age. In addition to fishing and hunting, the men carved, scrimshawed, made cooking vessels, and built canoes, while the women wove blankets, baskets, and clothing from wooden fibers and furs. The forms of artwork used on these crafted items were specified by gender. The men used a symbolic and quasi-representational style based on the shapes of natural and supernatural beings and beasts that were linked to clan, lineage, and legend, while the women created artwork that was secular and completely geometric.[88] Taken by the beauty of the Chinook artwork, Ross felt that "the art they display in the making of canoes, of pagodas, and of fishing tackle, and other useful instruments, deserves commendation, [because] they show much skill in carved work."[89]

During the trading season, the Chinook traveled all along the Pacific Northwest coast bartering for goods. Long before their contacts with Euroamericans, the Chinook refined and mastered the nuances of an elaborate trade network that existed along the Pacific coast. Over the course of generations, the Chinook became shrewd and clever traders, "never failing to ask at least three times what they considered to be the real value of an article."[90] Soon after Euroamericans became partners in their trade network, the Chinook began dictating prices to the traders. One trader lamented:

> We expected of course from the Information we hitherto had of these People that with the choice goods that compose our cargo, we should have been able to procure them [furs] in ways of Barter readily and with ease, but our disappointment might be better conceived than expressed when after bartering and shewing them a great variety of articles for the whole day we did not purchase a single Fur. Tea Kettles, sheet Copper, a variety of fine cloths and in short the most valuable articles of our Cargo were shewn without producing the desired Effect, and in the Evening the whole of them took to their cannoes, and paddled to the shore, leaving us not more disappointed than surprized.[91]

Blessed with the good fortune of occupying prime river real estate, the Chinook enjoyed the luxury of controlling the trade along the Columbia, a trade that enriched them and enabled them to reinforce their system of social gradation.

Like the Pecos, Mohawk, and Ohio Indians, the Chinook developed a rank-structured society based on prestige, wealth, and heredity. Individuals acquired wealth and prestige by engaging in the elaborate gift-giving custom of the potlatch, a custom that relied on the Chinook economic system of subsistence and trade to provide the commodities of exchange for this practice. As a result of this interconnected socioeconomic system, the Chinook developed and managed the frontier environment; created a complex preindustrial economy; developed and participated in an elaborate trade network that linked the entire northwest coast; became shrewd traders; and created a robust supply and demand for Indian and Euroamerican goods and services. In so doing, the Chinook laid the foundation for and possessed the ability to support the American and English settlement and development of the Oregon frontier by the time the first Astorians arrived in 1811.

The Pecos, Mohawk, Ohio Indians, and Chinook created preindustrial economies that enabled them to develop sophisticated rank-structured societies founded on the principles of gift exchange, obligation, prestige, kinship, and heredity. While this is important in its own right, it is even more significant when examining the broader course of the development and settlement of the American frontier. Rather than a wilderness when they arrived in North America, Euroamericans found Indian settlements and societies with well-developed economies that were connected by trade networks that stretched over large geographic regions. Coming to exploit the land and its resources, Euroamericans planted settlements like New Amsterdam, Santa Fe, Fort Orange, Fort Astoria, and Pittsburgh to obtain what Richard Hakluyt termed merchantable commodities: fish, furs, timber, sassafras, and a host of other items. Euroamerican traders sought these goods because they were items in great demand but in relatively short supply in European markets. For "if this was true," as historian William Cronon explained, it would "make sense to pay the cost of transporting it across the ocean."[92]

Fortunately for Euroamerican traders, through cultural practices like the Pecos act of godfathering, the Chinook potlatch, and the Mohawk and Ohio Indian principles of gifting, Indian settlements and societies created the demand for European goods, held the means to access Hakluyt's merchantable commodities, and created the markets to exchange them. In so doing, Indians provided the economic incentives for many Euroamericans to risk a journey to North America and settle in the region.

CHAPTER 3

American Indian Political Systems

As a result of the Neolithic Revolution, a period in history when people learned to domesticate plants and animals, the ancestors of the Pecos, Mohawk, Ohio Indians, and Chinook began the seven-thousand-year transition from nomadic hunting and gathering groups to settlement-oriented societies. As time lapsed, Indian populations and settlements grew, creating a need for the organization and management of their communities. To address these concerns, Indians developed sophisticated political systems to regulate the internal and external affairs of their communities. Tied to their socioeconomic systems, obligation, prestige, gifting, heredity, kinship ties, and personal relations governed Indian political systems. When the first Europeans arrived in North America, they came ashore in a region populated by over five hundred distinct Indian groups with independent political and economic systems that were connected through foreign relations and trade. Isolated from their parent nations and colonies in this politically dynamic world, these first Europeans needed Indian sponsors for physical protection, economic prosperity, and the permanent establishment of settlements. Driven by their desire for financial gain and reliant upon the interconnectedness between Indian political and economic systems, Euroamericans learned and adopted the nuances of these Indian practices to first survive, then prosper, then permanently establish their presence on the frontier. Euroamericans recognized the importance of these systems, adopted them, and then used them to further their political and economic aims, thereby creating and participating in Richard White's middle ground of mutual misunderstandings in conjunction with their Indian neighbors. Inexorably linked to their economic systems, Indian political systems became the framework that governed frontier relations and enabled, protected, and supported the Euroamerican settlement and development of North America's borderland regions.

A HIERARCHY OF POLITICAL SYSTEMS

While they meet Sjoberg's economic and social criteria for being preindustrial societies, the political systems that the Pecos, Mohawk, Ohio Indians, and Chinook developed fall outside his parameters for such civilizations. Egalitarian in nature, the political systems the four groups possessed were unlike the rigid hierarchical structures of preindustrial societies Sjoberg studied. According to Sjoberg, the political systems of preindustrial societies generally consisted of a power structure dominated by a small group of social elite who established an autocratic form of government.[1] In such systems, the elite group occupied most of the key positions in the society and tended to come from essentially the same small familial or kinship group. In many preindustrial societies, the sovereign (or king), ministers, and advisers enjoyed overwhelming temporal and spiritual authority and worked to maintain their economic and political positions through bureaucratic and/or coercive means that enabled them to control the masses.[2] The English and French monarchies of the seventeenth and eighteenth centuries are two good historic examples of preindustrial political systems.

Unlike the rigid nature of typical preindustrial political systems, the Pecos, Mohawk, Ohio Indians, and Chinook created rather liberal forms of government based on their rank, structured elaborate gift economies that afforded everyone the opportunity to become recognized, and sometimes institutionalized leaders in their society such as Shingas and Hendricks. The four groups actually created political systems that more closely resembled industrial rather than preindustrial societies, typified by liberal and loosely defined power structures where individual leaders and key personnel derived their authority by acquiring the consent of the governed through merit. In most cases, industrial and Indian communities selected key individuals to hold positions of authority with certain prescribed responsibilities and privileges but not with coercive power. The leader possessed such limited power and control over the community that it enabled the society to create and maintain less-rigid and more-fluid social and political systems. The Pecos, Mohawk, Ohio Indians, and Chinook based their decisions more on accepted sets of formalized rules and practices than on the decisions of a single person or group in positions of power and/or authority.[3]

At first glance, their governments may be mistaken for folk societies because of the liberality of their political systems. However, folk societies lacked any real governmental structure and developed limited divisions of labor or ranking systems because of the homogeneity that resulted from their small numbers.[4] In most instances, individuals of the community shared equal statuses based primarily on their sex. Similar to industrial societies, folk societies lacked a privileged stratum that exercised coercive authority and control over the general populace, but unlike the more advanced industrial and preindustrial groups, they failed to create organized rank-structured societies with institutionalized government offices.[5] Though certain charismatic and skilled individuals were consulted and solicited for their advice, these individuals held no institutionalized positions of authority affixed with certain responsibilities and powers and were essentially equal to their neighbors in regard to real authority. While they may have acquired more wealth and possessions because of their abilities or charisma, these individuals possessed no special rank or privilege in their community owing to a specific position or status they held.

THE FOUNDATIONS OF GOVERNMENT

Authority is a group-sanctioned right and responsibility for an individual to lead based on his or her capabilities or social position. In many societies, authority is bestowed by the consent of the general populace on an individual who sets the standards for others to follow and leads by example and not by coercion. The possession of authority then does not automatically grant someone coercive power. Rather, authority allows individuals in leadership positions to work out the realities of their daily lives through a socially accepted political process and not through the autonomous decisions of a single individual or body of leaders. In many societies, people compete for and maintain positions of authority in socially accepted ways and not through coercion.

In contrast, power is a measured source of control that an individual possesses over other members of the community. Power creates an environment that fosters an unequal relationship between members of the same society and enables individuals with control over the societal resources to essentially act autonomously without the consent or compliance of the general populace, as is the case with many preindustrial societies. In societies where a hierarchical system exists and places coercive power in the hands of a few select leaders, people actively seek those resources, economic and other, that allow them to secure positions of control within their community. As individuals seize power, the political process of a community becomes one that involves interplay between members with power and excludes those citizens with limited or no access to positions of control from influencing the affairs of their society.[6] Unlike authority, power enables leaders to coerce and control the actions of the members in their community to perform certain tasks or act in certain ways because of their ability to control the resources of society that allow individuals to acquire the prestige needed to rise in rank.

Control is the ability of an individual to restrain others from accessing the sources of power. Four types of power generally exist in most societies: social, economic, military, and ideological. Social power depends on an individual's relationship with the person's particular kinship group or community. The more powerful a family is, and the better supported one is by his or her family, the more control the individual enjoys. To exercise political control, individuals rely on the backing of their families and use social relationships (social power) to manipulate the society's power structure by engaging in activities such as strategic marriages, adoptions, and godfathering. Likewise, individuals seize economic, military, and ideological power by controlling the modes of commercial production, the loyalty of the "warrior" class, and the ability to direct the authority structure through the manipulation of the code of social order. By restricting others from accessing various sources of power, individuals establish and maintain their own positions of authority or power.[7]

Anthropologist Morton H. Fried best explains the relationship between power, control, and authority in a political society. Authority, Fried notes, exists as "the ability to channel the behavior of others in the absence of the threat or use of sanctions," the rewards or punishments that channel the behavior of an individual, while power is "the ability to channel the behavior of others by threat or use of sanctions."[8] In other words, authority is the ability to direct the actions of others without the use of power. Thus, while preindustrial groups rely more on power, industrial societies rely more on authority to rule, as was the case with the Pecos, Mohawk, Ohio Indian, and Chinook governments.

PECOS GOVERNMENT: A SECULARIZED THEOCRACY

By the time the Spanish stumbled into the New Mexican frontier in the sixteenth century, Pecos existed as a multiethnic trading settlement on the border of the plains and pueblo worlds. As the bridge between two worlds, the Pecos created a system of government designed to preserve their way of life and spread their influence over the plains and New Mexico frontier. To achieve this, the Pecos developed a liberal political system wherein no one group or individual could usurp the reins of government, and the leadership occupied institutionalized offices with varying degrees of power and authority. From these seats of power, Pecos leaders possessed the ability to influence the external and internal affairs of the pueblo world, but because of a system of checks and balances placed on them by the political system, they lacked the autonomy to rule society as autocratic leaders, making their system of government more akin to that of an industrial society.

To say the inhabitants of Pecos lived in relative harmony would be true, but to say they existed as a homogeneous folk society would be far from the mark. While its two thousand inhabitants lived in relative peace and prosperity, Pecos consisted of a diverse mix of people comprising pueblo and Plains Indians and lacked the homogeneity found in Sjoberg's folk societies. Prior to Spanish contact, small pueblo settlements with populations of upwards of a few hundred people dotted the landscape of the northern Rio Grande area of New Mexico. In the wake of the Neolithic Revolution, population pressures, increased farming needs, and security demands against nomadic Indian groups such as the Apache prompted the ancestors of the Pecos to abandon their small individual pueblos and consolidate into one large settlement.[9] Over time, Pecos grew and became the major center of trade and venue for cultural exchange between the pueblo and plains worlds. An eclectic group of inhabitants resided in Pecos consisting not only of the majority pueblos but also the Apache, Navajo, Comanche, Ute, and Jumano peoples.[10]

Due to the multiethnic nature of Pecos, the corps of authority and subsequently the seats of government derived from the various associations that governed the people's social lives.[11] To run the affairs of this large settlement, the Pecos created a theocracy based on a strict religious calendar and a system of ruling that relied on the leadership of two chiefs and a council of elders.[12] The leadership came from the prominent senior elders of the associations that dictated Pecos social life and addressed the five basic concerns of the settlement: weather, illness, warfare, environmental control, and harmony. Members of the medicine society, the most prominent and difficult association to enter, selected the town or inside chief, *cacique*, to lead the community and manage the religious affairs of the settlement based on the prestige and rank earned through deeds, age, and the Pecos gift economy. The war or outside chief, chosen by the *cacique* for his prowess as a warrior and prestige, came from any one of a number of associations and handled the protection of Pecos from external and internal enemies or potential disruptors of the peace. Under the war chief, the war captains—experienced men picked from the various associations by the *cacique* because of their social positions and knowledge in specific areas such as hunting, warfare, and weather control—made up the council of elders and managed the secular functions of Pecos, including irrigation projects, public works, and peace enforcement.[13] Unlike the *cacique* and war chief, who held their positions for life or until removed for incompetence or inappropriate behavior, the war captains remained in office for only one year. Derived from the various associations through an established selection process, Pecos leadership cut across clan and family affiliation, preventing one group from monopolizing the positions of authority in Pecos.[14]

The Pecos entrusted their leaders to control the internal and external affairs of the community. Like every other aspect of Pecos society, the five basic concerns occupied the attention, time, and efforts of the leadership. The *cacique* was the political symbol and center of Pecos and held the power to address the community's five basic concerns and control essentially every aspect of life.[15] As the head priest of Pecos, the *cacique*, in conjunction with the various association priests, saw to the spiritual and ceremonial needs of the community, those religious functions so essential to influencing the five areas of concern and to establishing the elaborate social hierarchy created by the obligation that resulted from the gift giving practiced during rituals. Maintaining communal harmony proved the most important religious role of the *cacique*.

The Pecos created communal harmony through the concept of reciprocity established by presenting gifts to their pantheon of deities and to each other at religious ceremonies to ensure that the cosmos essentially remained in order and to aid in the success of their crops, their offspring, and the outcome of battles, for example.[16] Through such ceremonies, the *cacique* not only addressed the immediate concern of the ritual but also fostered communal harmony by reinforcing the concept of obligation and by preventing the ever-present factionalism that existed in Pecos from rearing up and tearing apart the community.[17] When civil disobedience did occur, the *cacique* relied on the outside chief and war captains, who had the power to banish undesirables from the community, to maintain the peace.[18]

While religion played a central role in their lives, the Pecos and their leaders, unlike many non-Rio Grande pueblos, attacked the basic concerns of their community in more practical and secular ways. To address the concerns of weather and environmental control, the Pecos leaders coordinated community-level irrigation projects, planned the rotation of crops, ensured the collection of firewood, directed the clearing of farmlands, and conducted communal hunts.[19] While the ultimate decision on these projects rested with the *cacique*, he consulted the outside chief and war captains to solicit their advice and relied on them to plan and execute the projects. Under the direction of the outside chief, the war captains organized the citizenry into work parties and divided the labor according to sex. Women generally prepared the food, repaired the houses, and made pottery, while the men planted the crops, hunted, constructed the homes, and weaved.[20] Yet while they controlled and executed several secular duties, the outside chiefs' greatest power lay in their ability to influence and direct the external affairs of Pecos.

Because the Pecos lived in a state of nearly perpetual warfare with nomadic as well as pueblo groups, their physical protection was the most important duty of the outside chief.[21] To defend Pecos, the outside chief and war captains planned and coordinated the construction of buildings and walls. From these building heights, the outside chief and war captains directed the defense of Pecos when the settlement came under attack. Under the direction of the war chief, Pecos was a military power that spread its influence beyond its valley and subjected neighboring pueblos to its will.[22] When not engaged in war, the outside chief and war captains served as the political representatives and negotiators for Pecos when dealing with neighboring pueblos and, after contact, Europeans.[23] Thus, the *cacique* held power over and controlled the internal world of Pecos, while the war chief held sway over and directed the affairs of the external world.

Though endowed with great responsibility and power, the *cacique* and war chief ruled by the mandate of the people and lacked the overwhelming temporal and spiritual authority required to maintain their economic and political positions through bureaucratic and/or coercive means. To be a leader in Pecos, one first needed to acquire prestige and rank through benevolence or by performing personal, military, or social actions that proved beneficial to the pueblo in lieu of coercive means. When a person entered a position of authority, he or she, especially the *cacique* and war chief, needed to continue those actions and set the standard for appropriate behavior. Moreover, they needed to perform their duties without displaying emotion, act with moderation in their personal and public lives, refrain from quarreling, and avoid being spiteful. If leaders acted inappropriately, the *cacique* dismissed them from office. If the *cacique* acted inappropriately, the war chief and captains consulted the association heads and then, with their approval, removed the inside chief from power.[24] Though many wanted rank in Pecos, not all wanted to assume the mantle of leadership due to the expected level of behavior a leader needed to display.[25]

As Europe was in the throes of the Middle Ages and experiencing the institution of feudalism, the pueblo peoples of the Glorieta Pass region began populating Pecos. As migrants from the plains and pueblo southwest merged in Pecos, the settlers began developing an egalitarian society and a unique style of governing that, for lack of a better description, can be termed a theocratic democracy, a political system whereby the priests ruled with both divine and secular authority through the consent of the people and not by coercive means. In this theocratic democracy, the people, through association membership, bestowed on their leaders the authority to rule and granted them the power to control the resources and affairs of the community by way of a well-established and centralized political process. While the elite of society usually were the ones to rise to the positions of authority, they did so by way of their ability to redistribute the economic resources of the community to the populace and not by denying them access to them. Moreover, the organization of the government into an inside and outside world controlled by essentially two separate authorities set in place a system of checks and balances that prevented the abuse of power. These checks and balances, coupled with the ability to remove leaders peacefully from office, injected into the Pecos political system an element of liberality not present in preindustrial societies but typical of industrial governments. By the time of Spanish contact, the Pecos possessed a highly complex liberal government that influenced the affairs of the outside and inside worlds of the New Mexican frontier.[26] Thus, when the Spanish arrived in New Mexico, they found in Pecos an Indian sponsor with the ability to support their settlement of the region.

LEAGUE, NATION, AND SETTLEMENT GOVERNMENT OF THE MOHAWK

According to Mohawk legend, the Iroquois Confederacy or Iroquois League emerged from a period of struggle and warfare that engulfed present-day New York and its peripheral areas. Tired of the senseless and destructive violence, Deganawida, the son of a Huron virgin, traversed the Great Lakes region from present-day Canada to New York preaching a message of peace and enlisting followers. As a result of his efforts and those of an Iroquois convert named Ayonhwathah (Hiawatha), the Mohawk, Oneida, Onondaga, Seneca, and Cayuga formed the Great League of Peace known as the Iroquois Confederacy.[27]

As members of the confederacy, the Mohawk helped to create a political system with several levels of government based on their social structure and geared toward the preservation of the Great Peace. Essentially six levels of formalized authority and/or government offices existed in Mohawk and Iroquois society: the fireside, Longhouse, clan, settlement, national (tribal), and league.[28] In addition to the various levels of government, two spheres of control existed, the outside or international world and the inside or domestic world.[29] In both worlds, the concepts and reality of family, obligation, and peace stood at the heart of all levels of Mohawk government.

The Iroquois viewed the league as a large metaphorical Longhouse, with the Mohawk as the protectors of the Eastern Gate, the Seneca the protectors of the Western Gate, and the Onondaga the symbolic center and location of the sacred fire.[30] Like the Longhouse, the league operated on the premise of familial relationships, and the apparatus of government, the Council of Elders, existed as the forum for ensuring that the Iroquois kept the Great Peace intact by maintaining good feelings between groups through the creation of obligation and alliances.

The good feeling that the council strove to create came from the presentation of gifts and the principle of reciprocity. The council followed a ritualistic, almost spiritual, procedure typically begun with the condolence ceremony (or *hai hai*) to wipe away with gifts and kind words the grief of those who lost sachems, to raise new ones, and to rekindle the good feelings and relations of the Five Nations. Through the ceremonialism of the council; the gifts, which made words true; and the actions of the sachems, the league hoped to create, and for many years did, a mindset of consensus and good feeling between members of an organization where, in reality, any one nation could act independently of the others.

To ensure consensus prevailed at the council, no sachem reigned supreme over the others, all were equals, and no action was undertaken on an issue until all agreed on one. In such an atmosphere, where no real coercive power existed in any one person or group, the more influence and prestige one acquired, or the more gifted an orator was, the more he or she affected the outcome of the council.[31] Sachems strove to improve their positions by creating obligation and by improving their influence through gift giving.

The protocol of the council and the ideas of consensus, peace, and obligation prevailed and set the premise for the operation of government and leadership at all levels of Mohawk society. At the heart of the Mohawk political system stood the familial units, and the matrons were the core of the family and the two domestic spheres of government, the fireside and the Longhouse. The fireside consisted of a nuclear family, the matron and her children and the father, who, though he lived with his wife and offspring, had blood ties to his mother's household.[32] Usually, families consisted of about five members. Several families, anywhere from three or four to a dozen or more, formed the *ohwachira*, an extended family or lineage (kinship) group, and lived together to form the Longhouse.[33] Within each Mohawk settlement, the *ohwachira* belonged to one of three larger kin-based, both real and fictive, clans, the Bear, Turtle, and Wolf. In reality, clan affiliation within Mohawk settlements dictated personal and group relationships between individuals, such as whom one could marry or which groups buried each other's dead. Outside the settlement, clan affiliation established fictive kin ties to members of the same totem. For example, a member of the Bear Clan visiting Ossernenon from one of the neighboring Mohawk or other Iroquois nations received hospitable treatment, such as being provided with room and board from the members of the settlement's own Bear faction. Depending on the size of the settlement, each Longhouse accounted for just a single segment or *ohwachira*, and several combined to form a clan.

To direct the affairs of the settlement, each Longhouse and clan elected matrons they called *rotiyanehr* to represent them in a community council. Like all the offices in Mohawk society, the position of matron could be aspired to by any of the women who belonged to the group. Generally though, the Mohawk reserved this position for a senior woman who, like the leading men, was a "mild person who [spoke] easily and kindly [succeeded] to public roles." However, the authority and influence the matrons enjoyed in Mohawk society came primarily from a combination of their age and the economic positions they held in their community as the heads of households. As the primary owners of the fields, the foodstuffs, and the households, the matrons controlled the dominant physical resources (i.e., the gifts) of the domestic world. The power enabled the matron to exist as both a recognized and institutionalized level of leadership in the community.[34] Yet to say the women possessed the ability to "control"—in anthropologist Timothy Earle's definition of the word, "the ability to restrict access to the resources which are the media from which power can be fashioned"—the affairs of Mohawk society would be incorrect.[35] While women held great influence over the selection of male household and clan leaders, men could gain prestige and office through alternate means that fell outside the economic sphere or the hereditary lines of society, such as the pine tree chiefs who earned their positions based on deeds and, through their positions, influenced the outside political and economic spheres of Mohawk society. Due to this element in Mohawk society, the matrons lacked the ability to create a matriarchy or behave as all-powerful matriarchs.[36]

From their positions of authority, the matrons controlled the day-to-day affairs of the domestic world of the Mohawk. In addition to determining things such as the management of fields and settlement space, the matrons selected and removed the male leadership of not only their *ohwachira*, clans, and settlements, but of the league itself, giving them considerable sway in influencing international affairs. Father Joseph Lafitau, a Jesuit missionary among the Mohawk, noted, "The women are always the first to deliberate on private or community matters . . . hold[ing] their councils apart and, as a result of their decisions, advise the chiefs . . . so that the latter may deliberate on them . . . and the Elders decide no important affair without their advice."[37] As a result of their unique positions, the matrons not only directed the domestic world but significantly influenced the international world, functioning as the economic and social power behind the male-run councils.[38]

The Mohawk men assumed positions in society to direct the international affairs of the league, nations, and settlements. Three positions of authority and prestige existed as institutionalized levels of government: league sachem, an inherited position of leadership belonging to a particular lineage group; the male *rotiyanehr*, an *ohwachira*, or clan chief, appointed by Longhouse matrons to act as their counterparts and represent their extended families at councils; and the pine tree chief, an office gained through merit by individuals usually belonging to *ohwachira* or clans without inherited league titles.[39] In addition to the formalized levels of leadership, several informal positions of influence existed in Iroquois society, including the war captain, the wise old men, and the keepers of the faith, holy men selected by the matrons to supervise festivals and oversee religious affairs.[40]

Of all these positions, league sachem was the highest and most prestigious level of leadership earned by men in Iroquois society. In all the Five Nations, only fifty league sachemships existed—nine each for the Mohawk and Oneida, fourteen for the Onondaga, ten for the Cayuga, and eight for the Seneca. These positions were created at the inception of the league itself, and the Iroquois never expanded their number. They were permanently affixed to specific nations, clans, and *ohwachira*, making them hereditary titles with inherited personal names that the leader adopted on entering the position to remain in the hands of those particular segments of society for all time. The Mohawk divided their nine sachemships equally among the three clans, the Turtle, Bear, and Wolf.[41]

To become a league sachem, a man needed to be a successful and experienced senior possessed of goodwill, patience, unselfishness, and little emotion.[42] Nominated by the matrons, a man rose to the position of league sachem only after he was approved by the confederacy's Council of Elders through the *hai hai*, where they raised the new chiefs up during the ceremony. Once in this position of authority and influence, the league sachem, usually accompanied by an assistant or two of high rank, met at the confederacy council once a year, or more if the need arose, to discuss international affairs that concerned all Five Nations, such as war and peace.[43]

Though the principles of peace and consensus influenced the confederacy council, each of the Five Nations acted independently of one another.[44] On more than one occasion, for instance, the Mohawk acted independently of the league when the confederacy's leadership remained neutral in a war and they chose to engage in combat, as was the case in the Mohawk-Mahican War or in the many mourning wars they initiated.[45] To direct the affairs of the nation, the Mohawk matrons appointed chiefs to serve on a Council of Elders derived from a conglomeration of the league sachems, *rotiyanehr*, and pine tree chiefs who were taken from every settlement. Like the league framework and operation of government, the national council existed as the mechanism by which the leaders made and enacted decisions based on the same principle of consensus that influenced the confederacy's meetings. As a result of the unique Iroquois framework of government—separate, independently acting nations bound into a confederacy—the Mohawk council addressed issues pertaining specifically to its own nation, and it, not the greater league council, held the greatest amount of control over the actions of its people and settlements.[46]

While the fireside and Longhouse belonged to the matrons, and the league and national governments fell under the control of the men, the individual settlements were an arena where the two overlapped and where, in reality, the domestic world met the international world. Like their counterparts in the league, the settlement leaders worked to maintain the aura of good feelings within and outside their community. To accomplish this, the women *rotiyanehr* held their own councils and concerned themselves with the internal well-being of the community as previously mentioned. However, unlike the league and national councils that met only on occasion, the male *rotiyanehr* at the settlement level met almost daily at the Longhouse of the principal *ohwachira* and concerned themselves with the external affairs of the community. At these councils, the resident league sachems, *rotiyanehr*, pine tree chiefs, and any war captains, influential men, or even commoners participated, spoke their peace, and voted on the issues being discussed. As in the league and national councils, all who entered the meetings did so as equals despite their authoritative and/or prestigious positions in society. The more influence and prestige an individual attained through deed and the manipulation of the elaborate gift economy, the more sway the person usually held in the councils, and the more that person influenced the affairs of the Mohawk. Subsequently, the settlement government was perhaps the most liberal level of government and held the greatest amount of control over the people's lives.[47]

In the hydra that was the Iroquois political world, "factionalism, voluntarism, and individualistic patterns of leadership," as historian Daniel Richter suggests, created a unique system of government organized along familial lines that through the ceremonialism of a series of councils united the confederacy with the ideas of consensus, obligation, and good feelings. In this system of government, individualism, at the national and settlement levels, prevented the creation of a centralized state authority with the power to arbitrarily control league politics. Moreover, while some leaders in this system inherited positions of authority, they possessed no real coercive power, only a degree of prestige that carried with it some influence. Any prestigious person with influence and a substantial following could ignore the decisions of the councils. The selection and success of the leaders depended on the disposition of one's character and ability to create a power base founded on individual and group alliances through the creation of obligation and good feelings. While some scholars have labeled the Iroquois government an oligarchy, a society ruled by the few, and others a democracy on the verge of anarchy, in reality, because no real central state existed at the league and national levels, the Five Nations developed an intricate political system that was somewhat, but not truly, egalitarian, and followed a system where an established ceremonial process and the idea of consensus influenced the actions of the society. In the factionalized world of the Great League, the Mohawk helped to create this liberal political system that connected them diplomatically with a large geographic area while enabling them to preserve their autonomy. The Mohawk could control trade into and out of their land, marshal a significant number of allies to assist them with the defense of their territory or with the conquest of other regions, and influence the diplomatic world of the New York frontier. When the Dutch and English arrived in New York, they found themselves surrounded by two powerful groups, the Mohawk and Mahican, and isolated from not only Europe but also from the frontier environment that surrounded them. Out of necessity, the Dutch and English required and used Mohawk and Mahican sponsors and the preexisting Indian political network to support and secure their holdings and promote their interests in New York.

DEMOCRATIC SETTLEMENTS: OHIO INDIAN GOVERNMENTS

The political systems the Ohio Indians created in the eighteenth century varied in degrees depending on the Indian groups who formed each settlement. In some cases, one cultural group occupied an entire settlement and employed the traditional political system. However, the majority of Ohio Indian settlements housed myriad peoples from different cultural groups and developed governmental systems to meet the sociopolitical needs of their individual multiethnic populations. Of all the Ohio settlements, Logstown, perhaps the most influential Indian community of its day, provides an excellent example of the way many Ohio Indian settlements shaped their various political systems. To understand and appreciate the unique and multiethnic nature of the Ohio Indian political systems more fully, the roots of the Logstonian government must be gleaned from the traditional governments of the Shawnee, Lenape (Delaware), and Mingo. Similar to most features in Logstown, the Logstonians mixed together the various elements of Shawnee, Lenape, and Mingo cultures to develop a political structure that was unique to their own settlement. Despite the fact that the Shawnee, Delaware, and Mingo each came from societies with distinctly different governments, they drew on the similar features their various cultures shared and developed a new form of government that up to then was unique to eastern Indian frontier settlements.

The Shawnee

The Shawnee developed a system of governmental and societal organization known as a chiefdom, a political organization characterized by kin-based societies. In a chiefdom, social standing and political status depended on a person's position within a particular kinship group.[48] The Shawnee organized themselves into five distinct groups whose members inherited their affiliation patrilineally.[49] These five primary groups consisted of subgroups or name groups that signified an individual's particular kin group and social standing. An individual's name, for example, directly correlated to the person's name group. The Shawnee prophet Tenskwatawa explained to C. C. Trowbridge that "[the Shawnee] generally bestow a name descriptive of some act of the animal totem . . . a child from the Panther tribe is sometimes called the scratcher, or the leaper."[50] Though at one time these name groups represented over thirty distinct single family units, the historic Shawnee reduced these kin groups to twelve distinct units and assigned them specific animal names, such as the Turtle, Rabbit, Wolf, and Bear.[51]

The name groups provided the foundation for the relationships between individuals and various families in a community. Membership in a particular group placed certain responsibilities on its family members. For instance, the Turtle group normally carried the sacred bundle, a bag of ritual items, in each Shawnee community. Additionally, certain pairs of familial units buried each other's dead and were taught to feel a special affinity with individuals from their own and specified groups.[52] The name groups influenced Shawnee social organization more so than any other feature in an individual community.

While the name groups provided family units with the medium for individual community members to express social relations, the five primary groups, the Chalaakaatha, Mekoche, Thawikila (Hathawikila), Pekowi, and Kishpoko, created the organizational structure of the Shawnee. [53] Though they operated as a more cohesive and hierarchical society during the prehistoric period, the five Shawnee groups acted essentially independently of one another by the time of Euroamerican activity in the Ohio Valley during the mid-eighteenth century. Each group designated and created its chiefs and subcultures. In many instances, the subcultures created by the Shawnee more closely resembled other Indian groups than those of their fellow Shawnee. For example, the Mekoche shared many of the same ceremonies as the Creek, and in the case of the Logstonian band of Shawnee, the Pekowi and Hathawikila adopted many of the practices of the Lenape and Mingo. Although at times they joined forces and acted as collective units, each group essentially attended to its own political, military, and religious affairs.[54]

The Shawnee created two types of leadership positions in their society, peace chiefs and war chiefs. The peace, or settlement, chiefs attained their position through hereditary descent. Though hereditary, the eldest son of a deceased leader held no rightful claim to his father's former position. A collection of the community's chiefs and elders selected the most capable son of the deceased leader—the one who displayed the most skill and leadership potential—to assume his father's position as chief. Heredity merely supplied the minimum set of standards. If the deceased leader left no capable heir, the remaining chiefs and principle men in the community selected a skilled person to assume the vacant position. However, no matter whom they chose, they seldom selected anyone under thirty to become a chief.[55]

Unlike the peace chiefs, the war chiefs earned their positions through deed. To become a war chief, an individual needed to lead a minimum of four successful military excursions without suffering a friendly casualty and take one or more enemy scalps from each engagement. An individual who accomplished these tasks assumed the right to demand acceptance as a war chief. Once the individual made the request, the chiefs and elders of the community nearly always approved and acknowledged the person's right at a public feast.[56]

In addition to the male leaders, the Shawnee appointed female chiefs, whose duties were also divided into activities of war and peace. Usually, the female chiefs came from the same name or kinship group as the male chiefs and were close relatives or immediate family members of the paternal leader. Though this was somewhat of a women's auxiliary, the power of the female chiefs equaled that of their male counterparts. In most decisions on war and peace, the female chiefs influenced the actions of the male leaders.[57]

The duties of the chiefs encompassed both international and domestic responsibilities. In all matters of the community, the peace and war chiefs gave their input into the decision-making process of the leadership. Yet depending on the issue of discussion, the peace or war chiefs held the responsibility of making the final decision. For instance, in the case of land cessions, the peace chiefs took the lead and "in the councils, [the war chiefs] never preceded the village chiefs either in their speeches or propositions for the adoption of any measure." Likewise, in the declaration of war, the war chiefs listened to the opinions and concerns of the settlement chiefs but made the final decision.[58] Consequently, the Shawnee political structure limited the chiefs' abilities to exercise power or control over the community and to make decisions without the solicitation of the group's collective leadership.[59]

The rank of chief was a prestigious position of authority more than one of power. The individual gained the position and right to rule from the community. Though it was hereditary in nature, the people could remove a chief from office for abusive, poor, or inappropriate behavior.[60] Once it established the hierarchy of chiefs, the community willingly allowed the leaders to exercise control over the domestic and international affairs of their settlement and usually accepted their decisions on public matters.[61]

To assist the chiefs with their administration of the community, the Shawnee created an informal council made up of the significant members from all the name groups. Though these individuals possessed no formal power, the chiefs seldom made decisions without their consent and approval. "In important councils," Tenskwatawa explained to Trowbridge, "the aged men of the nation are invited . . . [and] sit behind the Chiefs . . . and explain the proceedings at any previous council . . . and generally afford their advice & assistance in the proceedings."[62] The council consisted of individuals who "were intelligent and staunch, fully able to advise about the affairs that affected the tribe" and assumed the responsibility of governing the community.[63] In most instances, chiefs chose prestigious and able councillors to become their subordinate chiefs.[64]

From hunting rights to punitive measures for crimes such as murder, the Shawnee developed a formalized system of rules. The Shawnee based their system of law on morality and custom. In domestic matters, the chiefs and councils based their decisions on this accepted code of behavior. For instance, the Shawnee regarded murder as an individual crime against a family or name group and not as a crime against the community. In regard to the punishment for such a crime, Tenskwatawa explained, "In the case of murder, if the guilty person be a man of power & respectability in the nation the chiefs assemble immediately and take measures to procure a large supply of wampum to compensate the friends of the deceased for their loss."[65]

Once they collected the unusually large amount of wampum, the chiefs visited the relatives of the murdered person and informed them of their intention to procure the appropriate payment for the crime, usually 60 fathoms, or 360 feet of beads, for males and 150 fathoms, or 900 feet, for females. However, the injured family could lessen or refuse the payment. If they chose to refuse the compensatory payment, the family had the right to take the murderer's life without fearing any reciprocation from the individual's name group or the community. If the murderer was of lower social standing, he or she negotiated with the victim's family on his or her own behalf. In all instances, the murderer accompanied the chiefs to the victim's family in a formalized ceremony and compensated them with the appropriate payment of wampum or forfeited their life.[66]

The Shawnee developed laws and forms of punishment for a number of crimes, including theft, adultery, incest, rape, and public drunkenness. Depending on the offense, the punishment could be banishment, flogging, death, public reprimand, or simple loss of prestige with no formalized type of reparation. In all instances, the chiefs, councillors, and community relied on their code of formalized and accepted behavior to determine the appropriate type and level of community and individual action.[67]

The traditional system of Shawnee government had features of preindustrial and industrial societies. While their system of government had positions of authority occupied by the prestigious "elite" from a common lineage similar to preindustrial groups, the community limited the power of the individuals holding these various posts, restricting the ability of Shawnee leaders to control the actions of the people much like more-advanced industrial societies, suggesting they were in a state of political transition or developed a governmental structure that was distinctly their own.

The Lenape

The social organization of the Lenape affected the development of their political system. Unlike the early Shawnee who organized themselves into five distinct groups, the Lenape developed a society oriented on individual frontier settlements and not on a well-developed clan system. According to historian Paul Wallace, the Lenape created "an atomistic society . . . one in which local communities were completely independent, each being subject to its own laws."[68] This lack of a group identity or organization caused the Lenape to develop autonomous political units oriented to their individual frontier settlements where each spoke varying dialects of the Algonquian language such as Munsee and Unami.[69] These individual communities acted as the focal point of Lenape society and provided the basis for their political, economic, and social structure.[70]

The Lenape frontier settlements consisted of a conglomeration of individual family units who possessed distinct geographical subsistence territories. Usually, each community consisted of one or more related groups who cultivated and hunted the lands immediately adjacent to their settlement.[71] Though these communities lacked a sense of a larger whole and were essentially autonomous and somewhat endogamous, the Lenape shared a similar culture belonging to one of three phratries or name groups—the Turtle, Turkey, and Wolf—and appear to have been loosely aligned, as members of neighboring groups intermarried and expanded familial relationships.[72] In most cases, members from all three groups lived in a single village, and for this reason, the phratries served to identify members belonging to the same kin group regardless of where they lived. Similar to the Shawnee name groups, members of these various phratries had names associated with their particular kin animal and usually wore or adorned themselves with a mark signifying this relationship similar to a European coat of arms.[73]

Lenape society was matriarchal, and the eldest female member of a family was the central and most influential figure of the family. Regarded as "chief-makers," the Lenape matriarchs could appoint and dismiss the male leaders of their family units, more commonly known as sakimas.[74] Though they chose the male leaders, elder females shared responsibilities with them in regard to administering the affairs of the family. In most instances, the sakimas attended to running the external political affairs of the community in regard to treaties, warfare, and land cessions, while the matriarchs ensured that their families performed and completed the domestic duties of the settlement, such as planting and harvesting.[75]

The position of sakima followed a hereditary descent along the matriarchal side to the family.[76] Unlike the Shawnee, the Lenape leadership generally passed from brother to brother, as opposed to father to son since sons and fathers belonged to different phratries.[77] A seventeenth-century writer described the Lenape descent explaining, "When the king dies it is not his children who succeed him, but his brother by the same mother, or his sister's, or her daughter's male children, for no female can succeed to the government."[78]

The responsibilities of the sachems encompassed political and ceremonial duties. For example, a sakima represented his group in the community council. But unlike the privileged kings of Europe, whom colonists compared them to, sakima participated in the rudimentary economic activities of the community and possessed no more wealth or power than any other male member in Lenape society.[79]

The governmental apparatus the Lenape used to manage the affairs of their community was a council made up of the male sakimas. "Nothing of importance," Thomas Holm wrote, "such as war, peace, the sale of land, or the like, is undertaken, without having been first discussed in council, to which are not only called the counsellors, but the common people."[80] Each settlement had a hereditary chief selected from one of the phratries who acted more as a mediator than as a ruler. Once the council began, the chief designated the order of the speakers from first to last. While an individual spoke, the entire gathering remained silent until the speaker announced he was finished. When all had spoken on an issue, the chief concluded the meeting by announcing his decision on the matter. In 1670, Daniel Denton explained that when "the Council having all declared their opinion, . . . the King after some pause gives the definitive sentence, which is commonly seconded with a shout from the people, every one seeming to applaud & manifest their assent to what is determined."[81]

To assist in governing their daily lives, the Lenape developed an unwritten moral code of behavior to control the general behavior and actions of the populace. The nineteenth century historian E. M. Ruttenber perhaps best summarized the historical literature and documentation regarding the Lenape code of behavior:

> Law and justice, as civilized nations understand those terms, were to them unknown, yet both they had in a degree suited to their necessities. Assaults, murders, and other acts regarded as criminal offenses by all nations, were regarded by them, but the execution of punishment was vested in the injured family, who were constituted judges as well as executioners, and who could grant pardons or accept atonements. The rights of property they understood and respected; and half their wars were retaliatory for the taking of their territory without making just compensation. There was not a man among them that did not know the bounds of his own land as accurately as though defined by a surveyor's chain. Their customs were their unwritten laws, more effective than those which fill the tomes of civilized governments, because taught to the people from infancy and woven into every condition and necessity of their being.[82]

Though dissimilar to Euroamerican justice systems, the Lenape code of societal conduct established the bounds by which members of the group behaved toward one another, a feature present in preindustrial societies but absent in folk societies.

Like the Shawnee, Iroquois, and Pecos, the Lenape developed a political system that had both preindustrial and industrial features. The position of sakima gave the male leaders authority and responsibility in the community but afforded them no real autocratic power. Power and control rested in the hands of the council and community in the form of a general consensus. For the most part, the sakima carried out the will of the people directly through the council and indirectly through informal pressures and controls.[83] To maintain their prestigious and authoritative positions in the community, the sakimas had to be "gracious, hospitable, communicative, affable, and their house . . . open to every Indian."[84] If they performed their duties poorly or proved to be individuals of questionable character, the community possessed the power and ability to remove the sakimas from their positions. "A more perfect democracy will never exist among the nations of the earth," Ruttenber concluded in 1872. "[T]he perfect liberty of the people was the fundamental law, and absolute unanimity the only recognized expression of the popular will. A more perfect system of checks and balances the wisdom of civilized nations has not devised."[85]

The "Refugee" Mingo

The political organization of the Mingo group is difficult to firmly identify. The Mingo were a mixture of several different refugee peoples—including Seneca, Wyandot (Huron), Erie, and Susquehannock—and their political system presumably consisted of elements from each of these groups. Since a complete study of their culture has yet to be undertaken, this may be one of the few works that attempts to put together the patchwork of material pertaining to the Mingo.

Of the four groups mentioned above, an abundance of primary and secondary resource material exists for the Huron and Seneca, while relatively little exists for the Susquehannock and Erie. Fortunately, historian and anthropologist Frederick W. Hodge concluded that the Erie political and social organization closely resembled that of the Huron, and several sources indicate that the Susquehannocks' culture virtually mirrored that of their Seneca neighbors.[86]

Like the Delaware, the Mingo traced their roots along a matrilineal line of descent and organized themselves into extended family units. The extended family units consisted of a "female ancestor and her children, together with the children of her female descendants."[87] The Seneca and Huron organized the extended family units, or *ohwachira*, into eight distinguishable clans. Six of the groups shared similar names—Wolf, Bear, Turtle, Beaver, Deer, and Hawk, while two of the groups differed. In the case of the Seneca, these two groups had the names Snipe and Heron, while the Huron used Sturgeon (or Loon) and Fox.[88]

The ohwachira and clans formed the foundation for the social and governmental institutions in the society and provided the basis for individual relationships. For instance, members of the same ohwachira held certain rights, privileges, and obligations because of their membership in a particular group. Belonging to certain ohwachira allowed individuals to elect or depose the group's sachem; prohibited individuals from marrying members of their group; gave them rights of inheritance to property of deceased kin; bound them to a reciprocal obligation to defend and redress injuries of fellow members; enabled them to bestow names on members; gave them access to a common burial place; and allowed them to be part of the ohwachira's council.[89]

Clan membership had no territorial or group limitations. Members of all clans lived in various communities among their own people as well as in neighboring groups' settlements. "Huron, Neutral, and Iroquois who belonged to clans named after the same animal regarded themselves as bound by many of the same ties of affinity as were members of a single . . . [clan] . . . within their home community."[90] Outsiders entering a community for the first time often sought out individuals with similar clan affiliations for shelter, food, and most of all protection. Clan membership transcended tribal affiliation, indicating that members of the Mingo group associated with one another before they merged in the Ohio Valley, lending proof to the hypothesis that individuals of the various nations—Seneca, Wyandot, Huron, Erie, and Susquehannock—came together to form the Ohio Mingo.

The various groups who made up the Mingo each developed essentially the same type of hierarchical government. The successive order of the hierarchy from bottom to top consisted of extended families (ohwachira), settlement-based clan segments, phratries (several different clans organized together), tribes, and confederacies. For instance, several ohwachira made up the Wolf clan; the Wolf clan belonged to the Wolf phratry, which also included the Hawk, Sturgeon, and Loon clans; this phratry was one of three (the others being Bear and Turtle) that made up one of the four or five Huron tribes, such as the Attignaouantan (People of the Bear) and Attigneenongnahac (Barking Dogs); and these tribes made up the confederacy.[91] Each level of this governmental apparatus consisted of a council of sachems that looked after community, tribal (national), and confederacy affairs, except for the phratry that acted more as a social organization.[92]

In this hierarchical system, the clan segments formed the basis of the governmental apparatus and saw to the management of the domestic and national affairs of their particular settlements and groups. Each clan segment created a council made up of the chosen heads of the individual extended families, also known as gentes, and selected two headmen, one to coordinate civil affairs and the other military. In regard to community affairs, the clan leadership usually met daily to address and resolve issues concerning their particular community. When dealing with national affairs, the community councils converged at a predetermined settlement and resolved matters that concerned the whole tribe. These matters included issues such as land seizures and sales and the election and removal of sachems.[93]

When the Mohawk and Huron met to resolve national or international affairs, the individual community councils designated their most prestigious people to speak on behalf of their group. These select individuals usually inherited this position from a brother or uncle. As a result, each settlement possessed a council made up of the sachems from each of the extended families and clan segments, and depending on the number of settlements that participated in the meeting, there could be several sachems representing each clan. Moreover, the head speakers of the various councils could very well be from the same clan.

The governmental mechanism of the Huron and Iroquois Confederacies consisted of the same elements as the tribal political apparatus. A composite of sachems chosen from the tribal leadership made up the confederacies councils. Similar to national affairs of the individual tribes, the various confederacy councils met only to resolve issues confronting the entire alliance.[94]

The sachems held either peace or war seats and were perhaps the most important and influential figures in Mingo society. Like those of the Shawnee and Lenape, the Mingo sachems held a position of authority but no real power or control over the community, nation, or confederacy. In addition to being chosen from a hereditary line of descendants by the matriarchs of the individual extended families, the clan, tribal, and confederacy councils validated the selection of war and peace leaders. Appointed to these prestigious positions, the sachems needed to conduct themselves in an appropriate manner or suffer the consequence of removal from office.[95]

At all levels of government, the Mingo used a council of sachems as the mechanism to govern and manage their lives. The sachems derived their authority from their extended families and made up each settlement and national council and represented their individual nations at the confederacy councils.[96] In most instances, the settlement, national, and confederacy councils consisted of and were led by the same individuals.

Whether declaring war, negotiating peace, or determining reparations for an individual's violation of community law, the Mingo addressed their domestic, national, and international affairs through their councils. Held in the presence of the governed and opened up to all who wished to express their views on a particular subject, including women, the council was a representative body, and unanimity was the fundamental law of its decision-making process.[97]

To assist with its decision making, the council relied on an ancient and accepted code of behavior. The Mingo system of law prohibited the general society or individual sachems from punishing a person for violating the behavioral code. In most cases, individuals literally paid for their crimes, even in the instance of murder. When dealing with an individual who habitually got into trouble, the council or the individual families and clan segments imposed restrictions or sanctions on that person's actions. On occasion, however, individual families and clan segments killed members of their group whom they deemed socially dangerous. Through their legal system, the Mingo sought to improve a person's behavior and "awaken a sense of responsibility" in the person and not merely punish an individual for poor judgment or inappropriate actions.[98]

Similar to their Shawnee and Lenape neighbors, the Mingo communities vested authority in the hands of a few proven individuals but prevented any control or abuse of power by any one person or group because of their style of government through a common line of hereditary descent. Bound loosely together by kinship, the individual frontier settlements served as the foci of Mingo daily life. Though the Mingo acknowledged the jurisdiction of the Seneca nation over the Ohio Valley in the eighteenth century, their community councils were the most influential and important element in the management of their daily affairs.[99] Hence, though they recognized a higher authority, the Mingo style of government enabled them to act autonomously in governing the domestic and international affairs of their individual communities.

The Logstonian Government

The diverse group of Indian peoples who resided in Logstown during the mid-eighteenth century led the Logstonians to create a governmental apparatus to manage their unique and diversified settlement. Though the basic elements of their system differed little from those of their former groups, the Logstonians adjusted their old institutions to accommodate the fragility of their fledgling multiethnic community. The basic components of this political system consisted of military and secular leaders, a community council of sachems, and an accepted code of behavior.

While there is some credence to historian Richard White's assessment that Logstown consisted of citizens who "were a potentially volatile mix of the discontented . . . who lived together as much from fear as from friendship," the Logstonians shared a similar kinship system that formed the basis for their social relationships.[100] Members of the Turkey clan continued to associate and share a reciprocal bond with other individuals from the same clan despite their affiliation with a particular tribal or national organization like the Seneca, Lenape, or Shawnee. The Logstonians associated along kinship lines more than along national or tribal lines, creating a significant degree of homogeneity and cooperativeness in the community. In fact, the kinship system of many Indian groups continues to exist today in one form or another, still providing the basis for social relationships between members of certain clans.[101] It is unreasonable to assume then that because the Logstonians of the eighteenth century departed from their ancestral groups, they ceased to use their preestablished clan systems to associate with one another. As in the days prior to Logstown's emergence, members of similar clans who were from different communities and nations identified with members of the same totemic group and maintained a reciprocal relationship of rights and responsibilities with related individuals.[102]

The position of sachem remained a post of authority with its rights and responsibilities outlined by the community and clan. As with their former groups, some clans continued to select a male leader to represent them as their sachem or to simply confirm a sachem's selection of a successor. While the position of sachem usually followed a matriarchal or patriarchal line of descent, by the mid-eighteenth century, the clans and community began selecting individuals outside the traditional lines, as in the case of Shingas.[103]

The sachems' roles in their communities changed little between the seventeenth and eighteenth centuries, encompassing both domestic and international affairs. Though the power of decision making generally rested in the hands of the clan or community members, the sachems began to enjoy more power and control in making international decisions. Usually, the sachem acted independently when dealing with matters of international trade, war, regional defense, and political alliances. The increase in power and control over international affairs occurred primarily for two reasons. First, due to the frequency and increasingly exclusive nature of their meetings with outsiders such as the English and French, the sachems lacked the ability to consult with the general public on every decision, with more meetings being held outside the community. Second, the Euroamerican practice to deal solely with the leaders of a particular group increased the need for sachems to act more independently in order to make timely decisions with the various outside groups.[104] Though they were given more freedom to govern, the sachems continued to consult their communities when possible. For instance, when approached by the government of Pennsylvania to forge an alliance, Scarouady, a Mingo leader of Logstown and its surrounding area, responded, "We will take the Belt home to Ohio where there is a greater and wiser Council than Us, and consider it and return you a full Answer."[105]

Tanacharison provides an excellent example of the Ohio Valley sachems. Born of a Catawba mother and Seneca father, Tanacharison established himself as one of the most influential men in the Ohio Valley. Though some scholars contend he was the "viceroy," "regent," or representative of the Iroquois Confederacy sent to watch over the Ohio Indians, the Half-King, a name Tanacharison later earned, gained his position by becoming a mediator between Ohio Indians and colonists. "Building upon a base of kin and personal allies, his authority enhanced by British generosity, Tanacharison eventually became the preeminent Iroquois in the Ohio Country" historian Michael N. McConnell notes.[106]

The wiser community council Scarouady alluded to consisted of the peace and war sachems from the individual clans. Within Logstown, three known clans existed that happened to coincide with three of the Lenape, Shawnee, and Iroquois Confederacy clans: the Wolf, Turkey, and Turtle. Like its former groups, the entire council deliberated over most of the domestic and international affairs and entertained the queries, ideas, problems, and solutions of its community members. Yet unlike its former groups, the Logstonian council consisted of members from all nations—Shawnee, Mingo, and Delaware—which created situations where decisions were made solely according to clan or tribal identity.

In his journal of 1753, Captain William Trent of the Virginia militia noted that on one occasion, he and the Half-King sent for Shingas, who resided primarily in Kuskuski, regarding a matter concerning the Logstonian Delaware. Trent wrote that "the Half King and myself sent for him [Shingas], and told him that it was not right for him to be out of the way when the Canaywagoes came, for it was with their Nation that their chief Business was."[107] Due to the diverse nature of the Ohio Indian settlements, the Logstonian council and sachems, like their neighbors, acted in accord and independently of one another depending on how a particular situation affected their clan, tribal group, or community. Unlike the hierarchy of the former groups that consisted of clans, nations, and confederacies, the components of the Logstonian and essentially the Ohio Indian political system consisted of clans, comprising members from all nations; tribal groups, which included only individuals of a particular nation, such as the Shawnee; and the community, which encompassed everyone in the settlement.

At the time of Euroamerican contact in the mid-eighteenth century, the most prominent sachems of the Logstonian council were Kakowatcheky, the Shawnee leader of the Wolf clan; the Delaware representatives Shingas and his brother King Beaver (Tamaque) of the Turkey clan; and the Mingo leaders Tanacharison and Scarouady of the Seneca and Oneida respectively.[108] While these were the more prominent sachems, several other leaders augmented the council with the support and participation of the community elders. In all, it could be conjectured that the Logstonian council consisted of members of the Shawnee, Lenape, Mingo, Wyandot, Erie, "Iroquois from the Sault St. Louis, from the Lake of the Two Mountains, and Indians from the Nepisiniques and the Abanakis, with Ontarios and other nations" based purely on documentation regarding the composition of the settlement's population and knowledge of the ohwachira and clan roles in the community.[109]

The sachems and council relied on the code of behavior used by their former groups to assist them in governing the settlements of the Ohio Valley. Designed more to mend relationships and rehabilitate offenders as opposed to punishing wrongdoers, the code governed the actions that the council could take when dealing with certain crimes. For many of the crimes, a victim's family or clan usually accepted payment in the form of wampum, skins, or other valuable items to compensate for the offense. In the new multiethnic settlements like Logstown, families, to avoid blood feuds or a rift in the community, seldom sought to repair damages with the death of the offender regardless of the crime. In crimes that affected the entire community, the Logstonian council often intervened to rectify a situation. At the Carlisle Conference in October 1753, for instance, Scarouady attempted to restrict the activities of rum traders in the Ohio Valley by appealing to the Pennsylvania government. Concerned with the adverse affect the liquor had on his people, Scarouady complained:

> Your [Pennsylvania's] traders now bring scarce any thing but Rum and Flour . . . the Rum ruins Us. We beg you would prevent its coming in such Quantities by regulating the Traders. We never understood the Trade was to be for Whiskey and Flour. We desire it may be forbidden, and none sold in the Indian country; but that if the Indians will have any they may go among the Inhabitants and deal with them for it. . . . In short, if this

Practice be continued We must be inevitably ruined. We most earnestly therefore beseech You to remedy it.[110]

Though the rum trade continued, the Pennsylvania government agreed to curtail the traffic of liquor by adopting a plan proposed by Scarouady to limit the goods to essentially three locations under the watchful eye of the Ohio Indians.[111] Due to the apparent adverse alcohol-related incidents caused by the rum trade, the Logstonian council intervened to restrict the trade and promote communal harmony.

Logstown had a well-developed government that efficiently managed the affairs of the settlement's population. Unlike preindustrial societies, Logstown lacked a political system dominated by a small group of social elite who occupied most of the key positions in the society. While many of the Logstonian leaders came from the same clans, the sachems never held complete autocratic power and control over the society. The sachems and their advisers never enjoyed overwhelming temporal and spiritual authority or directly controlled the economic and political institutions through bureaucratic and/or coercive military means. Therefore, Logstown's government cannot be classified as a preindustrial political system. Additionally, Logstown fails to meet all of Sjoberg's requirements for the governments of folk societies because of its clear division of labor, prestige-based social stratification, and the existence of discernible leadership positions in the community. Though the Logstonians clearly did not achieve an industrial status economically and socially, they did possess some of the political features present in industrial societies, such as an elected or appointed body of representatives and an accepted code of laws and/or customs.

Therefore, it would be inaccurate to label the Logstonian government as folk, preindustrial, or industrial. Because the position of sachem usually followed a hereditary line of descent and consisted of the more prestigious members of the community, Logstown's leadership closely resembled the leadership of preindustrial societies. Yet unlike preindustrial societies, the sachems merely occupied positions of authority with certain rights and responsibilities given to them by the community through a process of family and clan hereditary selection. Ultimate power and control rested in the hands of the governed because of the elaborate council system and code of behavior the sachems appealed to and relied on when making decisions resembling more closely the features present in industrial societies. The best description of the Logstonian government, then, would be to say that the political apparatus of Logstown was a system in transition from preindustrial to industrial.

Assigning a contemporary term to explain the Logstonian government is difficult. The four most likely terms to associate the Logstonian government with are "chiefdom," "democracy," "republic," or "oligarchy." While some scholars might argue that the Logstonians created a system of government that resembled a chiefdom, they lacked the population and territorial density to qualify for this type of government, thus ruling it out.[112] Likewise, Logstown could not be classified as an oligarchy seeing that the leadership consisted of a large body of members who possessed relatively little power in the way of societal control.[113]

Arguing that "republics destroyed hierarchy, order and authority," Richard White suggests that Logstown was one of the many "republican villages" of the Ohio Valley.[114] Yet a republic consists of a government composed of a representative body chosen by people who empower certain individuals to represent them and who thereby remove themselves from the decision-making process. Furthermore, an elected individual, not a monarch or chief, usually heads a republic.[115] Though they selected a body of representatives to represent their families, clans, and community, the Logstonians never relinquished their right to participate in the decision-making process. Rather, the community retained all power and control in governing the majority of the domestic and international affairs of the settlement through participation in the councils and the familial hold on the sachems. Thus, Logstown falls outside the parameters of a republic.

Of all the choices presented, "democracy" seems to explain the Logstonian system of government the best. A term originally used by the Greeks to describe the Athenian practice of laws being passed by a majority vote of all freeborn male citizens, "democracy" means "the making of law and policy by a majority of all."[116] Like many terms, however, the meaning of "democracy" changed over time, and it now includes concepts such as unrestricted access to public office. However, if taken in the purest sense of the word, the Logstonian political system resembled a democratic republic where the community, through its representative council of sachems, determined public policy and actions.

The Logstonians and their Indian neighbors connected the Ohio Valley politically through their family, clan, and national affiliations despite residing in politically autonomous settlements. When the French and English journeyed into the Ohio Valley in the mid-eighteenth century, they found this system of government in place and used Ohio Indian political support to first gain access to the region, then to exercise some control over it, and finally to erect permanent settlements. The Ohio Indian sociopolitical system provided the framework for the creation of the Ohio Valley's middle ground and for the permanent Euroamerican settlement of the region.

CHINOOK CHIEFTAINSHIPS

The Chinook developed a political system based on the rule of chiefs and the graduated levels of their social structure. The extended family, held together by blood ties and collocated in autonomous settlements, formed the basis of Chinook society. Three or four extended families banded together and formed the smaller settlements, while several hundred people from more than a few dozen families made up a clan and formed the five larger settlements.[117] Through this system of family, clan, and national affiliation, the Chinook controlled and influenced the political and economic affairs from the mouth of the Columbia River to The Dalles and along present-day Oregon's Pacific coast during the nineteenth century. When the Astorians journeyed to the region to settle it in 1811, they drew on and used this well-developed and firmly entrenched Chinook political structure to support their physical and economic presence in the area.

Like the family itself, the wealthiest male held the highest and most prestigious position in Chinook society and assumed the mantle of leadership. Below the clan and settlement chief, a handful of relatives and family chiefs, or *taises*, formed the social elite of the community and controlled the property and wealth of their respective families. Ordinary people, the *michimis*, and the lesser relatives of the chiefs stood below these ranking families and made up the remainder of the freeborn population, while the slaves rounded out the stratification by settling at the bottom of the graduated society.[118]

Authority to rule came from the extended family and was based on the wealth and prestige a person obtained through generosity and actions. "The creation of a chief," the American explorer Meriwether Lewis wrote, "depends upon the upright deportment of the individual & his ability and disposition to render service to the community; and his authority or the deference paid him is in exact equilibrio with the popularity or voluntary esteem he has acquired among the individuals of his band or nation."[119]

A family and subsequently the clan or settlement deemed one worthy to rule who fulfilled the needs of the family and community through gift giving, sharing, benevolent actions, and deeds that demonstrated abilities to successfully lead.

Though leadership generally passed from father to son because of the transition of wealth and the prestige that accompanied it upon the death of the former, the people approved the hereditary descent of the chiefdom.[120] If the community deemed the heir apparent unworthy to become chief, the people bestowed the position on the next adult male in the ruling family or in some instances to a high-ranking female in the hereditary kinship group.[121] "The politics of the natives of the Columbia are a simple affair: each village has its chief, but the chief does not seem to exercise a great authority over his fellow citizens," Explained Gabriel Franchere, one of the first Astorians.[122] The Chinook employed a ruling apparatus that more closely resembled liberal industrial political structures rather than preindustrial ones, lacking the complete autonomy that the more absolute preindustrial governments enjoyed. Individuals earned and kept their positions as a result of their success and performance in lieu of being born into them or coercing the populace.

Like the mayor of a Greek polis, the Chinook empowered their chiefs to direct and control domestic and foreign affairs. In regard to domestic affairs, the chief acted largely as an adviser, judge, or mediator over local disputes. In some instances, the chiefs convened a counsel of the most influential members of society when they needed to administer over difficult matters.[123] Externally, the chief negotiated foreign affairs with neighboring peoples or intrusive societies. In all instances, the Chinook chief acted with "foresight in matters affecting his own welfare and that of his people."[124] Franchere explained that "as all the villages form so many independent sovereignties, differences sometimes arise whether between the chiefs or the tribes."[125] In most instances, the chiefs easily resolved differences between neighboring groups, either by ensuring compensatory payments to offended parties or by negotiating disputes or concerns over fishing rights. However, in some instances, such as murder or the abduction of women, the chiefs usually rallied the men for war. In doing this, Alexander Ross mentioned, "every man belonging to the tribe is bound to follow his chief and a coward is often punished with death."[126]

In declaring war, the chiefs sent runners to their enemy's settlement to inform them of the day and time of the attack. Though this action violates modern-day military strategy, it afforded the enemy time to negotiate a peace and ensure that its women and children were properly safeguarded. If a peace failed to be reached by the appointed date and time, the Chinook embarked in their canoes to attack the enemy. However, the chance to obtain a peaceful resolution to the conflict remained. Once the attackers reached the defending village, the chiefs attempted to parley a peace agreement. In most instances, the chiefs averted war by this point. However, when armed conflict did occur, the hostilities usually concluded when a few individuals died on one side. Once a side suffered such losses, it admitted defeat and rewarded the enemy with presents.[127]

Perhaps this method of warfare and willingness to peacefully resolve most situations before they resulted in armed conflict led Reverend Samuel Parker in the mid-nineteenth century to write, "Probably there is no government upon earth where there is so much personal and political freedom, and at the same time so little anarchy; and I can unhesitatingly say, that I have no where witnessed so much subordination, peace, and friendship as among the Indians in the Oregon territory."[128]

Though they did not use force or exercise authority by command to rule their society, Parker noticed that "their influence [was] so great, [that] . . . [the chiefs] use their influence by persuasion, stating what in their judgment they believe to be right for the greatest good." Because of their status, Parker noted, "they rarely express an opinion or desire, which is not readily assented to and followed." Thus, the power and authority the chief was entrusted with came as a result of the prestige gained as a wealthy, successful, oftentimes brave benevolent individual and not through coercive measures. While they controlled the resources of the community and often the means to access them, Chinook leaders, because of the need to remain benevolent for the sake of prestige, lacked the latitude and the force necessary to act in coercive or dictatorial ways, making their government, in the words of Parker, one with "so much personal and political freedom," a government much more akin to the more advanced liberal industrial societies then to rigid preindustrial ones.[129]

The Pecos, Mohawk, Ohio Indians, and Chinook created unique and sophisticated political systems that were more advanced than those found in typical preindustrial societies. Unlike simple folk societies, those governments negotiated political alliances with neighboring Indians and later Euroamerican groups, defused potentially volatile domestic tensions, brokered trade agreements with foreign governments, and guided military actions against enemies. To accomplish these tasks, the four societies created governments designed to manage the affairs of families, communities, nations, and in some cases confederacies. At each level, the four groups selected people of prestige to see to their affairs. In some cases, people inherited their positions as in preindustrial societies, while in others they earned them through action or control of the economic resources as in industrial societies. Yet regardless of how one came to rule, leadership afforded an individual authority but not coercive power. Unlike heads of state in preindustrial societies, leaders in the four societies lacked the autocratic rule of the absolute monarchs of Europe. Rather, the ideas of consensus, obligation, and benevolence ruled the affairs of state, removing from them the controlling elements of preindustrial societies.

The Pecos, Mohawk, Ohio Indians, and Chinook created governments that consisted of institutionalized positions of leadership that followed deliberate and established political processes governed by culturally accepted and mandated social, religious, and/or moral codes similar to those of industrial societies. In all four cases, each group developed a system that possessed a high degree of liberality or political freedom nonexistent in preindustrial societies and achieved a level of sophistication that was unfamiliar to Europeans at first contact. Moreover, the development of these advanced governmental systems enabled Indians to connect themselves to a large geographic region diplomatically and militarily through group, clan, family, and settlement affiliation and relationships. Thus the political structures were in place at the time of Euroamerican contact for the Pecos, Mohawk, Ohio Indians, and Chinook to dictate, control, and influence the diplomatic and military affairs of their frontier regions. Though unfamiliar with them, Euroamericans, out of necessity in many cases, learned, to some degree, the intricacies of these Indian systems, adopted them, and then used them to connect them to the larger socioeconomic and political environments of the frontier to permanently establish their presence in North America.

PART 2

Resettling the American Frontier

To say the least, the North American environment offered Euroamericans many unique challenges and placed them in some rather precarious situations from the time they first began their settlement of the continent in the sixteenth century up through the mid-nineteenth century. Leaving "civilization" behind, Euroamericans set out for the frontier ill prepared to face the physical hardships that awaited them. Yet the one constant throughout American history is the recurring story of how the unprepared colonist and settler, on the brink of starvation and annihilation, found a trustworthy "noble savage," like the Pilgrims' Squanto, to rescue them. Most often, this noble Indian came from a settlement right "next door" or down the trail or stream from where the Euroamericans planted themselves. From these Indian settlements, Euroamericans acquired the resources, skills, and support they needed to survive and continue to function on the frontier in spite of their adverse circumstances and hardships until their frontier settlements became self-sustaining and firmly established.

While survival occupied the majority of their time, the initial Spanish, Dutch, French, English, and American pioneers ventured into the backcountry to make a profit from North America's natural resources, such as precious metals, furs, salt, fish, and timber. The first Euroamericans to establish settlements on the frontier often arrived in the company of traders, trappers, and soldiers to procure these resources from Indians or to personally acquire them. When they arrived in New Mexico, New York, the Ohio Valley, and Oregon, these Euroamerican trappers, traders, soldiers, and settlers realized that Indians were more efficient and skilled in procuring the resources they desired. Likewise, Indians viewed the pioneers as potential political and economic partners and desired to include them in their existing trade networks and to infuse European goods into their elaborate gift economies. Once they succeeded in keeping their newfound business partners alive, the economic activities between the Indians and pioneers broadened to include foodstuffs and the natural resources Euroamericans came to the frontier to seek. As trade between the various Euroamerican and Indian groups increased, the pioneers attempted to solidify their presence on the frontier, usually with the blessing and assistance of the Indians, by establishing permanent or semipermanent posts in and around the Indian settlements. Once these posts became established, the pioneers needed the continued economic support of the Indian settlements to ensure the profitability and existence of their own fledgling settlements.

As Euroamerican traders, trappers, soldiers, and settlers expanded the economic scope of their frontier settlements once they solidified their positions through Indian subsistence support, their respective governments attempted to establish a modicum of permanent economic and political control over the frontier zone. Lacking the manpower and resources to physically control such vast expanses of land, the pioneers' governments turned to the seats of Indian political power to buttress and secure their positions on the frontier. Presented with an opportunity to improve their own positions, Indians elected to politically support the pioneers' efforts by using policy and diplomacy. Indian leaders, with their seats of political authority located in their settlements, instituted domestic policy in a way that manipulated Euroamericans to reinforce Indian political and economic positions in their respective frontier zones. These plans and efforts included the negotiation of treaties, alliances, and agreements with colonial and neighboring Indian groups to strengthen and broaden their own influence, prestige, and political positions. Though the intention of their domestic policy was not to assist Euroamericans directly but to accomplish their own aims, some Indian plans required the use of certain measures that assisted Euroamerican settlers. Indians often adopted domestic policies that provided Euroamericans with the ability to access, exploit, and settle the frontier. Unlike their use of domestic policy to secure their own objectives, the Indians employed international diplomacy intentionally to assist Euroamericans with their efforts to establish permanent trading frontiers and primary settlements in their regions. In many cases, Indian leaders and settlements acted as the political sponsors for Euroamericans on the frontier.

While they attempted to improve theirs as well as their Euroamerican partners' positions through peaceful political negotiations, diplomacy often failed and war resulted. Lacking the manpower to properly protect their primary settlements and their claims to the frontier, the pioneers and their Euroamerican patrons relied on Indian military support to protect their interests. Whether an engagement between Indian groups, rival colonial governments, competing European powers, or a combination thereof ensued, Indians provided armed assistance to protect their as well as their allies' frontier interests. Moreover, Indian settlements usually acted as the logistical centers that supported Euroamerican military campaigns on the frontier. If no settlement existed, Indians assisted their Euroamerican allies with the construction of stockades and forts. These military settlements provided Indians and their allies with a connected network of supply depots, a centralized base of operations, and an ample and readily available pool of skilled and experienced frontier fighters. When they lacked Indian military support, Euroamericans found themselves hastily, whether permanently or temporarily, abandoning many of their frontier posts, as was the case with Fort Duquesne in 1758.

To maintain a presence on the frontier, Euroamericans not only needed to survive the physical, economic, political, and military hardships, but they also needed to keep open and safe the lifelines of communication and supply to and from their settlements. To keep these lines open, they relied on Indians to provide informational support. Indian settlements acted as waypoints along the major supply and communication routes to and from the Euroamerican frontier settlements. As waypoints, the Indian settlements provided havens of protection for messengers and convoys. The pioneer posts relied on Indians from the neighboring settlements to keep them informed of potential danger from opposing groups and to protect the lines of communication, supplies, and trade by raiding, scouting, and interpreting for their neighbors. Armed with intelligence of the area and its activities, sustained by an influx of supplies from their parent colonies, and able to travel virtually unmolested through the frontier, the pioneers strengthened their posts and positions on the frontier and ably thwarted attempts to disrupt their endeavors.

The resources Euroamericans needed to settle the American frontier consisted of more than just the rifle, plow, livestock, and knife as Frederick Jackson Turner suggested.[1] Euroamericans needed economic, political, and physical security and support to settle, control, and survive on the frontier. Constrained by natural barriers, an undeveloped infrastructure, and a lack of manpower, parent colonies could not provide the direct support the pioneers required to "plant' the settlements necessary to exploit and control the frontier. The pioneers and their respective governments turned to the only available support network on the frontier, the American Indians. What follows in this work is the presentation of four case studies that show how the Pecos, Mohawk, Ohio Indians, and Chinook actually aided the Spanish, Dutch, French, English, and Americans with the planting of their first settlements in New Mexico, New York, Pennsylvania, and Oregon between the late sixteenth and mid-nineteenth centuries by examining the political, economic, social, and military exchanges between the various groups in frontier borderland (i.e., contact) environments.

CHAPTER 4

For God, Glory, Gold, and Protection

The Establishment of Santa Fe, 1596–1700

NO HISTORIAN CAN IGNORE THE USE OF FORCE EMPLOYED BY THE Spanish to "pacify" the Pueblo Indians of present-day New Mexico during the sixteenth and seventeenth centuries. The story of their inhumane treatment by the Spanish is not a new one. Volumes of historical works detail Spain's colonization and subsequent harsh treatment and marginalization of the Pueblo Indians. However, the story of the Spanish colonization process remains incomplete. Over the past forty years, scholars revised this narrative, describing New Mexico's colonization process first as a story of great Spanish progress, then one of genocide, then one of passive resistance, and most recently one of attempting to understand the intercourse between Euroamericans and Indians on New Spain's northern frontier.[1] While these stories contributed much to the understanding of Spain's North American colonization, there is still one more story to be told, and that is how the Pueblo Indians significantly helped their Spanish oppressors lay the foundation for the Euroamerican settlement of New Spain's northern frontier.

While their harsh tactics successfully pacified and converted many of the Indians, the Spanish knew little about the harshness of New Mexico's arid summers and treacherous winters, or the resolve of the Pueblo to remain independent of a king several thousand miles away. Though the great pacifiers from New Spain were well prepared to defeat small autonomous groups of "heathen" Indians, they arrived in New Mexico at the dawn of the seventeenth century ill prepared to face the physical challenges and the unified efforts of the Pueblo to resist the Spanish *entrada* (conquest).[2] Existing as oases in the desert, pueblo settlements like Pecos contained everything the Spanish needed to survive the harsh New Mexico environment: food, shelter, clothing, a preexisting economic and political network, military forces, companionship, and a people who lived in the region for over four hundred years acquiring the knowledge to survive in it. Regardless of the fact that they marginalized and abused Indians, the Spanish used and relied on Pueblo settlements and their populations to supply them with the foodstuffs, shelter, clothing, heathen souls to convert for the Catholic Church, trade, warriors, intelligence, experienced individuals, and diplomatic connections they needed to survive the rigors of New Spain's northern frontier. In so doing, the Pueblo laid the foundation for the Euroamerican settlement of North America's southwestern frontier by spearheading the establishment of Santa Fe, the eventual focus of and logistical center for the development of New Mexico.

The importance of this narrative to this work is twofold. First and foremost, by including the Spanish study along with the Dutch, French, English, and American examples, this is one of the few works that looks at frontier settlement from a 360-degree perspective. Unlike Frederick Jackson Turner's and others' advancing waves of east-to-west settlement, the four studies provided in this work look at how Euroamerican settlement occurred simultaneously throughout North America. In short, while the Dutch settled New York from the east in the early seventeenth century, the French from the north in Canada, and the English from the southeast in Virginia, the Spanish entered and occupied North America from the southwest. Second, this study shows how even when they were reluctant and resistant to a Euroamerican presence in North America, Indians, simply through their existence, aided Spanish, Dutch, French, English, and American settlement on the frontier.

To appreciate the contribution the Pueblo made to the Euroamerican settlement of New Mexico, Spanish settlement must be looked at in two distinct phases that are marked by the Pueblo Revolt of 1680. The first phase of Spanish settlement occurred between 1598 and 1680, before the revolt broke out. During this stage of Euroamerican frontier development, the Pueblo, through their existence and supply of foodstuffs, clothing, shelter, and trade goods, kept the Spanish alive by fulfilling their basic physical and economic needs. In the second phase of Spanish settlement that occurred between 1692 and 1696, the Pueblo provided the Spanish with the diplomatic, military, and intelligence support that assisted them with their conquest and reoccupation of New Mexico following the revolt.

EARLY SPANISH INTEREST IN NEW MEXICO, 1536–1598

Though the Spanish did not actively begin to settle New Mexico's frontier until 1595, their interest and activity in the region started as early as 1536, when four survivors of an expedition who began their journey in Florida and shipwrecked near present-day Galveston, Texas, found themselves wandering through the southwestern desert of the Pueblo Indians until they stumbled upon Spaniards and made their way to Mexico City with their amazing story. Throughout his fateful journey, Cabeza de Vaca, the second in command of this failed expedition, chronicled his tale and described with no extraordinary zeal the small amount of mineral deposits he happened upon while in present-day New Mexico and Texas. Because Vaca was lost most of the time, his account of his journey provided little in the way of cartographical knowledge. However, because he and his three companions were the first to cross North America from Florida to New Mexico, Vaca's expedition, despite its description of little mineral wealth, sparked the interests of the two most powerful men in New Spain, Viceroy Antonio de Mendoza and Hernan Cortes.[3]

Wanting to explore the region before his rivals Cortes and Hernando de Soto, Mendoza sent the Franciscan Fray Marcos de Niza and one of Vaca's three companions, the former black Moorish slave Esteban, to search New Spain's northern frontier in present-day New Mexico. Esteban more than likely explored the region without Niza, and he died at the hands of Zuni warriors. Niza returned to Mexico City by summer 1539 with tales of a land he never saw.[4]

When he arrived in Mexico, Niza wasted no time in pronouncing that he had found the famed "golden" city of Cibola as well as several others with wealth beyond imagination. Lured by Niza's fanciful story about his discovery of the mythical city of Cibola, Mendoza ordered Francisco Vázquez de Coronado to explore, conquer, and lay claim to the lands of New Mexico in 1540. Though he failed to find and conquer Cibola, Coronado thoroughly explored the region and exposed the world of the Pueblo peoples to the Spanish crown through his detailed journal. Enticed by Coronado's reports of the region's untapped wealth in both heathen souls and natural resources, King Philip II of Spain authorized the official exploration and settlement of New Mexico in 1583.[5]

While motivated to expand his New World borders into the present-day southwestern United States, Philip chose to do so in a manner more aligned with the doctrine of the Holy Bible. Mindful of the colonizing and Christianizing difficulties brought about by the atrocities that the conquistadors inflicted on the native peoples of South America and Mexico, Philip changed Spain's colonial policy of conquest to one of pacification and prohibited the exploration and settlement of Indian lands without royal approval. To accentuate this new doctrine, he announced his "Orders for New Discoveries" in 1573, detailing his new protocol for the settlement of frontier lands. Using this act as the guideline for Spanish settlement, Philip elected to pacify, settle, and administer New Mexico through missionary expeditions that were accompanied by small military escorts.[6]

The Franciscans immediately answered the king's call to colonize New Mexico and launched the first expedition since Coronado into New Mexico in 1581 under the direction of Fray Agustin Rodriguez and Captain Francisco Sanchez Chamuscade. While Rodriguez and Chamuscade perished on this venture, Hernan Gallegos, the expedition's notary, returned to tell the tales of their adventure. Like Niza and Coronado, Gallegos described a land where the natives wore cotton clothing and lived in houses made of stone. Enticed by these tales, several would-be entrepreneurs began to concoct plans to try their hand at colonizing New Mexico.[7]

The first of these men, a successful cattle rancher named Antonio de Espejo, sought to make his way into New Mexico by offering the Franciscans his services as a possible rescuer for Rodriguez and another member of their order left behind on the 1581 expedition to administer to the souls of the Pueblo Indians. Though informed the Franciscans left behind were dead, Espejo, for a number of personal reasons, one of which was to escape the law, decided to take a reconnaissance party into New Mexico to ascertain the true condition of the men left behind and departed in November 1582. Exceeding the mandate of his mission, Espejo journeyed well beyond the lands of the Pueblo, traveling into present-day Arizona and onto the Great Plains. Like the accounts of the men before him, Espejo's report described a much larger country, rich with people and potential profits. Inspired by Gallegos's and Espejo's reports detailing the spiritual and economic potential of New Mexico's frontier, King Philip instructed his viceroy in New Spain to find a person qualified to pacify and settle the potentially rich lands of New Mexico.[8]

To lead the first royal-sanctioned entrada into New Mexico, Viceroy Luis de Velasco II selected Don Juan de Oñate, the son of the successful colonizer of Zacatecas and a capable "pacifier" of Indians in his own right, to head the

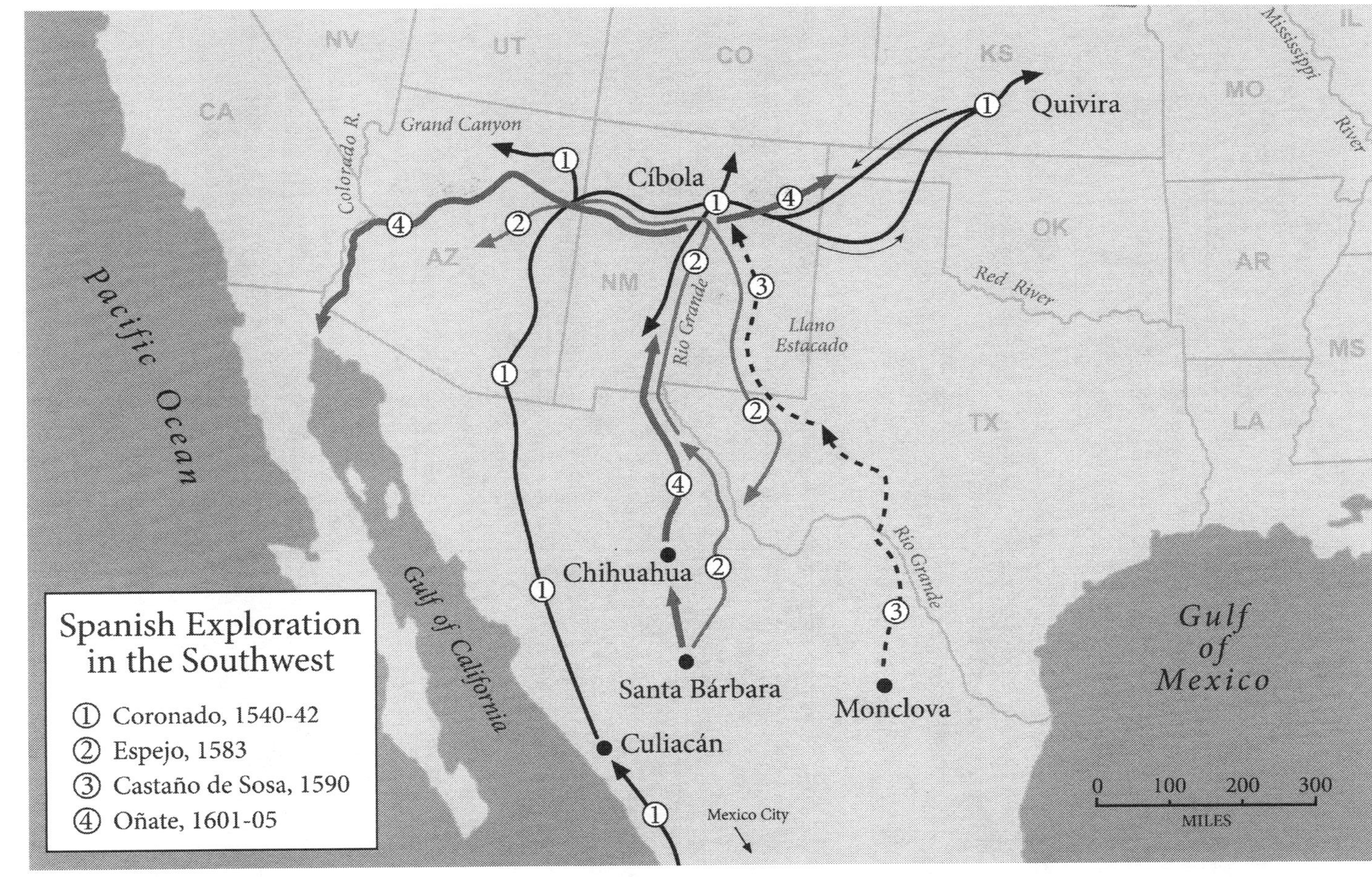
Spanish Exploration in the Southwest
① Coronado, 1540-42
② Espejo, 1583
③ Castaño de Sosa, 1590
④ Oñate, 1601-05
Pacific Ocean
Gulf of California
Gulf of Mexico
NV
UT
CO
KS
MO
IL
CA
AZ
NM
OK
AR
MS
TX
LA
Colorado R.
Grand Canyon
Cíbola
Quivira
Mississippi River
Red River
Rio Grande
Llano Estacado
Chihuahua
Santa Bárbara
Monclova
Culiacán
Mexico City
0 100 200 300
MILES

venture in September 1595. Though the contract called for him to depart for the northern frontier by 1596, court intrigue and political jockeying by his rivals caused a two-year delay in the project. Having personally bankrolled most of the project, Oñate departed for New Mexico frustrated and near financial ruin in March 1598 at the head of a column of 129 soldiers, nearly 400 colonists, and over 7,000 head of livestock.[9]

THE SPANISH TRIALS AT SAN JUAN AND SAN GABRIEL, 1598–1610

With the stories of Coronado, Espejo, and Gaspar Castaño de Sosa—a man who illegally attempted to colonize New Mexico in 1590—ringing in their ears, Oñate and his company embarked on their journey full of hope and religious zeal.[10] While the accounts of Coronado, Espejo, and Castaño described the peoples and potential riches of New Mexico, they also described the harshness of the land and the never-ending struggle to find food and water in a region subject to "*ocho meses de invierno y quatro meses de infierno*"—eight months of winter and four months of hell.[11] Informed and instructed that the "success of the expedition [would] not depend so much on their numbers as on . . . being so well provisioned that they [could] support themselves for some time," Oñate planned for what he perceived to be the worst conditions the expedition might face.[12] However, the conditions he and his band faced far exceeded anything the great pacifier and his company expected.

Before leaving Mexico, Oñate and his company of colonists, or *pobladores*, began to experience the hardships that were only a token of what lay in store for them in New Mexico. Unlike the first 750-mile leg of his entrada from Mexico City to Santa Barbara, Mexico, that included some semblance of a road system, Oñate's second 750-mile leg took him across broken and unforgiving lands. Leaving Santa Barbara, Oñate's caravan stretched nearly four miles long and followed tributaries, crossed rivers, trudged across a desert, weaved its way around sand dunes, and traversed dangerous mountain passes, seldom managing more than six miles per day. During the course of the six-month march, the company's stores, which they planned to be an integral part of beginning their colony in New Mexico, became entirely exhausted, forcing Oñate to send a vanguard through Pueblo settlements to procure food for their survival. As if these were not enough hardships, Oñate and his company found water scarce in the land, forcing them to rely on heavy rainfalls at times to quench their thirst and that of their livestock by sopping up what they could from mud puddles that dotted the landscape. Suffering the loss of over twenty wagons, hundreds of livestock, and a number of people from Indian attacks and the wretched conditions, Oñate limped his way into the Tewa pueblo of Okhe starving and parched from the bitter road. Exhausted from the long march and ignorant of the surrounding area, Oñate made the pueblo his temporary headquarters, renaming it San Juan.[13] After reconnoitering the area for a few months, Oñate moved his colony to the pueblo of Yunque, establishing it as the Spanish capital and renaming it San Gabriel.[14] With this less-than-glorious entrada, Spain officially began the first phase of its colonizing efforts in New Mexico.

Though the trials of the journey were over, the true test for Oñate and his company began as they faced the inferno that was the New Mexico summer. Charged with the threefold task of exploring the region, Christianizing the Indians, and establishing a colony, Oñate and the viceroy of New Spain laid out a plan for New Mexico that called for the implementation of the *encomienda* and *repartimiento* systems, legal methods employed to collect tribute and force labor from Indians, to support the fledgling operation.

Throwbacks from the feudal age, both systems essentially exploited the resources and labor of the native inhabitants of a land to ensure the success of Spanish colonization. The encomienda system authorized Oñate to reward trustees, or *encomenderos*, land grants that could be passed on hereditarily to successive generations of their families for their efforts on the frontier by allowing them to collect tribute from one or several pueblos. Oñate planned for the encomenderos to give a portion of the tribute they collected to him for the twofold purpose of supporting the colony and paying the crown. Unlike the encomienda system that taxed the peoples' resources, the repartimiento system authorized the Spanish to harness the labor of the Indians by levying Pueblo workers and assigning them throughout the colony to undertake public work projects, such as the construction of churches and towns. Through the implementation of both these systems, Oñate planned to fulfill the Spaniards' basic needs of subsistence and survival, while exploiting the reported wealth of the region. However, with his people on the brink of starvation when they entered San Juan in July 1598, Oñate decided to fulfill their subsistence needs by relying on the Indians for foodstuffs and elected to conquer and explore the region for Spain in lieu of employing the two systems to sow "a community plot [and] to feed his people."[15]

Several considerations probably influenced Oñate's decision to focus on exploring and conquering the region rather than firming up his tiny colony in a land occupied by an estimated sixty thousand less-than-jovial Pueblo Indians.[16]

First and foremost, before they could tap into and cultivate the land's riches, Oñate and his men needed to find and secure immediate profits for the Spanish crown and, more importantly, themselves. Having invested all they had on the hopes that New Mexico would be as profitable in gold, silver, and other commodities as Mexico, Oñate and his captains wanted to ensure that they would indeed secure their lifelong fortunes in New Spain's northern frontier.[17] Between the accounts of Coronado, Espejo, and Castaño mentioning the existence of silver veins; the low morale and mutiny of forty-five of his soldiers who fled after reaching San Gabriel; and the reports he received from the local Indians detailing great western settlements filled with riches and a nearby body of water believed to be the South Sea filled with pearls, Oñate sought to make his venture immediately profitable.[18]

Second, by the "Orders for New Discoveries," which were the actual impetus for the entire venture, Oñate and his men came to bring the Christian God to the Indians and were required to convert them to Roman Catholicism. Moreover, King Philip instructed Oñate and the friars to "attract the Indians, by good treatment and pay, to live in the homes of the Spaniards in order that they may learn trades and help in the necessary labors" required to ensure the success of the colony.[19] Equipped with ten friars bent on saving souls and mandated by the king himself to Christianize, Oñate had no choice but to see to the business of conversion.

Third, knowing that "the land could not be colonized . . . as the natives from all districts . . . would form a league, rebel, and destroy [the Spanish] easily" because of their success against the company during the march, Oñate wanted to demonstrate the lethality of his small force of men in the vast sea of Indians.[20]

Last, challenged by food and water shortages before they even arrived in San Juan, Oñate successfully provisioned his force of five hundred souls by sending out parties to neighboring pueblos to procure maize, squash, beans, and whatever else the Indians had in store. Having endured the draconian tactics of Coronado, Espejo, and Castaño, on most occasions the Pueblos temporarily abandoned their homes at the approach of Oñate's company and allowed the Spanish to waltz right into their settlements and confiscate anything they wished. If the Indians remained in their settlements and resisted the seizure of their food, Oñate and his men used force to make them surrender their goods. Successful with this modus operandi, Oñate saw this technique as the blueprint to sustain his colony and chose to forgo planting crops in a land "so poor and lacking in everything necessary to support life," electing instead to rely on the Pueblo Indians to provide his company with the supplies they needed to establish themselves in New Mexico.[21]

In a land where eight months of winter and four months of hell reigned, "corn [was] God," and the Spanish needed the Indian's golden deity to survive, leading them to plunder the pueblos' maize supplies to feed themselves and their livestock.[22] To procure their foodstuffs, Oñate, as he did on the march, routinely sent "people out each month in various directions to bring maize from the pueblos." As the Spaniards approached the pueblos, the Indians usually fled to the hills and left their large stores of food to be taken by the starving colonists. When they did remain in their homes, the Pueblo seldom resisted the conquistadors and only wept and cried out "as if they and all their descendants were being killed" when the Spanish confiscated their food.[23] So reluctant were they to part with their maize that the Spanish often found it "necessary to torture the chieftains, even to hanging and killing them" to "induce the Indians to furnish corn for food."[24] Compelled to use such tactics for fear of seeing their "women and children parish," even the friars, who deplored the practice, felt it was necessary to collect Indian corn "to keep from starving to death."[25] In just three short years, the Spanish tactic of confiscation significantly reduced the Pueblo stockpile of corn; where once seventy-eight thousand bushels of maize filled the kivas of settlements like Pecos, absolutely nothing remained.[26] Once they exhausted the Pueblos' stockpiles of goods, the Spaniards became so desperate for food that during Lent, they "ate meat three days a week for lack of anything else," despite it being an awful sin.[27] When they were lucky enough to find some corn, the Spanish treated it "as if it contained the most precious liquor," taking care to seal the containers with great diligence.[28] Due to the strain the Spaniards placed on the Pueblos' subsistence system, the Indians began killing the Spanish livestock for food, despite the potential punishment, and spent hours picking up every individual kernel of corn that dropped to the ground following harvests.[29] Beleaguered by such conditions, "any Spaniard," as one chronicler wrote, "who gets his fill of tortillas here feels as if he has obtained a grant of nobility."[30]

Coupled with starvation, the intolerably cold winters proved to be the other great thorn in the Spaniards' side. Unprepared to face such harsh conditions, the Spanish lacked the appropriate clothing to battle the freezing temperatures of the New Mexico winters. To compound matters, the land being almost devoid of trees forced Oñate and his people to travel distances of fifteen miles to gather enough firewood to stay warm and cook.[31] The temperatures reached so low that the wine often froze while Mass was being said.[32] As a result, the Spanish "robbed [the Indians] of the scanty clothing they had to protect themselves" and "took the blankets away from the Indian women, leaving them naked and shivering with cold."[33] To stockpile goods for successive winters, Oñate forced the Indians to pay a tribute of "one blanket, a skin, or a buckskin per house each year."[34] However, despite his best efforts, Oñate's blueprint for relying solely on the Indians to support his colonial efforts led to the starvation of many of the Pueblo and to the demoralization of his own people. In just three years, a large majority of the settlers asked the viceroy for permission to abandon the colony for fear of their certain demise.[35]

Aware that this strategy was hampering the Spanish efforts to establish a permanent colony in New Mexico, Oñate attempted to alleviate the privations of his people by enlisting the Indians to plant crops at San Gabriel and by hunting for buffalo. Within two years, the Indians devoted themselves "willingly to [the corn's] cultivation," successfully bringing in "more than 1,500 fanegas [24,000 bushels] of wheat" in just one year. Additionally, the Indians continued to "readily and willingly . . . supply without failing . . . fowls, corn, calabashes, and game" of every sort.[36] To augment these crops and the goods they confiscated from the Indians, Oñate sent an expedition to the Great Plains to hunt for buffalo meat. Though they found literally thousands of the beasts, the Spanish only managed to take a modest amount of meat and consumed what they did acquire within a matter of months.[37] Despite these accomplishments, Oñate's colony consumed over an estimated sixty-six thousand bushels of corn each year and continued to suffer from a lack of food, causing several members of the expedition to desert and risk the long, hazardous road back to Mexico on their own.[38] As Captain Diego de Zubia explained in a public inquiry to abandon the colony: "It has reached a point where this army is on the verge of starving to death or dying at the hands of the barbarous Indians, who will fall upon us when they see how helpless we are, without weapons, horses, or anything else. Provisions in this land are absolutely exhausted. All that the natives had has been consumed, and many of them are starving to death."[39]

The situation became so bad that Oñate, to prevent the colonial endeavor from going under, freed the horses to dissuade the people from desertion and killed some of the key mutineers pleading to abandon the province.[40] Despite these measures, over 350 of the 500-plus pobladores and soldiers who accompanied Oñate to New Mexico deserted when the governor was off exploring, leaving a mere two dozen colonists in San Gabriel.[41] To improve their position, Oñate and a number of his company appealed to King Philip III, who succeeded to the throne six months after Oñate began his expedition in 1598, for reinforcements and supplies to continue his exploration of the area and "to build a villa . . . in order that the foundations of the colony might be more stable."[42]

To accomplish this, Oñate and his brother in Spain attempted to persuade the king to finance a troop of four hundred soldiers to continue the business of colonizing New Mexico. While at first he entertained the idea, the king decided that discretion was the better part of glory in this case and denied Oñates's request. Questions about the integrity of Oñate and the benefits of the colony itself cast more than just a shadow of a doubt on the continuation of the New Mexico project. After all, the only thing Oñate and his company discovered was that the land was poor, the mines were of little value, and the people were "rustic, wretched in clothes and spirit."[43] As the king deliberated over his options, Oñate began assigning encomiendas while continuing to rely on the Indians for food. With San Gabriel reduced to fewer than one hundred people, the colony maintained itself despite the continued hardships of the land. In January 1606, the king finally decided to continue the colony solely to protect the seven thousand Indians the Spanish had converted.[44]

With this new missionary purpose guiding the project, the king redefined the parameters of the New Mexico colony and ordered the cessation of further discovery, recalled Oñate, disbanded his army, and appointed a new governor.[45] Feeling abandoned and betrayed, Oñate resigned his position in August 1607, allowing the viceroy to appoint Juan Martinez de Montoya interim governor until a suitable replacement was found. In early 1610, Don Pedro de Peralta, Oñate's replacement, marched into San Gabriel with orders from the viceroy to cease exploring trips, to immediately begin farming, to "promote the welfare of [the] Indians," and, before all else, "to found and settle [a] villa . . . so that they [the Spanish] may live with some order of decency."[46]

THE ESTABLISHMENT OF SANTA FE AND NEW MEXICO, 1610–1680

When he reached San Gabriel, Peralta immediately began to put the colony on firm footing. To accomplish this, the governor and New Spain's viceroy, Martin Lopez de Guana, intended to bring order to New Mexico by establishing a formalized municipal government to manage the affairs of the colony. "Since experience [showed] that greed for what [was] out of reach . . . always led [the Spanish] to neglect what they already had," Peralta devoted his efforts primarily "to maintain and make secure what [was] discovered, both in spiritual and temporal matters" by first establishing a new villa more appropriate for the missionary designs of the colony.[47] Within months, Peralta began the construction of Santa Fe, awarded more encomiendas, emplaced missionaries, and distributed the pobladores throughout the countryside in isolated farms and ranches in the proximity of the surrounding pueblos.[48] Though Peralta entered New Mexico with a clear vision and plan, the Spanish need for Pueblo assistance remained the major factor in determining the success of Santa Fe's establishment. For Santa Fe to become permanently and securely established, the Spanish needed Pueblo labor to build their settlement and cultivate their crops; Pueblo tribute and trade to finance their secular and economic endeavors; Pueblo souls to satisfy the Roman Catholic Church's need for converts; and Pueblo medical assistance and human companionship to help survive the rigors of the harsh New Mexico environment.

To construct Santa Fe, Peralta instituted the repartimiento system to levy the Indian labor required to build the villa. Relying on their skill as masons and carpenters, the Spanish used Indian laborers to haul the timber, mud, grass, and water required to build the scaffolding and to make the adobe bricks that were to be used in the construction of Santa Fe and the churches in the surrounding pueblos. To build some of the larger and grander buildings in New Mexico, such as the church at Pecos, the Indians needed to make and lay an estimated three hundred thousand adobe bricks and construct scaffolding four stories high for just one project that took years to complete. Over time, some of the Indians became skilled in European building techniques. The Pecos, for instance, earned a reputation as being the finest carpenters in New Mexico, causing many Spaniards to contract them for numerous jobs.[49] With each adobe brick weighing approximately forty pounds and the intricate woodworking required to bring the Catholics' churches to life, the Spaniards needed an army of laborers to build their settlements. Though they paid them a salary of a half to a full real per day's work, the Spanish continually required the Indians to pay an annual tax that was nearly the equivalent of their earnings. This essentially forced them to work for free and caused many of them to neglect the cultivation of their fields to earn money to satisfy their debt, which further increased the suffering of the Pueblo. With only sixty Spaniards in all of New Mexico in 1609, Peralta, his eventual successors, and the pobladores needed Indian labor to build their settlements, churches, farms, and ranches.[50]

Because the king and viceroy accepted the fact that New Mexico lacked the resources to turn a profit and so changed the objective of the colony to the harvesting and protecting of converted souls, Peralta journeyed to San Gabriel at the head of only sixteen men in lieu of the four hundred Oñate had requested. Because it was intended to be the administrative and logistical center for missionary activities in New Mexico and not a presidio, the king and viceroy planned for the sole Spanish settlement in the region to be protected not by regular troops but by militia and supported by the pobladores.[51]

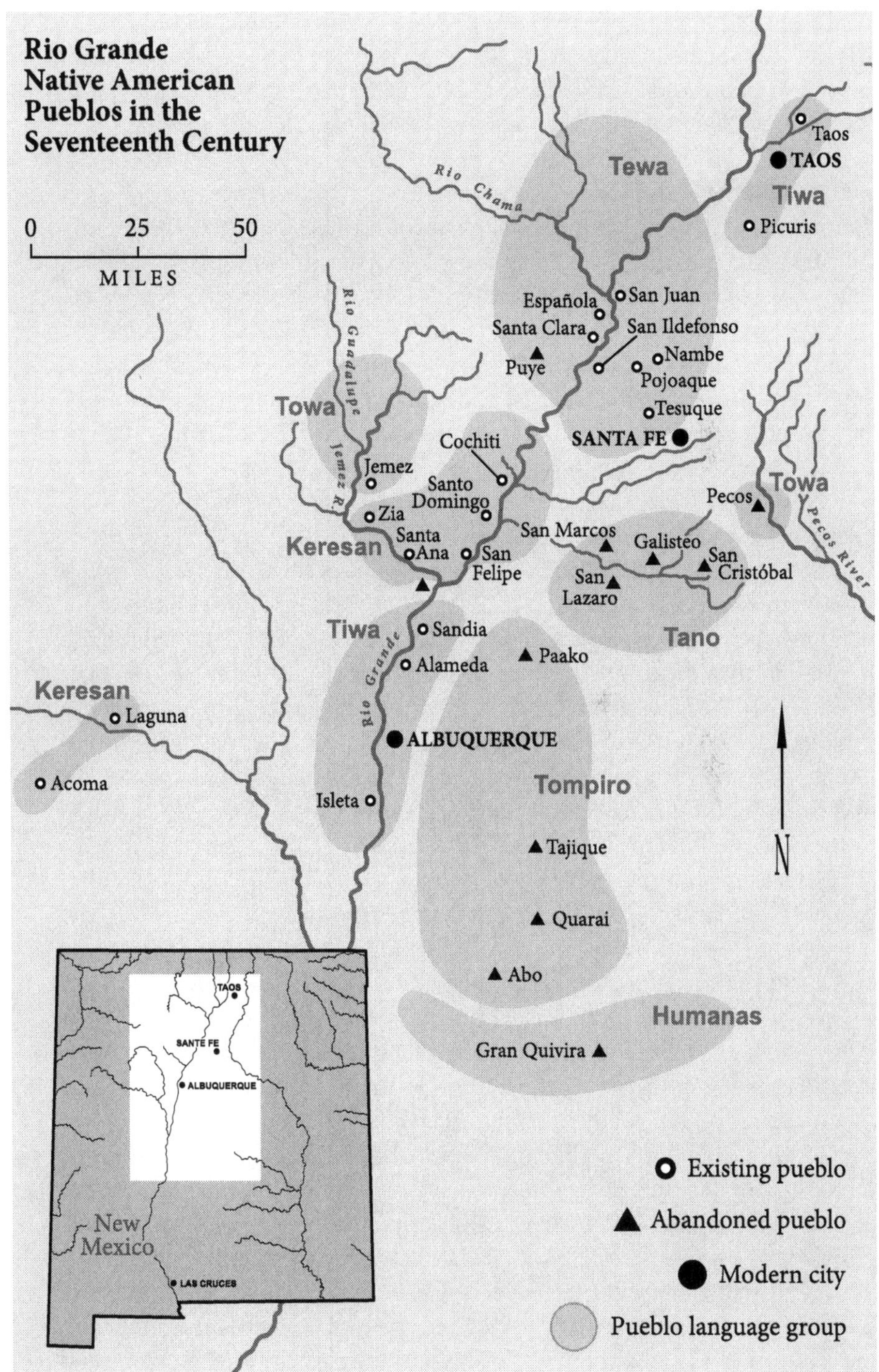
Rio Grande Native American Pueblos in the Seventeenth Century
0 25 50
MILES
Rio Chama
Tewa
Taos
TAOS
Tiwa
Picuris
Rio Guadalupe
Española
San Juan
Santa Clara
San Ildefonso
Puye
Nambe
Pojoaque
Towa
Tesuque
SANTA FE
Cochiti
Jemez R.
Jemez
Santo Domingo
Towa
Pecos
Pecos River
Zia
San Marcos
Galisteo
Santa Ana
San Felipe
San Cristóbal
Keresan
San Lazaro
Tiwa
Sandia
Tano
Rio Grande
Alameda
Paako
Keresan
Laguna
ALBUQUERQUE
Acoma
Tompiro
Isleta
Tajique
N
Quarai
Abo
Humanas
Gran Quivira
TAOS
SANTE FE
ALBUQUERQUE
New Mexico
LAS CRUCES
Existing pueblo
Abandoned pueblo
Modern city
Pueblo language group

To attract and keep the pobladores needed to maintain a colony in New Mexico, the king empowered Peralta to establish encomiendas in addition to what Oñate already granted with the twofold purpose of creating the militia and providing for the defense and spiritual welfare of the Indians.[52] By continuing this practice, Peralta hoped to attract and keep encomenderos with the promise of nobility, power, and the ability to secure their families' futures through the acquisition of land and the accumulation of Indian tribute for the simple price of military service. To make this system work, Peralta authorized the encomenderos to collect from every household a tribute of a blanket thirty-three inches long, one fanega of maize, usually in October following the harvest, and a piece of cotton manta or buckskin six palms square (approximately 5.6 feet square) in May.[53] To make the deal even more enticing, the governors organized the encomiendas to encompass entire pueblos, giving the encomenderos access to the tribute of thousands of Indians in some cases. In 1662, the accounting of Francisco Gomez Robledo's encomienda consisted of "all . . . of Pecos, except twenty-four houses, Two and a half parts of . . . Taos, Half . . . of Shongopovi, Half . . . of Acoma, except for twenty houses, Half . . . of Abo, [and] All . . . of Tesuque." In addition to the 976 bushels of corn he took each year, Robledo collected 340 "buckskins, mantas, buffalo hides or . . . elk skins from Pecos, 110 from Taos, 80 from Shongopovi, 50 from Acoma and 30 from Abo amounting to a sum of approximately 700 pesos."[54] From this Indian tribute, on which the entire encomienda system was based, the Spanish fed themselves, clothed themselves, and generated the revenue needed to invest in the development of their homes and their colony.

To accumulate the commodities necessary to fulfill their financial obligation to the Spanish, the Indians not only cultivated their fields but also engaged in an elaborate trade network that linked the worlds of the Pueblo and Plains Indians. The Pueblo acquired buffalo hides, elk, tanned skins, and a variety of other goods by exchanging corn, cloth, and turquoise with the Plains Indians. Located in the Glorieta Pass, the Pecos occupied a strategic position, enabling them to become one of the wealthiest pueblos in New Mexico by serving as middlemen in this elaborate trade network. Pecos was the closest pueblo to the plains, and the Apache and other Indians journeyed there and camped outside its gates, usually between August and October, engaging in an annual trade fair where a large number of commodities exchanged hands. The Pecos fair was also a venue to sell, buy, and trade slaves.[55]

Not long after they experienced the Pecos fair, the Spanish realized the economic and human potential of the yearly event, actively participating in the trade themselves, exchanging European trade goods for slaves, hides, and a variety of other items. Simultaneously, the friars used the fair as a way to impress upon the nomadic Apache the power of the Spaniard's civilization and God. Writing in 1622, Fray Andres Juarez alluded to this subliminal method of conversion, noting: "They come to this pueblo to trade . . . the items they bring us are very important to the natives and to the Spaniards. Many times when they come they will enter the church and when they see there the *retablo* [altar] and the rest there is, the Lord will enlighten them so that they want to be baptized and converted to our Holy Catholic Faith."[56]

Some of the Apache leaders who came to trade at Pecos were so impressed with the four-story church and the tales of the beautiful mother of God that they traveled to Santa Fe to see the image of the Assumption of Our Lady. When they arrived as night fell, a tapestry of well-lit candles surrounded the statue of the Lady while music rang out from the villa causing the Apache "to become very fond of her" and to proclaim their intentions of becoming Christians.[57] In a land that lacked everything but heathen souls, the Pecos trade fair was one of the few locations in New Mexico where the Spanish could actually trade goods, turn a profit, and attempt to convert the nomadic Indians. Without Pecos, Santa Barbara, 750 miles away from Santa Fe, stood as the only Spanish market where the pobladores of New Mexico could exchange their goods.

Being 1,500 miles from Mexico City, the pobladores and encomenderos, despite Spain's "Orders for New Discoveries," enjoyed nearly free rein over their lands, enabling them to abuse Pueblo labor and resources with ease. Unlike the richer Spanish districts where mines and markets provided Spaniards with much of their wealth, New Mexico's impoverished land required the encomenderos to rely almost solely on the items they took from the Pueblo to earn any sort of revenue. Though the encomienda system laid out strict guidelines that required them to reside in Santa Fe, the encomenderos justified living on their ranches and farms out in the countryside to more easily collect their tribute. Away from the Franciscans' prying eyes, the encomenderos illegally settled on Indian lands and regularly abused the encomienda and repartimiento systems by pressing the Pueblo to work on their farms and ranches as a form of tribute.[58]

The encomenderos continually used Pueblo laborers to tend herds, till fields, cut and haul firewood, serve as house servants, and act as load bearers for transporting goods. Sometimes these duties required that the men be separated from their families for long periods, placing great stress on the Indian women and children. In some cases, the men died in the service of the encomenderos and never returned from these projects. Likewise, women bore many hardships having to thwart or succumb to the unwanted and uncontrollable sexual approaches of the encomenderos themselves. To improve and sustain their revenue in the face of a declining Pueblo population, the encomenderos amended the encomienda system so that tribute collected was not per household but per individual, requiring the Indians to give four to five times more than the king required. "Instead of [going] to preach the word of God" as the king and viceroy intended, "the Spanish [only] blaspheme[ed] it" causing great angst among the Pueblo.[59]

Two other forms of available labor existed that the encomenderos exploited to their benefit, the *rescate* system and slavery. In the rescate system, the Spaniards paid a ransom to free captured Indians being held by other native groups. After a tragic affair in which four children were beheaded after the Spanish refused to pay a ransom, the king mandated that the system be enforced. Unfortunately for many of these ransomed Indians, liberation from their captors failed to guarantee their freedom. As they did with the encomienda and repartimiento systems, the Spanish abused the rescate program and, in lieu of returning the Indian children to their homes, placed them with Christian families to become civilized in return for household services. Though these Indians were officially considered servants, or *criados*, and not slaves, the Spaniards usually ransomed them at trade fairs, like the one annually held at Pecos, for the price of a good mule worth thirty or forty pesos. Separated from their families and placed in Spanish homes, the *criados* usually remained with their Euroamerican patrons, never returning to their native groups.[60]

Though the exploitation of these three systems fulfilled some of the labor needs of the Spaniards, Indian slavery remained a major component of New Mexico society. Since the labor of the Christianized Pueblo was easily manipulated through the encomienda and repartimiento systems, the pobladores of New Mexico took their slaves from the more nomadic heathen people of the plains who refused to accept God and resisted the Spanish presence in the region. Using the Pecos trade fair to exchange human flesh, the Spaniards either bought the slaves for their own purpose or sold them to mining towns in New Spain that needed the labor. If the trade fair failed to produce the number of laborers they desired, the Spaniards often formed raiding parties to acquire the slaves themselves.[61] The Spanish openly practiced the institution in New Mexico while the government officials there and elsewhere turned a blind eye to the matter since the king explicitly forbade Indian slavery. In many instances, the governors themselves used slave and forced labor to generate their own revenue by having the Indians run retail shops from the government palace, where they sold nuts, salt, shoes, tents, and an assortment of handmade crafts. By the time of the Pueblo Revolt in 1680, New Mexico had developed an export economy in slaves, profiting greatly from the practice. In 1714, slavery became such an issue that the governor of New Mexico, Juan Ignacio Flores Mogollon, ordered that all Indian captives be baptized before the pobladores "[took] them to distant places to sell."[62]

The Franciscans also placed a heavy burden on the backs of the Pueblo to save and protect them from their colonial masters, making their lives worse in the process. Never forgetting the king's renewed purpose for the colony, the Franciscans frowned on the negative impact that the Spaniards' harsh treatment and exploitation had on the Indians they were supposed to convert. The Spanish actions, Fray Francisco de Zamora noted, "brought great discredit on [their] teaching, causing the natives to wonder that if Christians caused so much harm and violence, why should they [the Indians] become Christians?"[63] Up against the encomenderos and governors, the Franciscans attempted to counteract the actions of the secular authority in New Mexico by literally trying to control the lives of the Pueblo. The Franciscans hoped to convert them to Roman Catholicism while freeing them from the oppression of the encomienda and repartimiento systems through the use of Indian labor to build their churches, tend their herds, cultivate their gardens, and take care of their *conventos*, or friaries. Ironically, the Franciscans only managed to make things worse.[64]

To convert the Indians to Christianity and free them from Spanish oppression, the Franciscans utilized a strategy known as the *cabecera-visita* system that centered on the pueblos and maximized the effectiveness of the limited number of friars on the frontier. Like the hub of a giant wagon wheel, the *cabecera* was the center of a fray's base of operations, where he established his church, or *iglesias*, and his *convento*. The Franciscans located their *cabeceras* in the larger settlements, such as Pecos, where a concentration of heathen souls dwelled and made routine visits to the smaller pueblos, or *visitas*, that neighbored the *cabecera* in the hopes of increasing his *doctrina*, or congregation.[65]

As they made their rounds from pueblo to pueblo, the frays attempted to convert the Indians by using gifts to create obligation and pomp and vigor to impress them, while employing essentially a two-pronged attack that targeted the leadership and youth of a community. By focusing on the caciques, the frays hoped that their status as the theocratic rulers of Pueblo society would alone facilitate the conversion of the masses. Likewise, the conversion of the outside chief and war captains usually meant the removal of any forcible opposition to the missionaries' efforts. If the cacique and his counterparts elected to remain heathens, conversion of the children created a future generation of leaders who were indoctrinated with the tenants of Christianity and who could hopefully resist and undermine the authority of the elders unwilling to accept the Spaniards' God. Being few in number and having literally thousands to convert, the frays relied on the Pueblos' preexisting political, social, and economic structures to accomplish their goal of turning heathens into Christians.[66]

From the time Oñate entered New Mexico to the period long after the 1680 revolt, the Franciscans and the secular authority constantly battled each other over the control of the colony and the Indians, leading to the excommunication and imprisonment of governors and friars respectively. Ordered by the Franciscans to do one thing and by the governors to do the opposite, the Pueblo, who became factionalized into Christian and non-Christian groups, watched probably in amazement and anticipation as their civilized neighbors battled each other for the use of Indian labor.[67] This competition between the Franciscans and pobladores over the use of Indian labor caused a rift between the two parties that nearly led to a Spanish civil war in New Mexico because both groups needed the Indians to accomplish their individual designs and goals.

Not all Spaniards treated the Indians with such harshness, despite the atrocities committed by the pobladores. From the onset of Oñate's initial entrada, the Spaniards sought and forged romantic and sexual relationships with Pueblo women, blurring over time the cultural lines that separated Indians from Euroamericans. Within one generation, Oñate and Peralta's Spaniards injected into New Mexico a mixture of "*mestizos*, *mulattos*, and bastards" who made up a majority of the non-Indian population.[68] Educated in mission schools alongside their Indian neighbors, the "half-breeds" and *espanoles*, or Spanish "pure bloods," played together, prayed together, and learned together, closing the cultural gap that separated the Pueblo and Hispanic worlds. Able to move in the social circles of both groups, the mixed bloods acted as go-betweens, interpreters, and friends of both Spaniards and Indians, enabling them to earn wealth as well as important Spanish government offices in New Mexico, such as that of the *alcalde* (mayor or constable) and the lieutenant governor of the colony itself, feats unheard of in the rest of Spain's New World empire. The Spaniards' quest for human companionship initiated a gradual process of acculturation and miscegenation that resulted in nearly 90 percent of New Mexico's population being mixed bloods who were natives of the colony by 1680.[69]

The Spanish borrowed and benefited from many of the Indian cultural practices throughout this process of acculturation. Of these, the Spanish adoption and use of Indian medicinal cures proved to be one of the most, if not the most, beneficial. With no school-trained physicians and doctors in New Mexico, the Spanish entrusted the most educated people, the friars, to cure and operate on their sick. To facilitate their efforts as caregivers, the friars established an infirmary at the pueblo of San Felipe located thirty miles from Santa Fe and stocked it with linens, herbs, and an assortment of surgical tools. One could only imagine how many Spaniards cringed at the prospect of going under a friar's knife. With only one infirmary in the area remotely situated and the small number of friars in the colony, the Spaniards turned to their Indian neighbors to provide them with the medical care they needed to stay alive on the frontier.

Since curing and religion were responsibilities of the Pueblo medicine societies, many of the medical techniques the Indians employed entailed the use of chants, songs, and healing totems, as well as an array of potions and cure-alls. Some women, like the *mestizo* Beatriz de los Angeles who moved in both Indian and Spanish circles, became noted healers, helping people such as the dona Maria Granillo overcome serious illnesses through the use of "spells." The friars viewed such methods as sorcery and witchcraft, and they condemned Spaniards who sought and used Indian cure-alls to heal themselves and their loved ones. On more than one occasion, friars arrested, flogged, sold into slavery, and in some instances hung Indian men and women who admitted to using "witchcraft" to heal people. Despite the Franciscans' objection, many Spaniards continued to employ local Indian healing practices, often relying on their Pueblo and mixed-blood relatives, servants, and acquaintances to cure them or introduce them to those who could.[70]

In the first phase of their settlement of New Mexico, the Spanish relied on the Indians to provide them with the physical needs—food, clothing, and shelter—to survive the rigors of the harsh New Mexico environment. Starving before they ever reached San Juan, Oñate and his company acquired nearly all their provisions from the Pueblo Indians. Unprepared to handle the challenges of the New Mexico desert, the Spanish lacked the know-how to effectively cultivate the land. Coupled with Oñate's choice to place exploration and conquest before the physical establishment of the colony itself, the Spaniards, despite the chagrin of friars and many pobladores, found it necessary to take food from the Pueblo by force to prevent their women and children from starving to death. Likewise, the bitter cold of the winter and the lack of available fuel sources caused the Spanish to rip the clothing off of Indian backs and to occupy by force temporarily abandoned pueblos for shelter. Even after Peralta put the colony on better footing, the pobladores and encomenderos needed Pueblo labor to tend their livestock, cultivate their fields, build their churches and towns, and provide them with nearly thirty-six thousand bushels of corn and thousands of hides, robes, and cotton mantas as yearly tribute to support the Spanish presence in New Mexico. If nothing else, the Spanish needed Pueblo souls to meet the goals of the colony following 1610: the conversion and spiritual welfare of the Indians. As many observers wrote, the Spanish effort in New Mexico hinged on the provisions, labor, and tribute provided by the Pueblo. Without the Indians, the Spanish pobladores had no reason, means, or way to settle New Mexico.

THE FIRST PUEBLO REVOLTS, 1639–1680

For over a century, the Pueblo endured the Spanish theft of their crops, exploitation of their women, religious persecution, and the unbridled demands for tribute. Believing that these atrocities were a result of their neglect for their ancient gods, many Pueblo medicine men clung to their traditional religious beliefs, continuing to practice their ceremonies in underground kivas in an attempt to resist the cultural onslaught of the Spaniards. On several occasions, some pueblos brought this resistance aboveground, attempting to throw off the yoke of their Spanish oppressors in a number of localized revolts between 1639 and 1675. As long as these rebellions remained localized and small, the Spanish could suppress them. However, in 1676, a religious leader from San Juan named Pope by the Spanish, who had been beaten for his use of sorcery, began unifying a large number of the Pueblo, Apache, and Navajo to drive the Spaniards from their home.[71]

Claiming to be guided by three spirits, Pope moved to the northernmost pueblo of Taos and rallied all of the pueblos to his cause with the exception of those belonging to the Piros in the south, Isleta Pueblo, and the pro-Spanish faction of Pecos. To strengthen his position further, Pope allied with the Apache, Mansos, and Moquis, who all suffered for years at the hands of Spanish slave traders. By August 1680, Pope had gathered to his side somewhere between seventeen thousand and thirty thousand Pueblo and Plains Indians.[72]

Pope amassed his army with great secrecy, intending to simultaneously strike the Spanish at Santa Fe, their mission pueblos, and their remote farms and ranches that dotted New Mexico's countryside. However, the pro-Spanish factions in Pecos and elsewhere learned of the rebellion and warned their Hispanic neighbors, nearly ruining Pope's plot. Losing the element of surprise, Pope sprung into action and launched his attack two days earlier than planned. Though momentarily bogged down with a siege at Santa Fe, the rebels pushed their attack and delivered a decisive blow to their enemy by killing four hundred Spaniards and forcing the remainder to flee to Isleta Pueblo. Intent on seeing their enemy utterly destroyed, the Pueblo forced the Spaniards out of Isleta and pursued them across the Rio Grande into present-day Texas. After a dogged pursuit, the rebels gave up the chase, apparently satisfied with their rout of the Spaniards. Freed from the relentless hounding of their pursuers, the exhausted and demoralized Spanish refugees decided to settle where they stopped and established the villa of El Paso, where they planned the reconquest of New Mexico.[73]

THE *RECONQUISTA* OF NEW MEXICO BEGINS, 1692

Following the success of their revolt, the Pueblo attempted to renew their traditional ways of life while maintaining the sense of unity that enabled them to repel the Spanish invaders. Promised by Pope that throwing off the yoke of the Spaniards' God would renew their prosperity, the Pueblo looked forward to reaping the benefits of their reward. But to their dismay, the prosperity Pope promised failed to come to fruition. Instead of rainfall and abundant yields, the Pueblo suffered continued drought, epidemics, and small harvests. Combined, these factors caused the factionalism that existed in Pueblo society before the Spanish entrada to resurface in postindependent New Mexico, leading to open hostility between pueblos for the economic and political control of the region.

One hundred years of Spanish occupation and acculturation changed the mosaic of New Mexico, adding to it people of mixed races and infusing in many Indians the tenets of Christianity and Western civilization. The acculturation that took place facilitated both intra and interpueblo divisions into pro- and anti-Hispanic factions. By 1689, the division between the various pueblos became so great that a violent civil war began that pitted the Pecos, Keres, Jemez, and Taos against the Tewas, Picuris, and Tanos, ending once and for all the unity that enabled the Pueblo to defeat the Spanish in 1680 and to hold off their numerous attempts to retake New Mexico from 1681–1689.[74]

The Spanish failed to retake New Mexico during the 1680s because of their preoccupation with other events and forces that threatened to significantly reduce their North American empire. While the Pueblos were enjoying the challenges of their renewed independence, the Spanish found themselves embroiled in several Indian revolts during the 1680s and 1690s that encompassed the provinces and villas of New Vizcaya, Conora, Sinaloa, and El Paso. The Spanish elected to suppress these rebellions in the richer parts of their empire prior to committing themselves to the reconquest of New Mexico. However, these uprisings proved to be only a few of the many problems nipping away at Spain's North American empire.[75]

The French attempted to stretch their colonial empire to the Gulf of Mexico, reaching as far south as Matagorda Bay along the Texas coastline in 1685, while the Spanish were in the midst of battling Indian rebels. With this move, the French threatened to disrupt the profitability of New Spain's mining and shipping operations along the Gulf Coast. To avert this potential disaster, the viceroy of New Spain concentrated his efforts on the expulsion of his European rival and promoted seven expeditions between 1685 and 1689 to stop the French intrusion.[76]

Combined, these factors taxed the Spanish coffers and forced them to concentrate their efforts on maintaining their colonial possessions in Texas and Mexico, essentially shelving the *reconquista*, or reconquest, of New Mexico until an enterprising middle-aged nobleman named Don Diego de Vargas offered to undertake the mission at his own expense in 1691. While the hope of riches prompted Oñate to colonize the region, and the salvation of souls kept the colony going, the need for protection against nomadic Indians, rebels, and French interlopers changed the colony's role once again in the grander scheme of Spanish colonization, causing Vargas and the viceroy of New Spain to actively pursue the reconquest of New Mexico.[77]

Stretched to the limits suppressing Indian revolts and attempting to stop the tide of a potential French threat, Vargas knew that the Spanish government could provide him with little support. He realized that he needed to exploit the factionalization that existed among the Pueblo to succeed in his *reconquista*. With this in mind, Vargas planned a two-part offensive that relied on diplomacy in lieu of the standard strong-arm tactics employed by the Spanish the previous century to woo the Pueblo away from one another and back into the arms of their Hispanic friends.[78] To accomplish this divide-and-conquer strategy, Vargas first planned to enter New Mexico with a small reconnaissance force in an attempt to establish diplomatic relations with the Pueblo still friendly to the Spanish. In 1692, Vargas initiated the first phase of his plan, departing El Paso bound for New Mexico at the head of a column of sixty Spaniards and one hundred Indian auxiliaries.[79]

With such a small force at his disposal, Vargas made a beeline for Santa Fe, hoping to regain the capital before all else. An unwanted visitor by many in New Mexico, Vargas turned to his Indian supporters to help accomplish his mission. Following the Rio Grande, Vargas used Indians scouts, interpreters, and guides to lay the groundwork for his diplomatic overtures. Luckily for the Spanish, Pueblo factionalism took its toll over a decade, and the Indians more often than not met with Vargas in the hopes of securing for themselves an alliance with the Spaniards against their Indian enemies. In such an environment, Vargas, in just four months and without a shot being fired, successfully gained the verbal commitment of twenty-three pueblos and ten independent Indian nations to return to the Spanish fold. More importantly, Vargas recaptured Santa Fe, freed 74 Christian captives, and baptized 2,214 Indians, many of whom were the relatives of the influential cacique and outside chief of Pecos.[80]

With the reconnaissance mission a complete success, Vargas returned to El Paso to begin the second phase of his operation, the reoccupation of New Mexico. From December 1692 to September 1693, Vargas assembled his army. Inspired by the success of his first mission, the viceroy of New Spain gave Vargas 40,000 pesos to fund the reoccupation project. Spending every last pesos and then some, Vargas organized an army of one hundred soldiers, nine hundred head of cattle, two thousand horses, one thousand mules, and nearly seven hundred colonists and Indian auxiliaries. After a series of delays, Vargas began the Spanish reoccupation of New Mexico in October 1693.[81]

Unlike his first entrada, Vargas's recolonization effort needed to be accomplished at the point of a spear and the muzzle of a harquebus. Using Indian diplomats, interpreters, scouts, and guides as he had on his first entrada, Vargas learned that the loyalty the Pueblo promised to give to the Spanish on their return was nothing more than mere words. Certain that the Spanish wanted retribution for the 1680 revolt, the majority of the Pueblo decided to resist Vargas's recolonization of New Mexico. But unlike their resistance effort in 1680, the years of interpueblo civil war created an irreparable schism between the Indians. Realizing that his goal of a peaceful entrada was beyond hope, Vargas, using the diplomatic, military, and informational support of the Pecos and their neighbors, immediately began employing his Indian allies and the pro-Spanish factions of the Pueblo to assist with the physical *reconquista* of New Mexico.

THE RESTORATION OF SANTA FE, 1693–1695

Before Vargas could effectively utilize Indian military and informational support to assist him with his reoccupation of New Mexico, the factionalization that existed in Pecos and the other pueblos with strong Spanish ties first needed to be quelled. To accomplish this, Vargas relied on the pro-Spanish caciques and outside chiefs in each pueblo to neutralize, or at least quiet, opposition to his reoccupation efforts while rallying warriors to physically assist with the reconquista. In Pecos, Vargas found his supporters in men like Juan de Ye and Felipe Antonio Chistoe, while he imported others from El Paso like the Spanish-speaking refugee hero from Zia Pueblo, Bartolome de Ojeda, who was wounded twice while fighting the Spanish and repented on what he believed was his deathbed to become a Catholic, only to survive the ordeal.[82]

On his first visit in 1692, Vargas laid the foundation for the success of his second entrada by recognizing Juan de Ye as the governor of Pecos and by choosing to treat the pueblo with kind diplomacy in lieu of violent force. When he entered New Mexico in 1692, Pecos stood ready to resist Vargas's meager force of sixty Spaniards. Influential in the revolt of 1680, the Pecos felt that the Spanish came to exact retribution for the pueblo's part in the siege of Santa Fe and for their murder of one of the friars in their settlement. Unsure of the Spanish intentions during their first entrada, the Pecos fled to the hills when Vargas approached their pueblo. However, some brave individuals who wanted the Spanish to return met with them and agreed to talk their people out of the hills and back into Pecos to meet with Vargas. Within time, a majority of Pecos returned to their pueblo and met with Vargas. Over the course of several days, Vargas baptized 248 people; recognized the pueblo's cacique, Juan de Ye, whom he called don Juan, as its governor; and stood as the godfather for his son Lorenzo. By befriending and relating himself to don Juan, Vargas had in Pecos an influential leader who was strongly supported by a large number of individuals who were either indifferent to or in favor of the Spanish presence in New Mexico. Pecos was one of the larger and more strategically located pueblos, boasting a population of an estimated 1,500 people, and don Juan kept several hundred warriors from supporting the rebel cause against Vargas when he returned in 1693. In fact, of all the pueblos that swore loyalty to Vargas during the first entrada, only the pueblos of Pecos, Santa Ana, and San Felipe honored their vow, welcoming the Spaniards with open arms.[83]

Vargas's treatment of the Pecos and don Juan in 1692 paid off almost immediately when the Spaniards reentered New Mexico in 1693. Unaware that the Pueblo intended to resist his second entrada, Vargas entered New Mexico prepared to peacefully emplace one hundred fifty Spanish families at Santa Fe; one hundred at Taos; fifty in the vicinity of Santa Ana; one hundred near Jemez; 100 dispersed along the Rio Grande; and fifty at Pecos.[84] Reaching the pueblo of San Felipe in November cold, hungry, and low on provisions, Vargas received information from don Juan that the "Tewa and Tano, [in concert with the Apache and Picuris], feigned . . . obedience . . . [and] . . . had made a pact with many people to attack the company."[85] The Indian plan, don Juan informed Vargas, called for the rebels to attack the Spanish with two converging forces that meant to strike simultaneously from the front and rear of the column.[86] If this attack failed, the rebels planned to dig in at Santa Fe, where they stored their provisions, "steal the [Spaniards'] horses . . . until [they] were on foot," and then kill them.[87]

Armed with this detailed information from his Pecos confidante, Vargas wasted no time in ordering his men to "be on the alert" and in dispatching Juan Ruiz, a mestizo, "to go immediately to the pueblos of Tesuque and Nambe . . . to . . . conclude [if] they were hiding in ambush."[88] In the interim, Vargas ordered

> the Captain and military leader, Roque Madrid, to gather the company together on the narrowest piece of land, occupying the smallest area possible. There, he should divide up and exercise care with all the companies to resist the enemy, alternating the patrols on each watch. He should also see that the best, most experienced soldiers have their horses saddled and their weapons ready. The horses, mules, and cattle should be brought near, so as to cordon off the company. In that way, with their forces united, they could defend themselves. Should fighting break out, luck would be with us. This was the only essential thing at present, and not to make an improvised response.[89]

Better prepared to face an assault, Vargas, for the twofold purpose of intimidating the Pueblo and acquiring provisions for his company, announced to the occupants and Indian visitors of San Felipe that two hundred soldiers were on the march to the settlement. With this ruse, Vargas continued his business of meeting with Indian diplomats from the surrounding area as if he was unaware of the proposed Pueblo attack.[90]

The Indian attack that threatened Vargas proved to be only one of many challenges the Spanish commander faced during the initial stages of his second entrada. Entering New Mexico late in the season, Vargas soon found that the winter was very inhospitable and that the men and women of his column were deserting the company. Though they brought nine hundred head of cattle with them, the Spanish still needed Indian maize to augment their diets and relieve their starvation. Knowing that an army moved on its stomach, Vargas sent out parties loaded with beef to trade with the Indians for their foodstuffs. Unfortunately for Vargas and his troop, the Spanish procured only small amounts of maize from the Pueblo, who feigned that a plague had left them little to spare. On the brink of starvation, Vargas appealed to his "compadre and relative" don Juan to "alleviate [the governor's] great concern, which [was] that most of the company not lack provisions." Answering Vargas's plea, don Juan procured seventy-three bushels of corn and sent word that he would fill his wagons and mules full of corn when the Spaniards arrived at his pueblo.[91] However, don Juan's previous warnings of potential Indian attacks coupled with the company's conditions spurred Vargas to forgo moving to Pecos until he first reoccupied Santa Fe, the symbol of the Spanish presence in New Mexico and of the Pueblo defiance to it.

Despite don Juan's multiple warnings of the ill intentions of the Pueblo Indians, Vargas hoped to reoccupy Santa Fe peacefully and to provide his beleaguered colonists with the provisions and shelter they needed to "defend themselves against the harshness of the weather." But when he and his company arrived at the villa, Vargas discovered that the "apostate Indians [took] over [the] land" and refused to vacate it for the Spanish.[92] Though he attempted to reoccupy the villa by employing diplomatic means, the Pueblo openly defied the Spaniards, "sneering" at them and allowing twenty-two Hispanic children and a number of colonists to die of their exposure to the elements. While he awaited a diplomatic solution to his problem, Vargas received word from several Indians, including don Juan and Bartolome de Ojeda, that the Pueblo in Santa Fe were planning to attack the Spanish. Concerned with the welfare of his people and the open defiance of the Pueblo, Vargas and his company knew they needed to restore Santa Fe, or "the Indians . . . [would] become insolent, and peace [would] not remain assured."[93] Yet despite these hardships and reports, Vargas, knowing that peaceful diplomatic actions would pay greater dividends in the long term, clung to the hope of a quick resolution to the situation.

While Vargas hoped for the occupants of Santa Fe to rethink their behavior, the Pueblo and their Apache allies gathered in a large council and devised a plan to divide the Spanish encampment, making it more vulnerable to attack. As days passed, the Indians from the pueblos surrounding Santa Fe sent runners requesting the presence of the Spanish friars to administer to the salvation of their lost souls. In cahoots with the Santa Fe defenders, the Pueblo hoped that the friars and the compliment of troops that always accompanied them would travel to the various pueblos, dispersing the

Spaniards throughout the countryside while reducing the size of Vargas's camp. Once in their pueblos, the rebels planned to attack the Spaniards piecemeal, forcing Vargas to withdraw to El Paso and surrender his position. However, don Juan, Ojeda, and others informed Vargas of the ruse, and he and the friars decided to save Pueblo souls after they effectively removed the enemy resistance.[94]

Their designs thwarted, the Pueblo and their allies remained steadfast in their desire to remove the Spanish from New Mexico and made Vargas's decision to employ force against Santa Fe easy on December 28. Before he could awake to the frigid morning air, an Indian boy and his blind companion, the Tano interpreter Agustin de Salazar, arrived at Vargas's tent warning him that the Pueblo were planning to attack the Spanish encampment that day. Immediately, Vargas ordered Captain Madrid to "reconnoiter the pueblo." When he arrived at Santa Fe, Madrid discovered that "the gate was already closed and the Indians were occupying their ramparts with great shouting, provoking the battle." Without haste, Vargas moved his camp to a more defensible position, asked don Juan to send for his "young warriors to come well prepared and armed," and went to Santa Fe to attempt to parlay with the rebel leader, Antonio Bolsas. "After many arguments," Bolsas informed Vargas that his "people would talk . . . and whatever they might decide, he would come out to tell." With that, Vargas returned to his camp to await Bolsas's reply. "As soon as night fell," Vargas received his answer when Bolsas and his compatriots at Santa Fe erupted into "furious screaming and war chants . . . calling . . . to the camp and generally to everyone with shameful words." Saddened by their response, Vargas "postponed the commencement of the war" to enjoy the benefits of a daylight assault and the reinforcement of 140 Pecos warriors.[95]

As morning dawned on the twenty-ninth of December, a stream of Pecos warriors entered the Spanish encampment with great fanfare as Vargas "embraced . . . don Juan many times" and promised to fulfill the needs of the Pecos from that day forward. Proceeding to the front lines, Vargas, with his force now doubled, began making his plan of attack. But in the midst of his planning, the defenders of Santa Fe unleashed a volley of missile fire, filling the morning sky with flights of arrows and sling bullets. While "the enemy was safe [behind the loopholes they built on the villa's ramparts] from being wounded," Vargas and his men found themselves easy targets in the open. Without delay, Vargas shouted, "Santiago, Santiago, kill those rebels," and with that, the battle commenced.[96]

As Vargas shouted out his command, a squadron of Spaniards and Indians dismounted and assaulted the main rampart of Santa Fe while others supported the attack with harquebus and arrow fire. Despite their opponents' fortitude, the Pueblo repulsed the Spanish-Indian assault and held the attackers at bay until the afternoon. Realizing that the enemy ramparts could not easily be taken, Vargas attempted to penetrate the Pueblo defense by reducing the villa's main gate to splinters. With axes in hand, the Spanish and their Indian allies tried once again to break through the Pueblo defense, but to no avail. All else having failed, the attackers elected to burn the gate. Successful with this maneuver, Vargas and his allies began to gain the momentum, but on the verge of victory, defeat needed to be averted as a band of Pueblo and Apache riders came from the mountains to relieve the besieged defenders of Santa Fe. To meet this threat to his rear and flank, Vargas dispatched three squadrons of Spanish cavalry and Indian allies to repulse the relief column. By the morning of the thirtieth, the defenders and their mortally wounded leader Bolsas surrendered the city to Vargas and his Indian allies. Without flinching, Vargas decided to show New Mexico the costs of Pueblo loyalty and disloyalty by executing seventy rebels and by announcing to all their support of the Pecos and the other Indian allies present.[97]

"Even though the royal banner wave[d] again above ice-encrusted Santa Fe," members of Vargas's company wrote a letter to the viceroy of New Spain informing him of the "precarious . . . hold" they had on New Mexico. With close to "a thousand colonists huddle[d]" in the snow, Vargas turned his attention to quashing the remainder of the defiant Pueblo. To assist him with the pacification of these hostile Indians, Vargas looked primarily to don Juan and Ojeda for help with the diplomatic and military conquest of New Mexico.[98]

Turning to the south, Vargas first marched out of Santa Fe in early February at the head of sixty soldiers, thirty militiamen, and a large contingent of Pecos allies to take the rebel stronghold of San Ildefonso located on the Black Mesa. Unlike his success at Santa Fe, Vargas, forced to battle heavy snow and rainfall as well as the Indian defenders, failed to uproot the staunch resisters of San Ildefonso and suffered twenty casualties and a fair amount of humiliation for his efforts. Besieged by the height of winter, Vargas elected to delay his military conquest until the spring and turned his attention to provisioning his colonists and to shoring up the defenses of Santa Fe.[99]

Like most shrewd politicians, don Juan took the opportunity of this tactical pause to push on Vargas his designs for Pecos. Though not known to Vargas at the time of his attack on Santa Fe, don Juan wanted the Spanish to remain in New Mexico for three reasons. First, the cacique wanted the military backing of the Spaniards. Located on the borderland between the plains and pueblo worlds, the Pecos continually battled nomadic Indians for their survival. With the Spanish at their sides, don Juan and his supporters believed their position would be more secure and free from marauding Indians. Second, the civil war that ripped the Pueblo world apart pitted Pecos against their traditional enemies, the Tewas and Tanos. It is no wonder that don Juan proved such a zealous supporter and informer for the Spanish when it entailed providing negative information about groups he and his people hated. Like the raids of the nomadic Plains Indians, years of warfare coupled with the factionalism that divided the pueblo significantly reduced Pecos's population from approximately 2,000 to 1,500 residents. Once again, a Spanish presence in New Mexico that recognized and rewarded the Pecos for their loyalty aided don Juan and his people greatly by preventing hostilities from their neighboring pueblos. Last, and perhaps most importantly, don Juan wanted to reinvigorate the pueblo-plains trade and restore Pecos as the dominant middleman in it. In so doing, don Juan hoped to bring prosperity back to his people and, more than likely, prestige to himself and his supporters.[100]

Almost immediately after capturing Santa Fe, don Juan made efforts to restore the Pecos-plains trade by bringing several Apache leaders to meet with Vargas. Like don Juan, Vargas saw an advantage in renewing the trade for two purposes. First, it might provide much-needed economic and subsistence relief to the Spaniards as it had done in the decades prior to the 1680 revolt, and second, through intercourse with nomadic Indians, Vargas hoped to gain a better understanding of the resources the plains had to offer. By the end of May, don Juan had brought Pecos, Apache, and Spanish leaders, including Vargas, together on several occasions to discuss the renewal of trading relations. In August 1694, don Juan saw the fruits of his diplomatic labor fulfilled when the trade fair was renewed at Pecos. To honor the event, Vargas delayed his military campaign to the northern pueblos, declaring a trading holiday. Ironically, the trade fair don Juan worked so hard to restore proved to be the eventual economic undoing of the Pecos economy, as Spanish traders with finely made European-crafted items replaced the Pueblo as the principal suppliers of goods.[101]

While he saw to the economic prosperity of his pueblo, don Juan, as did Ojeda, continued to assist Vargas with the military and diplomatic conquest of New Mexico. From April until his untimely death in July, don Juan and his Pecos warriors accompanied Vargas on nearly every military action he engaged in during his 1694 campaign. In April, the Pecos, along with Ojeda's Zia warriors, assisted Vargas with the conquest of the rebel Indians from Santo Domingo and Cochiti, earning for themselves the prize of two hundred head of cattle. Following this victory, the Spaniards and their Pueblo allies turned in two different directions. Learning of a proposed Jemez attack on Zia in early May, Ojeda turned west and launched an independent assault on these rebels, forcing them back to their pueblo. While Ojeda battled the Jemez, Vargas and an army of Pecos auxiliaries went on a foraging expedition to the north. Taking the vanguard, don Juan and his Pecos army led the way into each pueblo.[102]

As a diplomatic conduit for the intercourse between the Spanish and the rebels, don Juan entered each pueblo as an emissary first and a warrior second. Besides subduing the factionalism that existed in their pueblos of Pecos and Zia, don Juan and Ojeda often negotiated with the rebels and their Apache and Navajo allies to bring about a peaceful conclusion to the reconquista.[103]

Seeing their pueblos ripped apart by warfare, and reduced to rubble in the case of Zia, don Juan and Ojeda acted as impartial intermediaries seeking to reconcile the differences that existed between the rebels and the Spaniards to more than likely soften the blow of the eventual Euroamerican invasion of New Mexico. A fervent supporter and hero of the 1680 revolt, Ojeda, able to read, write, and speak Castilian very well, worked to keep the pueblos of Zia, Santa Ana, and San Felipe in the Spanish camp from the time of Vargas's first entrada until the completion of the reconquista. During the first entrada, the Zia stood ready to resist the Spaniards when Vargas's small company of men approached the pueblo. However, to their utter amazement, Ojeda, one of their cultural heroes, marched at the head of the Spanish column holding aloft a white cross. Entering the pueblo, Ojeda met with the Zia and "served as [the] interpreter," explaining "why [Vargas] had come." Following Ojeda's apparently successful intercourse, the pueblo's "captains and elder men received [Vargas] with great reverence," holding crosses in their hands as the Spanish governor entered Zia through arches the Indians made of evergreen branches.[104] Through Ojeda's efforts, Vargas maintained a steady supply of loyal auxiliary troops, interpreters, spies, and provisions throughout the entirety of his campaigns. Of the more than thirty occupied pueblos in New Mexico, Ojeda's individual efforts kept Zia, Santa Ana, and San Felipe in Vargas's camp along with the Pecos.[105]

Like Ojeda, don Juan acted as a mediator and cultural broker between the Pueblo and Spaniards, eventually paying the ultimate price by forfeiting his own life. An experienced diplomat who had seen and lived the pros and cons of life under Spanish rule, don Juan probably put his skills to use as an intermediary more to ensure the well-being and survival of the Indian peoples in the region than to promote the expansion of Euroamerican society. Though a strong supporter of Vargas's, don Juan remained a Pueblo first and foremost, stepping in to save the lives of potentially friendly and influential

Indians for the benefit of the Spanish and their Pecos allies. On one occasion, don Juan intervened to save the life of a respected Jemez elder who participated in the resistance effort against the Spanish. Arguing that he could be used as a force to woo the Jemez away from the influence of the rebellious Tewas, don Juan successfully convinced Vargas to spare the old man's life. However, don Juan's greatest contribution to the Spanish and, to many degrees, the Pueblo causes, came in 1694, when he acted as the vanguard and primary interpreter of Vargas's campaign.

Throughout 1694, don Juan barely left Vargas's side, often residing in Santa Fe to be close to the governor's ear. As leader of the Indian vanguard for the 1694 expedition, don Juan routinely entered pueblos before the Spaniards to lay the diplomatic groundwork for Vargas's eventual success. However, being Vargas's emissary proved to be don Juan's undoing. As Vargas's expedition journeyed north in search of food, the Spanish came across the pueblo of Taos, the once-famous haven of Pope and the rebellious leaders of the 1680 uprising. Though the Taos abandoned their pueblo, a group of Apache who came to trade with the settlement's occupants recognized their good friend don Juan and greeted Vargas and the Spaniards with much joy. After some discussion, the Apache agreed to arrange a meeting between Vargas and the Taos governor, Francisco Pacheco, another "old friend" of don Juan's. Arriving at the mouth of the canyon where the Taos were hiding, Pacheco met Vargas and, with don Juan acting as an interpreter, began to discuss the possibility of the rebels peacefully returning to the Spanish fold. After hours of discussion, Pacheco agreed to return to his people with Vargas's proposition. With the sun setting, Pacheco invited don Juan to come to his camp, where he and his friend could continue their dialogue. Despite several warnings from the Spanish governor and his captains, don Juan "removed his spurs and the powder pouches from his belt, handing them over with the mule and his cloak . . . along with the arquebus and his shield . . . [and] said good-bye to [Vargas], giving [him] an embrace and his hand." With that, don Juan departed with Pacheco, never to be seen again by Vargas, his family, or the Pecos. When he returned to Santa Fe, Vargas assumed don Juan had been killed and lamented the loss of his compadre, confessing to his godson Lorenzo de Ye that no man was more deserving of the title "reconqueror" than don Juan.[106]

After returning to Santa Fe, Vargas and Ojeda united once again to complete the subjugation of the Pueblo and their Indian allies. Beginning in late July, Vargas and Ojeda headed west and attacked the Jemez, who apparently had decided to go back on their promise of loyalty. Three days after leaving Santa Fe, Vargas's army laid the pueblo to waste, killing eighty-four Jemez rebels, capturing well over three hundred women and children, and confiscating nearly five hundred bushels of corn, much of which went to the Indian auxiliaries to compensate them for their efforts.

Capitalizing on the momentum of his victory, Vargas turned south to conquer the defiant and formidable pueblo of San Ildefonso. Unlike his earlier success at Jemez, Vargas met the stiff resistance of a rebel force comprising warriors from nine pueblos. With an uncoordinated attack, the Spanish struck at the Pueblo but soon found themselves beating a hasty retreat. The following day, the Pueblo, short on supplies, attempted a bold attack, but the Spanish repelled it. Encircled on their Black Mesa and unable to continue the fight because of their supply shortage, the Pueblo defenders of San Ildefonso surrendered to Vargas, momentarily ending the hostilities.[107] Secure for the time being, Vargas retired to Santa Fe; established a presidio with a one-hundred-man garrison; dispersed the friars to reestablish their churches in the pueblos, the first one being Pecos; and reoccupied the Spanish settlement of La Canada, renaming it Santa Cruz.[108]

THE SECOND PUEBLO REVOLT, 1696

Despite Vargas, Ojeda, and don Juan's best efforts to reconcile the Spanish and Indian peoples of New Mexico, Pueblo opposition leaders and forces remained strong and pushed once again for the Spaniards' expulsion when poor harvests strained the relations between the two cultures. In June 1696, the pueblos of Taos, Picuris, Cochiti, Santo Domingo, Jemez, and those of the Tewas saw their opportunity and launched an uncoordinated attack against the Spanish, killing five friars and twenty-one soldiers and settlers. To quell this latest Indian rebellion, Vargas called on his old ally Ojeda and his newest Pecos supporter, Felipe Antonio Chistoe.

Immediately answering Vargas's call for assistance, Chistoe arrived at Santa Fe at the head of one hundred warriors. When he reached Santa Fe, Chistoe asked Vargas to "issue an order for him to hang" the opposition leadership in Pecos because he feared "they would cause the people of the pueblo to rise" against the Spanish. With don Juan's death in 1694, the anti-Spanish faction in Pecos resurfaced under the leadership of several men to reportedly include Lorenzo de Ye, the Spanish governor's godson. Faced with this opposition, Chistoe chose to act decisively in lieu of using the milder tactics don Juan employed to suppress Pecos problems and devised a plan to essentially sever the head from the snake's body by eliminating the leadership of the anti-Spanish faction. Without much hesitation, Vargas supported Chistoe's plan and granted him permission to execute the rebel leaders.[109]

Armed with a license to kill, Chistoe got the opportunity to execute his plan just two days later when emissaries from the rebels journeyed to Pecos to meet with the anti-Spanish faction. Pretending to be interested in what they had to offer, Chistoe lured the rebel emissaries and the opposition leadership into an underground kiva filled with his loyal supporters. Questioning the opposition leaders, Chistoe learned that they supported the rebellion. In an instant, Chistoe jumped to action, shouting "here we are the king's men," and with that his coconspirators seized the rebels and hung them. To Chistoe's dismay, one of the opposition's younger leaders named Pock Face (Caripicado) escaped, but to no avail. Foolishly, the young rebel attempted to return and rally his supporters, but Chistoe and his harquebus met him instead. In seconds, Chistoe dispatched the young man with one shot through his temple, eliminating the last principal leader of the anti-Spanish faction in Pecos. Unfortunately for Pecos, Chistoe's shot not only ended Pock Face's life, it also divided the community, causing many neutral and anti-Spanish supporters to flee the pueblo in search of a less draconian leader and eliminated once and for all the possibility of Pecos support for the rebellion.[110]

With the domestic issues at Pecos solved, Vargas quickly used his Pueblo allies to pacify the Indian uprising. Adopting a total-war strategy that targeted the rebels' logistical assets, Vargas consolidated the civilian population in Santa Fe and moved his headquarters to Santa Cruz to deprive the northern pueblos of their provisions and to prevent them from linking up with their rebel allies in the west and south. Using sixty Pecos warriors and a small contingent of Spanish soldiers to fix the northern rebels in place, Vargas marched west that July at the head of a column of forty-five Pecos, eleven Tesuque, and one small Spanish cavalry regiment to attack Jemez. Clearing the pueblo of its defenders in a matter of days, Vargas and his Indian allies then moved to attack Acoma. Though Vargas failed to drive the Indians from their pueblo, Ojeda seized all of Acoma's foodstuffs and destroyed its fields during the course of the battle. With the west effectively secured by August, Vargas returned to Santa Fe to outfit his next expedition to the north. By early September, Vargas took to the campaign trail again, targeting the pueblos of Picuris and Taos. Finding the pueblos abandoned, Vargas seized their food stores, burned their fields, and forced the most zealous of the rebel leaders to flee to the plains. Vargas effectively ended the second Pueblo Revolt with this last foray into the northern reaches of New Mexico and present-day Colorado, despite the Hopi pueblos remaining independent from Spanish rule in the far-off west.[111]

Unlike the Spaniards' first phase of settlement in New Mexico that relied purely on Pueblo physical and economic support obtained more often than not by unscrupulous means to sustain themselves on the frontier, the second stage of Spanish settlement drew mainly on Indian political and military support through diplomacy to reestablish their northernmost American colony. Indian go-betweens such as don Juan, Ojeda, and Chistoe suppressed groups opposed to the Spanish within their own pueblos, consolidated military support for the Spanish, acted as Vargas's diplomatic vanguard throughout the reconquista, prevented Indian resistance in neighboring pueblos, and garnered logistical support for the Spanish. Moreover, when diplomacy failed, the Pecos and their Indian allies marshaled their support for the Spanish and provided the majority of military forces for Vargas's column. Combined, Indian diplomatic and military support enabled Vargas to move unmolested throughout New Mexico, stay well informed of his enemies' movements and plans, remain well supplied, and defeat his opposition on the battlefield. Without the assistance he received from groups such as the Pecos, it is unlikely Vargas's success would have been so swift and decisive. As Vargas himself said, Indian groups such as the Pecos and their leaders like don Juan were the ones who truly deserved the title of "reconqueror."[112]

AFTER THE REBELLIONS

With the end of the Pueblo rebellions, the Spanish took actions to establish themselves permanently on the New Mexico frontier. Determined never to lose the northern colonies again, the viceroy of New Spain began to flood New Mexico with droves of Spanish settlers, tools, and livestock. Over the next fifty years, the Spanish added a third settlement to the region, Albuquerque, and expanded the Hispanic population fivefold, increasing it from 800 colonists in 1693 to 4,353 by 1749. However, like the initial colonization under Oñate and the reconquista under Vargas, the Spanish needed Pueblo assistance to keep New Mexico on solid footing.

To remove the threat of another rebellion and to bring the Pueblo more securely into their camp, the Spanish adjusted their administrative and religious practices in New Mexico. In lieu of employing the oppressive encomienda system to exact tribute and labor from the Indians to provide for New Mexico's defense, the Spanish permanently garrisoned a presidial guard of one hundred men at Santa Fe and augmented it in times of trouble with Indian auxiliaries. Similarly, because creating a defensive buffer for Mexico became the main purpose of New Mexico, government officials chose a less-zealous approach to the conversion of Pueblo souls, using "good and gentle measures" and allowing them to continue practicing their traditional religious beliefs and ceremonies, to the chagrin of the Franciscans. Though the Spaniards continued to exploit the Pueblo in many ways, their postrebellion policy of toleration significantly reduced the tensions between the two cultural groups, bringing about a reconciliation of sorts.[113]

For both the Spanish and Pueblo, this change in New Mexico's administrative policy came at a very opportune time. From the 1680 revolt until well after Vargas's reconquista, bands of Apache Indians continually raided the individual pueblos to fulfill many of their subsistence needs. Taking foodstuffs, livestock, horses, and women, Apache raiders and their atrocities became more of a concern for the Pueblo than the Spanish abuses. Likewise, the Spanish suffered attacks from the bold Apache, who killed without discretion. Letting bygones be bygones, the Pueblo and the Spanish forged a new bond founded in the common need for protection against Apache and Comanche raiders. As they did during the reconquista, the Pecos and many other Pueblo groups combined with Spanish troops to keep their borders free of nomadic raiders. With the forging of this new relationship, the Spanish settlements of New Mexico, through the combined efforts of Pueblo and Spaniard alike, became permanent fixtures in present-day New Mexico, Arizona, Colorado, and Texas that eventually became the foci of Euroamerican settlement in the region.[114]

Pueblo support proved to be the most vital element in Spain's successful colonization of New Mexico and laid the foundation for the Euroamerican settlement of the American southwestern frontier in the seventeenth century. In 1598, as they lay huddled for survival in the abandoned pueblo of Okhe that had become their refuge in North America, Oñate's band of five hundred colonists probably wondered in amazement at their lack of foresight and judgment in leaving their homes in New Spain for the bleak "wilderness" of New Mexico's frontier. During this first phase of Spanish settlement, when they were desperate and starving, the Spaniards tapped into the only source of subsistence and survival that existed in New Mexico, the Pueblo Indians. Though not always actively or consciously, the Indians, through their possessions, their foodstuffs, their knowledge, indeed, through their very existence, enabled Oñate and Peralta's colonists to survive while they established Santa Fe. Once Santa Fe was built, the Pueblo helped the fledgling colony grow and prosper into a haven for salvaging heathen souls through their oftentimes-impressed labor until the 1680 Pueblo Revolt freed them from Spanish oppression. Following the loss of New Mexico and Santa Fe, the second phase of Spanish colonization in New Mexico began, and Pueblo groups such as the Pecos allied themselves with their Euroamerican counterparts and gave them the majority of diplomatic and military forces required to reconquer, expand, and protect the colony. Without Pueblo support, it is likely that Oñate's, Peralta's, and Vargas's efforts would have failed and caused the Spanish to abandon the colonization of New Mexico until a later date or surrender it altogether. In short, over the course of one hundred years, the Pueblo Indians provided the Spanish with a purpose for colonizing; the means to survive in the harsh New Mexico environment; the economic and religious capital to become prosperous; and the military and diplomatic resources to secure the colony and protect it.

Until their colony was firmly established in 1700, the Spanish continually lacked the physical resources such as food, clothing, shelter, medicine, labor, and the commodities of exchange necessary to survive on New Mexico's frontier. Though they attempted to supply themselves through caravans from Mexico, the irregularity of the convoys coupled with the unwillingness or inability of New Spain's viceroy to properly finance the colonizing effort failed to adequately support the Spaniards with the resources necessary to survive the frontier. In a constant need of supplies, the Spaniards looked to the Pueblo to fulfill all their basic needs. For food, the Spanish confiscated the Pueblo's stockpile of goods, and when the surplus of Indian maize was eventually exhausted, they employed the repartimiento system to conscript Indian labor to cultivate the colonists' crops and build their churches, homes, and Santa Fe itself. To protect themselves against the frigid winters, the Spanish literally ripped the shirts and blankets off the Pueblo's backs, leaving Indian women and children to freeze in the bitter New Mexico cold. And when they found themselves sharing the fate of their Pueblo neighbors, the Spaniards used Indian medicine to cure their illnesses rather than risk their lives under a friar's knife.

When their draconian tactics failed to alleviate their abysmal situation, all but a few dozen colonists fled to Mexico for relief in 1602. To rejuvenate and protect the colony after this exodus, Oñate and his successor, Peralta, used the encomienda system to entice encomenderos to settle in New Mexico and be its militia. Enabling the encomenderos to exact tribute in the form of corn, cotton, and hides from the various pueblos, Oñate and Peralta, through Indian labor and tribute, provided these men with the opportunity to fill their pockets and to secure their families' fortunes while fulfilling the colony's basic needs of survival and protection. To augment the tribute the encomenderos took from the Indians, Oñate and Peralta used the Pecos trade fair to obtain the food, hides, meat, and most importantly the slaves necessary to continue their colonizing efforts. Combined, these exploitative systems exacted a great toll on the Pueblo, provided the Spaniards with what they needed to maintain their existence in New Mexico, and drove the Indians to unite, revolt against, and expel, for a time, their Euroamerican oppressors. However, Pueblo independence lasted only as long as their unity.

Twelve years after removing the yoke of Spanish oppression, the Pueblo at Pecos, San Felipe, Zia, and Santa Ana turned on their former rebellious allies and significantly assisted Vargas with the reconquest, expansion, and protection of New Mexico. Motivated by several factors, the leaders of these pro-Spanish pueblos, men like don Juan, Ojeda, and Chistoe, diplomatically quelled the factionalism that existed in their respective pueblos, throwing their support behind the Spaniards and dooming any Indian revolt to failure. As informants, these men, and others like them, warned the Spaniards about the treacherous plans of rebels like Bolsas, enabling Vargas and his troops to prepare for and foil the enemy's designs. As interpreters and diplomats, don Juan and Ojeda literally led the way for Vargas, working to help promote the interests of Pueblo and Spaniard alike while paving the way for a more peaceful resolution to the reconquista. And finally, as warriors, don Juan, Ojeda, and Chistoe provided 75 percent of Vargas's troop strength on his military forays during the reconquista and afterward in the protection of New Mexico. Without Pueblo informational, diplomatic, and military support, it is highly unlikely that Vargas or his successors would have succeeded in their efforts to retake New Mexico.

Pueblo assistance in the Spanish development of New Mexico came at a great price to the Indians. Where 134 pueblos and an estimated sixty thousand Indians existed in 1596, just 46 settlements and seventeen thousand people resided by 1680. Like the decline of their physical world, the Pueblo also saw their cultural and spiritual worlds decay. Years of miscegenation and acculturation significantly altered the Pueblo's social world by slowly eroding the genetic lines that separated Indians from Spaniards. Similarly, like the mixing of races, the Pueblo melded together the concepts of Roman Catholicism with their ancient religious beliefs, forming their own unique brand of Christianity. But the greatest loss they suffered was their political autonomy. With the Spanish reconquest completed in 1696, the Pueblo subjugated themselves to the control and will of a foreign people. Though they lost much and suffered greatly, the Pueblo did not quietly pass from the scene. Through their support, the Pueblo Indians were the principle factor in Spain's successful colonization of New Mexico and enabled a demoralized band of haggard colonists to establish, build, reconquer, protect, and expand the colony that paved the way for the eventual Euroamerican settlement of the American Southwest.

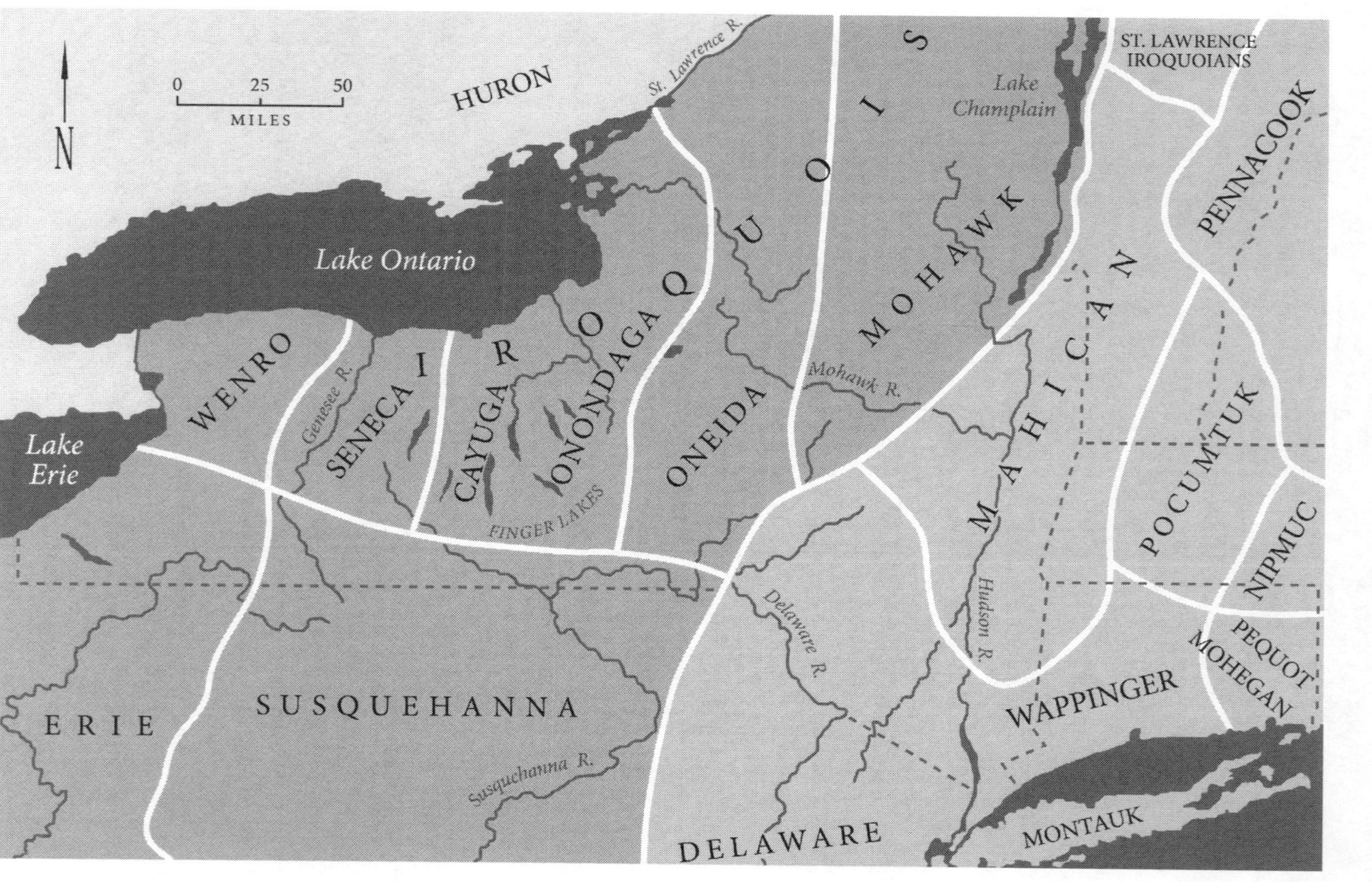
N
0
25
50
MILES
HURON
St. Lawrence R.
Lake Ontario
Lake Erie
IROQUOIS
MOHAWK
ONEIDA
ONONDAGA
CAYUGA
SENECA
WENRO
Genesee R.
FINGER LAKES
Mohawk R.
Lake Champlain
ST. LAWRENCE IROQUOIANS
PENNACOOK
MAHICAN
POCUMTUK
NIPMUC
PEQUOT
MOHEGAN
WAPPINGER
MONTAUK
Hudson R.
Delaware R.
DELAWARE
SUSQUEHANNA
Susquehanna R.
ERIE

CHAPTER 5

Settling New York's Frontier

Mohawk, Mahican, and Dutch Interaction in New Netherland, 1609–1664

The Dutch, Mohawk, and Mahican interaction on the New Netherland frontier and the establishment of Fort Orange (Albany), Rensselaerswyck, and New Amsterdam (New York City) in present-day New York during the seventeenth century offers a second case study in the development of the North American frontier. Unlike the religiously and militarily oriented Spanish colonization of New Mexico, where Pueblos and Spaniards laid the foundation for Santa Fe in a challenging environment, the Mohawk, Mahican, and Dutch intercourse took place in a setting influenced by favorable ecological conditions and based on economics, mutual dependency, and political parity. In this setting, the Hudson River Indians, predominately the Mohawk and Mahican, provided the Dutch with the motives and means to establish permanent settlements in New Netherland by creating a profitable fur trade that became dependant on Indian military prowess, provisions, diplomacy, and economic cooperation. The value of this case study to the overall discussion concerning the Euroamerican establishment of settlements on the North American frontier is not so much that it exposes the varied conditions and motives that existed in both locations but in the revelation that despite these differences, the interaction between the Dutch and Hudson River Indians produced the same result as the Spanish and Pueblo relationship in New Mexico: permanent Euroamerican frontier settlements.

HISTORICAL BACKGROUND OF THE DUTCH COLONIZATION OF NEW NETHERLAND

In 1568, after years of economic and religious persecution at the hands of King Philip II of Spain, the Protestant inhabitants of the Dutch lowlands revolted and battled their would-be masters across the globe to achieve their independence. Like many international conflicts of the sixteenth and seventeenth centuries, the war between the Dutch and Spanish proved to be a protracted affair, lasting eighty years and occurring in two distinct phases. In this contest, colonization and economic expansion were a double-pronged tactic employed by the Dutch to disrupt the flow of goods and wealth coming out of Spain's colonies, the items that fueled the powerful empire's ability to wage war on the Netherlands. Employing these strategies through the entire conflict, the Dutch won for themselves an independent state by 1609, and temporarily halted hostilities between the warring nations by negotiating and signing the Twelve Years' Truce. However, in their bid for independence, the Dutch alienated themselves from the rich colonial markets of the Spanish empire. Realizing that peace was just a momentary pause in its bid for complete autonomy, the Dutch government, the States General, actively sought new markets to fuel the nation's economy for a possible renewal of hostilities with Spain.[1]

THE EXPLORATION PHASE, 1609–1614

The Dutch development of the New Netherland frontier occurred in essentially three distinct phases: the exploration phase, 1609–1614; the trading phase, 1614–1623; and the settlement phase, 1624–1664. During the exploration phase, the Indians of the Hudson Valley influenced Dutch actions and settlement by their mere presence in the region. Aware of the potential profits that could be gained from participating in the North American fur trade, the Dutch journeyed to and explored New Netherland simply because they knew that the land possessed an abundant supply of fur-bearing animals and a number of people indigenous to the area who were willing to hunt, trap, and sell them to Holland's merchants. Motivated by this potential trade market that centered on the Indians' abilities to harvest furs, the Dutch began the first phase of their development of the New Netherland frontier.

While Don Pedro de Peralta was assuming the mantle of leadership in New Mexico and laying plans to establish Santa Fe, in 1609 the Englishman Henry Hudson sailed for the Dutch East India Company in his ship the *Half Moon* to the Arctic Ocean in search of a sea route to China. Hoping to find and open new economic markets for Holland in China, Hudson found instead the temperate woodlands of present-day New York, enriched with an abundance of fur-bearing animals, natural fruits and vegetables, fish, foul, and scores of Indian peoples who were adept at harvesting these various commodities and willing to interact with the Dutch. Hudson successfully met and exchanged commodities and information with the various native peoples along the Hudson River, laying the groundwork for the Dutch exploration and initial settlement of New Netherland, though trading with America's Indians was not the purpose of his journey.

Though historical evidence exists that suggests the Dutch seamen Hendrick Christiaensen and Adriaen Block may have been the first to discover the mouth of the Hudson River, Henry Hudson's explorations of the area, combined with the upriver accounts of his journey, created the motivation and the means for subsequent traders and explorers to travel to and settle the region. The chroniclers of Hudson's journey described New Netherland "as pleasant a land as one [could] tread upon" and told of an indigenous people who, while disposed to violence when ill-treated, welcomed the Dutch explorers with fine furs, wampum, tobacco, and foodstuffs in exchange for what the Euroamerican explorers considered to be "trifles," knives, beads, and cloth.[2] When the *Half Moon* returned to Holland in 1610, the Dutch East India Company, disappointed that no passage to China was found, showed no interest in Hudson's discoveries and allowed the accounts of his voyage to be passed on to Holland's merchants. The accounts of Hudson's expedition became the first documents translated and circulated in the merchant circles of Holland and England, though his journey upriver lasted only a month. In 1610, the same year the *Half Moon* returned to London from its voyage, Emanuel Van Meteren included the details of Hudson's voyage in his publication *History of the Netherlanders*. In it, Meteren told his readers: "In the lower part of the river they [Hudson's men] found strong and warlike people; but in the upper part they found friendly and polite people, who had an abundance of provisions, skins, and furs of martens and foxes, and many other commodities, as birds and fruit, even white and red grapes, and they traded amicably with the people."[3]

For Holland's merchants, Meteren's history, the *Half Moon*'s cargo, and the accounts of Hudson's journey exposed to Dutch traders the opportunity to open up and profit from markets they might create in New Netherland. Within less than a year of Hudson's return, several enterprising individuals sent ships to New Netherland in the hopes of participating in a lucrative trade with the Indians.[4]

Though the *Half Moon* was perhaps the first ship on record to navigate up the Hudson River, the Indians of the region already knew of Europeans and their trade goods. Since 1608, the Indians of the area had acquired European-made items from neighboring natives who had access to the French trade in Quebec. Seldom aware of the intended purpose of many of the European goods they obtained, the Indians used the items within the context of their own culture, employing axes and hoes as necklaces, copper pots for arrowheads and earrings, and stockings as tobacco pouches.[5] In some cases, the Indians used European goods to replace more-traditional items, such as their practice of using duffels (cloth) in place of furs to make leggings, loincloths, and capes.[6] Like many of the more-prized traditional commodities such as wampum, the Hudson River Indians held European-made goods in high regard, assigning to them a social significance that allowed individuals the opportunity to rise in rank and prestige by acquiring and redistributing such valuable items to their neighbors through the use of their gift economies. So the Hudson River Indians and their neighbors actively sought European goods more for the social benefit they provided than for their actual utility. Thus, when Hudson sailed upriver, the Indians of the region lined the banks to trade with the *Half Moon*, and in so doing, filled the ship's hull with the furs that motivated several Dutch merchant companies to fund their own ventures to New Netherland and pursue the Indian trade and eventually settle the region. With the advent of these expeditions, the exploration phase of the Dutch settlement of the North American frontier earnestly began.[7]

Between 1611 and 1614, several ships financed by merchant partnerships, such as that of Arnout Vogels and the Pelgrom brothers, fell upon the Hudson River in pursuit of the fur trade. Of the vessels that sailed to New Netherland, those guided by the supercargoes Christiaensen and Block, Thijs Mossel and Hans Hontom, and Cornelis May and Peter Fransen competed heavily for the trade. With such competition, a commercial conflict erupted and led to price wars, the pirating of one ship, and the creation of cartel agreements.[8] Yet to the merchants, the profits that could be gained by exploiting the trade far outweighed the risks.

Though no accounting records exist for the various partnerships for the period, Francoijs Pelgrom hinted at the allure of the trade, informing his wife in a letter dated July 30, 1613, "I cannot help telling you in this letter about the successful arrival of our ship . . . a good voyage, yes, a better voyage even than last year." Apparently, the voyage must have proved profitable, for just one month later, Pelgrom, in a second letter, informed his wife that he "could only send . . . this short letter . . . because I am so hard at work sending Aderiaen Block out again to the same place from where he returned . . . [sending] now . . . two ships thither" instead of one.[9] The rise of such a competition over the New Netherland trade alone indicates how Indian-procured furs and the accounts of Hudson's journey motivated the actions of Holland's merchants and gave them the sole reason for venturing to North America.[10]

As Holland's traders became more involved and interested in the region, the Dutch and the Hudson River Indians developed a general understanding of one another and created a middle ground on which to interact. In their process of mutual discovery, the Dutch and Indians saw each other from the perspectives of their own cultures, inhibiting each group's ability to fully understand the intricacies of its counterpart's society.[11] Yet despite all their misunderstandings, the Dutch and the Hudson River Indians managed to develop a lingua franca comprising "half sentences" and "shortened words" that was derived from the dialects of several native groups as well as the Dutch. In conjunction with this trade jargon, the Dutch and Indians developed and used a form of sign language.[12] Developed specifically to foster and standardize the bartering that took place during the exchange of goods, the jargon and sign language enabled the Dutch and Indians to learn various and incomplete aspects of each others' unique cultures. For example, while the Dutch discovered that the Indians placed a great value on wampum and continually exchanged it, they perceived it as being a form of currency and failed to comprehend the ceremonial and cultural significance when the beads changed hands.[13] As historian Daniel Richter so aptly noted, the exchange of wampum and other gifts in ceremonies and negotiations helped to determine one's place in society and signified the sincerity of one's actions because "words alone were merely words."[14]

Though they failed to understand the cultural significance of wampum, the Dutch learned the manners, customs, and commercial demands of the Indian trade and augmented their complement of European-made goods with healthy supplies of shell beads procured from the Indians at the mouth of the Hudson River near Long Island and along the New England coast to increase their profits. Wampum became so important to the Dutch that they stimulated its production by providing the Indians with intricate drills and tools to increase the amount and quality of shells they could produce.[15] More importantly, however, the Dutch learned that an elaborate Indian trade network connected New France to present-day Maryland and Illinois, a network they willingly used. Combined, the Dutchmen's increased knowledge of the country's native inhabitants, the Indians' desire to trade for European-made goods, and the creation of a viable and productive trade jargon further motivated Holland's merchants and supercargoes to continue their voyages to New Netherland.

As Dutch and Indian interaction in the Hudson River Valley increased between 1612 and 1614, the political and economic dynamics of the region gradually changed in favor of Holland's merchants. Before the *Half Moon* arrived, Algonquian-speaking middlemen along the St. Lawrence River monopolized the Indian trade originating out of Quebec, the source of European-made goods in present-day Canada and New York. Since the construction of Quebec in 1608, the Huron and their Algonquian neighbors had acquired a significant number of metal weapons and used this advantage in arms to subjugate and bully the Indians along the Hudson and Mohawk Rivers. As long as they were able to keep the southern Indians from directly accessing Quebec, the Huron and their northern neighbors maintained their advantage over the southern Indians. Thus, the arrival of the *Half Moon* offered groups like the Mohawk and Mahican the opportunity to strengthen themselves against their northern competitors. So the Mohawk, Mahican, and their southern neighbors encouraged and actively supported the Dutch trade during the exploration phase. In so doing, the southern Indians began to shift the political and economic dynamics of the area away from Quebec and toward the Hudson River, a shift that favored and encouraged Holland's merchants.[16]

While furs and profits motivated Holland's merchants, three critical outcomes resulted from the relationship created between the Dutch and the Indians during the exploration period that significantly facilitated the Euroamerican settlement of New Netherland. First, the Dutch and Indians created a trade jargon that transcended the linguistic barriers that existed between the two peoples, facilitating the flow of information and goods needed to develop the frontier. Second, the inclusion of the Dutch in the preexisting indigenous trade network began a shift in the political and economic dynamics of the northeastern frontier from Quebec in Canada to the Atlantic shores of New England by giving the powerful Iroquois Confederacy as well as the Mahican and other groups direct access to European goods that had otherwise been distributed throughout the region via Indian middlemen, an access to goods that motivated tribes like the Mohawk to encourage and support Dutch settlement. And third, the profits and competition generated by the fur trade coupled with the information traders learned and disseminated about New Netherland's rich, temperate, and prosperous landscape motivated the Dutch to invest even further in the region.[17]

Like many great discoveries of the day, what began as a search for a passage to East India ended up being the exposure of a new land full of potential profits and markets, profits and markets that revolved around and required the support of the Hudson River Indians. Though their influence and importance seems to be absent from the accounts of the various supercargoes and merchants who ventured to New Netherland, the Indians of the Hudson River Valley played a pivotal role in the exploration phase of Holland's frontier settlement by providing the Dutch with the motive and in some ways the means to explore and trade in the region. Without Indian hunters and trappers, the Dutch lacked the ability to procure the valuable furs they sought. If they had no way to accumulate furs, the Dutch had no real reason, save curiosity, to continue to venture to New Netherland, and curiosity, with no certainty of financial gain, only led to the depletion of a merchant's, a company's, and/or the government's capital. Since they wanted to compensate for the markets they lost as a result of their war with the Spanish, the Dutch actively pursued the New Netherland trade. The fact that the Indians actively sought European-made goods and that England and France allowed Holland's merchants to trade in New Netherland unmolested made the Hudson Valley an even more attractive and viable Dutch market, one that lured not only Holland's independent merchants but also the government itself.[18] Simply put, without the Hudson River Indians, no fur trade or economic market existed for the Dutch, and without the existence of a market, Holland's merchants and government had no immediate interest in venturing to and possessing New Netherland.

THE TRADING PHASE, 1614–1623

The trading phase of the Dutch development of New Netherland began with the creation of the New Netherland Company in 1614. Unlike the exploration phase, which was a period dominated by the sporadic activities of independent merchants isolated to the Hudson River proper, government interest and the goal to establish a more permanent and profitable presence and trade in the region motivated Dutch efforts during the trading stage. The Mohawk and Mahican actively supported Dutch designs during this period because they both saw an opportunity to counter the political and economic advantage the Huron and their Algonquian neighbors held over them. By acquiring and arming themselves with European trade goods, the Mohawk and Mahican hoped to strengthen themselves against each other as well as their northern neighbors. Combined, these Dutch and Indian objectives gave rise to Fort Nassau, Holland's first settlement in New Netherland; increased the profitability of the fur trade; and changed forever the political dynamics of the Hudson Valley by creating a center of trade that rivaled the effects of Quebec. More importantly, however, the economic and political changes brought about through Dutch-Indian interaction during the trading phase spurred Holland's government and merchants to eventually push for the creation of a permanent colony in New Netherland, a move that initiated the settlement phase of Dutch frontier development and brought about the creation of the Hudson Valley's first towns.[19]

In March 1614, Holland's government issued a general charter that promised any "good Inhabitants" who occupied themselves "in seeking out and discovering Passages, Havens, Countries, and places that have not been discovered nor frequented" the sole right to monopolize the trade in those regions "for six voyages as a compensation for their outlays, trouble, and risk."[20] Interested in obtaining what they rightly perceived to be a very profitable monopoly over the New Netherland fur trade, the various merchant companies who competed with one another along the Hudson banded together to form the New Netherland Company and petitioned Holland's government for the promised monopoly based on their combined "discovery" of New Netherland, in spite of Hudson's journey.[21] Aware that such an enterprise "would be honorable, serviceable, and profitable to [Holland]," the States General granted to the New Netherland Company a monopoly of the Hudson River fur trade for three years and four voyages.[22]

With the threat of competition eliminated by the government's monopoly and the consolidation of the rival merchant groups into a singular corporation, the New Netherland Company planned to exploit the Hudson River fur trade by establishing a year-round post where Indians could bring furs on a regular basis. Limited to the number of voyages by their charter and wanting to reduce their overhead by sending fewer ships, the company planned to locate a post in the northern portion of the Hudson where the waterway intersected with the Mohawk River, the Indians traded more amicably, and large seagoing ships could maneuver with little difficulty. For this purpose, the company chose a defensible and strategic spot south of the Mohawk River junction where its men built Fort Nassau on Castle Island (present-day Albany, New York).[23]

A simple redoubt, Fort Nassau consisted of just a solitary house surrounded by a shallow moat and a wooden palisade. If the size of the post was unimpressive, the garrison itself proved even more so, consisting of only twelve men, most of whom were clerks and traders. To make matters worse, though the post stood on defensible ground, the island on which it sat flooded several times a year, making the fort's position and permanency questionable at best. But despite its drawbacks, the simple post served the company's intent of being essentially a "ship on land" the Indians could access and bring furs to year-round.[24]

From the moment the Dutch arrived, the Mohawk and Mahican welcomed the company's merchants with open arms, assisting them with the establishment of Fort Nassau in three major ways. First, the Mahican approved the company's occupation of Castle Island. Second, the Mahican and their Indian neighbors kept the post provisioned with critical foodstuffs that allowed the Dutch to focus their efforts on the acquisition of furs and the exploration of New Netherland. And third, the Mahican entered into a trade agreement with the Dutch that broadened the scope of the company's fur market to include the St. Lawrence River, the Mohawk Valley, and the Delaware River, which in turn led the States General to claim and settle New Netherland for Holland.[25]

Like most groups of Euroamericans who ventured forth onto the North American frontier, the twelve traders and merchants who settled Fort Nassau came ill prepared to subsist off the land. To keep the post supplied with provisions, the company planned to send goods with its ships and to rely on the Indian trade in corn and meat to augment the pioneers' limited diets. While no historical documents exist detailing the day-to-day activities of Fort Nassau's twelve traders, evidence highlighting the exchange of goods between the Hudson River Indians and the Dutch suggests that Holland's pioneers relied on native foodstuffs to significantly augment their diets. In 1628, at New Amsterdam, for instance, the Reverend Jonas Michaelius commented on the poor conditions of a typical frontier settlement, noting: "The rations, which are given out here, and charged for high enough are all hard stale food, such as men are used to on board ship, and frequently not good, and even so one cannot obtain as much as he desires. . . . The savages also bring some things, but one who has no wares, such as knives, beads and the like, or seewan [wampum], cannot come to any terms with them."[26]

Because the twelve individuals at Fort Nassau focused on trading with the Indians and exploring the country, they more than likely lacked the ability, time, or desire to grow foodstuffs or subsist off the land and relied heavily on the Indian trade in meat and corn as Fort Orange did in later years to support the small garrison.[27]

However, the support the Mahican and Mohawk gave to the Dutch greatly exceeded the physical realm. In fact, Indian political and economic support of Dutch settlement during the trading phase had a far greater impact on Holland's eventual colonization of New Netherland than any other factor. Prior to the arrival of the Dutch, the Mohawk, Mahican, and their southern Algonquian neighbors received European trade goods from the French in Quebec through Algonquian middlemen. In this network of trade, the Hudson River Indians resided the farthest from the goods, causing the flow of items and their contact with Euroamericans to be irregular and slight. More than once, the Mohawk and other Indian groups of the area tried to become more involved in the trade by attempting to gain control over the St. Lawrence River through military means, but to no avail. Contrary to their objectives, the Mohawk excursions into the territory of their northern neighbors only yielded their own domination by the Huron. As a result of Quebec's location, the Frenchmen's preference to deal with the powerful Huron League and their neighbors, and the ability of the northern Algonquian peoples to maintain their hegemony over the fur trade through force of arms, the political and economic dynamic that developed in 1608 remained in effect until the Dutch established Fort Nassau.[28]

When the New Netherland Company established the fort, it essentially turned the back door of the Quebec trade network into the front door for the Hudson River Indians by planting an emporium of European goods directly in the land of the Mahican and only forty miles from the easternmost Mohawk settlement of Onekagoncka.[29] Seeing the Dutch, who brought only trade goods, and not settlers and missionaries into their country, the Mohawk and Mahican viewed a permanent Euroamerican presence as a blessing and not a curse. Though the Dutch attempted to purchase Castle Island from the Indians, the Mahican refused but granted the company permission to build its post.[30] "Our forefathers," the Mahican historian Hendrick Aupaumut wrote in 1754, "invited them on shore and said to them, here we will give you a place to make you a town . . . and after they went ashore some time, some other Indians . . . looked fiercely at them, and our forefathers observing it, and seeing the white people so few in number, lest they be destroyed, took and sheltered them under their arms."[31]

To the Hudson River Indians, the regular trade that Fort Nassau offered replaced the sporadic ship trade and made European goods more accessible, providing a temporary solution for some of the more important political, economic, and social issues the Mohawk and Mahican had.[32] Subsequently, the Mahican and their Indian neighbors enthusiastically supported the Dutch plan to build a post on Castle Island.

For the company to establish Fort Nassau, Mahican support proved critical. Without the approval of the 1,600 Mahican warriors residing near Castle

Island, it is doubtful that the twelve Dutch traders could build Fort Nassau without being molested and the fort possibly being destroyed before doing so.[33] For the southern Indians, the steady flow of European goods and weapons derived from Fort Nassau provided the Mahican and Mohawk with the opportunity to escape the influence of the powerful Huron League, a goal that overshadowed local disputes and drew the reluctant native groups together in an unlikely fellowship. With the influence of this mutual dependence driving the actions of the various Indian groups and the company, the Mahican encouraged and allowed the Dutch to plant their first settlement in the Hudson River Valley.

Upon Fort Nassau's establishment, the Hudson River Indians began a regular trade with the Dutch that revolved around the exchange of foodstuffs and furs for European-crafted items. Dutch success in this venture meant the company needed to acquire as many furs as possible in a single year as well as keep the Indians on friendly terms. To accomplish these two tasks, the Dutch elected to use their post like their ships, staying in one location and allowing the Indians to bring the furs to them. By employing this strategy, the Dutch hoped to open up and maintain profitable trade relations with the western and northern Indians like the land-locked Mohawk, who resided beyond the immediate periphery of the Hudson River. Also, the Dutch wanted to divert a portion of the Quebec fur trade toward Fort Nassau. Mahican cooperation proved critical to accomplish these aims in two important ways. First, the Mahican controlled Castle Island and the area surrounding it. If they wished, the Mahican could prevent other Indian groups from directly accessing Fort Nassau, thereby limiting or controlling the amount of furs exchanged at the post. If this were to happen, the Dutch stood to have their profits minimized, an idea they did not fancy. Second, long before the Dutch arrived, the Mahican positioned themselves as middlemen in the New England–St. Lawrence wampum trade. Acquiring wampum, which the French-allied Algonquians of the north lacked, from the New England Indians, the Mahican trafficked wampum, furs, and European goods between the two peoples. This trade arrangement enabled the Mahican to develop cordial relations with both groups, a relationship the Dutch felt would aid them in their effort to attract the northern Algonquians away from Quebec and toward Fort Nassau.[34] For these reasons, the Dutch sought and relied on the friendship and partnership of the Mahican, and to some degree the Mohawk, to make their trading endeavor worthwhile.

Mahican control of the area surrounding Fort Nassau and their sheer weight of numbers forced the Dutch to seek their permission to allow neighboring Indians to pass unmolested through their territory to ensure the profitability of the company's trade. Realizing the importance of Fort Nassau to their political and economic success, the Mahican reluctantly entered into a trade agreement with the Dutch and allowed their bitter rivals the Mohawk and other neighboring Indians to access the post. Once they enacted the agreement, the Dutch, Mohawk, and Mahican worked tirelessly to accomplish their independent political goals, goals that relied on and fostered the existence of Fort Nassau, the European goods it housed, and the fur trade.

Focused on acquiring Dutch trade goods, the Mohawk and Mahican directed their efforts toward accumulating furs and wampum. For the Mohawk to strengthen their position, they needed to control the flow of western and northern furs into Fort Nassau. To accomplish this, the Mohawk established themselves as middlemen between the Dutch and the other members of the Iroquois Confederacy by denying their confederates and other Indian groups free passage through their territory. While this strategy worked, the Mohawk also attempted to increase the amount of furs they acquired by actively raiding Indian traders along the Ottawa and St. Lawrence Rivers. By 1615, the Mohawk fur trade and friendship became so important to the Dutch that three of Fort Nassau's traders joined the Iroquoian group on a raid against the Susquehannock. Though the raid failed and the three traders were captured and later ransomed, the willingness of the Dutch to support this military excursion against another group of Indians who themselves were a potential trading partner for the company illustrates how dependant Fort Nassau became on the furs acquired by the Mahican and Mohawk.[35] Without Mohawk- and Mahican-procured furs and wampum, the company lacked a viable trade market and a reason to maintain its presence in the Hudson Valley.

Despite the mutual dependence of the Dutch and Indians, relations between them became violent at times. However, the willingness of each group to work through these episodes illustrates once again how important and influential the Hudson River Indians were to the Dutch settlement of New Netherland. The death of the skipper Hendrick Christiaensen provides an excellent example of how well the Dutch and Indians, for the sake of the fur trade, worked to prevent an escalation of violence that might have permanently damaged the relationship between the two peoples. One of the major traders on the Hudson since 1611, Christiaensen welcomed a group of Indians aboard his ship the *Swarte Beer* to trade. The Indians boarded the ship with the intention of killing Christiaensen, who had held one of their leaders for ransom a few years earlier, and attacked the crew, killing all but five men who successfully repelled the assault. Partly for their survival and their interest in the fur trade, the ship's crew made peace with the Indians by offering a present of knives. With the situation stabilized, the ship remained in the area for three weeks and continued to trade.[36] While episodes like this occurred regularly, both the Dutch and Indians, for a number of reasons, continually worked beyond the initial violence to maintain a trading relationship, supporting the idea that the presence of Holland's merchants in New Netherland depended almost solely on their rapport with the Hudson's native inhabitants.

The influence that Mahican and Mohawk relationships and diplomacy had on the Dutch settlement of New Netherland during the trading phase cannot be overstated. The trade agreement that the Mahican allowed to occur introduced Fort Nassau to the importance of the New England and Long Island wampum trade and broadened the Dutch market for furs. Subsequently, the profitability of the New Netherland Company's enterprise became greater and more enticing to the States General and Holland's merchants. Even after the company abandoned Fort Nassau following the expiration of the government's monopoly and a spring flood in 1617, the Mahican-Dutch trade agreement remained in spirit and enabled the New Netherland wampum-fur trade to continue, prosper, and grow.[37] Where the last voyage in 1614 of the independent merchants during the exploration phase yielded nearly 2,500 furs, for instance, Dutch traders extracted 4,000 beaver and 700 otter skins by the end of the trading phase in 1624.[38] By protecting and opening up Fort Nassau to other Indian groups and the wampum trade, the Mahican began shifting the attention and activities of native fur trappers away from Quebec and toward the small Dutch post, changing forever the political dynamics of New Netherland and Canada.[39] Moreover, the Mahican agreement decisively drew the Mohawk to the Hudson River and provided them with the opportunity to emerge as a major force in the region. Following the agreement, the Mahican moved to the eastern bank of the Hudson River and surrendered their physical possession of the territory on the western bank to the Mohawk. The agreement expanded the scope of the Mohawk-Dutch trade so much that one observer wrote "that furs sold too cheap among them, they [the Indians] come down themselves to the rivers and trade with the nations as best they can," acting as middlemen for native groups in the Ohio Valley and along the St. Lawrence River. Combined, the economic and political shift of the fur trade toward Holland's merchants and the relatively amenable treatment the Dutch received from the Mohawk and Mahican helped influence the States General to claim New Netherland as one of its colonial possessions and to create the Dutch West India Company in 1621 for the purpose of colonizing the region as well as South America and Africa's Gold Coast.[40]

THE SETTLEMENT PHASE, 1624–1664

The settlement phase of the Dutch development of New Netherland occurred in two stages, 1624–1650 and 1650–1664.[41] For the purpose of this work, this chapter deals only with the first phase, in which the Hudson River Indians helped the Dutch West India Company permanently establish New York's first Euroamerican settlements: Fort Orange, Rensselaerswyck, and New Amsterdam. As in the exploration and trading phases of New Netherland's frontier development, the Hudson River Indians, primarily the Mohawk in this case, sought to address their own political, social, and economic needs by using the Dutch and their trade goods as a means to gain an advantage over their Indian neighbors. In so doing, the Mohawk created a secure and economically prosperous environment for the company's settlements by providing a blanket of protection around Fort Orange and Rensselaerswyck that shielded the Dutch from their European rivals and hostile Indians. Once the Dutch were snug in this blanket of protection, the Mohawk and their Indian neighbors continued to facilitate Holland's development of New Netherland by increasing the profitability of the wampum-fur trade and by provisioning the colonists and traders with much-needed food, not only at Fort Orange and Rensselaerswyck but also at New Amsterdam. Because of this support, the Hudson River Indians enabled the Dutch to establish permanent agricultural settlements at Fort Orange and New Amsterdam, laying the foundation for the subsequent colonization and settlement of New York's and North America's frontier.

When the government monopoly granted to the New Netherland Company expired along with Fort Nassau in 1617, several merchants, many of them former members of the trading partnership, resumed old habits and began to trade along the banks of the Hudson River, bringing about a second round of trade wars and eroding, to some degree, the friendly relationship forged between the company and the southern Indians.[42] Concerned that its North American fur market was becoming threatened by the renewed competition between Dutch merchants, the newly arrived English in New England, and the French in Canada, the New Netherland Company appealed to the States General in 1620 for a second monopoly to protect its enterprise by permanently settling the land.[43] The States General denied the company's request several times, but, bothered by the growing European presence in the area, opted instead to create an entirely new organization to settle New Netherland, the Dutch West India Company (WIC).

Motivated by the Twelve Years' Truce with Spain ending in 1621, the States General wanted a state-sponsored armed mercantile organization to resist rival European powers from interloping on Holland's colonial possessions. In short, the States General wanted an organization to protect, maintain, and carry on "navigation, commerce, and trade . . . for the common weal . . . and welfare of the inhabitants of the country."[44] To accomplish this, the States General granted the WIC a twenty-four-year monopoly, agreed to provide troops and ships to protect any and all territory the group settled, and provided the mercantile organization with a million guilders (nearly half a million dollars) to fund its efforts. For its part, the States General expected the WIC to establish forts, settlements, and trade routes, as well as to negotiate treaties and alliances with the rival European groups and native inhabitants located in the various regions covered by its charter.[45] Challenged with the task of developing markets on three continents, the WIC elected to focus its efforts on acquiring African gold, Brazilian sugar, and Caribbean salt, while adopting a policy of agricultural colonization to support the fur trade in New Netherland.[46]

By adopting a plan of agricultural colonization, the WIC faced several challenges, the most important being the enlistment of colonists who wanted to depart their homes in civilized Europe for the unsettled land of North America. While many proved willing, the WIC needed the right people to plant the initial seeds of settlement in New Netherland. Studying the initial negative English experience in Virginia and the later success of its families in Plymouth, the WIC directors realized that the usually all-male monopolistic ventures of their European predecessors failed because the people involved with the endeavor generally consisted of individuals bent solely on adventure and immediate financial gain with little or no interest in making a home. To avoid this problem, the company's directors looked for a mixture of people and families who were self-motivated, willing to develop the New Netherland frontier, skilled as farmers and artisans, and who would willingly support the overall trading objectives and authority of the company. By 1624, the company found its ideal colonists and enlisted thirty Walloon families, French Protestants from southern Holland, along with a multiethnic group of traders and clerks to build and populate four posts in New Netherland, two of which were Fort Orange and New Amsterdam.[47]

The WIC realized that to colonize New Netherland successfully it needed to control the waterways into and out of North America's interior. The company planned to control the Hudson by building two posts, one in the vicinity of Fort Nassau and the other at the river's mouth on present-day Manhattan Island, New York, where the Long Island Indians arguably produced the best wampum on the Atlantic coast. Of the two posts, the company elected to invest the majority of its efforts and resources in the vicinity of the abandoned Fort Nassau where the prosperous fur trade existed during the previous decade. When the WIC's ships reached Fort Nassau, eighteen of the thirty Walloon families, along with a complement of traders and clerks, disembarked and began constructing a post on the western bank of the Hudson River just two thirds of a mile north of Castle Island and the abandoned Fort Nassau.[48]

Over the course of the next year, the Walloons and the company's traders built Fort Orange on the western bank of the Hudson overlooking a deep ravine and opened up trade with the Mohawk and Mahican. Like Fort Nassau, Fort Orange was a "miserable little fort" with four bastions armed with few artillery pieces, connected by wooden walls fifty-eight feet long, enclosed by a moat eighteen feet deep, and susceptible to flooding. On the post's interior, the Walloons constructed a single building for the storage of company personnel, arms, supplies, and equipment.[49] Relatively small, the post lacked enough space to house the Walloon families and the farms they were to cultivate. To accommodate their needs, the Walloons built their homes, farms, and a company mill outside the periphery of the fort, laying the foundation for what later became the settlement of Beverwyck (Beaver Town) in 1652.[50]

The site selected for Fort Orange illustrates just how important Indian political and economic support was to the WIC's establishment of a colony in New Netherland. With its presence and prosperity threatened by the French in Canada and an increasing and expanding English population in New England, the company desired a safe, stable, and strategically located spot where it could access northern Algonquian furs and New England wampum, while at the same time isolating the Hudson River trade from its European rivals. For this purpose, the company elected to build a post near the juncture of the Hudson and Mohawk Rivers. By nestling their post within the political, economic, and military bosom of the powerful, friendly, and well-connected Mahican, the Dutch felt they could easily expand and exploit the fur trade in relative peace and prosperity. The Dutch believed this because of the political state of affairs that emerged around Castle Island following the demise of Fort Nassau.

With the collapse of Fort Nassau, the Mahican reasserted their physical control over Castle Island and the western bank of the Hudson River by forcefully removing the Mohawk presence after a series of assaults between 1616 and 1618. With their victory, the Mahican successfully drove the Iroquoian nation back to the safe confines of the Mohawk Valley and reassumed control over Castle Island, the western bank of the Hudson River, and the

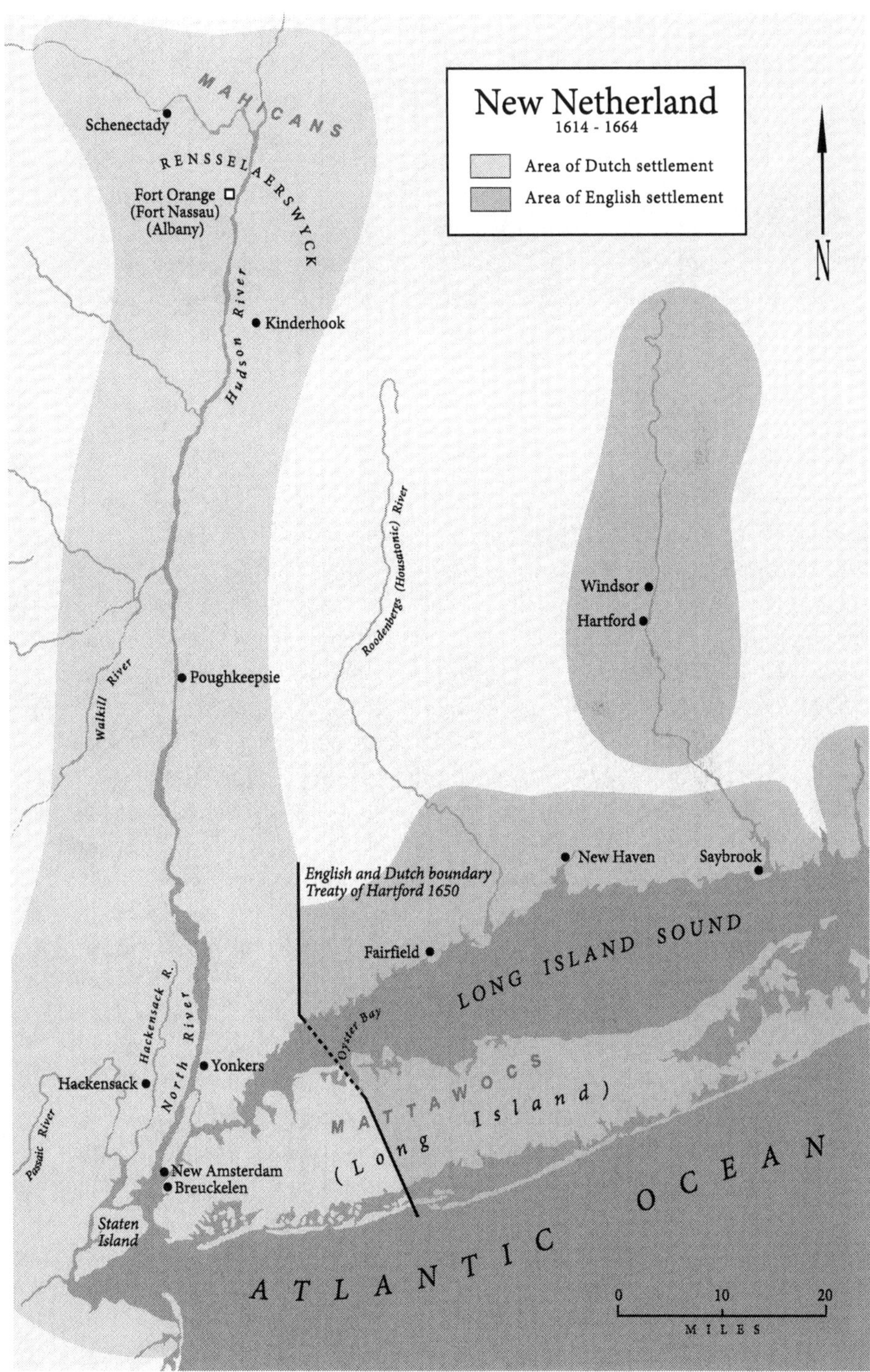

New Netherland
1614 - 1664
Area of Dutch settlement
Area of English settlement
N
MAHICANS
Schenectady
RENSSELAERSWYCK
Fort Orange
(Fort Nassau)
(Albany)
Hudson River
Kinderhook
Roodenbergs (Housatonic) River
Windsor
Hartford
Walkill River
Poughkeepsie
New Haven
Saybrook
English and Dutch boundary
Treaty of Hartford 1650
Fairfield
LONG ISLAND SOUND
Oyster Bay
Hackensack R.
North River
Yonkers
Hackensack
Passaic River
MATTAWOCS
(Long Island)
New Amsterdam
Breuckelen
Staten Island
ATLANTIC OCEAN
0
10
20
MILES

mouth of the Mohawk River. Once reestablished in those areas, the Mahican became middlemen in the Hudson Valley's trade once again by being the conduit of exchange between New England wampum and St. Lawrence furs. Wanting to maintain a post near the strategic juncture of the Mohawk and Hudson Rivers where they could access the rich New England–St. Lawrence wampum-fur market, the Dutch realized they needed the permission and goodwill of the Mahican to ensure their economic and physical survival. So the WIC directors took care not to disturb or annoy the Mahican by forging relationships with neighboring Indian groups like the Mohawk. However, the company also wanted access to the fur markets under the influence of the Mohawk.[51]

With relations between the Mohawk and Mahican strained, the last thing the Dutch wanted was to provoke the animosity of either group by forging friendly relations with the other. By positioning Fort Orange on the western bank away from the Mahican settlements and literally overlooking a ravine that acted as a passageway between the Mohawk and Hudson Rivers, the Dutch hoped to avoid problems and to foster positive trade relations with the Mohawk, who could access the rich furs of the western and northern Indian markets.[52] With access to both markets at stake, the Dutch needed to place their post in a position where it could be visited by all and monitored by few. While the company could have carried on an active trade with the Hudson River Indians without the construction of a post, a Dutch settlement, as Fort Nassau proved, increased the scope and profitability of the fur market.[53] The company's choice for Fort Orange's location indicates just one way in which Mohawk and Mahican political and economic support and objectives influenced Dutch settlement in New Netherland. Without Mohawk furs and Mahican permission, trade connections, and protection, the Dutch lacked the military strength, manpower, and motivation to arbitrarily establish a post in such a populated, contested, and strategic location. And without a post, the company stood to gain little, making Indian political and economic support for such an endeavor vital.[54]

The initial reaction of the Hudson River Indians to the return of the Dutch more than likely overjoyed the company's directors. Immediately after the establishment of Fort Orange, the Mahican, Mohawk, and their Indian neighbors jumped at the opportunity to rekindle their trading relationship. As one of the Walloons recalled, the "Mahikanders [Mahican], or River Indians, the Maquase [Mohawk], Oneydes, Onnondages, Cayugas and Sinnekes [Seneca], with the Mahawawa or Ottawawaes Indians . . . made covenants of friendship [with the Dutch], bringing . . . great presents of bever and other peltry."[55] While all sought to become Dutch trading partners, the

Mahican maintained hegemony over the area and the trade surrounding Fort Orange. Wanting to be the company's principal and most-favored partner, the Mahican renewed their trade agreement with the Dutch that granted the Mohawk and other neighboring Indian groups permission to pass unobstructed through their territory to trade at Fort Orange. Because of its ideal location and Mahican support, things appeared to be going quite well at Fort Orange by December 1624, with the Walloon's crops "as high as a man" and the fur trade producing 27,000 guilders worth of revenue. Inspired by this prosperous beginning, the company sent ships laden with livestock and additional colonists to supply Fort Orange and to construct a second settlement on Manhattan Island.[56] By the end of 1625, the company's position in New Netherland seemed to be headed in the right direction, with the construction of New Amsterdam underway and the traders at Fort Orange nearly doubling the return of furs taken in 1624. However, despite the fruitful and promising beginning, Mohawk and Mahican political designs, fierce competition, and independently thinking Walloons exposed the fragility of the Dutch position in New Netherland and threatened the colony's very existence.

Between 1624 and 1628, Mohawk and Mahican conflicting objectives led to a war that disrupted the Hudson River fur trade and permanently altered the political dynamics, as well as the Dutch settlement of New Netherland.[57] According to Samuel de Champlain, Canada's governor, the Mahican failed to abide by the spirit of their pact with the Dutch and continually inhibited the Mohawk from trading at Fort Orange. With access to Quebec being controlled by the Huron, the Mahican placed the Mohawk in a vulnerable position by obstructing their ability to obtain European goods from Fort Orange. To make matters even worse for the Mohawk, the Dutch began to encourage and foster friendly relations between themselves, the Mahican, the St. Lawrence Algonquians, and the New England Indians in an attempt to reinvigorate and exploit the old Fort Nassau north-south wampum-fur trade.[58] In this new political arrangement, it appeared to the Mohawk that the Dutch had little need of them. If they allowed things to continue as they were, the Mohawk realized they would be surrounded by hostile neighbors—the French, Huron, northern Algonquians, and Mahican, all of whom wanted to see the power and influence of the aggressive Iroquois nation curtailed.

Fearing their own demise, the Mohawk elected to change their problematic position by taking two actions. First, they decided to make a peace with the French and their Indian allies, and second, they planned to remove the Mahican from the Fort Orange area by force. By taking these two actions, the Mohawk hoped to replace Mahican hegemony over the Fort Orange trade with their own.[59] By controlling Fort Orange, the Mohawk knew they could prevent other Indian nations from trading directly with the Dutch. With no one else to trade with, the Mohawk rightly predicted that if the Dutch were to prosper, they had to deal directly with or through Mohawk middlemen.

For their plan to work, the Mohawk needed to free up the full complement of their warriors by ensuring that diplomacy in lieu of force maintained the security of their northern borders. To the joy of Champlain, who had been seeking an Algonquian-Iroquois entente, the Mohawk sent emissaries to Quebec in 1624 and quickly struck a peace that benefited both parties as well as the Frenchmen's northern Algonquian allies.[60] With peace in the north secure, the Mohawk launched their war against the Mahican later that year. Though they had the element of surprise, the Mohawk failed to cripple the Mahican, who gained the upper hand one year later by destroying the Mohawk's easternmost settlement.[61] Over the course of the next year, the war raged, and Mohawk harassment of Mahican and northern Algonquian hunters greatly debilitated the Fort Orange trade.[62] To compound matters for the Dutch, the Walloons realized they could essentially "get rich quick" by acquiring furs directly from the Indians and elected to forgo their farming duties and assumed a sort of middleman position between the natives and traders. Because of this, a fierce competition broke out between the Walloons and traders, driving up the demand and price of furs and forcing the company to purchase all the colonists' wampum "to take the fur trade away from them," for fear of losing it.[63] "If there is anything to be had it is the colonists who get it," the company's secretary in New Netherland, Isaak de Rasiere, wrote: "The wife of Wolfert Gerristsz came to me with two otters, for which I offered her three guilders, ten stivers. She refused this and asked five guilders, whereupon I let her go, this being too much. The wife of Jacob Lourissz, the smith, knowing this, went to her and offered her five guilders, which Wolfert's wife again told me. Thereupon, to prevent the otters from being purchased I was obliged to give her five guilders."[64]

Things became so bad for the company at Fort Orange that by July 1626, the traders only acquired 40 otter and 305 beaver skins after "great troubles and many threats" from the Walloons, compared to the 463 and 5,295 purchased in 1625.[65] Unhappy with Fort Orange's deteriorating market, the post's commander, Daniel van Krieckenbeeck, decided to reverse this unfavorable situation by shipping off ten of the Walloon families to New Amsterdam and assisting the Mahican with the neutralization of the troublesome Mohawk.

As winter 1626 approached, Krieckenbeeck led a party of six Dutchmen along with a retinue of Indians to assault the Mohawk. For the Dutch, this proved to be a fatal day. The Mohawk surprised the war party and killed Krieckenbeeck, three other Dutchmen, and a number of Indians. Alarmed by this, Rasiere wanted to raise a troop of fifty or sixty men to attack the Mohawk.[66] Concerned that a war with the Mohawk might cost it everything, the company sued for peace and shipped the remaining eight Walloon families to New Amsterdam to assist with the settlement of Manhattan and left only sixteen men to promote the trade at Fort Orange.[67] With the Mahican threat and Dutch presence curtailed by this war, the Mohawk relocated some of their settlements closer to Fort Orange and began to set up a veritable web around the post by regulating the flow of Indian furs coming out of the north and west. As historian Ian K. Steele put it, Fort Orange took its first step toward becoming a "Mohawk hostage" that prospered only when the Iroquois prospered.[68] But the web the Mohawk began to create around Fort Orange shielded the Dutch from the French threat in Canada and produced so many furs for the company that it enjoyed its greatest returns by the end of 1626, earning over 45,000 guilders worth of revenue.[69]

While the Indian and Dutch struggles played out around Fort Orange, the nearly 270 colonists and Walloons who arrived at Manhattan in 1625 and 1626 were just beginning to construct what the company planned to be its administrative headquarters in New Netherland, New Amsterdam. Though consolidated and secure on Manhattan, the company's personnel found themselves faced with the unexpected challenge of constructing a multiethnic company-oriented settlement while simultaneously having to feed a much larger population than the administrators originally planned.

Unlike the homogenous settlement of Walloons at Fort Orange, the company, in desperate need of bodies to make the colony work, broke from its original plan and sent to New Amsterdam a large multiethnic and diverse population of families, traders, clerks, administrators, and adventurers who went primarily to make money in the pay of the company and who "might as well have staid home."[70] Due to the nature of Manhattan's population, the leadership found it difficult to get the construction of New Amsterdam underway because the colonists were a "rough lot who . . . [had] to be kept at work by force."[71] Hampered by the poor character and lazy quality of many of the colonists, the company only succeeded in staking out Fort Amsterdam and constructing thirty bark houses, an administrative building, and a few small farms. By November 1626, the colony's governor, Peter Minuit, explained that what the company had planned to be the well-established nerve center of New Netherland was little more than a "place of . . . hovels and holes in which . . . they [the colonists] huddled rather than dwelt."[72]

Focused primarily on sheltering themselves and swamped with refugee Walloons from Fort Orange and Fort Nassau on the Delaware River, the colonists failed to cultivate enough ground to support the entire population. To amend this, the company augmented the colony's supplies with food and livestock. However, the supplies ran short, and poor soil and poisonous foliage limited the production and longevity of crops and animals. Moreover, based on the progress made at Fort Orange and the supplies sent in 1625, the company chose to reduce its investment in New Netherland and focused its efforts on Brazil, which exacerbated the situation in New Netherland.[73] Things became so bad that many of the Walloons and traders planned to abandon the colony once their term of employment with the company ended.[74] Minuit himself became so dissatisfied with the appalling situation in the colony that he wrote a scathing letter to the directors informing them:

> The promise of the Lords Masters to grant me 6 or 7 morgens [12 or 14 acres] of land to support myself in place of freeboard, otherwise would be my perquisite, is worth nothing. For their Honors themselves knew perfectly well that neither horses nor cows nor laborers are to be had here for money. And this is the first item of the bill; time will show what else will follow. Thus we lead a hard and sober existence like poor people. This should otherwise be forsooth, though suffering is salutary, as the saying is among the nuns, for they themselves know quite well, that empty cupboards make dull Beguines.[75]

On the verge of losing its colony in New Netherland, the company elected to sell "beads at one guilder a pound" to the settlers for the purpose of purchasing "maize, fish, and various other things" from the Indians.[76] With Indian subsistence support augmenting their diets, the colonists gained the food and time necessary to cultivate six of the twelve planned farms to support the settlement. But despite the construction of the six farms, New Amsterdam continued to rely on Indian foodstuffs to augment its meager diet and failed to meet the expectations of the company's directors, who viewed the colony as being only "a slight success."[77]

The colony having barely survived the first two years of settlement, the company attempted to make it more profitable by broadening the type of commodities it could extract from New Netherland, experimenting with timber, tar, pitch, lime-burning, and brick-making industries.[78] Unfortunately for the company, the colony lacked the manpower, resources, and people experienced enough to make any of these industries profitable, leaving the fur trade as the only real way to make a profit.[79] Slowly becoming entrapped in a web at Fort Orange and on the brink of starvation at New Amsterdam, the Dutch relegated themselves to the new trading environment and began to cultivate a south-to-north wampum-fur trade between the Mohawk and Long Island Indians, earning for the company nearly 57,000 guilders worth of revenue in 1627, its most prosperous returns to date in New Netherland.[80]

Despite the quiet and prosperous year of 1627, the colony's permanency and survival remained in doubt.[81] In 1628, a war broke out once again between the Mohawk and Mahican that directly impacted the Dutch existence in New Netherland. The origin of the war is unknown, but scholars generally agree that the Mohawk grew concerned that the Dutch were acquiring furs from the northern Algonquian, which, if allowed to continue, might threaten their existence. To prevent this, the Mohawk needed to take total control of all the territory surrounding Fort Orange and elected to do so by attacking the Mahican. In an attempt to strike a blow at what was quickly becoming the lifeblood of Mohawk economic and subsequently political power, the Mahican planned an attack on the weakly defended garrison at the decaying Fort Orange, but it failed because of "the gracious interposition of the Lord."[82] Fortunately for the Dutch, the "interposition" came in the form of Mohawk warriors who successfully defeated the Mahican before their plan came to fruition. Without Mohawk military support, it is highly unlikely that the sixteen to twenty traders who occupied the post could have ably defended Fort Orange's crumbling perimeter.[83] If attacked by literally hundreds of Mahican warriors, the Dutch traders would have been left with just two choices: fight and probably die, or retreat and abandon Fort Orange to its fate. Luckily for the traders, the Mohawk presented a third choice for the Dutch and made their decision easy: stay and live. Once the Mahican were defeated, the Mohawk pushed them into Connecticut and tightened their grip on the Fort Orange trade, controlling the flow of goods and personnel to and from the post. As the patroon Kilian van Rensselaer later recalled, "the savages, who are now stronger than ourselves, will not allow others who are hostile and live farther away and have many furs to pass through their territory."[84] Yet despite Fort Orange's entrapped state, the Dutch experienced their greatest level of security and economic prosperity, earning 61,000 guilders worth of revenue, the company's highest return since becoming involved in New Netherland.[85]

The year 1628 proved to be both a blessing and a letdown for the WIC. Though it planted two settlements in New Netherland, Fort Orange and New Amsterdam failed to become the self-contained agricultural communities the company hoped to establish. Moreover, the Dutch position in New Netherland became inexorably linked to the prosperity of the Mohawk and oriented around a single industry, the wampum-fur trade. With a growing English presence in New England and the French firmly established in Canada, the permanency and prosperity of the WIC's settlements in New Netherland were far from a foregone conclusion. Yet despite the letdown in New Netherland, the company literally struck it rich in other parts of the Americas when it defeated and captured the Spanish silver fleet off the coast of Cuba that was valued at more than eleven million guilders.[86] But as hopeful as this was to the company, this great victory proved problematic for the development and prosperity of New Netherland. With the source of Spanish silver being located in South America, the company made an even greater commitment to developing its presence in Brazil and left New Netherland to fend for itself.[87]

Unable to finance its increased effort in Brazil and fund the colony in New Netherland, the company decided to privatize settlement in the latter by initiating the patroonship program in 1629. Under this program, the company granted an investor or a group of investors a tract of land on which to finance and settle fifty colonists within a four-year period. In return, the patroon owned and held jurisdiction over the land. By privatizing colonization, the company hoped to create the type of permanent self-contained agricultural settlements it originally sought to establish but without bearing much, if any, of the cost.

With the enactment of this policy, the Dutch plan to create permanent self-supporting settlements in New Netherland became a reality when one of the company's directors, Rensselaer, formed a group of investors to settle the area around Fort Orange. Rensselaer chose Fort Orange as the site of his settlement because of its rich soil and relatively secure and peaceful location. Though other individuals became patroons, Rensselaer succeeded in building the only real profitable and stable settlement in New Netherland. Rensselaer's settlement, Rensselaerswyck, enabled the Dutch presence in the Hudson Valley to become firmly established, leading many modern historians to credit Rensselaer with much of New Netherland's success. While much of the praise is deserved, many of these scholars overlook the role the Hudson River Indians played in the development of Rensselaerswyck and New Netherland following 1628.

The Dutch relied on Indian foodstuffs to help support their meager diets and growing population throughout the first part of the settlement phase.

Though the colonists attempted livestock and arable farming techniques, the lack of labor, fertilization, and equipment, as well as intense flooding, prevented the Dutch from developing enough surplus crops to put the colony on solid footing until well into the 1640s. In a scathing memorial to the company's directors in 1633, Rensselaer explained the tenuous situation in New Netherland:

> [S]ince there were now farmers and animals, they [the company directors] decided that little or no provisions ought to be sent, not considering that it takes time to clear the land before it can be plowed or cultivated and that in the beginning several horses and cows perished which they [the directors] would not replace, whereby the people were forced to take the merchandise and trade it for provisions, thus damaging the Company to an incredible number of thousands.[88]

The demand for food became so important to Dutch colonists in the mid-1630s that Rensselaer tried to begin a venison-wampum trade market that flowed from Fort Orange to New Amsterdam.[89] This industry never developed to the extent Rensselaer hoped it would to sustain the colony, and the Dutch throughout the New Netherland frontier continued to rely on Indian meat, fish, poultry, and maize to help sustain their existence. In one instance, the Dutch even delayed the capture and prosecution of an Indian who murdered a colonist "until the maize trade ended" to ensure that Indian traders did not become distressed and withhold their food.[90] The Dutch were poorly provisioned, ill equipped, and undermanned, and Indian food gave them enough time to build up a large enough labor pool to enable agriculture to take hold and prosper by the 1650s. Without an ample source of food, a large labor force could not be recruited and sustained, and without a large labor pool, the land could not produce the yields necessary to support a population large enough to develop more-profitable industries and stave off the encroachment of Holland's European rivals. Thus, Indian foodstuffs provided the surplus provisions necessary for the Dutch to increase their labor, and once increased, the labor cultivated enough land for both Rensselaerswyck and New Amsterdam to take root.

Like the subsistence support, Mohawk military and political support remained a constant feature in the Dutch settlement of New Netherland and greatly aided in the economic growth of the colony until well after the English assumed control in 1664. Throughout the 1630s and 1640s, for instance, Dutch economic fortunes greatly benefited from the Mohawk Mourning/Beaver Wars. Ravaged by European-introduced diseases, the Mohawk population plummeted from nearly eight thousand to just under three thousand people in the first half of the 1630s. Moved to recoup their losses and ensure their economic and political survival, the Mohawk launched and orchestrated, in conjunction with the other members of the Iroquois Confederacy, a series of wars against the western and northern Indians that lasted nearly twenty years.[91] In this contest, the Mohawk and their Iroquoian allies successfully defeated the Huron and many of their northern Algonquian allies, as well as the Cat (also known as the Erie), Petun, and Neutral peoples. Through their conquests, the Mohawk spread their political and economic control over the region between the Hudson and Mississippi Rivers, giving the Dutch access to the far western and northern furs they so long desired. However, access to this rich supply of furs continued to come by way of Iroquoian middlemen who controlled the flow of goods and, in many ways, Dutch fortunes. Moreover, with their victories, the Mohawk proved a viable and potent obstacle for the Dutch against the French trade in Canada. In June 1660, for instance, the Mohawk and Seneca "attacked a fort, defended by seventeen Frenchmen and one hundred savages." Overpowering the garrison, the Mohawk and Seneca suffered only thirty-three casualties and killed all of the defenders "with the exception of two Frenchmen and twenty savages, whom they carried as prisoners back to their fort."[92] Writing to the company's directors in 1661, the governor, Peter Stuyvesant, commented on the effect Mohawk warriors were having against the French:

"The French prisoners, brought away by the Maquas [Mohawk] savages from under their forts every year, and occasionally ransomed by our people, declare unanimously, that if the French receive no assistance by soldiers from France, they will shortly be obliged to leave the country; the gracious God may grant, that the Maguas will not begin with us, after they have destroyed and finished the French."[93]

With the fur trade being the only profitable industry in New Netherland, the Mohawk almost single-handedly fed the colony's economy by expanding and securing the Dutch market and presence in North America through their victories. Without Mohawk-procured and trafficked furs, the colony lacked any revenue-producing industry, and without at least some revenue, New Netherland was virtually useless.

Mohawk military actions and diplomacy affected not only the economic fortunes of the Dutch but their physical fortunes as well by assisting with the defeat of hostile Indians such as the Wappinger and Esopus located in the lower Hudson Valley. For years, relations between the lower Hudson Indians and the Dutch teetered between open warfare and mutually dependent trading. More than once, the Dutch and lower Hudson Indians launched raids and assaults on each others' homes for a number of reasons. On one occasion, an armada of lower Hudson Indians in sixty-four canoes attacked New Amsterdam, killing a number of colonists and torching the settlement.[94] While the colonists often fared well when in large protected groups, the lack of trained soldiers prevented the Dutch from ably defending the isolated pockets of farmers and traders living outside the settlements. Thus the security of the colony rested primarily on farmers, traders, and clerks who "were little conversant with the use of the arquebuse."[95] As could be expected of such ill-trained and unprepared colonists, they often fell prey to hostile Indians, losing in excess of "two hundred thousand guilders [worth of property] and more than 200 persons" when a force of nearly one thousand warriors attacked the small settlements outside of New Amsterdam at Pavonia and Staten Island.[96] To assist them in dealing with these groups, the Dutch appealed to the Mohawk, who on two occasions sent warriors and emissaries to bring the Wappinger to their knees and to negotiate a peace with the Esopus.[97]

While the Mohawk and Dutch literally slept side by side and aided one another at Rensselaerswyck, they also experienced several outbreaks of violence between each other.[98] Yet despite these attacks, the Dutch decided to arm the Mohawk with four hundred firearms in 1644 to aid them in their war with neighboring Indians.[99] It is interesting that while the Dutch were willing to go to war with the southern Indians, they found it in their best interest to work through their problems with the Mohawk, which in many ways shows a great need for Indian assistance.[100] The decision to sell firearms to the Mohawk, despite the risks, is perhaps the best example of how the Dutch relied on their assistance to prosper. Determined never to sell the Indians firearms on pain of death, the Dutch ignored their policy because they feared they would lose Mohawk support to the English colonists in New England who were selling them guns.[101] Stuyvesant, in a resolution dated February 1654, clearly articulated the Dutch need for Mohawk friendship and support. Addressed to the "The Honorable Director General and Council," the resolution noted:

> the incessant demands, which they [the Mohawk] consequently make on the inhabitants of the Fort Orange, the village of Beaverwyck and the people of the Colony, and have further considered, that, if the aforesaid ammunition were entirely and suddenly denied to the said nation, the good inhabitants of the aforesaid village and places might have to suffer some mishap or at least that thereby the whole trade might be diverted and that the aforesaid nation might ask for the ammunition from the English, our neighbors, and obtain it there, a circumstance which in this dangerous

> situation would bring more and greater misfortune on this province. As the Aforesaid Maguaas are now our friends, who, obliged by want of the said ammunition to look for it among our neighbors, from whom they also can get a larger quantity of wampum for their beavers, have already received large gifts and presents for the English, in order to attract their trade, and as the consequence of this would likely be, that with the loss of their trade, we would also lose the friendship of the Maguaas and hence heap more misfortunes upon us and our nation. Therefore, we . . . have thought and deemed it proper and highly necessary . . . to accommodate the aforesaid nation.[102]

In lieu of war, the Dutch and Mohawk elected to appease each other with gifts.[103] It is clear by Stuyvesant's resolution that the Dutch relied heavily on Mohawk assistance, so much so that despite the fact that Mohawk warriors were killing Dutch colonists and cattle outside of Rensselaerswyck, they armed them. This fact alone demonstrates the great lengths the directors of the company went to to maintain the friendship of the Mohawk.[104] The reason for this disparity between Dutch relations with the Mohawk and southern Indians is simple. In the Mohawk, the Dutch found a willing ally who secured the fur trade, decimated and crippled hostile Indian and European nations, and peacefully resolved troublesome quarrels. Having the assets of such a formidable partner at their disposal, the Dutch used the Mohawk to promote the security and growth of their colony. Likewise, the Mohawk appeased Dutch complaints to promote their own welfare. Simply put, the Dutch and Mohawk needed each other to achieve their independent political and economic objectives. Based on this mutually supporting and beneficial economic, military, and political relationship, between 1628 and 1650, the Dutch and Mohawk enabled the fledgling posts of Fort Orange and New Amsterdam to firmly take root. And with that, the spearheads of New Netherland's frontier's development were formed.

Soon after, settlers radiated out from Fort Orange, Rensselaerswyck, and New Amsterdam to establish the second wave of Dutch settlements in New Netherland: Nieuw Utrecht (present-day Bensonhurst in Brooklyn, New York) in 1657, Nieuw Haerlem (present-day Harlem, New York) and Wiltwijck (present-day Kingston, New York) in 1658, and Schenectady and Nieuw Dorp (present-day Hurley, New York) in 1662. Though it slowly grew to 1,500 inhabitants by the 1660s, the Dutch colony in New Netherland paled in comparison to the English colonies in New England, which totaled nearly thirty thousand people.[105] Unfortunately for the Dutch, in their bid to alienate Spain from New World markets, they became overly aggressive and ruptured their earlier friendly, almost familial, relationship with England, bringing about the Anglo-Dutch Wars. In these contests, the English defeated the Dutch and took possession of New Netherland, renaming it New York. With the Dutch defeat, the Mohawk found themselves embattled by diseases as well as enemies on their northern and eastern borders. Like the true diplomats they were, the Mohawk sued the English for peace and forged the famed Covenant Chain, simply replacing one Euroamerican partner with another.[106]

Mutually supporting Dutch economic and Indian political interests simultaneously surfaced during the first decade of the seventeenth century, enabling Euroamerican settlements to emerge on the New Netherland frontier. At the same time and place that the Dutch sought new economic markets to offset the loss of Spanish trade following their war for independence against Spain, the Hudson River Indians looked for a way to counter the technological advantage French arms and equipment gave to the Huron and northern Algonquian following the establishment of Quebec in 1608. With these two forces in motion, what simply began as an expedition for a sea route to China turned into the formation of a Dutch colony in North America. In the process of this colony's development, the Hudson River Indians provided the Dutch with the motivation to come to and settle New Netherland, the means and security they needed to extract furs and expand the market, and the foodstuffs required to see their colony safely through its first years of existence. In so doing, the Hudson River Indians significantly influenced and assisted the Dutch with their development of New Netherland by first drawing them into the region, then leading them to build remote trading posts that evolved into pioneer settlements, and finally aiding these settlements with their efforts to become firmly established. Combined, Dutch and Indian efforts created New York's first Euroamerican settlements, the economic, political, and social centers that eventually became Richard C. Wade's civilizing spearheads through the intercourse of exchange undertaken on Richard White's middle ground.

While Henry Hudson looked for a western sea route to China, he found instead the Golden Fleece that acted as the lure for Holland's involvement and subsequent settlement of New Netherland: North American furs. From the onset, Hudson and his crewmen exposed the bountiful land of New Netherland furs to the merchant community of Holland. Hearing and reading about the "friendly Indians" and seeing the *Half Moon*'s cargo of Indian-procured furs, Holland's merchants became instantly interested in New

Netherland. With no furs, no interest existed. Even the Dutch East India Company turned a blind eye to New Netherland, leaving its economic exploitation to independent merchants and later to ad hoc organizations like the New Netherland Company. Yet for many independent merchants, the New Netherland fur market was a viable way to make their fortunes, and so began the exploration and trading phases of the Dutch development of present-day New York.

Though the stories and furs attracted Holland's merchants, the Hudson River Indians stood at the heart of the fur trade. Without the Indians' ability and interest in procuring and selling furs, the Dutch had no real reason for going to and later staying in New Netherland. Indian hunters procured the furs, and their political and social interests in European trade goods led them to participate in and help create a new and elaborate network of trade that encompassed myriad native peoples. Along this trade network, goods, ideas, and information, about both Dutch and Indian cultures, flowed and led to the standardization of a trade jargon, a language in signs, and a currency (wampum) that helped further facilitate Holland's development of the New Netherland frontier. Though they traded to fulfill their own needs, the Indians provided the Dutch with the economic motive to journey to and settle New Netherland. Once established in New Netherland, the fur trade remained the anchor for the Dutch presence in North America, an anchor that rested on Indian hunting, wampum, and diplomacy.

Primarily there to make money and to occupy land for the benefit of Holland, the administrators of the WIC knew that positive relations with the Indians were the key to their success and took note to cultivate their relationship with the various nations who occupied the Hudson Valley and its periphery. With Indians to provide it with furs and foodstuffs, the company planned to limit the expenditure of funds and resources in New Netherland. To the Dutch, Indian furs and wampum made the market, and without it, no trade existed and New Netherland was useless. To make the market successful, the Dutch knew they needed to keep the Indians happy with a vibrant trade and a limited presence.

As some historians stated, the Hudson Valley remained a hostage of the Mohawk following their victory over the Mahican in 1628, prospering only when the powerful Iroquoian group prospered.[107] However, from the moment Holland's ships arrived at Fort Orange, the affairs and whims of the Hudson River Indians, especially those of the Mohawk and Mahican, significantly influenced and in many cases dictated the course and outcome of Dutch settlement in New Netherland by controlling nearly every aspect of the fur trade. When the New Netherland and later the Dutch West India

Companies arrived, the Dutch needed the approval and cooperation of the Mahican to build Fort Orange and ensure its, as well as New Amsterdam's, prosperity. Without Mahican trade agreements in 1614 and 1624, for instance, the Dutch presence, let alone their trade market, in New Netherland might have become threatened. Likewise, once the Mohawk "imprisoned" Fort Orange, the Dutch trade and security in New Netherland, especially around Rensselaerswyck, rested almost entirely on the goodwill and influence of the powerful Iroquoian group. As disease reduced Mohawk numbers, the successful Mourning Wars in the 1630s and 1640s placed the furs of the Ohio Valley and western reaches of Canada within the grasp of Fort Orange and Rensselaerswyck. With their political fortunes being tied to Dutch prosperity and trade, the Indians wanted, and in many cases needed, Fort Orange and New Amsterdam to prosper, leading them to make every effort to support the existence of the fledgling posts. Whether it was intentional or not, Indian efforts, though sometimes detrimental to the temporary prosperity of Fort Orange and New Amsterdam, provided Dutch posts with the security to firmly establish and expand their fur market to the far reaches of the St. Lawrence River and the Ohio Valley. Due to their political maneuvers and military prowess, the Mohawk broadened the fur market and provided Dutch settlements with the security and economic viability to become firmly entrenched in New Netherland. Without Indian support, it is doubtful that the Dutch posts in New Netherland would have fared and developed into something any better than what Fort Nassau became, a temporary and short-lived trading post.

Though political and economic motives shaped the broader course and outcome of the Dutch settlement of New Netherland, all would have been for naught had Holland's merchants and colonists starved. From Henry Hudson's first voyage until well after the British conquered New Netherland, both Fort Orange and New Amsterdam needed and bartered for Indian foodstuffs. Food became such a principal commodity of exchange between the Indians and the Dutch that even Rensselaer tried to capitalize on the trafficking of venison procured from the Mohawk and southern Algonquian at Fort Orange by trading it and selling it to New Amsterdam for furs, trade goods, and wampum. Simply put, the Dutch population of New Netherland exceeded the capacity of the local farms and livestock. Thus, the Dutch lacked the foodstuffs necessary to support a large unprepared population and looked to the Hudson River Indians to fulfill their needs. As always, the Indians leaped at the opportunity to participate in this exchange of goods to satisfy their own needs. In so doing, the Hudson River Indians kept the Dutch from starving and afforded them the time to build an adequate pool of labor that was capable of stabilizing the colony long enough to develop the type of agricultural industry required to allow permanent settlements in New Netherland to take root.

Only the abandoned remains of Fort Nassau and the fur trade existed in New Netherland when eighteen Walloon families broke the ground at Fort Orange in 1624. Though the WIC planned for its settlements in New Netherland to be self-supporting entities that could direct and control the Hudson River fur market, they lacked the military forces and economic resources necessary to expand and become permanently established. Without Indian food, furs, and partnership, the Dutch presence, let alone their prosperity and trade market in New Netherland, hung in the balance. However, when the Dutch received Indian support, the frail and oftentimes vulnerable settlements of Fort Orange, Rensselaerswyck, and New Amsterdam stayed afloat long enough to develop into the agricultural self-supporting settlements Holland needed to establish a permanent presence in New Netherland. While they may have been successful in establishing posts without native assistance, it is clear that the Dutch settlement of New Netherland greatly benefited from Indian support. With it, the Dutch gained the security and resources necessary to turn Fort Orange, Rensselaerswyck, and New Amsterdam into the spearheads of New York's and eventually North America's frontier development.

CHAPTER 6

The Emergence of Pittsburgh

Middle Ground Diplomacy between the Ohio Indians, French, English in the *Pays d'en Haut*, 1744–1764

THE STORY OF THE EMERGENCE OF PITTSBURGH IN THE MID-EIGHTEENTH century in the *pays d'en haut* (Ohio Valley) is different from the previous studies presented in this work in two distinct ways. First, where Santa Fe, Albany, and New York emerged during the initial stages of Indian and Euroamerican contact on the New York and New Mexico frontiers, the interaction between the Ohio Indians, English, and French in the Ohio Valley occurred following nearly a century and a half of contact. As a result, the Ohio Indians and their Euroamerican counterparts knew of each other's cultures and did not need to discover one another. Rather, the Ohio Indians consisted of groups such as the Iroquois and the Lenape who already forged political, economic, and social relationships, both negative and positive, with Euroamericans long before the settlement of the Ohio Valley began. Second, unlike seventeenth-century Euroamerican settlements where the lines of colonial possession were just beginning to be drawn between European rivals, the lines that separated English, French, and Spanish claims in North America clearly existed by the mid-eighteenth century. Thus ownership of the Ohio Valley, which stood at the periphery of each nation's borders, was a hotly contested issue between England and France, an issue that could either be ignored or pushed.

Due to these unique circumstances, the English and French establishment of Fort Pitt reveals three important aspects about the Euroamerican settlement of North America that the previous studies do not. First, the frontier moved as both Indians and Euroamericans moved or as they came in contact with one another and attempted to form political relationships. Whether the groups had previous contact with one another or not, each time Euroamericans attempted to make inroads into Indian-occupied lands, a new middle ground, one that fit that particular moment in time, emerged between the various parties involved. Subsequently, the interaction that took place on these newly formed middle grounds generated unique outcomes based on the particular situation that Indians and Euroamericans faced at the time. Second, despite having well-established colonies in North America, Euroamericans remained dependent on Indian support when they established frontier posts because the distance between their logistical centers on North America's Eastern Seaboard and in Canada proved too great to keep their isolated settlements adequately supplied and protected. Third, Euroamericans did not always dictate the timing, course, and outcome of their settlement. In some cases, Indian political objectives and maneuvers dictated the time, place, and in many ways, the successes and failures involved in the establishment of frontier posts.

HISTORICAL BACKGROUND OF OHIO VALLEY SETTLEMENT

In the decades that made up the later part of the seventeenth and first half of the eighteenth centuries, England and France engaged in a series of military and economic conflicts that led to several wars for control of North America and its lucrative fur trade. To achieve their political goals in this conflict, the two European powers sought the aid of their colonies as well as the various Indian groups who occupied the strategic Ohio Valley. With the assistance of its Indian allies, France intended to block the westward expansion of the English colonies that threatened its monopoly over the Ohio Indian trade.[1] Similarly, the English sought Ohio Indian support to expand their colonial holdings and to increase their activity in the valley's lucrative trade. Like an intricate chess game between two masters, England, France, and their respective colonies maneuvered to ally with Ohio Indians to legitimize their claims to the valley's trade. However, the claims for the valley included not only contentions between England and France but also between the English colonies.

Of these disputes, the most significant was between the colonies of Pennsylvania and Virginia, each of which claimed the Ohio Valley belonged within its borders. Almost like the contest between England and France, the two colonies attempted to make inroads into the Ohio Valley and strengthen their claims by purchasing land from and making treaties with the Ohio Indians. Understanding their unique, opportunistic, and fragile position of being members of "a country between" the various European and colonial factions, the Ohio Indians actively sought to increase their political autonomy and control over the region by capitalizing on the rift between these various groups, and in so doing initiated the Euroamerican settlement of the Ohio Valley.[2]

INDIAN DIPLOMACY OPENS THE WAY TO SETTLEMENT, 1744–1747

Events beginning in New York in 1744 motivated Ohio Indian political maneuvers beginning in 1747 that led to the establishment of Fort Pitt and subsequently Pittsburgh in the Ohio Valley in the mid-eighteenth century. The parties involved in the establishment of Fort Pitt and later Pittsburgh consisted of a "skewed triangle" of powers: England and her colonies of New York, Pennsylvania, Virginia, and Maryland; France and her agents in Canada and Louisiana; and the autonomous Ohio Indians based primarily out of Logstown and Kuskuski.[3] While each group had its own reasons for attempting to control the rich Ohio Valley, Fort Pitt emerged because the Ohio Indians desired to become politically independent from the Iroquois Confederacy. To accomplish this, the Ohio Indians antagonized the already tumultuous relations between the English and French and brought about a war that altered the political dynamics of the world and led to the establishment of Fort Pitt.

The Ohio Valley remained free of Euroamerican settlement between the area of the Allegheny Mountains and Mississippi River prior to 1747 for essentially two reasons. First, Euroamericans lacked the logistical assets and resources required to support remotely situated outposts in the region, and second, the Ohio Indians did not want Euroamerican settlements next to their homes based on their experiences with Dutch, Swedish, English, and French colonization in the seventeenth and early eighteenth centuries. Consequently, England, France, and their respective colonies chose to forgo settlement in the valley and attempted to control the region's trade indirectly by using "Indian proxies" based out of the major Ohio Indian settlements of Logstown and Kuskuski and through diplomacy with the Iroquois in New

York.[4] However, the idea of merely being a proxy to exchange trade goods did not sit well with the Ohio Indians. They wanted to control trade and political affairs in the Ohio Valley by becoming a separate and powerful entity in the region.

The goal of the Ohio Indians to become politically independent from the Iroquois Confederacy stemmed from the results of the Beaver (Mourning) Wars. The Iroquois Confederacy claimed hegemony over the Ohio Valley by right of conquest with its victory over the Huron, Cat (Erie), Petun, and Neutral Indians in the mid-seventeenth century. Though the confederacy was victorious, its direct control of the region proved short lived. Not long after conquering the territory, the Iroquois allied themselves with the English during King William's War (1689–1697). An extension of a European war that set England against France, King William's War pitted the Iroquois against France's Indian allies in North America. Engulfed by war on all sides, the Iroquois eventually succumbed to the weight of force and lost a major engagement on the shores of Lake Erie against the Ojibwa that freed the Ohio Valley from the direct control of the league. From the close of King William's War until the mid-eighteenth century, the Iroquois attempted to maintain control over the valley by garnering Indian and Euroamerican recognition of their "right of conquest" over the region through diplomatic maneuvers. Because of the "chain of friendship" that existed between the English and the league, England's North American colonies went through the Iroquois council at Onondaga when dealing with the selling, purchasing, and administration of Ohio lands. Displeased with this arrangement, the Ohio Indians aggressively sought a Euroamerican trading partner who would recognize their autonomy from the Iroquois Confederacy and fulfill their economic needs.[5]

The Ohio Indians viewed Pennsylvania as a potential partner that might help them achieve their goals. To lure the colony into a benefical partnership, the Logstonians sent two successive delegations to Pennsylvania and negotiated the Philadelphia Treaty of 1747 and the Lancaster Treaty of 1748. With these treaties, the Logstonians sought to accomplish two objectives. First, they wanted to establish their political autonomy from the Iroquois Confederacy, and second, they sought to forge a permanent economic and political relationship with Pennsylvania that would strengthen their control over the Ohio Valley.

The Ohio Indians initiated the Philadelphia Conference of 1747 as a result of a series of events that began in 1744 at Onondaga, New York, with the signing of a treaty between the Iroquois Confederacy and the English colonies of New York, Pennsylvania, and Maryland. With the 1744 Treaty of

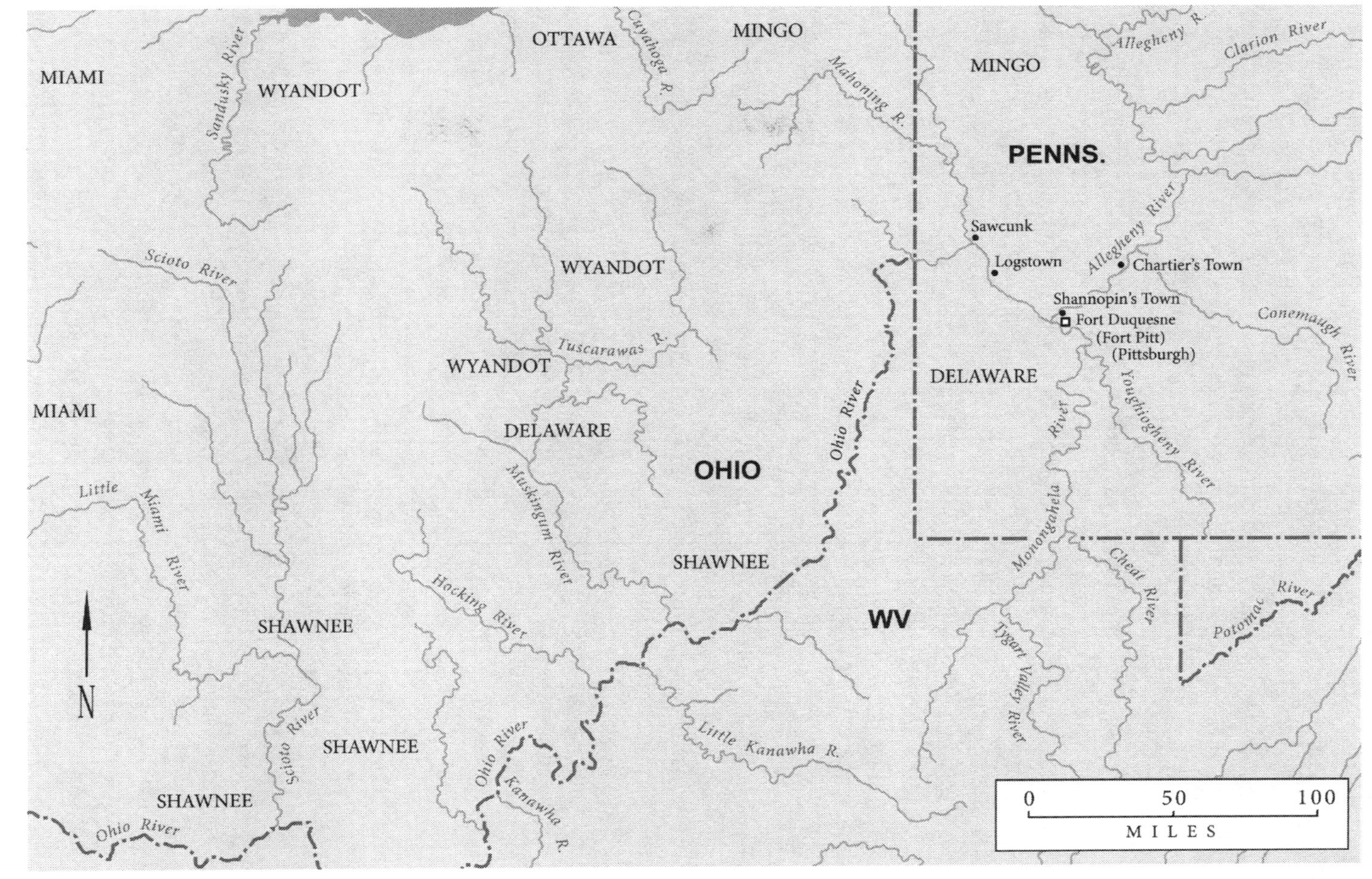
MIAMI
Sandusky River
WYANDOT
OTTAWA
Cuyahoga R.
MINGO
Mahoning R.
MINGO
Allegheny R.
Clarion River
PENNS.
Sawcunk
Logstown
Allegheny River
Chartier's Town
Shannopin's Town
Fort Duquesne
(Fort Pitt)
(Pittsburgh)
Conemaugh River
Scioto River
WYANDOT
Tuscarawas R.
WYANDOT
MIAMI
DELAWARE
Ohio River
DELAWARE
OHIO
Youghiogheny River
Monongahela River
Little
Miami River
Muskingum River
SHAWNEE
Hocking River
Cheat River
WV
SHAWNEE
Tygart Valley River
Potomac River
N
Scioto River
SHAWNEE
Ohio River
Kanawha R.
Little Kanawha R.
SHAWNEE
Ohio River
0 50 100
MILES

Lancaster, the Iroquois council at Onondaga ceded to Pennsylvania, Virginia, and Maryland the land that now makes up present-day Kentucky, West Virginia, and western Pennsylvania, an area that encompassed the eastern half of the Ohio Valley.[6] Though only a small number of English traders went to the Ohio Valley as a result of this agreement, the treaty excluded Ohio Indians from claiming ownership of the ceded territory and gave Pennsylvania, New York, and Maryland the right to intrude on Ohio Indian lands. Subsequently, the Ohio Indians sought to broker a deal with the English that would recognize their ownership of the eastern portion of the Ohio Valley and prevent the Onondaga council from directly controlling their political affairs.

The French viewed the Treaty of Lancaster, which occurred at the onset of King George's War (1744–1748), as an aggressive move to occupy, or at least control, the Ohio Valley by their English rival, although it proved only a minor threat to France's monopoly.[7] To undermine the English traders and to gain allies for its war with England, the French colonial government opened negotiations with the Ohio Indians to prevent them from embracing the British trade.[8] The French began by attempting to bring the Shawnee into the their fold in 1745, and convinced the mètis trader Peter Chartier, who lived among the Indians, to make a clean break from the British and to support France's political and economic claims to the region. Though a majority of the Shawnee—including those at Logstown—continued to back the British, Chartier led his band in several raids against English traders, forcing the few who were in the valley to flee.[9] Despite Chartier's break, the French attempt to woo the Ohio Indians to their cause proved to be an utter failure.

Believing they had lost their economic hold over the region, the French sought to reestablish their presence in the region and to win the Ohio Indians to their cause by increasing the number of voyagers, *coureurs de bois* (fur traders), and diplomats they sent into the areas of the Ohio Valley they perceived to be the most vulnerable to English advances, Logstown and Kuskuski. However, a sharp decline in fur prices, the high cost of France's trade goods, and an English plea to "take up the hatchet" against their European enemies, accompanied by a gift of coats, hatchets, and guns, pushed the Ohio Indians further away from aligning with the French and led them to attack Canada and Louisiana's traders.[10] Unfortunately for the French, the success of these raids motivated the Logstonians to send the first Ohio Indian diplomatic envoy to Philadelphia in 1747 with the intent to coax Pennsylvania into a relationship that would help them gain their political autonomy and strengthen their position in the valley.

The Logstonian delegation went to Philadelphia in November 1747 to accomplish three goals. They wanted to solicit logistical and economic support from the English colonies in their war with the French; restrict the traffic of liquor; and gain recognition of their political autonomy from the Iroquois Confederacy.[11] Conrad Weiser, a New York Indian agent selected by Pennsylvania to meet with the delegation, recognized the opportunity to make the "Indians around the Lakes their . . . warm friends," and encouraged Pennsylvania to acquiesce to the Logstonians' requests. Pennsylvania's governor, Anthony Palmer, heeded the advice of the experienced Indian diplomat and authorized a gift worth £200 that included weapons, powder, flints, and lead to express his government's friendly intentions. Weiser volunteered to take the present to Logstown the following spring to acknowledge the autonomy of the Ohio Indians and to assess their military strength.[12] With this action, the Logstonians took the first step toward establishing a permanent English settlement in the Ohio Valley and toward bringing about a war that reshaped the political dynamics of the world, the French and Indian (Seven Years') War.

The Philadelphia Conference proved beneficial for the Logstonians and the English. For the English, the conference gained Indian support for their presence in the valley and opened the area to an influx of traders who gravitated toward and settled in Logstown and Kuskuski, the primary political, economic, and social centers of the region. By 1748, over twenty English, as opposed to only five French, traders lived in Logstown and had established trading houses in the settlement. To make things even better for the English, the Logstonians promised to safeguard Pennsylvania's traders against both French and Indian aggression.[13] For the Ohio Indians, the most significant and beneficial outcome of the conference was Pennsylvania's acknowledgment and support of their political autonomy. With Pennsylvania's recognition of Ohio Indian political autonomy, the Logstonians and their neighbors became independent from the powerful Iroquois Confederacy. No more would the French and English colonies deal with the Iroquois at Onondaga to determine the political and economic fate of the valley; they now dealt directly with the Ohio Indians.

This conference proved significant to the Euroamerican settlement of the Ohio Valley in two ways. First, the conference enabled the Logstonians to draw Pennsylvania into the Ohio Valley and maneuver the English colony into a position that made it dependent on the Ohio Indians for its economic success in the region. Without Ohio Indian support, the English traders lacked the motivation and the ability to engage in the lucrative fur trade of the area. Second, the Ohio Indians gained the recognition of a Euroamerican partner to influence the international affairs of the Ohio Valley directly without first gaining the approval of Onondaga. The importance of these two outcomes to the establishment of Fort Pitt cannot be overstated. Without the political maneuvers of the Ohio Indians, it is likely that England and France might have remained content, at least for that moment in time, to preserve the status quo in North America, meaning the eastern half of the Ohio Valley would have remained free of Euroamerican settlement for who knows how long. With the Philadelphia Conference, however, the Logstonians set in motion a series of events that placed England and France on a collision course that directly led to the establishment of Fort Pitt and the initiation of the French and Indian War.

RAMIFICATIONS OF THE COUNCIL FIRES AT LOGSTOWN, 1748–1752

The results of the Philadelphia Conference concerned many who watched the partnership between the Ohio Indians and Pennsylvanians form, which only served to hasten the establishment of Fort Pitt and the initiation of the French and Indian War. Learning of Pennsylvania's intention to treat separately with the Ohio Indians, Shikellamy, a significant Oneida sachem at Shamokin near present-day Sunbury, Pennsylvania, informed Weiser that the western Indians were subject to the Iroquois Confederacy and had no legitimate right to make treaties or sell land.[14] Furthermore, Shikellamy told Weiser that the council at Onondaga planned to send a delegation to visit Philadelphia and Shamokin in spring 1748 and expected him to attend. Shikellamy suggested to Weiser that his journey to the Ohio Indians would be a fruitless and unrewarding venture and encouraged him not to make the trip.[15] Eager to gain the friendship of the Ohio Indians while maintaining its relations with the Iroquois, Pennsylvania elected to keep Weiser in Philadelphia for a conference with the league and to send the trader George Croghan, who actually suggested a diplomatic mission to the region in May 1747, to Logstown in his stead.[16] By taking these steps, Pennsylvania hoped to lay the foundation for future economic and political relations with the Ohio Indians by presenting a small gift that signified their autonomy from the Iroquois Confederacy.[17] Though the Iroquois protested, Pennsylvania remained steadfast in its support of Ohio Indian political autonomy because the colony needed Indian warriors to protect its traders and their markets. Where the Iroquois could only offer words, the Ohio Indians provided a physical presence to support Pennsylvania's designs in the valley.

With their partnership established, the eastern Ohio Indians and Pennsylvanians wasted no time in pursuing their independent political and economic goals, actions that caused the French in Canada to adopt a more forceful approach to controlling the Ohio Valley. The Logstonians and Kuskuskians hoped to improve their positions in the valley by broadening their relationships with the Ohio Indians located west of Old Briton's

Twightwee group living in Pickawillany, present-day Piqua, Ohio. They wanted Pennsylvania to recognize the independence of Old Briton's group from the French and to establish trade relations with the western Ohio Indians in present-day Illinois via a Logstown, Kuskuski, and Pickawillany trade route. By doing this, both the eastern Ohio Indians and Old Briton's Twightwee hoped to become wealthy and influential middlemen in a lucrative Ohio Valley fur monopoly.

When he arrived at Logstown in April 1748, Croghan immediately met with the Ohio Indians, explained the pertinent items on his agenda, and delivered Pennsylvania's gift.[18] After Croghan concluded his business, the Logstonians and Kuskuskians informed Croghan that Old Briton's band sought to break from the French and to "open up a Council Road to the English Governments."[19] To strengthen their position, the eastern Ohio Indians invited Old Briton to meet with the English colonies.[20] Pleased with this news, Croghan departed Logstown with a letter to the Pennsylvania government from the Logstonian leaders Scarouady, Tanacharison, and Kakowatcheky explaining their intentions to visit Lancaster in the summer with the Twightwee delegation to be headed by Old Briton's son Assapausa.[21]

The impact of this eastern Ohio Indian diplomatic move had far-reaching implications. In their willingness to accept the Twightwee into their chain of friendship and to act as mediators with the English on their behalf, the Logstonians directly threatened French trade in the region. In previous decades, the French enjoyed an uncontested monopoly over the Twightwee trade, located far from the English colonies. The French felt the Twightwee would remain in their interest and trade solely with either Canada or Louisiana because of the distance to the English colonies. However, because the eastern Ohio Indians and Old Briton's band desired to become the dominant middlemen in the Ohio Valley trade, they created a competitive market that favored themselves and their English allies and threatened the French. Determined not to lose their monopoly, the French began organizing for several military excursions into the Ohio Valley to improve their now-unfavorable economic situation.[22] Because of their political maneuvers, the eastern Ohio Indians created the motivation for the English and French to increase their activities in and pursue the settlement of the Ohio Valley.

Delayed by inclement weather, the Ohio delegation reached Lancaster in July 1748. Though the delegation began as a small party of only eighteen people, by the time it reached Lancaster, it had ballooned to fifty-five and included Mingo, Shawnee, Delaware, Twightwee, and Nanticoke. Led by the

Logstonian leader Scarouady, the delegation came to petition the Pennsylvania government to admit the Twightwee people into their chain of friendship and to act as intercessors for the members of Chartier's band that desired to return to the English interest.[23] After only four days of deliberation, the Pennsylvania government established the Logstonians as mediators for the Ohio Indians, forged an alliance with the Twightwee that directly threatened French claims to the valley, and repaired relations with the renegade Shawnees now under the leadership of Logstown's newest sachem, Neucheconneh.[24]

The true impact of the Lancaster Conference occurred not at the meeting itself but several months later at Logstown. Shortly after the conference concluded, Weiser finally journeyed to Logstown to give the Ohio Indians the gift that Pennsylvania promised them in Philadelphia in 1747.[25] When he arrived, Weiser formally established a separate council fire for the Ohio Indians at Logstown and confirmed their allegiance to the English colonies despite the tentative Treaty of Aix-la-Chapelle signed April 19, 1748, that ended the overt hostilities of King George's War.[26] With the Logstown Conference of 1748, Pennsylvania essentially cut the Iroquois Confederacy directly out of any deals concerning the Ohio Valley and, in so doing, placed the eastern Ohio Indians in a strong position to influence the affairs of the Ohio Valley. Though Weiser's journey marked the first time an official delegation went to the Ohio country to negotiate with the Ohio Indians, thereafter, every English colony, as well as the French in Canada, went through the council fire at Logstown to promote its political and economic agendas in the region.

While Pennsylvania's establishment of the council fire was monumental, the eastern Ohio Indians' move to expand the scope of their economic and political influence in the valley proved just as important. Like Weiser, the Ohio Indians promoted their own agenda in 1748 and sought to expand their sphere of control by bringing the Wyandot and their ally the colony of Virginia into their chain of friendship. The Logstonians hoped to increase their military and political strength as well as open profitable trade relations with Virginia. On both accounts, the conference proved successful for the Ohio Indians. Under the leadership of Scarouady and Tanacharison, the Ohio Indians were able to bring the Wyandot into their chain of friendship, thereby bringing along their Virginia ally. Much to the chagrin of Pennsylvania, the Ohio Indians drew into the valley their colonial rival, which only served to heighten the intensity, scope, and frequency of French and English actions in the region.[27]

Because of these events, Canada's governor, the Marquis de la Galissonière, made the first military move to lay direct claim to the Ohio Valley and its lucrative trade by sending Monsieur de Celoron and 245 officers, Canadians, and Indians on a trek throughout the Ohio country to assert France's ownership of the territory.[28] On July 8, 1749, Celoron arrived at Logstown, known to the French as Chiningue, and discovered ten English traders in the town. Concerned that the French intended to drive the English traders off, some the Logstonians planned to attack Celoron's column. Alarmed by the Logstonians boldness, Celoron stepped up his guard, ordered the English flag Weiser raised in 1748 torn down, and met with the head of the English traders to warn him and his compatriots off the land.[29] Additionally, Celoron met with the Logstonians and informed them that he came "only to do good," to rid the territory of English traders, and not to attack the Ohio Indians. Unnerved by the presence of armed troops, the Logstonians agreed to renew relations with the French but petitioned Celoron to cease his aggression against the English traders.[30] With this expedition, Galissonière intended to drive the English from the territory and to "make those return who had gone astray."[31] However, Celoron's mission failed to have the impact Galissonière hoped and only worked against the French by strengthening the bond between the Ohio Indians and the English.[32]

Several months after Celoron left Logstown, Canadian traders and Indian diplomats began to deal with the Logstonians and their Ohio Indian neighbors. In response, Pennsylvania sent Croghan and Andrew Montour to counter the activities of the principal French trader and Indian diplomat in the Ohio country, Chabert de Joncaire Jr., with the offer of a large present to the Ohio Indians in spring 1751.[33] When they arrived in Logstown on December 15, 1750, Croghan and Montour learned that Joncaire planned to build a fort at an Indian town 150 miles up the Ohio River with the consent of the residents. Additionally, Croghan and Montour discovered that Joncaire petitioned the Logstonians to "meet him and clear the Road for him," but to no avail. The Logstonians remained steadfast in their support of the English and suggested to Croghan that Pennsylvania build a fort on the Ohio to secure the trade in lieu of the French.[34] Concerned that the construction of a fort on the Ohio would renew the hostilities between the English and French, Pennsylvania chose to shelve the proposal despite the Logstonians' apparent desire to "remove closer to their Brethren the English, with a view, no doubt, of receiving Protection."[35]

The request that the eastern Ohio Indians made to Croghan is significant in regard to the eventual establishment of Fort Pitt. Because of Celoron's expedition in 1749, the Ohio Indians adopted a foreign policy that ran counter to the very reason they journeyed to the Ohio Valley in the first place, to rid themselves of Euroamerican neighbors. Less than a decade after they wanted to keep Euroamerican settlements at a physical distance, by 1751, the Logstonians and Kuskuskians felt so threatened by the French that they made a clear and conscious choice to invite Pennsylvania to build a stockade right next door to their Indian settlements. Once they adopted this new political agenda, the eastern Ohio Indians pushed for the establishment of an English post in western Pennsylvania, which eventually brought about the establishment of Fort Pitt.

The Philadelphia and Lancaster Conferences not only motivated the French to make a move but spurred Virginia into action. Following the 1748 conference at Logstown, the Virginia government authorized the creation of the Ohio Company to claim the Ohio real estate ceded to it in the 1744 Lancaster Treaty and to purchase new lands. Once the company was formed, King George III of England granted it five hundred thousand acres of Ohio land, with two hundred thousand acres to be settled immediately by one hundred families and a fort.[36] With royal petition in hand, the company sent Christopher Gist to the Ohio country to survey the land and to gather an "exact Account of the Soil, Quality, & Product of the Land."[37] Though this expedition accomplished little save the collection of topographical data, the creation of the company marked Virginia's intent to claim the lands it purchased from the Iroquois at the Lancaster Treaty of 1744. Moreover, the move pitted Virginia, which planned to build settlements in the area, against Pennsylvania, which intended to extract vital resources from the area by creating strong political and economic ties with the Ohio Indians and by keeping settlers out of the region.

Aware of Virginia's petition, Pennsylvania sent Croghan and Montour back to Logstown with the present they promised on their visit in 1750 in an attempt to maintain their advantage with the Ohio Indians.[38] Luckily for the English, Croghan and Montour arrived just two days before Joncaire brought forty warriors to Logstown in an attempt to sway the Ohio Indians back to the French interest. Like Celoron before him, Joncaire failed to turn the Logstonians away from the English. Rather, the Logstonian sachems informed Joncaire, "We ourselves brought them [the English] here to trade with us, and they shall live amongst us as long as there is one of us alive. . . . Our Brothers are the People we will trade with, and not you."[39]

The Logstonians and their neighbors realized that their bold stance alienated the French and brought themselves closer to war. To avert possible French hostilities, the eastern Ohio Indians turned their recommendation for an English post on the Ohio River to a formalized request.[40] In a speech to the Pennsylvania government, the Lenape sachem Beaver, the brother of Shingas, and several Mingo leaders explained:

> Now, Brothers, we have been considering what the French mean by their Behaviour, and believe they want to cheat us out of our Country, but we will stop them, and Brother You must help us. We expect that you our Brother will build a strong House on the River Ohio that if we should be obliged to engage in a War that we should have a Place to secure our Wives and Children likewise to secure our Brothers that come to trade with us. . . . Now, Brothers, we will take two Months to consider and choose out a Place fit for that Purpose, and then we will send You word.[41]

Still concerned that a post on the Ohio might draw it into a war with the French, Pennsylvania elected to ignore the Ohio Indians' request.

With the Philadelphia, Lancaster, and Logstown Conferences, the Ohio Indians motivated both the English and the French to attempt to control the eastern half of the Ohio Valley by occupying it with troops, posts, and/or traders. Prior to the Philadelphia Conference, the French enjoyed a monopolistic hold on the valley's trade. With no threat to their economic activities in the area, the French remained content with the valley's trade being generated by independent and company traders who operated out of Ohio Indian settlements. Though they primarily focused their efforts in the western half of the valley, a limited number of French traders such as Joncaire operated in the eastern part out of Logstown and Kuskuski.[42] The English, though they realized the unlimited potential of the valley, lacked the resources to support large-scale trade in the region and opted instead to maintain and nurture their lucrative trade with the Iroquois Confederacy. As a result, few English traders ventured into the French-controlled Ohio Valley. However, with their initiation of the Philadelphia Conference of 1747, the Ohio Indians provided the English with a reason, the means, and the security to establish themselves in the Ohio Valley.

To exploit this reversal of fortunes, the English agreed to recognize the political autonomy of the Ohio Indians and subsequently established a council fire at Logstown that served to manage the international affairs of the valley. To start the operation of this newly forged relationship, the English and Ohio Indians met in a series of conferences at Logstown and Lancaster between 1748 and 1751. These various meetings resulted in the Logstonian request for a Euroamerican post on the Ohio River and increased the membership of the chain of friendship to include the Twightwee, Wyandot, and Virginians. The French, in turn, began to assert themselves in the region with the use of military force as a result of the increased English activity in the Ohio Valley. Consequently, the eastern Ohio Indians found themselves between the two European rivals and chose to support the English in lieu of the French efforts by making a second request for the establishment of a stockade. Though Pennsylvania elected not to establish the post that the Ohio Indians wanted, the conferences caused the French and the colony of Virginia to attempt to control the region directly with their physical presence in lieu of using traders and Indian proxies.

THE LOGSTOWN CONFERENCE OF 1752

Of all the political maneuvering they conducted prior to 1750, perhaps the most significant diplomatic move the Ohio Indians made with regard to the establishment of Fort Pitt was the inclusion of Virginia into their chain of friendship. With this move, they took the first step toward influencing the establishment of a permanent Euroamerican settlement in the valley. Though Pennsylvania rejected the Logstonian request for a post in the Ohio Valley, Ohio Indian leaders continued to push for a military settlement on the Monongahela River to help protect their interests as well as their families from French aggression. Undeterred by Pennsylvania's reluctance, the Ohio Indians saw a chance to establish an English post on the river with the inclusion of the colony of Virginia into their skewed triangle. Once Virginia was included in the chain of friendship, the Ohio Indians negotiated with it and assisted the colony in building Fort Prince George, the foundation for Forts Duquesne and Pitt.

While Croghan and Montour worked to secure Pennsylvania's relationship with the Ohio Indians, Virginia's governor, Robert Dinwiddie, planned to send a diplomatic expedition to Logstown in May 1752 to "treat with the said Indians in order to confirm what was agreed upon at the Treaty of Lancaster [in 1744], and to secure that Nation to the Interest of His Majesty and this Colony."[43] For this purpose, Dinwiddie selected Gist to take a present, and the Ohio Company commissioners selected land surveyor Joshua Fry, member of the Virginia House of Burgesses Lunsford Lomax, and former British naval officer and real-estate investor James Patton to negotiate with the Ohio Indians at Logstown.[44] In addition to Dinwiddie's instructions, Gist received directions from the Ohio Company, a private land-speculation group from Virginia, to proceed to the Ohio country prior to the official expedition to invite as many of the Ohio Indians to the conference as possible and to secretly "[take] Notice of any Quantity of good Land . . . [on] the River Ohio . . . convenient for . . . building Store Houses & other Houses for the better carrying on a Trade and Correspondence."[45] With instructions in hand, Gist set out for the Ohio country on November 4, 1751.

After he took Dinwiddie's invitation to the Ohio Indians, Gist led the Ohio Company commissioners to Logstown in May 1752 to ratify the Lancaster Treaty of 1744 on behalf of the colony of Virginia. With this conference, the Virginians hoped to accomplish two things. First, they sought the Ohio Indians' approval of the Lancaster Treaty of 1744. In the original treaty, the Iroquois Confederacy agreed to cede "all the Lands that are or shall be, by his Majesty's Appointment in the Colony of Virginia," for the mere sum of £200 worth of presents.[46] If successful in doing this, the Virginians would, by right of "his Majesty's Appointment," be able to settle the five hundred thousand acres King George III granted the Ohio Company in its charter. Second, the Virginians sought the approval of the Ohio Indians to build a fort and settlement on the banks of the Ohio River.

The conference started off poorly for the Virginians. After being introduced by Croghan, Gist and the commissioners elected not to give the Ohio Indians the present they brought from the governor of Virginia due to the absence of some key individuals such as Tanacharison. Disgusted at the Virginians' reluctance to distribute the gift—a sign of good faith and intentions in Ohio Indian treaty negotiations—two Shawnee leaders decided to leave the conference.[47] Soon after they made this decision, Tanacharison and the other key individuals arrived and convinced them to stay. With all the key persons present, Gist and the commissioners distributed the gift, and the conference commenced, with the Virginians immediately addressing the issue of the treaty ratification. Yet tensions remained high because of the commissioners' stipulation that the Ohio Indians already ratified the Lancaster Treaty of 1744 when they accepted Weiser's gift from Pennsylvania in 1748. Believing their land claims resolved, the Virginians continued to address the various points on their agenda and requested permission of the Ohio Indians to build a settlement on the Ohio River. In an attempt to make the proposition sound better to the Ohio Indians, the commissioners noted, "From such a settlement greater advantages will arise to you than you can at present conceive, our people will be able to supply you with goods much cheaper than can at this time be afforded, will be ready to help in case, you should be attacked and some good men among them appointed with authority to punish and restrain the many injuries and abuses . . . by disorderly white people."[48]

After the Virginians made their requests, the Ohio Indians transacted some business among themselves to end Shawnee and Lenape hostilities against the southern Indians (Cherokee) and to acknowledge the admittance of Croghan as a permanent member of their council fire. With these actions completed, the conference ended the first day without the Ohio Indians addressing the major concerns of Virginia.[49]

After several days of concluding business among themselves and their neighbors, the Ohio Indians addressed Virginia's issues. In regard to the Lancaster Treaty, the Ohio Indians acknowledged the land cessions up to the "hill on the other side of the Allagany hill," meaning the western side of the Allegheny Mountains, which failed to include the location of present-day Pittsburgh. The second point, concerning the establishment of a fort and settlement, worked somewhat into the hands of the Ohio Indians. Though Pennsylvania ignored their requests for a "strong house," the Ohio Indians saw a perfect opportunity to have Virginia establish the post that both groups desperately wanted. However, the Ohio Indians disliked the idea of having an English settlement on their lands and informed the Virginians that:

> Our brothers of Virginia may build a strong house at the fork of Monaungahela to keep such goods, powder, lead, and necessaries as shall be wanting, and as soon as you please. . . . In regard to your request, to build a strong house at the Monaungahela, you told us it would require a settlement to support it with provisions and necessaries; it is true, but we will take care that there shall be no scarcity of that kind.[50]

Despite their immediate rejection of a settlement being constructed adjacent to the proposed fort, the Ohio Indians humored the Virginians and informed them that they would consult the council at Onondaga for advice on the situation and rethink the issue at a later date.[51] The Logstonians also requested that Virginia prove its support of the Twightwee and personally deliver a portion of the present to them. With this gesture, the Logstonians believed the Twightwee would remain in the chain of friendship and not go back to the French. The Virginians ended the conference with one final request and offer. They asked the Ohio Indians to consider either sending their children to an Indian school in Virginia or to entertain the possibility of sending English teachers to their towns. With kind words, the Ohio Indians refused both offers, and the conference ended.[52]

The Logstown conference of 1752 is important for four reasons. First, the Ohio Indians and Virginians gained the fort they both wanted in the Ohio Valley near Logstown at present-day Pittsburgh. With this conference, the Ohio Indians essentially selected the place and, in many ways, the time of the establishment of Fort Prince George, later Pittsburgh. Second, Virginia replaced Pennsylvania as the dominant English colony in the Ohio Valley owing in part to its willingness to build the post the Ohio Indians wanted, thereby shifting the general English policy from one concerned with trade to one concerned primarily with settlement. Consequently, the Ohio Indians opened their region to English traders and their forts, creating an even greater chasm between themselves and the French. Third, the conference established the bounds of the Lancaster Treaty of 1744 and limited the unchecked advance of Euroamerican settlement. Moreover, the treaty ratification reaffirmed the Ohio Indians' autonomy with the colony of Virginia. Following this conference, Virginia and Pennsylvania dealt directly with the Ohio Indians in regard to the westward advancement of their colonies. Last, the conference established the Ohio Indians' resolve to support English as opposed to French claims in the Ohio Valley. Combined, these factors prompted France to adopt a military strategy to recapture the Ohio Valley trade. Hence, because of Ohio Indian political maneuvering, the militarily weak English gained the permission and support they needed to establish a "strong house" in a region hotly contested by colonial and European powers.

THE CONSTRUCTION OF FORTS PRINCE GEORGE AND DUQUESNE, 1752–1754

Though the eastern Ohio Indians invited the English to build a stockade in the valley, the task remained uncompleted until tensions between the French and English colonies heightened in spring 1754. Concerned with the boldness of the English colonies to build forts along the Ohio River, the French began to feel that the king of England personally orchestrated the actions of Virginia and Pennsylvania. In a letter to Jean Baptiste Machault, France's comptroller-general of finances, Canada's newly appointed governor, Marquis Duquesne, wrote that "it is not possible that the King of Great Britain has not consented to and even ordered all the movements which the English are making on this Continent."[53] Though many French officials wanted to more forcefully assert France's claims to the valley, Baron de Longueuil, the interim governor of Canada, wished "to leave the Belle Rivière at peace, having a special respect and consideration for the Iroquois who dwell there."[54] More poignantly, however, Longueuil contended that "the English were trading there before us; that it was not just to chase them out; that at most the river belonged to the Iroquois; and that we had only to supply their needs, as the English were doing, for these last to withdraw of their own accord, when they saw they could not earn a living there."[55]

Unfortunately for the English, not all of France's officials felt the same way. When he arrived in Canada in 1752 to replace Longueuil, the Marquis Duquesne had orders in hand directing him to "drive the English from our territory, and to prevent them coming there to trade."[56]

Duquesne wasted no time in dispatching his orders and organized an expedition of 2,200 men to establish a string of four forts descending from Fort Niagara south into the Ohio Valley. By the end of 1753, the French had established three of the four posts, Fort Presqu'Isle (Erie), Fort Le Boeuf (Waterford), and Fort Venango (Venango), all in Pennsylvania.[57] Because of poor weather and a lack of supplies, the French failed to build a fort at Logstown, the site selected for the fourth post. Though displeased with their progress, the French commander, Claude de Contrecoeur, enjoyed few human obstacles in the form of the Ohio Indians or their English friends. Throughout their advance, neither Contrecoeur nor his command came under any hostile attack. On the surface, it appeared to the French that their plan to repossess the Ohio Valley trade had all but succeeded in winter 1753.[58]

Unbeknownst to Contrecoeur, the French actions drove the Ohio Indians closer to the English and essentially opened a Pandora's box. When the French landed at Presqu'Isle and began to erect a fort, the Ohio Indians sent a delegation to Virginia to ask for military aid.[59] Governor Dinwiddie immediately dispatched Captain William Trent to Logstown "with a Present of Powder, Lead, [and] Guns."[60] When he arrived at Logstown, Trent met with Tanacharison and discovered that the Logstonians sent a reconnaissance party to scout out the French activities at Presqu'Isle. After the party returned, Trent held a formal council with the eastern Ohio Indian leaders where the chain of friendship determined their next move.[61] After fourteen days of deliberation, the eastern Ohio Indians and Trent agreed on two actions. The Indians decided to send a delegation to the French to warn them off their lands and another to meet with Dinwiddie to discuss the affairs of 1753 in depth. Trent agreed that Virginia would honor its commitment to the Ohio Indians and build the fort it promised as soon as possible and also send an emissary to the French to request their departure from the region.[62] With these actions determined, Trent set out for Virginia.

En route to Virginia, Trent sent a letter to Governor James Hamilton of Pennsylvania detailing the situation in the valley and informing him, "The Indians are in such confusion that there is no knowing who to Trust. I expect they will all join the French except the Delawares, as they expect no assistance from the English."[63] When he returned to Virginia, Trent made Dinwiddie privy to the same information. In response to this information, the governor sent a young George Washington to the French at Fort Le Boeuf with a warning to "require . . . [their] peaceable Departure."[64] Before Washington departed, Tanacharison initiated his part of the plan made with Trent and met with the French to inform them:

> This is our land, and not yours. . . . If you had come in a peaceable Manner, like our Brothers the English, we should not have been against your trading with us, as they do, but to come, Fathers, and build great houses upon our Land, and to take it by Force, is what we cannot submit to. . . . I desire you to withdraw, as I have done our Brothers the English. . . . I lay this down as a Trial to both, to see which will have the greatest Regard to it, and that Side we will stand by, and make equal Shares with us . . . for, I am not afraid to discharge you off this Land.[65]

Despite Tanacharison's proposal of a "trial" to determine who the Ohio Indians would support, the French remained committed to their plan to take back the Ohio Valley trade by a show of force. In his response to Tanacharison's speech, Le Boeuf's commander, Le Gardeur de St. Pierre, pointedly stated the French position, informing the Mingo sachem:

> You need not put yourself to the Trouble of Speaking, for I will not hear you: I am not afraid of Flies, or Musquitos, for Indians are such as these, I tell you, down that River I will go, and will build upon it. . . . I have Forces sufficient to burst it open, and tread under my Feet all that stand in Opposition, together with their Alliances. . . . It is my Land, and I will have it.[66]

Frustrated by his failed attempt, Tanacharison accompanied Washington on his journey to officially return the wampum given the Ohio Indians by the French in earlier years that affirmed their friendship toward one another. This gesture made clear the Ohio Indians' open intent to cast their lot with the English against the French. St. Pierre refused to except the wampum and the Ohio Indians' rejection of French friendship and promised Tanacharison that "he wanted to live in Peace, and trade amicably with them, as Proof of which, he would send some Goods immediately down to the Loggs-Town for them"[67] Though St. Pierre promised amicable trade, the Ohio Indians remained leery of the French and chose to support the English efforts to erect a fort on the Ohio River.

While Ohio Indian diplomacy played out at Fort Le Boeuf, Governor Dinwiddie authorized Trent and Washington to raise a company of one hundred men each and John Carlyle to acquire enough supplies to support five hundred men for a military excursion into the Ohio Valley. After he conferred with the Ohio Indian delegation sent to him following Trent's visit at Logstown, Dinwiddie ordered Trent to erect the fort they promised at the site dictated by the Logstonians, the confluence of the Allegheny, Ohio, and Monongahela Rivers. Meanwhile, Washington and Carlyle received orders from Dinwiddie directing them to assemble their respective companies and to meet with Trent.[68] With these plans set in motion, the British colonies raced along a collision course with the French that the Ohio Indians initiated with their diplomacy in 1747.

While Virginia planned for its armed expedition into the valley, Pennsylvania sent Croghan and Montour to Logstown to assess the situation, deliver a present, and appraise the losses the colony would suffer if the French continued with their plans. When they arrived at Logstown, Croghan discovered that the Twightwee had returned to the French interest following a successful raid that brought about the demise of Old Briton and displayed the inability of the English to assist the Ohio Indians with any type of military force.[69] Trade between the English and Ohio Indians virtually stopped at this point because of the French military presence in the Ohio Valley and their successful attack against Old Briton. Because of the inability of the English to protect their own traders or deliver goods, the Ohio Indians began to rethink their strength and capabilities.[70] Thus, English doddering over a period of three years threatened their, as well as the Ohio Indians', position in the valley.

While Croghan and Montour met with the Ohio Indians at the site of their council fire, a vanguard of French soldiers arrived at Logstown and made camp adjacent to the settlement. Despite the French efforts to convince the Ohio Indians they "were coming here to visit," Tanacharison, following a run-in with the French commander, met with Croghan and Montour and voiced a desire to have a second fort built on the Ohio River and for English troops to man the posts.[71] In a speech to Croghan, Tanacharison stated:

> We now request that our Brother the Governor of Virginia may build a Strong House at the Forks of the Mohongialo, and send some of our young Brethren, their Warriors, to live on it; and we expect our Brother of Pennsylvania will build another House somewhere on the River where he shall think proper . . . as our Enemies are just at hand, and we do not know what Day they may come upon Us.[72]

With the diplomatic wheel set in motion, the Ohio Indians cast their lot against the French at the beginning of 1754 and made an all-out military and economic commitment to support the English. Moreover, the eastern Ohio Indians pushed even harder for the establishment of not only one but two posts in the Ohio Valley and for the first time regarded the French as their enemies. Thus, despite the presence of over two thousand Frenchmen in their lands, the Ohio Indians chose to remain in the English interests and set the conditions for the establishment of Fort Prince George.

When they heard Trent had received orders to raise a company of men to erect a fort at the confluence of the three rivers, Tanacharison and Scarouady sent a letter that urged the captain to "come immediately and build a Fort at the Forks of the Monongahela." To accommodate this request, Trent hastened his departure before he gathered his complement of one hundred men and arrived at the confluence on February 1, 1754, with only thirty-three militiamen.[73] To assist Trent, Tanacharison brought a company of men to help erect the fort and personally laid the first log of Fort Prince George.

Though things began to appear more favorably to the Ohio Indians with the establishment of the post in full swing, Trent and half his company left the uncompleted stockade to quicken the delivery of Carlyle's supplies.[74] As fate would have it, soon after Trent departed, a French force of 1,100 men attacked the hastily constructed and weakly defended Fort Prince George and forced Ensign Edward Ward, the acting commander, to surrender without a shoot being fired. To many, the weak display of force proved the English lacked the ability to support Ohio Indian interests in the valley. Displeased with the English colonies' lack of support, a small number of Ohio Indians became neutral or returned to the French interests. However, the strong support of Tanacharison, Scarouady, and Shingas kept a majority of the Ohio Indians aligned with the English despite the fact that the stockade they so strongly desired fell into French hands.[75]

Like a freight train moving down a track, the establishment of a Euroamerican settlement in the Ohio Valley in 1754 began very slowly in 1747. With the Philadelphia, Lancaster, and Logstown Conferences in 1747 and 1748, Ohio Indian political maneuvering laid the track and got the English train slowly rolling toward the Ohio Valley, prompting the French to roll their train with Celoron's expedition in 1749. Locked onto their respective courses, the two trains picked up steam during the whirlwind period between 1751 and 1754. Not wanting to be outpaced by its rival, each train continued to pour on the steam. Where one tried diplomacy to settle issues in the Ohio Valley, the other used a military presence, and vice versa. This exchange between the Ohio Indians, French, and English continued until the two Euroamerican trains were speeding down the track out of control and toward an inevitable collision. All along the track, the Ohio Indians manipulated the course of both trains to fulfill their own political objectives and unsuspectingly paved the way for the construction of Fort Prince George. Without Ohio Indian involvement, the English lacked the ability and initiative to establish such a formidable position in the Ohio Valley that it threatened French interests and perpetuated their military actions. Moreover, without the Ohio Indians, the militarily weak English lacked the ability, and perhaps the desire, as Pennsylvania's reluctance to build a post shows, to establish Fort Prince George. Hence, the establishment of Fort Prince

George required more than just a mere trader and his stock of supplies as Kenneth Lewis suggested. The establishment of a Euroamerican frontier settlement in the Ohio Valley in the mid-eighteenth century required the Ohio Indians to initiate the process with their diplomacy, approve the project, and support it with their much-needed military and political assistance.

THE END OF LOGSTONIAN POLITICAL POWER, 1754

Shortly after they took Fort Prince George, the French used the poorly constructed stockade as the foundation for Fort Duquesne. With Duquesne situated in such a strategic location, the French elected not to build a post at Logstown. Rather, they elected to conduct military operations from Duquesne. Ironically, had it not been for the poor weather conditions in 1753, the French would have erected their fourth fort at Logstown and prevented the construction of Forts Prince George and Duquense, thereby delaying the establishment and emergence of Pittsburgh. With Duquesne established, the French completed the string of forts they believed would keep the English traders out of the valley and motivate the Ohio Indians to return to their interests. However, the establishment of Duquesne only led to overt Indian hostilities.

In May 1754, following Ward's surrender of Fort Prince George, Tanacharison and a group of Indians accompanied Washington and his command up the Ohio River beyond Duquesne to erect a second fort. En route, Tanacharison and Washington came upon a French detachment under the command of Ensign Joseph Coulon Jumonville. Tanacharison, Scarouady, and Washington believed the detachment came to reconnoiter their forces and agreed to attack the unit. In just a few minutes, the English and their Indian allies killed ten, wounded one, and captured twenty-one. More importantly however, Jumonville, a prominent member of French society, died at the hands of Tanacharison.[76] Elated at their first joint victory and complete rout of the enemy, Tanacharison "declared to send these Frenchmen's Scalps with a Hatchet to all the Nations of Indian's in union with them" to prove the abilities of their English allies.[77] Unlike their previous diplomatic activities, the attack on Jumonville marked the first military action the Ohio Indians took against the French and firmly established their alliance with the English.

The success that the chain of friendship enjoyed in May proved short lived and stood as the high point in a series of English and French engagements that ended in defeat for the former. Only two months after his victory over Jumonville, Washington suffered a defeat at a stockade he hurriedly constructed and aptly named Fort Necessity. Jumonville's brother handed

Washington his defeat and made him sign a document of capitulation that claimed he assassinated the officer's younger brother. Spurred by these events, the English sent General Edward Braddock to capture Fort Duquesne. However, Braddock suffered an embarrassing defeat at the Battle of Monongahela. These successive defeats coupled with the English inability to support their economic, military, and political needs caused the Ohio Indians to divide into two camps: a pro-English camp led by Tanacharison and Scarouady and made up primarily of Mingo people, and a pro-French sect led by Shingas and comprising mostly Delaware and Shawnee. More importantly, however, Scarouady burned Logstown, the site of the Ohio Indians' council fire. Two settlements, Aughwick and Kuskuski, became the locations for the pro-English and pro-French factions respectively and replaced Logstown as the location for Euroamerican and Indian conferences.[78]

Once divided, the two factions momentarily assumed secondary roles in the political and military affairs of the Ohio Valley. In a conference held at Aughwick in 1754, for example, the English informed the Mingo that the Iroquois had sold them a large tract of land that encompassed their current settlement and a large portion of the Ohio Valley. When the Mingo objected to this, Weiser, the English delegate, informed them that they may "look upon the [Ohio] lands as lost to them" because of these transactions and the French occupation.[79] In addition to this issue, the Ohio Indians raised a number of points that concerned their military involvement against the French. When they questioned Weiser about their role, the Englishman instructed them, "Make yourselves quiet and easy and mind nothing but Council affairs till you see Us first stir." Weiser continued, telling the Ohio Indians to visit their kin on the Ohio to gather "News of our Friends . . . and also the Proceedings of the French."[80] To compound matters, the Mingo lost their most prolific political and military leader shortly after the conference with the death of Tanacharison. Though Scarouady remained, Tanacharison's loss proved a great blow to the Anglo-Indian alliance and caused many Ohio Indians to join Shingas and his brother the Beaver at Kuskuski in their support of the French.[81]

The Aughwick Conference marked a turning point in Ohio Indian political affairs. For the first time since 1744, the English negotiated directly with the Iroquois in regard to valley politics without consulting the Ohio Indians. Also, the English decided to use their Ohio Indian allies solely to gather information as opposed to conducting independent raids or other offensive maneuvers against the French because they no longer viewed them as a significant military force. Consequently, after 1754, the pro-English faction of Ohio Indians was a marginal political and military force in the valley and no longer controlled their international affairs. Rather, the English essentially made Scarouady and his peoples puppets, virtually directing which of their policies the Ohio Indians supported. In contrast, Shingas, who joined the French, retained his political autonomy and remained at Kuskuski and in position to dictate many of the valley's affairs. Shingas's people reoccupied Logstown and convinced the French to build thirty cabins complete with fireplaces for the inhabitants.[82] Following its reconstruction, Logstown remained the major trading center in the Ohio Valley and became a lifeline of military and physical support for Fort Duquesne.[83] With the French occupation of the valley, the political dynamics of the region changed considerably with the Ohio Indians in Logstown and Kuskuski abandoning the English and supporting the French in the defense and establishment of Fort Duquesne.

OHIO INDIAN SUPPORT OF FORT DUQUESNE, 1754–1758

Though they defeated the weakly defended Fort Prince George, the French required the assistance of the Ohio Indians to ensure the security and success of Fort Duquesne. Challenged with protecting all of Canada and the Ohio Valley, and resourcing both endeavors, the French sought to hold Fort Duquesne and their other frontier posts by relying on the Ohio Indians to provide the bulk of their military force and provisions. The Reverend Claude Godfroy Cocquard, a Canadian priest, hinted at the faith the French placed in their Ohio Indian allies in a letter he wrote to his brother. Despite the likelihood of an English attack, Cocquard noted that "M. Dumas, Commandant of Fort Duquesne . . . is awaiting without fear; that his fort is well fortified, and that 2,000 Indians in cabins around that fort, were a strong defense which the English would not readily approach."[84]

To the French, Fort Duquesne was the keystone of their defense of the Ohio Valley because it stood as the first line of defense against Pennsylvania and Virginia. Unlike the other posts that descended from Fort Niagara into the Ohio Valley, the location of Fort Duquesne proved ideally suited to thwart the two most aggressive English colonies and to control the Indian trade. Writing in 1757, the Marquis de Vaudreuil, the governor general of New France (present-day eastern Canada, the Great Lakes region, and the trans-Appalachian West), explained the importance of Fort Duquesne to his superiors: "But for the Preservation of the Beautiful river on which depends the security of all the posts of the Upper countries [Canada], 'tis indispensable that we fortify Fort Duquesne in such a manner as to enable it to sustain a siege."[85]

Despite Fort Duquesne's strategic importance, the post continually stood in a miserable state of disrepair owing in part to the ineptness of the commanders who built and first administered the garrison. Several French administrators and officers, including Fort Duquesne's commander, Captain Jean-Daniel Dumas, noted in 1755 that "no foresight had been employed to supply that fort with provisions," and that the post "[had] never been completed . . . [and could not] resist an attack with artillery."[86] Additionally, Vaudreuil stressed the inadequacies of the post's defense to his superiors, explaining in 1757: "Fort Duquesne, in its present condition, could not offer any resistance to the enemy; 'tis too small to lodge the garrison necessary on such an occasion. A single shell would be sufficient to get it so on fire, that it would be impossible to extinguish it because the houses are too close. . . . Besides, 'tis so near the confluence . . . that it is always exposed to be entirely submerged by the overflowing of the rivers."[87]

Moreover, Fort Duquesne's distance from Canada made provisioning it near impossible. Duquesne himself explained to Vaudreuil that "too much time was consumed in going in one trip from the fort on River au Boeuf to Fort Duquesne, to the loss of a great quantity of provisions which have been spoiled by bad weather."[88] Due to their unfavorable situation and wretched conditions, the French garrison at Fort Duquesne turned to their Ohio Indian allies for assistance.

The garrison at Fort Duquesne relied on the Ohio Indians to provide them with enough resources to augment their insufficient amount of provisions from the time the French first arrived until they burned the post in 1758.[89] Charles de Raymond, a captain in the Troupes de la Marine (Troops of the Navy), wrote that "the soldiers of the . . . Belle Rivière . . . require . . . if one wanted to . . . feed them . . . the same food that all the voyageurs live on, that is Indian corn, venison, and other meat that the Indians kill."[90] With the assistance of the Ohio Indians, Duquesne believed the post would be self-sufficient in two years. In the first year of its existence, the garrison, in conjunction with the Ohio Indians, produced "seven hundred *minots* [bushels] of Indian corn" and planted a secondary crop of peas. The soil in the area proved so rich that the garrison's corn field extended up both the Allegheny and Monongahela Rivers for a quarter of a mile.[91] Moreover, a number of Ohio Indians moved to the post and grew crops conjointly with the garrison. With the increased manpower and favorable weather conditions, Duquesne calculated "that if the harvest were good, at least 2,000 *minots* could be saved" per year and easily provide for the garrison's subsistence needs.[92]

Unfortunately for the French, poor harvests prevented the fort from producing the intended supplies and forced it to rely heavily on subsistence trade with the Ohio Indians. In a letter from Logstown, Michel Maray de La

Chauvignerie, a Canadian officer, expressed the French reliance on Ohio Indian subsistence support: "we are on the verge of going without food. The great quantity of Brandy . . . poured out . . . Prevents the Indians from hunting, and as a result we are at the point of lacking everything."[93] Similarly, the French trader at Logstown, Joncaire, noted that "the . . . Residents . . . increase the price of their Corn in the hope of selling it very expensively . . . the high price of Corn obliges me to get rid of all my animals due to the bad forage . . . this winter."[94] Unable to forage for food and defend the post at the same time, the French sought and relied on Ohio Indians to fulfill their subsistence needs. However, even with Ohio Indian support, poor harvests coupled with the ravages of war caused Fort Duquesne to be insufficiently supplied throughout its existence.[95]

Limited resources coupled with inadequate garrison space forced the French to rely heavily on the Ohio Indians to help defend Fort Duquesne. In fact, the military support the Ohio Indians gave the post enabled it to survive. Only one year after the French erected the post, General Braddock marched on Fort Duquesne with a force of over two thousand English regulars and colonial militia. Outnumbered four to one, the commander of the beleaguered French post rallied his Ohio Indian allies to provide for the fort's defense.[96]

In an effort to spoil the English offensive against his uncompleted and scarcely defensible post, Contrecoeur, Fort Duquesne's commander at the time, sent eight hundred men comprising six hundred Ohio Indians and two hundred Frenchmen and Canadians to ambush Braddock's force. The French commander reacted too slowly, however, and his forces met Braddock's troops in an open and frontal engagement. Within minutes of fighting, the British halted the French advance with three quick volleys, killing their commander, Captain Daniel Lienard de Beaujeu, and demoralizing the French and Canadian troops. Undeterred, the Indian forces, "yelping and screaming like many Devils," pushed forward and began enveloping the flanks of Braddock's column, "coming very swift" and cutting off and killing "the small British parties on the slopes to either side of the column."[97] Unaware of the Ohio Indian envelopment, George Washington estimated the enemy strength at only three hundred men and attempted to make a stand.[98] Unfortunately for Washington, the Indian move along the English flanks happened so quickly and with such devastation that according to Captain Dumas, Beaujeu's second in command, "the enemy, who were already shouting their 'Long Live the King,' thought now only to defend themselves."[99]

Within moments of the initial British volley, the French gained the upper hand and routed the English back to their supply trains. Though Washington attempted to rally his troops along the way, Dumas recounted that "the whoop of the Indians, which echoed through the forest, struck terror into the hearts of the entire enemy" and prevented the British reorganization.[100] By the battle's end, the Ohio Indians and their French allies had killed or wounded 1,200 of the 1,459 Englishmen they encountered.[101] Though over one thousand troops remained at his disposal, Colonel Thomas Dunbar, Braddock's second in command, feared the Indian threat so much that he retreated to Fort Cumberland in eastern Pennsylvania. With this retreat, the English military threat to Fort Duquesne ended until its renewal in 1758, when the Ohio Indians abandoned the French.

Many historians point to poor generalship on the part of the English commanders and the undisciplined performance of the British regulars as the reason behind Braddock's defeat.[102] However, the nearly six hundred Ohio Indian warriors who aided the French caused the British rout at the Battle of the Monongahela in 1754. Without the aid of the Ohio Indian warriors, Fort Duquesne's survival was surely in doubt. The Ohio Indians rallied to Contrecoeur's side, engaged the enemy, held their position against well-trained British regulars, and then used the terrain that was so familiar to them as an advantage to outflank the English column. As historian Thomas A. Lewis more poignantly put it, "without them [Contrecoeur] was lost."[103]

Following Braddock's defeat, Fort Duquesne's garrison needed Shingas's warriors to keep the British forces at bay. Concerned with Fort Duquesne's poor defenses, the newly appointed commander, Captain Dumas, believed he needed to assume an offensive posture to prevent the English from attempting a second attack on his post. To accomplish this, Dumas employed hundreds of Ohio Indian allies to conduct raids on military and civilian settlements throughout the colonies of Pennsylvania, Virginia, Maryland, and South Carolina. In 1756 and 1757, the Ohio Indians launched a series of raids from Kuskuski and Logstown and decimated the English colonies, inflicting over one thousand civilian and military casualties, capturing hundreds of prisoners, burning several stockades, severing communications between the British colonies and their frontier posts, and plundering or destroying numerous goods and livestock, all while the French garrison remained at Fort Duquense.[104]

The success of these raids paralyzed the English frontier and enabled Fort Duquesne to escape defeat for three years. In a letter to Marquis de Machault, the Canadian minister of marine and controller-general, Vaudreuil explained the impact of the Ohio Indians' successes. Vaudreuil wrote that "our continual incursions have placed it out of the power of Virginia to undertake anything . . . even to construct [a] fort to protect herself . . . on account of our

Indians, who are always in the field . . . the entire frontier of the three Provinces is in the like condition. . . . The English are in daily dread of being attacked." The Ohio Indian raids proved so devastating to the English colonies that when threatened with the likelihood of an attack on Fort Duquesne in 1756, Vaudreuil brushed the notion aside, claiming, "if the enemy was really marching against . . . [Dumas] . . . he could . . . have raised the Indians of the Beautiful river . . . by means of whom he would . . . prevent the former making any progress."[105] The military prowess and success of the Ohio Indians proved critical to the existence of Fort Duquesne. Without the Ohio Indian preemptive raids and their augmentation to the French force, Braddock's advance on Fort Duquesne would have more than likely succeeded in its mission to take the fort in 1755. Due to the military efforts of the Ohio Indians, however, Fort Duquesne lasted as a keystone in the French defense of the Ohio Valley and New France for nearly four years.

Unfamiliar with their surroundings, the French relied on the Ohio Indians to keep Fort Duquense well informed of events going on outside its walls. From the outset of their tenure at Fort Duquesne, the French used their Indian information network to keep them abreast of the movements and actions of the English and their allies. Vaudreuil described the informational support Fort Duquesne received from the Ohio Indians. In reference to Braddock's attack, Vaudreuil explained:

> We had confirmation of this intelligence from some reliable Indians belonging to different villages, who had given us pretty strong assurances of it, not admitting of a doubt. They have also added, as a very sure thing, that 4,000 men were going to Choueguin; that the 5 Nations would form the wings of this army; that the English were desirous of seeing Niagara and Fort Frontenac, and that 600 bateaux had . . . been built and . . . that 5,000 men were encamped outside Orange, covering two leagues of country.

Based on this information, Vaudreuil sent four hundred men to Fort Duquesne to buttress the post's defenses and kept another four hundred at Fort Presqu'Isle that he planned to move to Niagara.[106]

Ironically, the movement of the four hundred reinforcements prompted Contrecoeur to send out the force that routed Braddock's column. Without the reinforcements, Contrecoeur doubted that his force could withstand the attack of such a formidable and well-organized column and made preparations to abandon the post.[107] Ohio Indian intelligence reports directly influenced the affairs of what was perhaps the pivotal point in Fort Duquesne's early period. Though this is only one instance of Ohio Indian informational

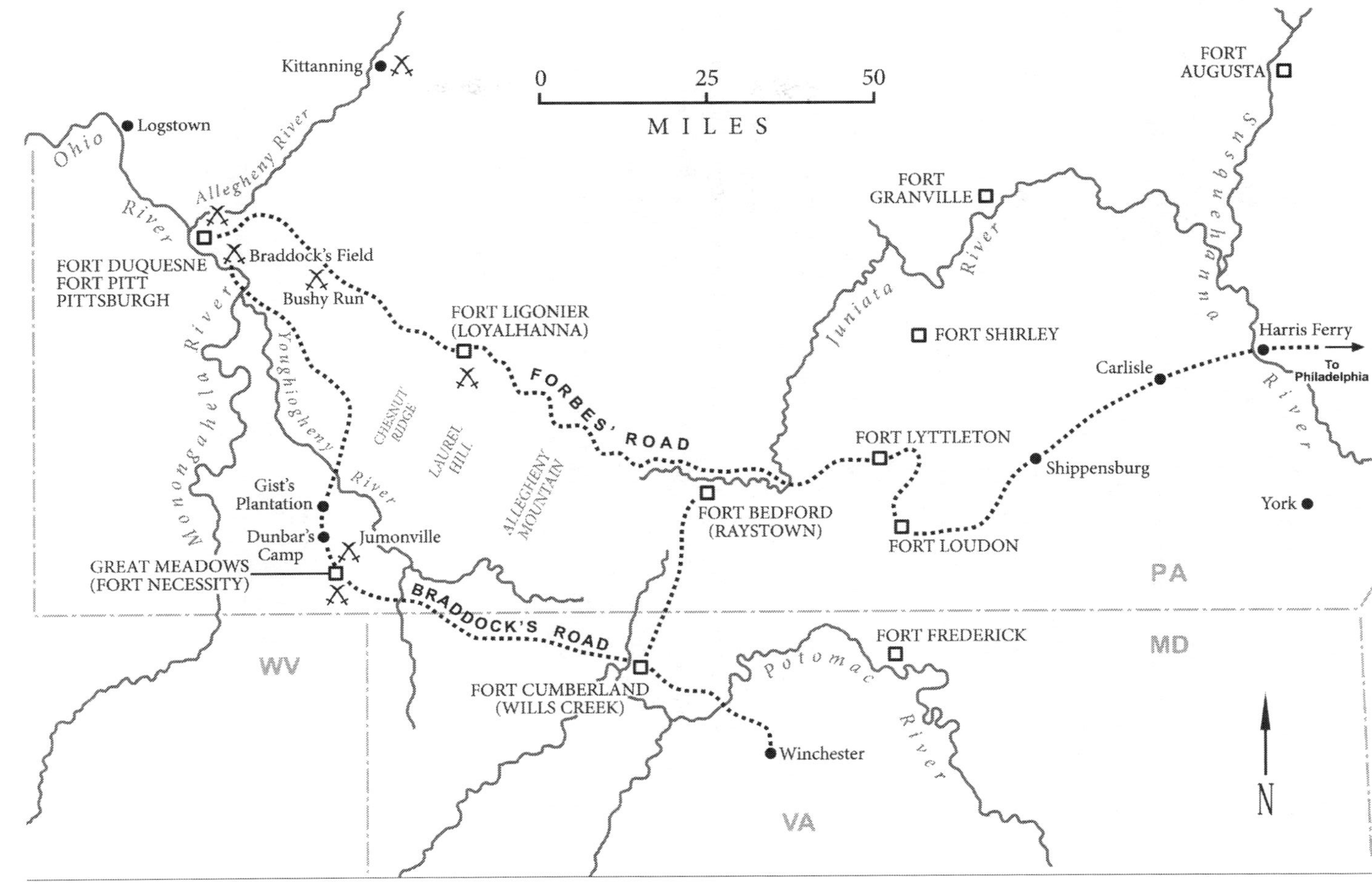

Kittanning
Logstown
Ohio River
Allegheny River
0
25
50
MILES
FORT AUGUSTA
FORT GRANVILLE
Braddock's Field
Bushy Run
FORT DUQUESNE
FORT PITT
PITTSBURGH
Monongahela River
Youghiogheny River
FORT LIGONIER
(LOYALHANNA)
FORBES' ROAD
CHESNUT RIDGE
LAUREL HILL
ALLEGHENY MOUNTAIN
Juniata River
FORT SHIRLEY
Susquehanna River
Harris Ferry
To Philadelphia
Carlisle
FORT LYTTLETON
Shippensburg
York
Gist's Plantation
Dunbar's Camp
Jumonville
FORT BEDFORD
(RAYSTOWN)
FORT LOUDON
GREAT MEADOWS
(FORT NECESSITY)
PA
BRADDOCK'S ROAD
FORT FREDERICK
MD
WV
Potomac River
FORT CUMBERLAND
(WILLS CREEK)
Winchester
VA
N

support, the literature is filled with accounts of the French using the Ohio Indians to gather information—so many, in fact, that it would require several chapters to touch on each affair.[108]

Despite Ohio Indian support, Fort Duquesne seemed almost predestined to fail. Though the French enjoyed great successes with their Ohio Indian allies, the lack of provisions coupled with the poor location and construction placed the post in an unfavorable condition before the hostilities of the French and Indian War heightened. Moreover, the offensive approach of Fort Duquesne's commanders and the limited number of garrisoned troops left little time and people for the post's physical improvements. In the four years it existed, the French constructed only one building of any significance and failed to improve on the post's defensibility. To compound matters, an unpopular and inept French commander, the Marquis de Ligneris, replaced the effective and popular Dumas and Contrecoeur at a time when the French could not supply the Ohio Indians with trade goods.[109] Furthermore, because of their offensive raids into the English colonies, the Ohio Indians neglected their harvests and left their corn to rot in the fields.[110] When the garrison at Fort Duquesne relied on them to defeat a second English attempt on the fort in November 1758, the Ohio Indians abandoned the post in the face of a large British force and returned to their settlements to hunt.[111] To the French, the Ohio Indian withdrawal signified the end for their most important post in the valley. The Marquis de Bougainville, the aide-de-camp of General Louis-Joseph de Montcalm-Grozon (more commonly referred to as General Montcalm), expressed the inevitability of Fort Duquesne's fall after the Ohio Indian exodus. Bougainville wrote that "the Indians . . . have quitted Fort Duquesne, to return to their villages . . . it was found impossible to retain them; yet, the Beautiful river is almost certain of being attacked . . . its success is more than probable."[112] Without Ohio Indian support, the French burned the post and left the southern gateway to the Ohio Valley, never to return.[113]

Ohio Indian support proved vital to the establishment and development of Fort Duquesne between 1754 and 1758. Restricted by wartime activities, the Ohio Indians and French focused their efforts on the protection and survival of Fort Duquesne. Continually overmatched by their English opponent and underfed, the French relied on the Ohio Indians to ensure the stability of their post. In their Ohio Indian allies, the French possessed a force that successfully defended Fort Duquesne on two occasions from an English attacker twice their size. Likewise, the Ohio Indians proved to be the only offensive weapon employed by the French to prevent an English advance in the Ohio Valley. When informed of the loss of the Ohio Indians, General Montcalm, the commander of French forces in New France, plainly stated that it "'tis to be feared."[114] The importance of the Ohio Indians to the success of Fort Duquesne is perhaps best summarized in a comment made by Colonel Henry Bouquet, an English officer involved in the post's capture. After the English concluded a peace with the Ohio Indians, Bouquet said, "the treaty struck the blow which has knocked the French in the head."[115] George Washington likewise pointed to the French loss of Ohio Indian support as being a major cause of Fort Duquesne's demise. In a letter to Virginia's lieutenant governor, Francis Fauquier, Washington wrote that "the possession of this fort has been a matter of great surprise to the whole army, and we cannot attribute it to more probable causes than those of weakness, want of provisions and the desertion of their Indians." Ironically, all the items Washington cites as reasons for the downfall of Fort Duquesne proved to be factors directly related to and dependent on Ohio Indian support.[116] Simply put, the Ohio Indians saved Fort Duquesne, the keystone of France's Ohio Valley defense, from destruction and kept its garrison alive with much-needed foodstuffs and intelligence, and, when they stopped their support, doomed the post to failure.

THE BUILDING OF FORT PITT, 1758–1762

Unlike the sad saga of Fort Duquesne, the story of Fort Pitt and the emergence of Pittsburgh stands, to historians such as Frank C. Harper and Richard C. Wade, as a monument to the English settlement of the frontier that "had a world significance . . . and determined that ours should be an Anglo-Saxon . . . civilization." However, Wade, Harper, and scholars like them overlook the important role played by the Ohio Indians to bring about the construction of Pittsburgh. More often than not, they view the Ohio Indians as being passive victims who "faced [the] loss of their hunting lands . . . [and] their total extinction as a people" with the establishment of the post.[117] Yet even if they ignore the political role the Logstonians and Kuskuskians played between 1747 and 1754 that motivated, and in some cases directed, the English and French actions in the Ohio Valley, scholars must recognize that the Ohio Indians protected Fort Pitt during its first four years of existence through military and political means, provided the preponderance of provisions needed to keep the post operating and growing, and through their intelligence gathering served as the eyes, ears, and envoys for the English garrison. Without the assistance of the Ohio Indians, Fort Pitt may have gone the way of its predecessor, Fort Duquesne.

Ohio Indian political support proved vital in the early establishment of Fort Pitt. Even before Fort Duquesne fell, the English solicited the political support of the Ohio Indians to ensure the success of their expedition against the post, a plan that caused the French to abandon the garrison. In an effort to weaken the military strength of Fort Duquesne, General John Forbes, the English commander who led the attack on the post in 1758, sought the neutrality of the Ohio Indians with their ratification of the Treaty of Easton.[118] "If no Indians were to Join the Garrison," Forbes and many Englishmen believed, "Fort Du Quesne could easily be carried."[119] To accomplish this, Forbes petitioned Shingas and his brother the Beaver to "establish as sure as the Mountains between the English Nation and all the Indians . . . an everlasting Peace."[120] To Forbes, Bouquet, and many others, the Ohio Indians proved to be the key to Fort Duquesne's defense, and the Beaver and Shingas, who led some of the largest and most lethal attacks on Pennsylvania's frontier while in the French interest, were the two most capable leaders to broker an English peace.[121]

Shingas and the Beaver embraced the opportunity to support the English because of the French inability to carry on a prosperous trade with the Ohio Indians and to defend themselves without the assistance of Indian warriors.[122] The Ohio Indians lacked such confidence in their French alliance that the Logstonians removed their women and children to Kuskuski with Forbes's advance.[123] When Forbes approached them with his proposal, Shingas and the Beaver jumped at the opportunity to reinvigorate their economy and agreed to secure a peace between the English and the Ohio Indians.[124] In a letter to a female friend, Bouquet alluded to the role the Ohio Indians' neutrality played in Fort Duquesne's fall:

> The glory of our success must after God be allowed to our General, who from the beginning took those wise measures which deprived the French of their chief strength . . . [and] kept such a number of Indians idle during the whole campaign, and procured a peace with those inveterate enemies, more necessary and beneficial to the safety and welfare of the Provinces than driving the French from the Ohio.[125]

Once the Ohio Indians brokered their neutrality with Forbes, the French hurriedly abandoned and burned Fort Duquesne without a shot being fired.

With the Indian threat neutralized, Forbes triumphantly marched into Fort Duquesne at the head of nearly ten thousand men in November 1758. Though he successfully seized the strategic location, the English position at the confluence remained tenuous.[126] Bouquet explained the English position as, "A sad state of affairs, camping 300 miles from Philadelphia, with neither tents nor baggage, and in need of clothing, with the weather bitter cold (the thermometer at 16°), and getting supplies only with the greatest of difficulty."[127]

If the physical conditions they faced were not bad enough, George Croghan warned the English commanders that "although the military conquered the French, they 'had nothing to boast from the War with the natives' who must be conciliated."[128] In poor health and unable to sustain a large force at the newly named Pittsburgh, Forbes left a detachment of 280 men under the command of Bouquet with orders to secure the peace with the Ohio Indians.[129] To Forbes and Bouquet, the security of their detachment and the future designs of the English to control the Ohio Valley rested on the goodwill and support of the Ohio Indians.[130] Bouquet, in a letter to General Jeffrey Amherst, the overall commander of English troops in North America, expressed this belief when he wrote "the visible disafection of the Ohio Indians gives me more uneasiness than the exagerated Preparations of the Ennemy, as it is their Power to cut off the Supplys of our advanced Post."[131] Likewise in a series of letters with Amherst, Forbes reinforced Bouquet's belief and explained:

> The Governors . . . ought to attend . . . to . . . for the safety, and welfare of these Provinces, Peace with the Indians . . . the State of the Indians all along the Ohio . . . is I'm afraid not understood. . . . I beg you will not think trifflingly of the Indians or their friendship; when I venture to assure you that twenty Indians are capable of laying half this province to waste.[132]

Moreover, Colonel Hugh Mercer, who succeeded Bouquet as commander at Fort Pitt and had orders to abandon the post in the face of an assault, received information from his Ohio Indian allies that the French proposed to attack Pittsburgh with the winter thaw.[133] In the face of such potential danger from an enemy that still forcefully occupied the greater portion of the Ohio Valley, Bouquet and Mercer knew they needed an alliance with the Ohio Indians to preserve their position and arranged to meet with the Indian leaders to turn their newly forged neutrality into a lasting peace.[134]

Throughout Fort Pitt's formative period, the English relied on Ohio Indian diplomacy to create a peaceful environment essential for the post's prosperity. From the commencement of Mercer's command in November 1758 until July 1760, Croghan met with the Ohio Indians in a series of conferences to reestablish their economic and military alliance.[135] To Bouquet and Mercer, Croghan's success was imperative to the security of Pittsburgh. In a letter to Mercer, Bouquet informed him that "Mr. Croghan with your assistance will I hope be able to support our Interest with the Indians, till we can raise the Troops, and Inforce your arguments by the weight of an Army."[136] In the initial stages of their negotiations, Croghan and the Beaver worked to pacify the Ohio Indians to provide Mercer and his command with the time and resources necessary to construct a formidable defense at Pittsburgh.[137]

Unfortunately for Croghan and the Beaver, many of the Ohio Indians believed that the English force came and remained at Pittsburgh to possess their land.[138] Pesquitomen, a Mingo sachem, explained to Christian Frederick Post, a missionary selected to meet with the Ohio Indians, "We are always jealous . . . [that] . . . the English will take the land from us."[139] To thwart this perceived English attempt at occupation, many of the Ohio Indians gathered at Kuskuski with their still French allies to plan an attack on Pittsburgh.[140] To prevent this attack, the Beaver, on three occasions, suggested to Croghan and the English that they withdraw "back over the mountains . . . till the other nations have joined the peace, and then . . . come and build a trading house."[141] Likewise in a conference with Post, Ketiushund, a Mingo sachem, told the missionary, "All the nations had jointly agreed to defend their hunting place . . . and suffer nobody to settle there . . . and if the English would draw back over the mountain, they would get all the other nations into their interest; but if they staid and settled there, all the nations would be against them; and he was afraid it would be a great war, and never come to a peace again."[142]

Though it appears the Beaver was attempting to reverse the Ohio Indians' decision in 1751 to invite the English to settle in the valley by asking Bouquet to "draw back over the mountain," Croghan and his commanders ignored the sachem's request and remained insistent that a post be erected as soon as possible to prevent the French reoccupation of Pittsburgh.[143]

Having failed in their mission to persuade Bouquet to leave the area and still wanting to renew trade relations with the English, the Beaver and Shingas decided to accommodate the British by assisting them with their establishment of a permanent fort in the valley. It is unlikely the two sachems realized they were about to be almost solely responsible for securing a peace that would enable the English to build the most formidable and costly fort ever constructed in North America by Europeans. In concert with the Mingo leaders on the Ohio, the Beaver and Shingas set out to broker the peace that the English desired. In July 1759, the Beaver and his compatriots gathered nearly five hundred Ohio Indians from nine nations to meet with Croghan at Fort Pitt to talk of peace.[144] At the conference, Croghan assured the Ohio Indians that the English came to rid the country of the French and to "secure . . . [the] . . . Trade" with them. For this purpose, Croghan petitioned for their "Sensible" understanding of the situation and explained the English intention "to build a trading house" for the purpose of securing the trade. Additionally, Croghan requested that the Ohio Indians show their intentions for peace "by restoring . . . all our People who yet remain Prisoners amongst you." In support of Croghan's request, the Beaver told the Ohio Indians, "I desire you would sit and smoke your Pipes till I give you a call; I assure you the English have no intention of Injuring you, and I must insist on your . . . immediately quitting the French." As an "example" to the Ohio Indians of his own support for the British, the Beaver delivered two English prisoners whom he considered his "Mother . . . [and] . . . sister" to Croghan.[145]

Through the efforts of the Beaver and Croghan, the Ohio Indians at Kuskuski, who remained in the French interest, elected to make a peace with the English. Only the brother and nephew of the Lenape sachems Teedyuschung and Cutfinger opposed the reconciliation and expressed their intentions to assist the French with their expulsion of the English, who would "lull asleep the Indians . . . [and] . . . Cut their Throats."[146] Within one month, the Beaver's efforts at the conference came to fruition when sachems from the Lenape, Shawnee, Wyandot, Ottawa, Ojibwa, Kaskaskia, Miami, and Potawatomis journeyed to Fort Pitt to make peace with the English. In a ceremony of peace, the Lenape war sachem White Eyes "buried the French war hatchet" with a "Belt of Wampum" and petitioned the Ohio Indians to "go hunting and travel this Road of Peace . . . and exchange your skins and furs, for Goods to clothe your Women and Children."[147] Mercer gleefully relayed to Bouquet the impact of the Beaver and Croghan's efforts, informing him, "A happy opportunity offers itself . . . of clearing the Ohio intirely of French Men, Their Indians are wavering to a Man, & many drop off from them dayly, & will be fixed in the British Interest."[148] The favorable results of these conferences, coupled with the French expulsion from and abandonment of Forts Niagara and Venango, gave Mercer and his command a more secure environment to erect Fort Pitt.[149] In a letter to Pennsylvania's Governor William Denny, Mercer noted, "We can now talk to our new Allies in a proper Stile . . . the Consistency of our Plan in bringing them entirely over to the British Interest, ought to be preserved by treating them with a great kindness, but suffering none of their insults."[150]

One month later, General John Stanwix, Forbes's replacement as commander of British forces in the Ohio Valley, began the construction of Fort Pitt.[151] Though momentarily safe from an immediate French attack, the English knew they needed the continued efforts of the Beaver and the other key sachems to ensure a lasting peace while they constructed the fort.

To preserve the peace, Croghan once again solicited the Beaver and his supporters to gather the Ohio Indians to Pittsburgh for a series of conferences. Between October 1759 and August 1760, the Beaver and Croghan orchestrated no less than three large conferences. The Beaver's efforts culminated with a conference in August 1760 that attracted 919 Ohio Indians to Pittsburgh.[152] At this conference, the Ohio Indians agreed to consider, along with the Onondaga Council, an English proposal to build forts in the Ohio Valley. Additionally, the Ohio Indians agreed to quit any and all violence toward the English and "to return to [their] former Employment of Hunting," while the British "settled to offer trade goods at the cheaper prices."[153] Through their combined diplomatic efforts, the Beaver and other key sachems prevented an Ohio Indian attack on the weakly fortified Pittsburgh and enabled the English to set the conditions for the establishment of Fort Pitt and subsequently the settlement that followed.

The Ohio Indians aligned with the French continued to harass English convoys and small parties that operated on the periphery of the post despite the Beaver and Croghan's efforts to check the potential for a large and unified Franco-Indian military action against Fort Pitt. This harassment, coupled with the inadequate amount of supplies that Fort Pitt received because of transportation and requisition problems, kept the English garrison at an intolerably low number of troops. With the English lines thinly stretched and an enemy force poised at Quebec and the French forts of Niagara and Venango, Bouquet coldly informed Mercer that "this is a Critical time for you but we confide entirely in your Prudence, and Industriousness to extricate yourself from the difficulties that surround you."[154] Unable to build a sufficient force to defend and construct Fort Pitt simultaneously, Mercer solicited Ohio Indian warriors to amend the bleak conditions that existed beyond Fort Pitt's meager walls.

The major security problem Mercer and Bouquet faced was the protection of the long and indefensible supply line between Fort Pitt and the English colonies. "Beginning in June," one trader noted:

> The Indians began to infest the Communication by several Parties constantly kept upon the Roads from Pittsburgh to Fort Loudon, & Attacked our convoys by which the Horses provided . . . were near all lost being either kill'd or taken by the Enemy, or destroy'd by forced Marches for want of time to feed; and that in the beginning of July out of Eight Hundred . . . purchased, I found only about One Hundred and Twenty fit for Service.[155]

Bouquet contracted for provisions and gave Mercer the responsibility to outfit and support Fort Ligonier (present-day Ligonier, Pennsylvania) with supplies, however, poor weather conditions, inept traders, and inadequate amounts of packaging and shipping resources compounded the ill effects of the hostile Ohio Indian raids.[156] Colonel James Burd, the commander of Ligonier, described the impoverished situation of the frontier forts when he wrote Mercer: "I must begg that this Garrison and at the Crossing may be immediately & constantly supplied with Provisions; The want ever since I came here has been very severe upon the Troops, and the Arrears due them considerable & for the want of Provisions the Service has been much impeded which I hope will no more be the Case."[157]

James Kenny, the keeper of the king's stores at Pittsburgh, expressed the desperate situation Fort Pitt's garrison faced, noting in his journal of 1759 that "being almost out of provisions, there was some hints that we must soon eat horses & dog, if relief did not come soon."[158] In an offer to expedite and secure the convoys, Colonel Robert Monckton, the English officer in command of Pennsylvania affairs, offered to reinforce Mercer and Burd with an additional one hundred men. Bouquet refused this offer because of the inability to supply the frontier posts and opted to "dissemble till . . . better provided at Pittsburgh . . . trying what Croghan could do by way of Negotiations . . . as we have not yet sufficient Forces to afford Escorts to all the Convoys."[159]

To relieve his embattled supply lines and to provision his haggard posts, Mercer turned to his Ohio Indian allies, who willingly came to the relief of the beleaguered English forts. Faced with two tasks—construction and protection—Mercer immediately began to employ Ohio Indian escorts to protect the supply trains to Fort Pitt. Despite the heavy cost in trade goods that it took to employ Indians, Mercer informed Bouquet that "we are under a Necessity of employing Indians for most of our Expresses . . . [that] . . . You will no doubt be of Opinion that the expence arising from thence is not to be mentioned at so critical a juncture."[160] For the success of this plan, Mercer and Bouquet turned to Croghan to "use all . . . [his] . . . Influence & Address to persuade . . . a Number of Young Warriors to take The Hatchet . . . to clear The Communication & Secure our Convoys."[161] To the joy of the English commanders, Croghan successfully enlisted a number of Ohio Indians who took up the hatchet with great zeal and relieved the embattled supply lines, enabling provisions, though still of low quantities, to flow into the post with little difficulty. Mercer, overjoyed with the success of his plan, wrote Bouquet:

> We are all along in good spirits, preparing for a resolute defence; you may judge how happily circumstanced for the Enemy, with Not an Ounce of Flour, or Beef, but a few Milch Cows of the Sutlers, and Horses enough. The Convoy with supplies will be in tomorrow; and every week must now

> add to our Force & accomodation. The Delawares & Other Indians have showd great zeal & fidelity on this Occasion; but for them our Circumstances could scarcely have been made known to you, or supplies so readily obtained.[162]

With their lines of communication opened and the exterior regions of their posts secured by Indian warriors, Mercer and his men gained the time they desperately needed to concentrate on the construction of Fort Pitt, the post England required to become firmly entrenched in the valley.

Three elements were the key factors for the establishment of Fort Pitt: the control of the ground, the speed of construction, and the quality of materials used in the post's erection. In the initial stages of the fort's establishment, the English needed to defend the ground from a French incursion while they hastily erected a post to hold Pittsburgh. Without the ground and a defensible position to build on, the English had no need for construction materials. Unfortunately for the English, the manpower they needed to undertake the completion of these two tasks depended not simply on the availability of troops but on the quantity of provisions gathered to sustain a garrison sizable enough to accomplish them. "The King's orders," Bouquet pointed out, "are to build a Fort . . . which cannot be Effected without a large body of Men, and it is not possible to Send them as long as all the Provisions . . . are consumed."[163] In short, food dictated the number of men that could be housed and employed for the construction and defense of Fort Pitt. General Stanwix alluded to this fact when he informed Governor Denny that work progressed "unequal" to his wishes because he was only able to employ "as many troops as [he] could feed for the Works."[164] Under the continuous and ominous threat of a French attack, the English needed to man Pittsburgh with a force large enough to establish the post and withstand an enemy assault. Left in a miserable "state of affairs" with few resources and options at hand, Mercer turned to his Ohio Indian allies to augment Pittsburgh's stores and provide them with the provisions necessary to maintain the force required to accomplish the objectives of his command.[165]

The lack of provisions and manpower plagued the English construction of Fort Pitt from the outset. Because of a shortage of supplies, Forbes, who had triumphantly marched into Fort Duquesne at the head of nearly 10,000 men, left a force of 280 soldiers at Pittsburgh to face an enemy garrison of 1,000 Frenchmen located only forty miles away at Fort Venango.[166] To make matters worse for the English, of these 280 men, twenty percent were poorly trained and unreliable provisional soldiers who, according to Mercer, were "the most worthless individuals of the Pennsylvania troops."[167] Due to these obstacles, the English commanders at Fort Pitt dedicated the majority of the garrison's manpower to protect the post, which severely hindered its construction. Stanwix explained this problem to Bouquet, noting, "We break ground for our Fort only the 3rd Instant [nearly one year after the occupation of Pittsburgh] . . . [we] have so many call's for other services in the woods Escorts & Covering partys that for want of hands we advance as yet but slowly."[168]

Because of these circumstances, Mercer held a tenable position with troops who had relatively little food, no shoes, tents, or baggage and faced an enemy four times their size. Bouquet perhaps best summed up the English position at the forks, noting that "the regulars are not suitable on their present footing, and the provincials are not good for much."[169] In the face of this adversity, Bouquet ordered Mercer to make a peace with the Indians, send spies to Venango, place Pittsburgh's garrison on half rations, and solicit the Ohio Indians for much-needed support.

Unable to spare men to till the soil and hunt for meat, Mercer wasted no time in prosecuting his orders and turned to his Indian allies to provide Fort Pitt with the provisions necessary to maintain a force large enough to accomplish the objectives of his command.[170] During the first four years of Pittsburgh's existence, the English relied heavily on Ohio Indian subsistence support to augment the post's beleaguered provisions.[171] Nature, enemy attacks, and Ohio Indian visits made provisioning Fort Pitt a constant battle for the English commanders. The effects of nature proved to be the most difficult factor for the garrison to overcome. Though Bouquet contracted for numerous supplies to be delivered to the post, poor harvests, heavy rains, and the seasonal unavailability of certain supplies prevented the garrison from acquiring a level of provisions necessary to station a large number of soldiers at Pittsburgh.[172] To compound the problem, frequent raids on convoys prevented ample provisions from being brought to the post. Consequently, the post continually lacked the supplies necessary to sustain a large force. On several occasions, Mercer dispersed troops to other frontier posts such as Fort Ligonier to alleviate the food shortages.[173] To stop the raids and increase provisions, Mercer employed large numbers of Ohio Indians to protect the supply lines, which proved to be a double-edged sword for the English.

Preoccupied with defending English convoys, the Ohio Indian guards ceased their traditional subsistence activities and required foodstuffs like the rest of the garrison. Because of Pittsburgh's precarious situation, Mercer, not wanting to lose the support of the Ohio Indians, supplied his Indian guards with twice the normal allowance of rations. “All the Indians upon the Communication cannot be more hurtfull to us,” Bouquet expressed to Croghan, “than our pretended friends are in destroying our Provisions at Pittsburgh, the Consequences are the same, as it is Equal if the Convoys are destroyed upon the Road, or devoured by them at Pittsburgh.”[174] Placing an unexpected strain on the very provisions they protected against attack, the Ohio Indian warriors who were helping rid the post of enemy activity actually prevented the English commanders from increasing the garrison's strength. The English exacerbated the food shortage problem even further each time they invited large numbers of Ohio Indians to make peace treaties at the fort.[175] Because of the strains of war and unexpected population expansions, the poorly provisioned garrison risked increasing its troop strength without first increasing its provisons, which forced the English commanders to appeal to their Ohio Indian allies for subsistence support.

Despite the negative effects that nature, enemy attacks, and treaty negotiations had on the post, Ohio Indian subsistence support proved to be an essential factor in the establishment of Fort Pitt. The Indians supplied Fort Pitt with essentially two kinds of provisions, meat and corn. The meats consisted of turkey, bear, buffalo, raccoons, and venison.[176] The meat trade proved so vital to the survival of Fort Pitt that approximately 51 percent of daily rations consumed by the post's garrison came from the venison sold to them by the Ohio Indians for trade goods, powder, lead, black wampum, and, for the first time, British sterling.[177]

Though the meat trade made up the bulk of their subsistence support, the Ohio Indians continually supplied Fort Pitt with corn to feed the garrison as well as the livestock and pack animals. To augment the lack of forage for the livestock, Mercer made it his first order of business to harvest the “Corn field left Standing opposite Loggs Town” and to purchase corn from the Ohio Indians.[178] Though the garrison attempted to plant crops of their own, floods, insects, and poor weather conditions often reduced the yield. Of four hundred cabbages planted at Fort Pitt in 1762, for instance, Kenny noted that there were “only forty left but what ye Grasshoppers has Eatten.”[179] Consequently, the Ohio Indian corn trade became a needed and dependable food source for the post. Lieutenant Elias Meyer, an officer at Pittsburgh, best described the importance of the Ohio Indian food trade to the garrison, explaining, “In our present unfortunate position . . . we [have] need of [the neighboring Indians] both for the hunt and for Indian corn.”[180] With Fort Pitt unable to acquire food effectively from any other source, Ohio Indian subsistence support relieved it from the restrictive and undependable flow of military provisions and freed the garrison to attend to the tasks of protection and construction, as opposed to being consumed with foraging for survival.

While Pittsburgh's garrison never reached the one thousand men Bouquet desired due to food shortages, Ohio Indian subsistence support provided enough provisions to the post's stores that it enabled the English to double the fort's troop strength within the first six months of their occupation.[181] Several months after he transferred 100 men to other posts because of inadequate supplies, Mercer noted that the Ohio Indian support enabled him to retain a force of 350 men at Pittsburgh. Invigorated by the Indian food trade, Mercer informed Bouquet that "the Indians . . . gave [the garrison] the advantage" of relieving two hundred men to "carry on some publick work . . . [and to] check any . . . Indian [attacks]."[182] With the increased security and provisions, the Ohio Indians enabled the English commanders to double the number and types of skilled artisans employed to construct the post. By October 1760, the post's complement of skilled workers ballooned from fifty-five to ninety-one and consisted of bricklayers, wheelwrights, blacksmiths, carpenters, limeburners, sawyers, brickmakers, masons, and a master smith.[183] With this increased supply of manpower, one observer wrote that the army is "now . . . employed in erecting a most formidable fortification; such a one as will . . . secure the British empire on the Ohio . . . [and] be a lasting monument."[184] As another observer poignantly noted, "The presence of . . . General [Stanwix] . . . [and] the friendship and alliance of the Indians has been of the utmost consequence . . . for continuing the fortifications and supplying the troops here and on the communications" of Fort Pitt.[185] By early 1760, the increased manpower generated by Ohio Indian subsistence support enabled Stanwix to complete the outer walls, the barracks, and lay the groundwork for Bouquet's completion of the post in 1761.[186]

Because of their defensive posture, limited number of troops, and lack of knowledge concerning the backwoods of western Pennsylvania, Fort Pitt's garrison relied heavily, if not solely, on Ohio Indian intelligence reports to keep them abreast of activities beyond the immediate periphery of the post. The Ohio Indians provided the fort with essentially two types of intelligence, military and political. Military intelligence pertained to enemy troop movements and fortifications, while political intelligence concerned the intentions of neutral Ohio Indians to support French or English interests. Ohio Indian couriers were the primary means of communication to and from the English colonies and their frontier posts. Through their use, Fort Pitt remained updated on the disposition, composition, and strength of Franco-Indian forces, as well as the political designs of the neutral Ohio Indians. In their remote environment, where a numerically superior and offensively minded enemy was only six days away by land and three by water, Mercer made the Ohio Indians the eyes, ears, and lifeblood of communications for the weakly garrisoned post.

Bouquet and Mercer made the gathering of enemy intelligence a primary concern of Fort Pitt. Threatened with an imminent French attack, Bouquet ordered Mercer "to keep constant Spies about Venango, Presqu' Isle, and down ye River to discover the forces of the Ennemies." Bouquet also instructed Mercer that "no Surprise can happen where you command . . . and . . . as the Ennemies could perhaps attemt this Post . . . your Scouting Indians must keep a Look out." Information of the enemy situation proved so vital to the security of Fort Pitt that Bouquet authorized Mercer to "pay the exorbitant demands" of Indian spies "to gather the intelligence." With orders in hand, Mercer turned to the only source of information available to the post, the Ohio Indians.[187]

Ohio Indians continually provided Mercer and Fort Pitt with the latest and most detailed information about enemy troop movements. The account of Captain Thomas Bull, a Lenape employed by Mercer to spy on the French in 1759, is a perfect example of the type of detailed intelligence Ohio Indians provided Fort Pitt. Bull journeyed to the French forts of Presqu'Isle, Venango, and Le Boeuf and informed Mercer:

> Prisque Isle the Garrison consisted of . . . One Hundred and three soldiers . . . The Fort is a square, with four Bastions, Square Log Work . . . The Wall only Single Logs; no Bank within or Ditch without. . . . La Beef . . . is of the same shape but very Small, The Bastions, Stockaids, and joined by Houses for the Curtains, the Logs mostly rotten; Platforms are erected in the Bastions, and Loop holes properly Cut. One Gun is Mounted on One of the Bastions and Points down the River. Only One Gate, and that fronting this Way on the Side Opposite the Creek. The Magazine is on the Right of the Gate going in, part of it Sunk in the Ground, and above is some Casks of Powder to Serve the Indians. Here are . . . One Hundred and Fifty Soldiers. . . . He found at Venango Forty Men . . . but gives the description of the Fort as I received formerly.[188]

Never satisfied with only one report, Mercer usually employed several spies at one time to gather information. Based on this report, Mercer dispatched a second spy, the Lenape sachem Killbuck, to meet the Ohio Indians at Kuskuski to "draw them off from the French" in an attempt to weaken their enemy's position further and to confirm Bull's intelligence. Killbuck succeeded on this second mission, getting the Lenape and Mingo to agree not to fight for the French in the event of a conflict and discovered that "500 soldiers besides Indians" planned to reinforce Venango.[189]

With this newfound information, Mercer sought to capitalize on the weakened state of Venango and petitioned Stanwix to authorize an attack. Stanwix responded favorably to Mercer's request and instructed him to "Seize the opportunity . . . to burn Venango." To accomplish this mission, Stanwix suggested that Mercer "engage" the help of "three hundred . . . Warriors," and since his "Chief dependence [was on] the 300 Indians," he was "not to move from Pittsburgh" without their assistance.[190] Before Mercer could enact his plan, the English attacked and captured Fort Niagara, forcing the French to abandon Venango.[191] Though his plan to attack Venango never materialized, Mercer and his commanders used Ohio Indian information to make strategic moves to counter the French in the Ohio Valley. With the vital information gathered by Ohio Indians, the English remained secured from enemy attacks and succeeded in their efforts to construct Fort Pitt.

Always uncertain of the Ohio Indians' political position, the English relied on Indian informants to warn them of potential swings in their loyalties. By being forewarned of potential breaks in their newly forged chain of friendship, the English, through Indian proxies, prevented shifts in loyalty that might subject Fort Pitt to Franco-Indian attacks and inhibit or delay the post's construction. In the primary literature concerning Pittsburgh's early years, myriad examples exist of Ohio Indian informational support. In June 1759, for instance, Croghan received information from two Ohio Indians that a French officer at Venango wanted eighty Indians to "go on the Road, and annoy the English Convoys." In response to this request, the informants told Croghan that "the Indians agreed" to attack the English convoys. To preempt these strikes, Croghan sent word to Stanwix about these potential raids, dispatched the two spies back to Venango to gather more information, and sent a group of Indian envoys to dissuade the eighty Indians from attacking Fort Pitt's already-embattled supply lines.[192] To Croghan's joy, the Ohio Indian spies and envoys returned with news that, "The Indians with The French told them that they heard that the Heads of all the Indian Nations were to meet me [Croghan] here to settle a Peace, & that as soon as they heard the Peace was settled they would to a Man abandon the French."[193]

Though this is only one example, the intelligence that the Ohio Indians provided Fort Pitt enabled Croghan and envoys like the Beaver to prevent attacks on the post's fragile supply lines and to keep the vital provisions needed to generate the manpower behind the fort's construction flowing.

In addition to keeping the English abreast of Ohio Indian and French political and military activities, the Ohio Indians also served as guides, interpreters, porters, and couriers. Armed with a knowledge of the woods and the people that few Euroamericans mastered, the Ohio Indians hauled goods to the post at a dollar a day, delivered messages, and acted as interpreters and guides for the English.[194] Croghan explained Fort Pitt's reliance on Ohio Indians to perform these tasks in his journal of 1759:

"This day I sent . . . five . . . Indians to Ligoneir with Letters, & to pilot a small Escort through the Woods here, with Provisions as we were quite out of Flour, and the Enemy watching the Road & neither of the Garrisons having a Sufficient number of Men to bring up an Escort in the face of the Enemy."[195]

From 1758 to 1762, Ohio Indian support provided the English with the vital security and resources necessary to establish the first permanent settlement in the Ohio Valley. In only four years, Fort Pitt and its surrounding outpost rose from a poorly provisioned garrison of 280 men huddled in the snow on a barren piece of ground for security to a settlement with a civilian population of 332 people and a military garrison of 400 men who lived in 162 houses and huts as well as the barracks of the post.[196] In addition to the homes, Pittsburgh's population built a hospital, a sawmill, brick kilns, outdoor ovens, forges, a blacksmith shop, a boat-building yard, a seine, private trading houses, gardens, corn fields, apple orchards, and a company store that regulated the major industry of the settlement, the fur trade.[197] Yet the most impressive feature of Pittsburgh was the post itself. When completed, it spanned eighteen acres and was surrounded by a moat.[198] The post was the largest and costliest ever built by the British in North America, and the perimeter of its main works stretched almost a mile long and took an estimated sixty-six thousand cubic yards of dirt and a projected £60,000 to £100,000 to construct.[199] To put its size in perspective, Fort Duquesne, complete with bastions, could fit into the perimeter of Fort Pitt's interior parade field "with room to spare."[200]

The emergence of Fort Pitt in the mid-eighteenth century reveals three significant aspects about the Euroamerican settlement of North America. The first two aspects that Pittsburgh's story exposes support the idea that Euroamerican settlement required the creation of a middle ground that was the forum of economic, political, and social interaction between Indians and

Euroamericans on the frontier. Unlike the previous studies, however, Fort Pitt's tale brings to light the knowledge that at each point of intersection between Indians and Euroamericans on the frontier, new middle grounds formed based on the places and times the groups came in, or renewed, contact with one another. In the case of Fort Pitt, the middle ground that the Ohio Indians and Euroamericans created centered on France and England's European rivalry for power, which encompassed the globe. Though the groups had been in contact with one another since the seventeenth century, the dynamics of the interaction between Indians and Euroamericans in the Ohio Valley in the mid-eighteenth century revolved around conflicting political objectives of the day. Essentially politically and militarily equal on the frontier, the Ohio Indians, French, and English each had their own goals, and the actions of one group often influenced or dictated the actions of another party. Celoron's expedition into the valley in 1749 as a reaction to the Logstown Conference of 1748 is a prime example of this dynamic of the *pays d'en haut*'s middle ground. In some instances, Ohio Indian goals aligned with those of the English and generated a common objective, as was the case with both groups' desire to have a Euroamerican post established in the Ohio Valley. Because of this unique politically charged environment, Ohio Indian diplomatic moves that began with the Philadelphia Conference of 1747 provided the motive and virtually dictated the place and time for the establishment of Fort Pitt.

The third aspect of Euroamerican settlement that the study of Fort Pitt shows is that while politics dominated middle ground interaction, Indian economic and social activities played significant roles in the establishment of frontier posts. While economic and social activities usually generated financial profits for Euroamericans, the importance of these activities to the French and English establishment of posts in the Ohio Valley were not in their ability to make money but in their capacity to build relationships and to provide the vital resources frontier forts needed to be built and to operate effectively. Unlike the Dutch, who settled New York to make money, the English and French settled the Ohio Valley for political reasons and used the economic and social interaction of the middle ground to promote their political agendas and to provide Forts Duquesne and Pitt with the vital resources they needed to exist. Despite the fact that England's and France's North American colonies were well established by the mid-eighteenth century, both groups desperately needed Ohio Indian military, subsistence, and informational support to keep Forts Duquesne and Pitt operating because of their distance from resource centers like Philadelphia in the east. On the frontier, a delicate balance between supplies and manpower significantly hindered the French and English efforts to establish their Ohio Valley forts. To create equilibrium between these two elements, the French and English relied on the Indian trade generated out of Logstown and Kuskuski to provide them with the food and warriors needed to keep their posts supplied and protected. Whether it was providing six hundred warriors to defend Fort Duquesne, venison to supply Fort Pitt with 51 percent of its daily rations, or emissaries like Killbuck and the Beaver to collect information and negotiate peace treaties, economic, political, and social interaction between the Ohio Indians and Euroamericans provided Forts Duquesne and Pitt with the resources they needed to become established, grow, and survive.

The story of the emergence of Fort Pitt is a tale of interaction between the Ohio Indians, French, and English on a middle ground created in the Ohio Valley in the mid-eighteenth century. In only seven years, Indian, French, and English interaction motivated and supported the establishment of Fort Pitt, the largest Euroamerican post built in a region of North America that was previously unsettled by Euroamericans. Throughout those seven years of development, the Ohio Indians paved the way for the establishment of Fort Pitt by providing Euroamericans with the reason to settle the region and the resources necessary for a weak and dependent fort to survive, grow, and eventually mature into the settlement of Pittsburgh. With the emergence of Fort Pitt, the English successfully established a settlement in the Ohio Valley that became the spearhead and hub for the further Euroamerican development and settlement of the American frontier. Unfortunately for the Ohio Indians, the English finished Fort Pitt just in time to face and help defeat Pontiac's Rebellion, changing forever the political dynamics of the Ohio Valley, North America, and perhaps the world.

CHAPTER 7

The Building of Astoria

Thomas Jefferson's Germ of Empire, 1811–1850

THE SETTLEMENT OF THE OREGON TERRITORY IN THE EARLY NINETEENTH century by the United States unveils two important aspects about the Euroamerican development of the North American frontier. First, it shows that despite over two hundred years of mixed experiences and knowledge concerning the harshness and challenges of the frontier environment, no matter how well Euroamerican pioneers planned, they always seemed to lack what they needed to operate solely without Indian assistance. Second, the story of Astoria shows that the settlement and development of North America's frontier did not always take root with the establishment of the larger and more famous centers like Santa Fe, New York, and Pittsburgh. Rather, Astoria's tale reveals that Euroamerican frontier settlement and development took root in the first posts firmly established in the region. Once established, Astoria, like the larger centers, acted as the hub of logistical resources that enabled Euroamericans to expand their settlement activities in Oregon.

HISTORICAL BACKGROUND OF PACIFIC NORTHWEST SETTLEMENT

While it was Meriwether Lewis and William Clark who opened up the United States' far western frontier to settlement in 1806 with their expedition from

St. Louis to the mouth of the Columbia River in present-day Oregon, it proved to be the men of John Jacob Astor's Pacific Fur Company who actually planted the United States' first settlement in the American Northwest. A group of mercenary traders, the Astorians consisted of an assortment of Canadian voyageurs, Englishmen, Sandwich (Hawaiian) Islanders, Americans, Montreal Scots, and Missourians.[1] These traders went to the Oregon Territory with the sole aim of procuring pelts from the Indians who occupied a fertile land teeming with an abundance of fur-bearing animals. As Alexander Ross, one of the fur company's clerks, described on the first page of his book, *The Fur Hunters of the Far West*, "the great Astor project . . . had for its object the monopolizing of all the fur trade on the continent."[2] However, to Astor and many others, the planting of a post on North America's far western shore would be more than just an economic enterprise; it would be, in the words of Thomas Jefferson, "the germ of a great, free, and independent [American] empire."[3] To accomplish this monumental task, Astor planned for his company to establish a trading post in the Oregon Territory that was to act as a supply depot linking America's northwestern fur trade with markets in China.[4] While Astor and Jefferson planned for this post to be the germ of an empire, the first Astorians arrived at the mouth of the Columbia River, the predetermined location for their emporium of trade, unprepared to face the challenges of the inhospitable country. Because of this lack of preparation, the Astorians needed to rely on their Indian neighbors not only for help but also for survival. Seeing an opportunity to strengthen their own positions on the Columbia River, the Chinook, Clatsop, and their Indian neighbors willingly assisted the Astorians with the establishment of their post and with the foundation of the first Euroamerican settlement in the Pacific Northwest.

THE HARDSHIPS OF THE FRONTIER: THE ASTORIANS' FIRST MONTHS

When Astor's ship, the *Tonquin*, sighted the mouth of the Columbia River in March 1811, the Astorians reveled at the opportunity to begin the designs of their mission following nearly a year aboard ship. Almost instantly, the Astorians discovered the unforgiving harshness of the frontier. As per regular protocol, the ship's captain dispatched a boat to take soundings of the Columbia's mouth. Unfortunately, the small boat capsized, and the status of the crew was unknown. For four days, the captain sent several boats to sound the river's mouth, losing another boat in the process. Finally, the *Tonquin* managed to enter the mouth of the Columbia, passing over its deadly shoals after a harrowing experience that nearly sank the ship. Overjoyed with this small victory, the *Tonquin* anchored in Bakers Bay on March 26. Yet the glee it entered the mouth of the Columbia with soon turned to gloom.

Once the ship settled in the bay, Alexander Ross headed a recovery mission to find the missing boats. Like the boats they searched for, Ross and his crew became embattled by inclement weather and soon found themselves rowing for their very lives. Seeing the Astorians being tossed about on the water like driftwood, four Chinook Indians paddled their canoe over to the struggling boat and offered to aid Ross and his men by escorting them back to their ship. But a gale overtook Ross's boat and capsized it. Noticing the small craft in danger, another group of Chinook along the shore dispatched two canoes, and the *Tonquin* one longboat, to assist the capsized crew. However, the four Chinook with Ross successfully saved the Astorians and returned them safely to the *Tonquin* before the three craft arrived. Describing his near-death experience, Ross noted:

> We had on this occasion a specimen of Chinook navigation . . . overtaken by a storm . . . our craft was upset in the middle of the passage. . . . At this time we were upwards of two miles from the shore, while eight people unable to swim were floating in every direction; coats, hats, and everything else adrift, and all depending on the fidelity of the four Indians who undertook to carry us over; notwithstanding the roughness of the water and the wind blowing a gale at the time, these poor fellows kept swimming about like so many fishes, righted the canoe, and got us all into her again, while they themselves stayed in the water, with one hand on the canoe and the other paddling.[5]

Although they were rescued, the ordeal had only just begun. Momentarily safe, the four boats headed for the *Tonquin*. En route, Ross explained "the boat which had put off [from the *Tonquin*] to our assistance was upset on her return to the ship; had it not been for the two canoes that followed us, its crew would have perished."[6] As if a grim story line to a novel were being established with these initial events, the Astorians began their great pioneering project with a series of fiascos that cost the lives of eight crew members, giving them a sign of the hardships to come and the source for their relief, the Indians.

With their first trial behind them, the Astorians set out to find a proper location for their emporium of trade. After days of examining both sides of the river, they chose a location twelve miles inland from the mouth of the Columbia. Sullen because of the recent events, the first Astorian work party landed on shore, and with "heavy hearts . . . began the toil of the day."[7]

Though some of the group's leaders has read the accounts of Lewis and Clark's ordeals at Fort Clatsop only a few miles from the location they now occupied, none of them were quite prepared for the environment surrounding them. Before them stood fir, hemlock, spruce, and cedar trees from forty-two to fifty-four feet in circumference and upwards of three hundred feet in length, and around them were undergrowth and vines so thick that visibility was reduced to under one hundred feet. To tackle the taming of this environment, Astor assembled a pioneer corps of traders, shopkeepers, Hawaiians, and voyageurs that would "make a cynic smile" (as Ross wrote), the majority of whom never handled an axe or gun before or knew how to use them.[8]

Inexperienced as they were, this corps of lumberjacks began clearing the land. With axe handles of different shapes and sizes, the Astorians haplessly hacked away at the mammoth trees. Having no rhythm or coördination to their swings, the would-be loggers took days to fell just one tree, and even after cutting it through had no guarantee it would fall. On more than one occasion, before the final cut was made, the Astorians surveyed the tree fifty or so times in a futile attempt to gauge the angle of its fall only to have the stubborn log remain in place or get hung up in the surrounding vegetation, which left the crew in an awful suspense after the last blow was made. Like a comedic opera, one of the frustrated loggers spewing the vilest of obscenities at his wooden opponent jumped onto the scaffolding they constructed around the trees and hacked away with dull axe in hand until the behemoth moaned out a final roar and fell. As the descent began, the mad lumberjack beat a hasty retreat, dodging while limbs, foliage, and the tree itself fell to his side. However, the true work began with the clearing of the deadfall and the nine-foot-stump that was left after the tree fell. Like cutting the tree itself, the clearing of the stump took days and proved quite hazardous when the Astorians used volatile gunpowder to finish the job.[9]

As if this were not enough of a challenge for the pioneering corps, the Astorians, consisting of only thirty-three men, found themselves surrounded by a population of Indians in excess of one thousand warriors.[10] With the Astorians unsure of Indian intentions, the darkness, dampness, isolation, and limited visibility of the place created an aura of paranoia that overtook them. With every ruffle of the leaves or movement in the bush, the group of skittish pioneers ceased work to investigate the noise. Ever fearful of an Indian attack, they spent hours looking about to prevent such an incident from occurring, slowing their progress considerably.

To make matters even worse, the Astorians found themselves critically short of food. Though they took heed of Lewis and Clark's notes concerning the limited variety of food in the region and stocked themselves with fresh fruits and other foods from the Hawaiian Islands, most of the food they brought rotted or was consumed by them and their livestock aboard ship before or soon after landing.[11] Reduced to a diet of boiled fish and wild roots, the Astorians suffered greatly from stomach problems related directly to the poor diet, causing several men and in some cases the entire party to be laid up sick for days.[12]

While facing these challenges, Duncan McDougall, the corps' acting leader and a partner in the company, experienced quite a different set of circumstances. Like a Chinook extended family, a hierarchy existed within the framework of the company, and each position carried with it a set of prescribed responsibilities and privileges. Because McDougall was a partner, his responsibilities called for him to exercise his mind in lieu of his muscles, drawing complaints and accusations of laziness and ineptness from clerks like Ross and the laborers. Because he chose to forgo physical labor at the expense of "leading," Ross explained that, like a "great pasha," McDougall was "served in state" and frustrated many of the men.[13]

Embattled by hard labor, sickness, and unsavory Indians while simultaneously enduring the frustrations of being led by a great "pasha," the Astorians grew discontent and quickly became demoralized. Within just a few months, the trials and tribulations of the expedition so wearied and challenged the group that many desired to abandon Astor's project outright and return east overland. Yet cooler and more optimistic heads prevailed, and a party of members approached McDougall to attempt to rectify the situation in some manner, but to no avail. With things unchanged, ten men deserted the post, trying their luck with the Indians and a long trek east through inhospitable, unfamiliar country rather than remain at the fledgling and possibly doomed post of Astoria.

Short on food, lacking shelter, uncertain of the Indians, unequipped with proper medical care, demoralized, and inexperienced, Astor's great pioneering corps faced a bleak situation. It is no wonder that between the escapades of logging, scouting, and surviving, it took the Astorians nearly two months of incessant toiling to clear only one acre of ground at the cost of six individuals—three of whom were killed by Indians, two injured by falling trees, and one injured from the use of gunpowder.[14] To alleviate their dire situation, the Astorians turned to the Chinook and their Indian neighbors to provide them with the physical, political, and informational support they needed to survive and firmly establish their post.

THEIR NEEDS AND WANTS FULFILLED: CHINOOK PHYSICAL SUPPORT

Before a far-flung fur empire could exist in Oregon, the post needed to be established and its occupants kept alive. From the time the first Astorians arrived at the mouth of the Columbia until the establishment of the Puget

Sound Agricultural Company by the Hudson Bay Company in 1839, the traders continually relied on the Chinook and their neighbors to provide them with most of their food. In fact, the Astorians planned on acquiring most of their meat and fish products from the Indians while augmenting their diets with post gardens consisting of corn, turnips, potatoes, and a host of other vegetables.[15] However, like many other things Astor and his partners planned, their idea of productive gardens and livestock failed to materialize, and the post's occupants found themselves relying almost solely on Indian foodstuffs to stay alive.

Unlike Lewis and Clark's boring diets at Fort Clatsop, the Astorians planned to maintain an array of foodstuffs and laid out a plan to ensure the post was not wanting for provisions. To accomplish this task, the Astorians loaded goats, sheep, pigs, and chickens in the Hawaiian Islands and brought them to augment the fish, elk, venison, and bear they expected to get from the Indians along the Columbia. However, the livestock intended to liven up and add a nutritional variety to the Astorians' diets proved to be both a blessing and a curse. The goats, by far the most productive of the livestock, provided small amounts of milk; the two sheep vanished from the historical record and are never mentioned again following spring 1811; and a storm killed nearly all the chickens before the *Tonquin* reached the Columbia. The pigs, on the other hand, proved to be the only livestock that survived in any great number, and to the chagrin of the Astorians, they menaced the post by tearing up gardens and paths after several escaped following their arrival.[16] By 1820, the wild hog population had multiplied so much that residents of the post killed the "vile" creatures at only twelve paces and left them where they lay to rot.[17] Despite their best efforts to ensure they had enough food to support themselves once they arrived, the Astorians failed to plan properly and discovered they needed to rely on alternate food sources produced by their Indian neighbors to stay alive.

As was the case at many trading posts of the day, the pioneers at Astoria planned to plant gardens to fulfill many of their subsistence needs. Soon after the company arrived, McDougall tasked four Hawaiians to begin planting the post's gardens. The Hawaiians planted an assortment of vegetables that included Indian corn, turnips, potato eyes, cucumbers, radishes, and rape leaves for their livestock with the intent to harvest the crops five months later in September. Of all the crops planted, turnips proved the hardiest and most productive, yielding extraordinary specimens measuring over thirty inches around and weighing in excess of fifteen pounds.[18] Like turnips, potatoes eventually took at the settlement and by fall 1813 contributed to the Astorian diet. Within time, the Astorian farmers discovered and followed a planting cycle that improved the yield of their crops. However, the poor clay and gravel-filled soil that surrounded the post retarded the growth of the majority of the crops, leading to a complete failure of the corn, cucumber, and radishes.[19] While the turnips and potatoes added to the Astorian diet, the time it took for the crops to mature coupled with the actual number planted and harvested contributed valuable but limited amounts of food to the post. In fact, one of the major reasons the Hudson Bay Company moved operations from Fort George—the name given Astoria after the British fur-trading group the North West Company purchased it—was the inability of the post's inhabitants to produce enough crops to sustain themselves.[20]

In addition to the produce from their gardens, the Astorians planned for hunting to be a primary means to feed the post. Unfortunately for the traders, hunting also proved to be a difficult endeavor for the Astorians. The thick underbrush and heavily wooded and broken ground prevented ample growth of the foliage preferred by large game creatures such as deer and bear. The only large animals that resided in any great numbers near Astoria were elk, but when they were sighted, even the most skilled hunters often lost the beasts in the thick underbrush. To make matters worse, when one of Astoria's three hunters managed to acquire a target in the thick growth, the rain and moisture in the air often prevented their black powder flintlock muzzleloaders from discharging.[21] Despite all the efforts to ensure the subsistence of Astoria through hunting, farming, and managing livestock, McDougall placed the post on two rations a day within only six months of beginning the post, living on a "very meager diet . . . [of] smoked fish."[22] By November 1812, the situation had become so dire that the Astorians began to develop scurvy as a result of their poor diet.[23]

Despite their subsistence woes, the Astorians possessed a 286-ton mobile market in the *Tonquin*. In addition to the gardens and livestock that were to produce local foodstuffs for the post, Astor and the partners intended to keep their Pacific enterprise supplied through regular shipping visits from vessels like the *Tonquin*. The partners intended for Astoria to be a way station for the Pacific trade. The plan called for the Astorians to plant smaller trading posts upriver from the mouth of the Columbia and to traffic goods and pelts to and from Astoria. As Astor's ships made regular visits, they would move goods from Astoria to Chinese markets. In this sort of triangular trade, the partners intended to keep Astoria supplied, but yet again, fortune dealt the Astorians another unexpected situation.[24]

The *Tonquin* remained at Astoria for only two months after depositing its human cargo in March 1811. Unfortunately for the Astorians, the *Tonquin*'s captain, Jonathan Thorn, elected to unload only part of the foodstuffs and trade goods intended for Astoria. Apparently, McDougall and Thorn agreed to have the captain begin the second leg of the *Tonquin*'s trip leaving Astoria to fulfill Astor's agreement to supply Russian trading posts located in present-day Vancouver and Alaska. After trading with the Russians and Indians along the coast, the two men planned for the *Tonquin* to return to Astoria to unload the remainder of its cargo. But while journeying to the Russian posts, Thorn offended a headman from an Indian settlement named Newity, leading to the killing of his crew and the destruction of the ship. This left Astoria "almost destitute of the necessary articles of trade" and, more importantly, food. The ship's destruction and a failed overland expedition McDougall sent to report the pioneering corps' progress left Astor back in New York uninformed of the post's situation.[25]

Left in this "destitute" state, the Astorians relied almost solely on the Chinook and their Indian neighbors not only to augment but literally to feed their post by providing it with much-needed provisions. "From the commencement of the month of July," the clerk Gabriel Franchere wrote, "we were forced to depend upon fish . . . [and] venison on the precarious hunt of one of the natives . . . for which we had to pay, notwithstanding, very dear. The ordinary price of a stag was a blanket, a knife, some tobacco, powder and ball, besides supplying our hunter with a musket." By the middle of June, the Indians visited the post regularly, trading between seventy and eighty salmon a day. With such a regular supply of fish, the Astorians nearly exhausted their supply of salt in an attempt to store enough salmon to see them through the coming winter. As Ross so simply put it, as their provisions began to diminish, the Astorians depended on "the success or good-will of the natives for our daily supply" of food.[26]

While the Astorians relied heavily on the Chinook and their neighbors for food, provisions did not come easily or cheaply. The Chinook, though experienced traders, held fast to their cultural traditions and reluctantly exchanged salmon with the Astorians when they first arrived. According to Chinook religious practices, the first salmon caught each season needed to be prepared and eaten in very specific ways. If improperly prepared, the Chinook and their neighbors believed that the salmon might not return to the river. Before they agreed to trade salmon to the Astorians, the Chinook made them agree to follow the strict rules of the salmon ritual. Worried more than a little that the Indians would not sell them the much-needed salmon, the Astorians accepted the Chinook ritual despite its "superstitious" nature.[27]

As winter 1811 drew near for the Astorians, conditions grew worse because of the absence of Chinook fishermen and hunters. "When the Indians quit

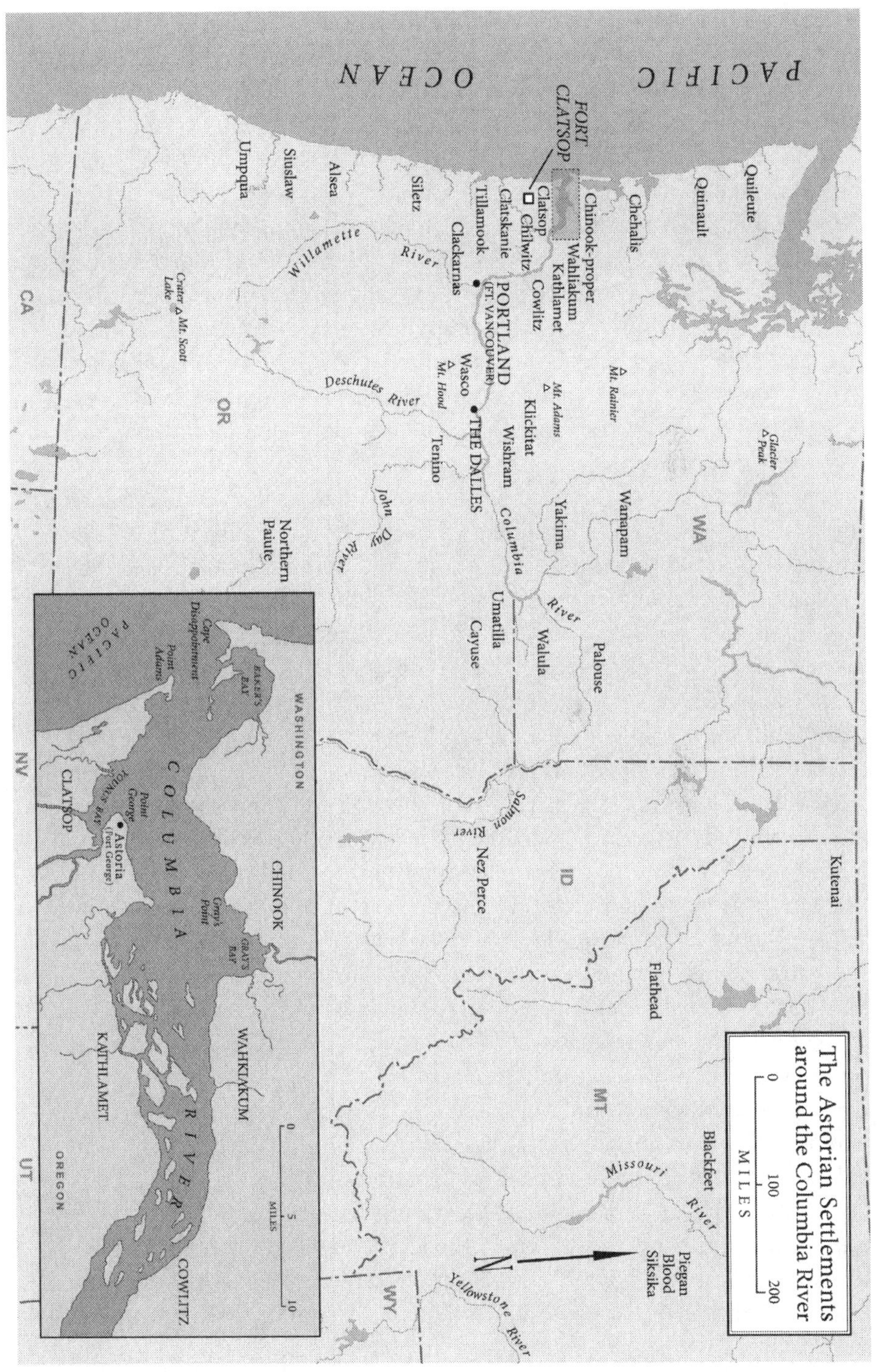

The Astorian Settlements around the Columbia River

the seashore," Franchere mentioned, the Astorians "were able to get almost no food" and became so desperate that they "determined that Mr. R. Stuart should set out in the schooner with Mr. Mumford for the threefold purpose of obtaining all the provisions they could, cutting oaken staves for the use of the cooper, and trading with the Indians up the River."[28] After twenty days on the river, the Astorians successfully accomplished all three of their objectives, trading for a large number of geese, ducks, and smoked salmon.[29] Luckily for them, they accomplished this venture a few months prior to the arrival of a party of thirty people from the company's overland expedition. Franchere speculated that it "would have embarrassed [the post] had [the arrival of the overland party] taken place a month earlier," when the Astorians were desperately short of supplies. But "happily," Franchere continued, "the natives . . . brought . . . fresh fish in abundance" and, in conjunction with the "shopping trip," provided enough supplies for the post.[30]

The Indians not only provisioned the post with food, they also supported the overland expedition and individual parties departing from Astoria by providing them with food, shelter, clothing, and protection. As the overland expedition journeyed to Astoria, circumstances forced it to divide the party. Two of the company's travelers, Ramsay Crooks and John Day, temporarily fell in with a group of traveling Snake Indians after they separated from a party led by Wilson Price Hunt, the partner Astor selected as overall commander for the entire Oregon endeavor. While in their company, the Snake fed and protected Crooks and Day, but once the Indians departed, the two were left to fend for themselves. Taking note of the roots the Snake ate, Crooks and Day attempted to follow the example and dug some up to eat. Unfortunately for them, neither man knew how to cook the root properly and they poisoned themselves, causing them to lie in a "torpid state" for a day and night. As fortune would have it, two traveling Indians found, revived, fed, and stayed with them for a couple of days, nursing them back to health. However, for Crooks and Day, their trials had just begun.

Motivated by their mishap with the roots, Crooks and Day decided to set out for Astoria on their own in lieu of waiting out the winter. After several days of traveling starved and frozen with their clothing reduced to rags, the two stumbled onto the Columbia River and into an Indian village, where an elderly man named Yeck-a-tap-am took them in and "treated [them] like a father." Two days later, Crooks and Day again attempted to reach Astoria but met a group of unruly Indians who robbed and stripped them naked. Destitute, ill equipped, and in the most precarious state imaginable, the two were rescued again by Yeck-a-tap-am, who appeared from virtually nowhere. Eventually the two men happened upon a group of Astorians trading along the river and fell in with their company to complete their event-ridden journey.[31] So dire was the Astorians' situation at times that when traders like Crooks and Day were unable to trade with or run into friendly Indians, they found themselves trying to subsist off of anything they found, including salmon half eaten by eagles.[32]

Of all the support the Astorians received from the Chinook and their neighbors, subsistence proved to be perhaps the most important. Stranded in the Oregon country without anyone knowing of their situation, the Astorians lacked the woodcrafts and hunting skills needed to survive off the land. Knowing this, they attempted to augment their diets with crops and produce derived from the post's gardens and livestock, but poor luck, weather conditions, soil, and a hazardous journey upended their plans. Though they realized that part of their diet would come from the Indian trade, it is doubtful that the Astorians estimated that their post would depend so extensively on the Chinook and their neighbors for food. So reliant were the Astorians and their Euroamerican successors on Indian foodstuffs in Oregon that the Hudson Bay Company administrator who eventually moved operations from Fort George to Fort Vancouver, Dr. John McLoughlin, wrote that "had it not been for the . . . absolute necessity of being independent of Indians for provisions, I never would have encouraged farming in this Country."[33]

In addition to provisions, the Chinook and their neighbors provided the Astorians with other physical needs such as transportation, female companionship, and, most importantly, the furs they went to acquire in the Oregon Territory. Once they fulfilled their basic needs such as food and shelter, the Astorians set out to accomplish the sole purpose of their endeavor, the acquisition of furs from the Indians. The partners always intended for Astoria to act only as a supply depot for interior trading houses where the company men would exchange goods for furs. The company planned to traffic trade goods each season from Astoria to the houses in exchange for the furs acquired during the winter from the interior Indians. Once assembled at Astoria, Astor planned to move the furs from Astoria to foreign markets in China, where the company would exchange them for Asian goods such as tea and silk. Luckily for the Astorians, the Chinook and their neighbors had established a trade network centuries before Astor's men arrived that linked the northwest coast economically to areas beyond the Cascade Mountains.[34]

The exchange of goods played such an important role in their sociopolitical relationships that trading and gifting became a way of life for the Indians of the northwest coast. Fish, because they were plentiful along the Columbia, became a principal commodity of exchange between the coastal and interior Indians. The Chinook and their neighbors often exchanged fish and crafted items such as their finely scrimshawed artwork for horses and the pelts of fur-bearing animals from the interior Indians. To facilitate this exchange of goods, the Indians in the region developed a shell currency known as *higua* to gauge the value of an item.[35]

Because of this established system of trade, the Chinook and their immediate neighbors seldom hunted the beaver along the coast, preferring instead to trade for pelts with the interior Indians.[36] When the Astorians arrived in 1811, the Chinook already existed as the dominant traders along the Columbia River. To ensure they remained so, the Chinook headman Comcomly welcomed the Americans with open arms and used less-than-scrupulous tactics to corner the market on the Astorian trade by informing the interior Indians that the traders came to enslave them. Likewise, Comcomly informed the Astorians that the interior Indians were a hostile bunch bent on the extermination of the traders. By employing this strategy, Comcomly and his people intended to monopolize the trade, but to no avail. Within weeks, the Astorians discovered Comcomly's designs and sent out an expedition to head upstream on what would be a 350-mile trek inland to establish trade relations with the interior Indians as well as build the houses they planned. In the interim, Captain Thorn and the company traded with the Chinook and Clatsop from the decks of the *Tonquin* before its destruction.[37]

Comcomly and the Chinook commanded great respect along the river despite their hold over the trade being partially disrupted. Occupying and controlling some of the best and richest fishing areas, Comcomly and the Chinook granted neighboring Indians the right to hunt, fish, trap, and in some cases trade in their territory.[38] Within time, the Astorians realized that if goods were to be trafficked along the river, the old one-eyed chief and his people needed to be appeased. In recognition of this fact, the Astorians presented Comcomly with a large sum of gifts symbolizing his status as the major trade broker along the lower Columbia. Soon afterward, goods began to flow freely at Astoria. In addition to the food they exchanged at the post, the Astorians and Chinook traded canoes, horses, and, most importantly, fur pelts. Between April 1811 and May 1812, the Astorians acquired 3,500 pelts, including 1,750 beaver, 61 sea otter, 15 squirrels, and 1 red fox. With the assistance of his people and their trading tendencies, Comcomly, "by his skill and perseverance, bent the company to his will" and made Astoria itself a major hub of exchange, thereby preserving its existence for at least another year by enabling the post to turn a profit.[39]

To traffic goods up and down the Columbia and to supply the interior trading houses they eventually built, the Astorians needed a means of transportation. Though they had brought the *Dolly*, a 30-ton schooner, with them for the purpose of trading along the river, the roughness of the Columbia's waters near Astoria and its famed falls known as The Dalles rendered the vessel virtually useless.[40] With no logistical centers in the area, the Astorians relied on the Indians to provide them with the means of transportation—canoes and horses—needed to navigate the Columbia and to traverse the terrain beyond the river.

Shorthanded and overtasked as they were, the last thing the Astorians needed was to waste valuable time constructing canoes or assembling the *Dolly*, a coasting vessel brought aboard the *Tonquin* to be used to trade with the Indians, in lieu of clearing the ground and building their post. Soon after they landed, the Astorians discovered from an Indian that traders from the North West Company occupied trading houses near Spokane a few hundred miles upriver. In an effort to preempt their Canadian competitors and to explore the region, the Astorians purchased canoes from the Chinook to paddle upriver to claim the Lower Columbia as their domain. Designed to navigate the river, the canoes enabled the Astorians, after numerous travails, to explore the interior and establish communications with the Indians along the Columbia up to The Dalles. Throughout their occupation, the Astorians continually purchased canoes from the Indians to facilitate their movement and traffic of goods along the Columbia.[41] The Astorians knew that these finely crafted and plentiful vessels were better than anything they could construct and elected to trade for transportation rather than expend the time and energy required to make canoes of inferior quality.[42]

Like the canoes, the Astorians purchased horses from the Columbia and interior-region Indians to facilitate their movement beyond the river and to continue the progress of their overland expedition. On more than one occasion, the Astorians purchased enough horses to outfit entire pack trains that required a hundred or more animals to move their goods.[43] Like fish and furs, horses and canoes became a regular item of exchange between the Indians and Astorians.

Animals and goods were not the only things traded at Astoria; human companionship, along with all the transmitted diseases associated with it, also became an item of exchange between the Astorians and their neighboring Indians. Despite their unappealing looks in some cases, after a year aboard ship, the men of the company found themselves wanting the touch and companionship of women. Active traders themselves, the women often exchanged their wares with the Astorians, sealing the deal with the "shameless profligacy" of their bodies.[44] Though viewed as a "shameless" practice by some individuals, sex existed as a medium of exchange on the Columbia long before the introduction of Euroamericans and continued after the Astorians entered the region.[45] Apparently, sex proved to be such an important medium of exchange that one headman of the Arikara inquired of Henry Brackenridge during the overland journey whether or not "white people" had any females, seeing how fond the Astorians were of Indian women.[46]

Similar to supply depots, the Indian frontier settlements were the logistical centers and possessed all the items the Astorians needed to survive and pursue their goals in the Columbia region; establish their post and move and traffic their trade goods. Without Euroamerican settlements to procure these items from, the Astorians relied on Indians to fulfill their needs.

THE NEGOTIATORS OF WATER AND WOODLAND: CHINOOK POLITICAL SUPPORT

Before the Astorians ever set foot in Oregon, Astor and the partners anticipated some of the challenges they would face and knew that the success of their mission relied on the goodwill of the Columbia Indians. Peaceful intercourse and fair trading, the partners believed, would not only further their own aims but serve to hinder the progress and success of their Canadian competitor, the North West Company. Likewise, Comcomly and other Chinook and Clatsop chiefs such as Daitshowan and Calpo saw an opportunity to strengthen their own position as well as that of their people along the river by acting as the political and economic negotiators between the Astorians and other Indians, by establishing familial bonds through strategic marriages with the traders, and by manipulating Astorian/Indian relations with stories of kidnap and intrigue.[47]

Before they landed, the Astorians realized that their physical security was tenuous at best. As increasing numbers of Indians came to trade with the *Tonquin* and the "embryo settlement" of Astoria, the Astorians felt more insecure. Yet the presence of the *Tonquin*, armed with several cannon, provided the fledgling post with some degree of protection, and its mere presence acted as a force to deter Indian aggression. Secured by the ship's presence, the Astorians focused their initial activities on clearing the ground, unloading the ship, exploring the area, and trading with the Indians. When the ship departed only two months after their arrival, "not a gun was mounted, not a palisade raised, nor the least precaution taken," proclaiming the defenseless state of the Astorians "to all the hostile tribes around.[48] In lieu of waiting for an attack to catch them by surprise, the Astorians instituted a local patrol that reduced the number of hands available to construct the post's protective palisade. Though actively engaged in patrolling the woods, the Astorians remained vulnerable to attack as long as the post remained unfinished. To ensure the safety and the success of their pioneering endeavor, the Astorians looked to leaders such as Comcomly to negotiate for their protection and for the success of their economic endeavors by acting as mediators between the Indians of the Columbia and the members of the fledgling American post. Ross explained how circumstances dictated that the Astorians place "much confidence" in the "assurance of fidelity and protection from Comecomly, [in whom they] reposed much confidence."[49] However, the assurances Comcomly gave the Astorians were far from a guarantee that no harm would befall the pioneering corps. Surrounded by a warrior population that numbered somewhere between one thousand and two thousand, the thirty-three Astorians, even after they were reinforced by their overland expedition, knew that their limited numbers and lack of a formidable post left them exposed to attack and possibly complete annihilation.[50]

Within days of the *Tonquin*'s departure, Ross, Franchere, and Cox's fears became reality when "Indians from all quarters . . . began to assemble in such swarms that [the Astorians] had to relinquish all labor and think only of defense."[51] Concerned for their well-being, the Astorians hastily began to construct their post and sent for Comcomly several times to assist them in dealing with the growing crowd of Indians surrounding Astoria. Though summoned to help, Comcomly disappointed the Astorians and chose not to come until offered a rather large present. Eventually, however, Comcomly, as Ross described, arrived and "opened a friendly intercourse with the strangers, traded with each tribe in turn, [and] made some presents. . . . Apparently well satisfied with the friendly reception they had experienced," the Indians left the Astorians, who were "agreeably relieved by their departure." Ross concluded his account of this affair by mentioning that to "Comecomly and his two sons . . . influence and good offices we not only owed our safety, but were indebted for all the furs obtained from our distant visitors."[52] Even after the completion of the post and its purchase by the North West Company, the Astorians felt they were left "at the mercy of chance, on a barbarous coast, among natives [who] . . . threatened to descend on the fort in large numbers to drive away what few people were left there."[53] As a result, the Euroamerican trading companies who occupied Astoria continually used leaders such as Comcomly to buttress their position in Oregon by acting as political go-betweens with neighboring and sometimes hostile Indian groups.

As with the affairs at the post, the Astorians relied on the goodwill and influence of many Indian headmen to ensure their welfare along the river. From the onset of their first journey upriver, the Astorians faced many obstacles emplaced by the Indians. With so few men at Astoria, the expeditions sent inland to establish trading houses and to reconnoiter the area consisted of only a handful of men. On more than one occasion, the Astorian traders found themselves outnumbered by an ever-growing crowd of Indians intent on either trading for or seizing their precious goods. Greeting them in full warrior regalia one day, the Indians appeared to the Astorians as "objects of terror." In a "painful state of anxiety," the Astorians, who felt their "fate [hung] upon a hair," appealed to the chiefs of the group to stay within their encampment to prevent any of the Indians from doing them harm. The chiefs exclaimed that they were the friends of the Astorians and agreed to sleep in their camp and speak to the Indians who in fact had some ill designs.[54]

Even when they successfully traded with certain groups, the Astorians found themselves under attack by their recently acquired friends, resulting in the death of several members of an expedition, or in one case, the entire party.[55] In nearly every instance, whether they were being bombarded by stones, threatened with arrows, robbed by sly men offering a helping hand, or having to pay exorbitant trade goods to have their items hauled around The Dalles or elsewhere, the Astorians, who usually were not "in a situation to hazard a quarrel," regularly sought the assistance and protection of the headman along the river to secure their safety.[56]

In the autonomous Indian world of the northwest coast, personal relationships established political relationships, and the best way to bond groups together was through marriage. Blessed with several daughters, Comcomly more than willingly married four of them to Astoria's own Duncan McDougall and Thomas McKay, as well as to the "Nor'westers" and Hudson Bay men Archibald MacDonald and Louis Rondeau.[57] After McDougall offered a price in goods for Comcomly's oldest daughter, Illchee, that took years to pay, the old one-eyed chief took advantage of his newly forged relationship with the proprietor of Astoria, making daily visits to the post and regularly burdening the blacksmith to have weapons and items forged and repaired. While McDougall's was the most important union, several Astorians married into influential Clatsop and Chinook families, forging strong political bonds with the significant members of both groups.[58] Whether these couples wed for political or personal reasons, their relationships, despite the production of offspring, seldom lasted, and usually ended with the departure of the trader. However, while they did last, the Astorians and Indians used their marriages to manipulate the social, economic, and political affairs of the Oregon Territory.

When the Astorians arrived in Oregon in 1811, they and their ship stood alone in a world surrounded by a large number of potentially and oftentimes hostile Indians. Unprepared to face the physical challenges of the country itself, the Astorians relied on the goodwill of friendly Indian groups and leaders such as the Chinook and Comcomly to provide them with food, furs, and the assurance of protection they needed to plant their post in the region. While no Indian leader was a potentate who controlled the entire Columbia region and could guarantee the protection of the Astorians, men like Comcomly, Daitshowan, and Calpo offered what protection they could and acted as mediators between the pioneering corps and Indians, thereby providing Astor's men with the political support they needed to establish Astoria.

EYES AND EARS OPEN: CHINOOK INFORMATIONAL SUPPORT

Unfamiliar with the Indian language, too few in numbers to act aggressively, and challenged by rival companies wanting to make the Columbia trade their own, the Astorians needed and relied on the Chinook and their neighbors for information concerning the affairs of the Oregon country to plan for and prevent trouble from befalling them. Lacking the linguistic skills to effectively communicate with the peoples of the Columbia River, the Astorians needed Indian guides, interpreters, and informers fluent in the Chinook trade jargon to break down the barriers of communication. On numerous occasions, the Astorians took actions based on information gathered by the Chinook and their neighbors, successfully pursuing their goals and protecting the fledgling, weak, and poorly provisioned Astoria.

The Indians along the Pacific coast and Columbia River spoke six distinct languages with sharp localized dialectical variations. To communicate between groups, the Indians created and accepted the Chinook trade jargon as the lingua franca in the region. It was a malleable language, and the Chinook and their neighbors expanded the jargon to meet the growing demands of an ever-increasing trade network. By the time the Astorians arrived, the Chinook trade jargon enabled Indian groups to communicate effectively despite their unique cultural differences in some cases. As early as 1788, Chinooks like Comcomly interacted with explorers such as James Cook as well as Lewis and Clark and learned and created a language that consisted of words from the Nootkan, Spanish, and English languages. With the majority of the pioneering corps unable to speak the language, the Astorians, in almost every case, used the Chinook and their neighbors to effectively communicate with the interior Indians.[59]

Establishing their post only one year before the War of 1812, the Astorians, many of whom were English subjects, not only had to face the trials of establishing a settlement in hostile territory but also had to tackle the challenges thrown at them by an aggressive Canadian company that wanted to possess the Columbia trade. Bent on pushing the Astorians from the region, the North West Company planned to send a large party to the Columbia with designs to build trading houses along the river in 1811. Aware of this fact, the Astorians used Indians to keep them abreast of the movements and actions of the Pacific Fur Company's Canadian and English competitors.[60]

Eighteen days after the *Tonquin* arrived at the mouth of the Columbia, an Indian from the interior journeyed to Astoria and informed the post that a party of thirty Nor'westers was building a trading house near The Dalles. Alarmed by this news, McDougall sent a party of seven men upriver to investigate and enlisted the support of Calpo to guide the small expedition. Calpo's efforts and skills as a guide enabled the Astorians to uncover a ruse designed by their supposed friend Comcomly, explore the region, and establish relations with the interior Indians.[61]

As they navigated the river, the Astorians discovered that Comcomly had attempted to monopolize the Columbia trade by convincing the interior Indians that the pioneers were bent on harming them. As they advanced, the interior Indians "flew to arms, and made signs [for the Astorians] to keep at a distance." Informed by Comcomly that the Indians upriver were hostile, the Astorians became concerned for their safety as the Indian "forces [began] collecting fast." However, Calpo and some friendly Indians arrived on the scene and spoke to the hostile crowd, explaining the peaceful intentions of the Astorians. Within moments, the crowd calmed down and Calpo explained to the Astorians that Comcomly had informed them that the traders were evil. To accentuate this point, the Indians showed the Astorians a stockpile of furs prepared for shipment to the Chinook. Taken aback by this information, the Astorians offered the groups prices for the furs much higher than the ones Comcomly agreed to pay them. Once they heard these great prices, the Indians "put their hands to their mouths in astonishment" and urged the traders to return, informing them that they would never sell their furs to the Chinook chief again. However, despite this sincere proclamation, Comcomly's status on the river enabled him to influence significantly the flow of goods to and from Astoria.[62]

Even with a capable guide like Calpo, the Astorians faced many perilous moments, including a couple of scrapes with the Indians that caused them to spend more than one evening when "it was impossible [for them] to close [their] eyes." On their way back from The Dalles, the Astorians came under attack from a band of "sordid and treacherous rogues," losing one of their men in the mix. To avoid these types of encounters, Calpo guided the Astorians to settlements he knew were friendly, such as Kalama, "the chief of which was a young man called Keasseno," a relative of the guide. Because of his relations with these people, Calpo guaranteed the safety of the Astorians and enabled them to rest peacefully in a place of "freshness and beauty . . . nature seemed to have adorned with her most precious gifts."[63]

When they eventually reached The Dalles, Calpo refused to travel beyond the falls because of the negative relationship he and his people had with some of the Indians occupying that region of the Columbia. The Astorians realized they could not advance without Calpo and decided to turn back. However, they did discover from the Indians who lived by The Dalles that no Euroamerican post had been built.

While he failed to escort the Astorians beyond the falls, Calpo greatly aided them with the success of their economic and political dealings with the interior Indians, introducing them to chiefs like his relative Keasseno, negotiating for them, and showing them the lands upriver that teemed with an abundance of the fur-bearing animals they desired. Though the Astorians eventually intended to push inland to establish trading houses, the news the Indians provided prompted them to step up their plans and initiate a fruitful expedition that exposed Comcomly's ruse, opened relations with the interior Indians, and gave them a better understanding of the Columbia.[64] Without guides like Calpo to assist them, one could only hazard a guess at what hostilities may have befallen the Astorians and led to their possible demise.

When they were not guiding the pioneers throughout the region, the Chinook, Clatsop, and their Indian neighbors provided the Astorians with valuable information concerning the affairs of the Oregon Territory. After the *Tonquin* failed to return to Astoria, the pioneers became concerned about the safety of the vessel and asked the Indians about its whereabouts and disposition. With the help of Calpo and Comcomly, the Astorians soon discovered "that the *Tonquin* had been destroyed by the natives along the coast."[65] Unsatisfied with this report, the Astorians hired and outfitted two Chinook to search for the ship. En route, the Chinook found an Indian survivor from the ship named Kasiascall. The Chinook took Kasiascall to Astoria, where he provided a detailed account of the ship's fate. The Astorians eventually accepted the story about the ship's demise, without having to embark on a time-consuming and potentially dangerous expedition to confirm it. Armed with this knowledge, the Astorians knew their post would not be supplied and took measures to procure provisions from the Chinook and their neighbors for the coming winter.[66]

With an information network at their disposal, the Astorians utilized the Chinook and their neighbors to assist them with their efforts to build Astoria. Sometimes a double-edged sword, the information the Astorians gathered from the Indians was not always completely accurate. In some cases, such as Comcomly's ruse, the Indians purposely misinformed the Astorians about the activities of rival groups to buttress their own position along the Columbia. Yet as interpreters, guides, and informers, the Chinook and their Indian neighbors provided the Astorians with knowledge of the Oregon Territory that they lacked and were incapable of acquiring without assuming great risk. Fluent with the language and customs of the people who occupied the Columbia, these guides and interpreters acted as the go-betweens for the Astorians who lacked a means to communicate with the interior Indians. Utilizing the Chinook trade jargon that became the standard of communication along the Columbia, the guides and interpreters enabled the Astorians to escape attack and forge profitable trade relations with the interior Indians. When they could not or would not mediate on behalf of the pioneers, these guides took the Astorians to settlements that acted as havens of security where they enjoyed moments of peace that were rare while traversing the Columbia alone. Armed with the informational support of the Chinook and their neighbors, the Astorians possessed eyes and ears all along the Columbia that enabled a fledgling, ill-prepared, scantly defended post to stay abreast of the movements of Indians and European rivals and make sound decisions.

CHINOOK MILITARY SUPPORT

Before the Astorians reached the mouth of the Columbia River, Comcomly, Calpo, and many other chiefs along the coast wanted Euroamericans to construct a trading post in their territory. After years of successfully dealing with Euroamerican traders, the Chinook and their neighbors not only established a trade jargon but also understood the benefits and power a Euroamerican trading settlement would bring a group or man who could control the traffic of trade goods along the river. Before the Astorians laid the first log of their post, Comcomly, a wily veteran of the coastal trade, attempted to monopolize and manipulate the fur industry on the Columbia through strategic marriages, deceit, and strong-arm tactics, leading more than one raid against the Indians of the interior. These successful attacks and the marriage of his daughter to Astoria's commander Duncan McDougall enabled Comcomly to establish himself as the middleman in the Columbia trade. The last thing Comcomly wanted was to jeopardize his relationship with McDougall and Astoria. To secure this relationship, Comcomly made a conscious effort to go to any lengths to support the Astorians, including going to war. However, though Comcomly jumped to arms to support his son-in-law and Astoria in the hopes of maintaining his status along the river when the British ship *Racoon* appeared in the mouth of the Columbia in December 1813, the Chinook never needed to preserve Astoria through force of arms.[67] Yet it is important to note that while military support was not needed by the Astorians, it was at their disposal.

As the English warship entered the waters outside the mouth of the Columbia River, Comcomly rushed to Astoria and informed McDougall "that King George had sent a ship full of warriors, and loaded with nothing but big guns, to take the Americans, and make them all slaves." Since his son-in-law and the company were the first Euroamericans to settle the country and treat the Indians well, the Chinook "resolved to defend them from King George's warriors, and were . . . ready to conceal themselves in the woods close to the wharf, whence they would be able with their guns and arrows . . . to shoot all the men that should attempt to land from the English boats."[68] Able to muster a force of eight hundred warriors, Comcomly offered "this proposition . . . with an earnestness of manner that admitted no doubt of its sincerity." So powerful were Comcomly's words and sentiments that as two armed boats from the *Racoon* rowed ashore, the Astorians believed that "had the people in the fort felt disposed to accede to the wishes of the Indians, every man in them would have been destroyed by an invisible enemy."[69]

Unbeknownst to Comcomly, McDougall and the other partners had agreed earlier that year to quit Astoria because of the hardships they faced and sold the post to the North West Company. McDougall gave Comcomly a nice suit of new cloths to thank the chief for his support and assured him that the British, unlike the Chinook and their neighbors, did not enslave the people they conquered. When the ship's captain, William Black, arrived on shore, McDougall and company turned the post over to the English, much to the chagrin of Comcomly, his people, and his neighbors. However, Comcomly's grief and disappointment in his son-in-law were both short lived. Only one day after they surrendered the post, Comcomly met with Captain Black and confirmed his undying loyalty to the English, expressing this acclimation by arriving at Astoria, newly named Fort George, with the Union Jack hoisted above his canoe and dressed in a British regimental uniform.[70]

Though the Chinook never actually needed to defend the post, Comcomly and his people stood ready to support their partners and relatives by providing them with military assistance. Though it is not truly known if Comcomly really intended to attack the English and their warship, the Astorians believed he was sincere and capable of doing so, taking into consideration that the coastal Indians destroyed the *Tonquin* and several other ships over the years. Moreover, Comcomly, a veteran of many wars, further convinced the Astorians of his intent and capabilities when he offered a viable plan of action hinging on the destruction of the *Racoon*'s landing party and captain. With eight hundred men at his disposal and Astoria's guns recently mounted, the plan might have worked. However, McDougall rebuffed his offer and sealed the fate of Astoria despite Astor's desire to maintain the post in American hands.[71]

AFTER ASTORIA: FORT GEORGE, FORT VANCOUVER, AND PORTLAND, 1813–1850

Following the War of 1812, the Oregon Territory fell legally under the dominion of the United States by way of the Treaty of Ghent. Yet the British-owned North West Company remained in possession of Fort George and continued to monopolize the Indian fur trade along the Columbia River. In 1821, eight years after McDougall finalized the sale of Astoria to the North West Company, the Hudson's Bay Company merged with the North West Company and sent Dr. John McLoughlin to administer the Oregon country. After several years in Oregon, McLoughlin moved the center of operations to a new post at Fort Vancouver because of the inability of the post to survive without the extreme physical support of the Indians and left only a few buildings at Fort George to continue the salmon trade and collect furs.[72]

In an effort to become independent of the Chinook and their neighbors, McLoughlin petitioned the company's administrators to create a group of settlers to establish an agricultural community in Oregon focused on providing the fort with food and other necessary products. Responding to McLoughlin's request, the company created the Puget Sound Agricultural Company. Once these settlers reached Fort Vancouver, they began to develop the area around the post, beginning the germination of the settlement seed planted by the Astorians in 1811.[73]

With the creation of this company, Euroamerican settlers began emplacing their logistical spearhead in Oregon's frontier. From this post, Portland spawned and became the resource center that subsequent generations of settlers needed to develop the territory. By 1849, Fort Vancouver stood as a testament to the Euroamerican resolve to settle the region. It consisted of a hospital, forge, warehouses, two churches, stables, bakery, carpenter's shop, "three farms under cultivation, a flouring mill, sawmill, large herds of the finest English cattle, droves of hogs & horses & large flocks of sheep, nearly everything [one] want[ed] to render [themselves] independent."[74] A stable and self-supporting logistical center, Fort Vancouver lured settlers away from their eastern homes and convinced them to travel the routes of Lewis and Clark's and Astor's overland expeditions to begin anew.[75] Within time, these and subsequent travelers established the Oregon Trail, with Fort Vancouver, Oregon City, and eventually Portland as its endpoints. Thus, what began as a small and isolated fur post manned by a desperate and ill-prepared group of thirty-three traders became the "germ" of America's far western settlement.

Arriving in the Oregon country "ignorant in [their] new walk of life," the Astorians relied on the physical, economic, political, and informational support of the Chinook and their neighbors to see them through their early endeavors. Though Indians often were barriers to Euroamerican efforts, for every Indian that stood against them, the Astorians and their English successors found one willing to help them plant their "germ of . . . empire" in the Oregon country. Though they planned to provision themselves with post gardens, the livestock they brought, and supplies from ships like the ill-fated *Tonquin*, their plans failed, and the Astorians needed to rely on the Chinook and their neighbors for the food, human companionship, transportation, guides, informants, interpreters, and political negotiators necessary to survive and plant a settlement in Oregon. Once the post was established, the Astorians planted the seed for the Euroamerican development of the Oregon frontier, initially at Astoria, later renamed Fort George, and then at Fort Vancouver and Portland, where the resources and security necessary to survive the rigors of the land became fully developed with the establishment of institutions like the Puget Sound Agricultural Company. As Ross so aptly put it, in a land where their life hung by a hair, the existence and prosperity of the trader relied on the goodwill and support of the Indians to stay alive and plant their germ of settlement.[76]

Conclusion

WITH A SINGLE LOOK AT ROBERT GRIFFING'S PAINTING *UNCONQUERED*, one can almost immediately understand the connection between Indian and American history. At first glance, a connoisseur of art might marvel at the majestic presentation of the three Indians who stand in the foreground of the picture, the depiction of the beautiful western Pennsylvania frontier in the mid-eighteenth century, and the bustling post of Fort Pitt. But to the historian, the image Griffing so ably brings to life offers much more. In the foreground, three Ohio Indians watch as Fort Pitt blossoms into a town that would prove to be the gateway to the Ohio Valley and one of the major spearheads for the Euroamerican settlement of the American frontier. Where a stockade once stood, an elaborate fort now commands a region filled with Euroamerican farms and homesteads. Realizing that the English are there to stay, the three men watch as their way of life is eclipsed by another.[1] One can almost hear the Seneca Red Jacket's words of lament to a friend:

> [Their] forefathers crossed the great waters, and landed on this island. Their numbers were small. They found friends and not enemies.... They asked for a small seat. We took pity on them, granted their request, and they sat down amongst us.... [They] have now become a great people, and we have scarcely a place left to spread our blankets. [They] have got our country.[2]

However, Indians did not fade from the scene or exist as innocent bystanders as part of a larger backdrop to America's history. Indians mattered and significantly contributed to the growth and development of America, as Griffing's painting suggests. Residing in frontier towns like Logstown that acted as resource centers, Indians laid the very foundation for the establishment of Euroamerican frontier settlements such as Fort Pitt by actively seeking the construction of the posts and providing them with the support and protection they needed to survive during the first several years of their existence. Thus, the three Indians in Griffing's painting look upon a settlement they helped to create, a settlement that, once built, became a resource center for the Euroamerican development of the American frontier.

The four case studies presented in this work reveal seven important aspects about the Euroamerican settlement, colonization, and development of the North American frontier. First, the Euroamerican establishment of settlements on the frontier, whether they occurred in the seventeenth century with the debarkation of Walloons on Castle Island or two hundred years later in Oregon, took place in borderland settings. Second, the motive behind the Euroamerican settlement was almost always economic in nature. Third, the frontier, regardless of how prepared pioneers thought they were, always proved to be a hostile and unforgiving place to Euroamericans. Fourth, the interaction between people on the frontier took place on a middle ground created by the participants and resulted in the creation of Euroamerican settlements. Fifth, despite the motives, time, place, or people involved, the Euroamerican construction of towns in North America followed a general process that began with the establishment of Indian settlements on the frontier and ended with the creation and expansion of towns like Pittsburgh, New York, Santa Fe, and Portland. Sixth, the location of Indians played at least as big a role as geography in determining where Euroamericans built their settlements. Seventh, and most importantly, though often resistant to Euroamerican progress or abused by it, Indians played an integral part in the development of the United States by motivating and assisting with the establishment of frontier towns from New Mexico to New York, the towns that became the logistical spearheads for the development of North America.

Not until the fifteenth century did the term "frontier" become part of the English language. When it did, the term referred to the region of a country that fronted or bordered another country. The North American frontier was in fact a border region and not merely the region at the edge of a settled area. The Pecos, Mohawk, Ohio Indians, and Chinook all had limits and boundaries to their territories. There is a reason, for example, that Coalpo refused to advance beyond The Dalles when escorting the Astorians up the Columbia River, or why the Mohawk waged a war against the Mahican to control Castle

Unconquered by Robert Griffing. (*Courtesy Robert Griffing and Paramount Press, Inc.*)

Island and the vicinity surrounding Fort Orange. Indians created and maintained recognized borders around land that ranged from family hunting and fishing properties to areas adjacent to politically independent settlements like Pecos and Logstown to even larger regions like the Mohawk River Valley controlled by the Mohawk. Limits existed, and Indians established, acknowledged, and respected them.

Within the confines of their respective borders, Indians created preindustrial settlements like Pecos, Ossernenon, Logstown, and Comcommoley that acted as the venues for the major political, economic, and social activities that took place in virtually every part of North America before Europeans arrived. Interconnected by infrastructures comprising elaborate gift economies, age-old political relationships, and broader, often-times fictive kinship ties, Indian preindustrial settlements proved to be the predominant universal feature in nearly every frontier region in North America. The ground Euroamericans found when they arrived in North America or traversed its landscape was not uninhabited, virgin, or widowed, as Francis Jennings and many other scholars suggested, but regions occupied by Indians with existing political, social, and economic infrastructures that were the venues of exchange and interaction. Whether or not it was the haunt of Indian and animal that Richard Wade perceived it to be, North America was a divided and socially sophisticated land with well-established borders long before Europeans arrived.

Indians willingly invited Euroamericans to settle, or, in the case of the Pecos, resettle in their territory because they desired European- and American-made products. Once this happened, new borders emerged between Euroamericans and Indians. Thus many border regions or frontiers surfaced and existed in North America. Where two or more groups converged, whether they were Indian or Euroamerican, a frontier existed. Subsequently, when Euroamericans settled the various parts of North America, they found a borderland region occupied by Indians.

The overarching drive behind the Euroamerican settlement of North America proved to be economic motives inspired by the potential of the Indian trade. Drawn in by the allure of Indian-procured and extracted commodities such as furs and gold, merchant companies, traders, and clerks spearheaded the Euroamerican settlement of North America. In the case of New Mexico, Don Juan de Oñate's search for gold, furs, and minerals spurred his self-financed expedition into New Spain; in New York, the New Netherland Company and later the state-financed Dutch West India Company went to New Netherland in search of furs and to open new markets for Holland; in the Ohio Valley, men like Conrad Weiser and George Croghan, and the Ohio Company journeyed into present-day western Pennsylvania in search of furs; and in Oregon, John Jacob Astor's American Fur Company went to the far-off Pacific Coast to link the United States' fur markets with China. In each case, Indians and their products motivated the actions of these companies, which included the establishment of trading posts, stockades, and forts, the seeds for the Euroamerican settlement of North America. Without the Indians who wanted, encouraged, and provided the commodities they sought, Euroamericans lacked any real reason to go to and settle North America. Though other factors became important, such as the salvation of Pueblo souls in New Mexico and the physical control of the strategic Ohio Valley, economic gain, either on the part of Indians, individuals, merchant companies, or state governments provided the initial drive for the Euroamerican advancement into North America. While this idea in and of itself is not new, it is very important when combined with the third point of this discussion in understanding how Indians played such a pivotal role in the establishment of America's earliest towns.

Since it was generally self-financed merchant companies, traders, and clerks who led the way for Euroamericans into North America, they usually came ill prepared to face the challenges of the frontier environment. To turn the greatest profit, traders, more often than not, filled the hulls of their ships and the packs of their animals with mercantile goods and not provisions. Subsequently, when they attempted to plant settlements, they failed to bring enough supplies and personnel to provision and protect themselves. Even though Don Juan de Oñate in New Mexico and the Astorians in Oregon thought they prepared properly by bringing several thousand head of livestock and enough produce to begin bountiful gardens, for instance, poor weather like New Mexico's decade-long drought and misfortunes like the destruction of the *Tonquin* often strained Euroamerican resources and abilities beyond their breaking points. As the accounts of Alexander Ross, Colonel Henry Bouquet, and Fray Lope Izquierdo suggest, the first Euroamericans failed to plan well and would have starved to death or died at the hands of their enemies without the intervention of Indians. In Ross's own words, their efforts to plant settlements on the frontier proved so inadequate that a cynic would have smiled at the misfortunes Euroamericans suffered owing to their lack of preparedness.

Because of these conditions, the interaction between Euroamericans and Indians in North America's multiple frontier settings took place on middle grounds created between the various groups involved in the regions. According to Richard White, a middle ground was "a mutually comprehensible world" constructed by groups who wanted to interact with each other but were essentially ignorant of one another's cultures. So the parties used aspects from both cultures to create a world where they could successfully interact.

For a middle ground to emerge on one of North America's many frontiers, several conditions needed to be met. First, the middle ground required the involvement of three or more parties, at least two of whom needed something from each other. In the case of the settlement of New Mexico, for instance, it consisted of the Pecos, Spanish, Apache, and the independent pueblos of the Rio Grande Valley. Second, many elements usually made up the dynamics of the middle ground based on what was needed between the groups. With the Ohio Indians, English, and French, for example, the middle ground consisted of primarily an economic and political element, while the New Mexico middle ground had both of these elements as well as a religious component. Likewise, where the Dutch, Mohawk, and Mahican middle ground contained a mixture of elements, the Oregon middle ground was founded almost purely on economics. Third, a shared condition of weakness generally led to the creation of a middle ground. Seldom did one group have enough power to act freely without regard to the other members of the middle ground, or with their neighbors who lived immediately beyond its periphery. For example, the creation of the Dutch, Mohawk, and Mahican middle ground occurred because all three groups had an economic need and were not strong enough to stand on their own against the northern Algonquians and French. Mutual need drew the parties together. Without parity, one group could simply act unilaterally and take what it wanted from another group, as was the case with the Dutch relationship with the southern Hudson River Indians and that of the Spanish and Pecos prior to the Pueblo Revolt of 1680. For successful interaction and accommodation to take place between these groups, military, political, economic, and social power needed to be virtually equal. Finally, tensions always existed between at least two or more members of the middle ground, which increased the need for cooperation and accommodation among the other parties. For instance, King George's War combined with England's and France's goals to check the advancement of each others' North American colonies provided the tensions that created the middle ground in the mid-eighteenth century Ohio Valley. Similarly, the Pueblo Revolt of 1680 created such tensions between the various members of New Mexico's middle ground that it shifted the political dynamics of the region and drew former enemies, the Spanish and Pecos, into a mutually beneficial partnership. In each of these situations, as was the case when the Dutch aided the Mahican in a failed military action against the Mohawk, the mutual need and dependence on one another forced parties to set differences aside to achieve their broader political and economic goals. Thus a sense of mutual dependence, political tensions, and military weakness combined to create the dynamics of the middle ground relationships between Indians and Euroamericans, which eventually led to the establishment and growth of America's frontier towns.

Though they eventually settled North America, Euroamericans never created a plan on how they would actually do it and essentially left it up to the whims and actions of traders and explorers to determine the locations of settlement. Subsequently, the establishment of the United States' early frontier towns followed a general pattern because of the location of Indians and the operation of the various middle grounds that were created. Since the Euroamericans came for economic reasons and were ill prepared to meet the challenges of the many frontier environments they encountered, their settlement of North America began in Indian preindustrial settlements. Long before Henry Hudson sailed down what would later be called the Hudson River or Cabeza de Vaca washed up on the Gulf Coast, Indians set the conditions for the successful establishment of Euroamerican settlements in North America by simply existing and establishing preindustrial settlements of their own. Over the course of centuries, Indians created large community-based settlements like Pecos with its two thousand inhabitants with highly developed and efficient subsistence economies tailored to overcome the unique challenges of the frontier environments they occupied. Because of these efficient subsistence technologies, most Indian communities maintained populations in excess of two hundred inhabitants and developed preindustrial societies with social hierarchies, complex political systems, and elaborate gift economies. Whether it was the potlatch of the Chinook, the irrigated fields of the Pecos, the elaborate confederacy politics of the Iroquois League, or the societal organization of the Ohio Valley's multiethnic settlements like Logstown, Indian communities possessed everything Euroamericans needed to survive in and settle North America.

Though geography influenced where Euroamericans established their colonies, the location of Indian settlements played, perhaps, an even greater role. In the case of Fort Orange (Nassau) and New Amsterdam, the Dutch chose the location of the former because of the friendly nature of the Mahican Indians. Likewise, they selected the site for New Amsterdam based not only on its strategic importance in controlling the flow of sea traffic along the Hudson River but also for its importance as being the home of arguably the most skilled and productive wampum-making Indians on the Eastern Seaboard. Similarly, the French and English chose to build Pittsburgh where they did because of its proximity to Logstown and Kuskuski. The French initially planned to build the fourth fort in its line of defenses linking the Ohio Valley to Canada at Logstown. The fact that William Trent already laid the foundation of Fort Prince George in the spot the Ohio Indians specified to the English is the prime reason for it being the site chosen for Fort Duquesne when two thousand Frenchmen descended on the confluence of Pittsburgh's three rivers and later Fort Pitt's location once the English reclaimed it. Oñate even chose the site for Spain's first home in New Mexico to be the vacated pueblo of San Gabriel. Not until Don Pedro de Peralta arrived in 1609 and impressed the labor of the Pecos and other Pueblo Indians did he successfully build Santa Fe. The location of Indian settlements played a more significant role in determining the site of America's first frontier towns than geography.

When Euroamericans did arrive in North America and eventually traversed its landscape, they gravitated toward these resource centers, redrew the frontier's boundaries, and slowly developed a middle ground with the local Indians. As their needs and desires to build a more permanent presence in North America became greater, Euroamericans became more dependent on Indians to provide them with the resources and manpower they needed to establish frontier settlements. Likewise, as the needs of Indians grew, they also became more dependent on and intertwined with a permanent Euroamerican presence on the frontier. Within time, these wants and needs, which were played out through middle-ground interaction, produced the trading posts, stockades, and forts that eventually replaced Indian settlements as the resource centers for the Euroamerican development of the frontier. Once these settlements emerged, the process of frontier development generally followed the pattern outlined by Kenneth Lewis in his book *The American Frontier*.

Though they have a unique culture and a history unto themselves, Indians mattered and contributed to the development and creation of the United States in many ways and need to be given a bigger role in the broader picture of American history. As Jennings, White, and other scholars suggest, Indians touched every Euroamerican world in North America between the sixteenth and nineteenth centuries, from New Mexico to New York. Because the majority of the last 513 years of history in North America involved Indians and the development of the various borderland environments that made up the American frontier, a history that fails to include Native Americans as something greater than the noble other who resisted and succumbed to Euroamerican progress does a disservice to both American and Indian history. In short, Indians mattered as much for what they did to develop North America as for who they were. Indians not only laid the foundation for their own settlement of North America, they resourced, protected, encouraged, and created the infrastructure for the Euroamerican establishment of frontier settlements and, in so doing, helped plant the germs of Thomas Jefferson's great, free, and independent American empire.

Notes

ABBREVIATIONS

ABFP	A Beautiful and Fruitful Place
DCHNY	Documents Relative to the Colonial History of the State of New York
JMGW	The Journal of Major George Washington
MPC	Minuetes of the Provincial Council of Pennsylvania
NNN	Narratives of New Netherland, 1609–1664
ORRD	The Official Records of Robert Dinwiddie
PA	Pennsylvania Archives
PHB	The Papers of Henry Bouquet
VRBM	Van Rensselaer Bowier Manuscripts
WGJF	Writings of General John Forbes
WGW	The Writings of George Washington

INTRODUCTION: THE URBAN FRONTIER REVISITED

1. J. Miller, "Old Religion among the Delawares: The Gamwing (Big House Rite)," *Ethnohistory* 44 (Winter 1997): 113-134; Rob Harper, "The Politics of Coalition Building in the Ohio Valley, 1765–1774," in *Borderland Narrratives: Negation and Accommodation in North America's Contested Spaces, 1500–1850,* ed. Andrew K. Frank and A. Glenn Crothers (Gainesville: University Press of Florida, 2017), 18-45; Pekka Hamalainen, "The Shapes of Power: Indians, Europeans, and North American Worlds from the Seventeenth to the Nineteenth Century," in *Contested Spaces of Early America,* ed. Juliana Barr and Edward Countryman (Philadelphia: University of Pennsylvania Press, 2014), 31-68.
2. Richard White, *The Middle Ground: Indians, Empires, and Republics in the Great Lakes Region, 1650–1815* (Cambridge: Cambridge University Press, 1991), ix-x, 517.
3. Donald L. Fixico, *Rethinking American Indian History* (Albuquerque: University of New Mexico Press, 1997), 3.
4. Donald L. Fixico, "Methodologies in Reconstructing Native American History," in ibid., 125; Eugene D. Genovese, "Scholar Spearheads New Historical Society to Reshape the Profession," interview by Courtney Leatherman, *Chronicle of Higher Education* (March 20, 1998): A12-A13.
5. Genovese interview, "Scholar," A12-A13.
6. Frederick Jackson Turner, *The Frontier in American History* (New York: Holt, 1920), 20; Frederick Jackson Turner, "The Significance of the Frontier in American History," in *Does the Frontier Experience Make America Exceptional?*, ed. Richard W. Etulain (Boston and New York: Bedford/St. Martin's, 1999), 29.

7. Richard C. Wade, *The Urban Frontier: Pioneer Life in Early Pittsburgh, Cincinnati, Lexington, Louisville, and St. Louis* (Cambridge, MA: Harvard University Press, 1959), 1.
8. Ibid., i.
9. Kenneth Lewis, *The American Frontier: An Archaeological Study of Settlement Pattern and Process* (Orlando, FL: Academic Press, 1984), 10. See also J. R. V. Prescott, *The Geography of Frontiers and Boundaries* (Chicago: Aldine, 1965), 34-55, 264.
10. Lewis, *American Frontier,* 10.
11. Ibid., 277.
12. Ibid., 285-286, 288.
13. For quote see Andrew R. L. Cayton and Fredrika J. Teute, *Contact Points: American Frontiers from the Mohawk Valley to the Mississippi, 1750–1830* (Chapel Hill: University of North Carolina Press, 1998), 5. For explanation and sample of the frontier being a multidimensional place see Jeremy Adelman and Stephen Aron, eds., "From Borderlands to Borders: Empires, Nation-States, and the Peoples in between in North American History," *American Historical Review* 104, no. 3 (1999): 815.
14. Francis Jennings, *The Invasion of America: Indians, Colonialism, and the Cant of Conquest* (New York: W. W. Norton, 1976), 30. For frontier zones see Cayton and Teute, *Contact Points,* 2.
15. Turner, "Significance," 25.
16. Jennings, *Invasion,* 30.
17. Henry Gannett, *Statistical Atlas of the United States 1900* (Washington, DC: US Census Office, 1903), 40.
18. Office of the Secretary of State, *First Census of the United States* (Philadelphia: Childs and Swaine, 1791), 1-56.
19. Ibid., 53.
20. *Webster's II: New Riverside University Dictionary* (1984), s.v. "frontier."
21. Turner, "Significance," 4.
22. Ibid., 3.
23. Jack D. Forbes, *Frontiers in American History and the Role of the Frontier Historian,* Desert Research Institute 21 (Reno: University of Nevada, 1966), 22.
24. Ibid., 6, 14, 15.
25. Richard White, *It's Your Misfortune and None of My Own, A New History of the American West* (Norman: University of Oklahoma Press, 1991), 85.

PART 1. THE FRONTIER'S FIRST SETTLEMENTS

1. Roderick Nash, *Wilderness and the American Mind,* 3rd ed. (New Haven, CT: Yale University Press, 1982), xii.
2. Daniel K. Richter, *Facing East from Indian Country: A Native History of Early America* (Cambridge, MA: Harvard University Press, 2001), 3-5; Alice Beck Kehoe, *America before the European Invasions* (New York: Longman, 2002), 172-178, 252.
3. Jennings, *Invasion,* 30.
4. John P. Radford, "Testing the Model of the Pre-industrial City: The Case of Ante-Bellum Charleston, South Carolina," *Transactions of the Institute of British Geographers,* New Series 41, no. 3 (1979): 392.
5. Gideon Sjoberg, *The Preindustrial City: Past and Present* (Glencoe, IL: Free Press, 1960), 5.
6. Ibid., 5, 8.
7. Ibid., 7.
8. Ibid., 8.
9. Ibid.; *Encyclopedia Britannica Online,* s.v. "Siriono," accessed April 7, 2020, https://www.britannica.com/topic/Siriono. See also *Encyclopedia Britannica Online,* s.v. "South American Nomad," accessed April 7, 2020, https://www.britannica.com/topic/South-American-nomad;

for more on the Siriono see Allan R. Holmberg, *Nomads of the Long Bow: The Siriono of Eastern Bolivia*, (Washington, DC: Smithsonian Institution Press, 1950).
10. Sjoberg, *Preindustrial City*, 10. See also Allan R. Holmberg, "Nomads of the Long Bow," *Smithsonian Institution, Institute of Social Anthropology* no. 10 (Washington, DC: Government Printing Office, 1950).
11. Sjoberg, *Preindustrial City*, 11.
12. Ibid., 12.
13. Ibid., 27, 30.

CHAPTER 1. AMERICAN INDIAN SUBSISTENCE TECHNOLOGIES

1. Sjoberg, *Preindustrial City*, 30; Jared Diamond, *Guns, Germs, and Steel: The Fates of Human Societies* (New York: W. W. Norton, 1999), 85-92.
2. John L. Kessell, *Kiva, Cross and Crown: The Pecos Indians and New Mexico, 1540–1840* (Tucson, AZ: Western National Parks Association, courtesy University of New Mexico Press, 1987), 489-492.
3. Fray Alonso de Benavides, *A Harvest of Reluctant Souls: The Memorial of Fray Alonso de Benavides, 1630*, trans. and ed. Baker H. Morrow (Niwot: University of Colorado Press, 1996), 22; Pedro de Castaneda, "Relacion de la jornada de Cibola," in "The Coronado Expedition," *Fourteenth Annual Report*, Bureau of Ethnology, Smithsonian Institution, 1892–1893 (Washington, DC: Government Printing Office, 1896), 1:329-613.
4. Don Francisco de Valverde, "Investigation of Conditions in New Mexico, 1601," in *Don Juan de Oñate: Colonizer of New Mexico, 1595–1628*, ed. George P. Hammond and Agapito Rey (Albuquerque: University of New Mexico Press, 1953), 6:626.
5. Ann Rasor, "Pecos Pueblo," in *Pecos: Gateway to Pueblos & Plains*, ed. John V. Bezy and Joseph P. Sanchez (Tucson, AZ: Southwest Parks and Monuments Association, 1988), 32.
6. Edward P. Dozier, *The Pueblo Indians of North America* (New York: Holt, Rinehart and Winston, 1970), 38.
7. Fray Alonso de Benavides, *The Memorial of Fray Alonso De Benavides, 1630*, trans. Edward E. Ayer (Chicago: privately printed, 1916), 22; Valverde, "Investigation," 626, 646, 660.
8. Rasor, "Pecos Pueblo," 32.
9. Hernan Gallegos, "Relation of the Chamuscado-Rodriguez Expedition," in *The Rediscovery of New Mexico*, ed. George P. Hammond (Albuquerque: University of New Mexico Press, 1966), 85.
10. Valverde, "Investigation," 626, 634-635.
11. Gaspar Castaño de Sosa, "Castaño de Sosa's 'Memoria,'" in *The Rediscovery of New Mexico*, ed. George Hammond (Albuquerque: University of New Mexico Press, 1966), 278.
12. Rasor, "Pecos Pueblo," 32.
13. Henry Harvey, *History of the Shawnee Indians* (Cincinnati: Ephraim Morgan & Sons, 1855), 146-148.
14. Jerry Clark, *The Shawnee* (Lexington: University Press of Kentucky, 1993), 31; Richard Aquila, *The Iroquois Restoration* (Detroit: Wayne State University Press, 1983), 32-33.
15. Herbert C. Kraft, *The Lenape* (Newark: New Jersey Historical Society, 1986), 115; David De Vries, "From the 'Korte Historiael ende Journaels Aenteyckeninge,' 1633–1643 (1655)," in *Narratives of New Netherland, 1609–1664* (hereafter *NNN*), ed. J. Franklin Jameson (Washington, DC: Scribner & Sons, 1909; New York: Barnes and Noble, 1937), 218; Johan De Laet, "From the 'New World,' 1625, 1630, 1633, 1640," in De Vries, *NNN*, 49.
16. James H. Howard, *Shawnee* (Athens: Ohio University Press, 1981), 48.
17. *Webster's II*, s.v. "girdle."
18. Howard, *Shawnee*, 48.
19. For fertilization process see William Cronon, *Changes in the Land* (New York: Hill and Wang, 1983), 45, 48, 150-153; for ability to occupy sites for decades and centuries see C. Hale

Sipe, *The Indian Chiefs of Pennsylvania* (Baltimore: Wennawoods Publishing, 1995), 35; George Mercer, *George Mercer Papers*, ed. Lois Mulkearn (Pittsburgh: University of Pittsburgh Press, 1954), 477.

20. Clark, *Shawnee*, 32.

21. Oliver Spencer, *The Indian Captivity of O.M. Spencer*, ed. Milo Milton Quaife (Chicago: Lakeside Press, 1917), 85.

22. Cronon, *Changes*, 44.

23. John W. Jordan, ed., "Journal of James Kenny, 1761–1763," *Pennsylvania Magazine of History and Biography* 37 (1913): 22.

24. Howard, *Shawnee*, 49.

25. Isaack De Rasieres, *Narratives of New Netherland, 1609–1664* (hereafter *NNN*), ed. J. Franklin Jameson (Washington, DC: Scribner & Sons, 1909; New York: Barnes and Noble, 1937), 107.

26. Thomas Campanius Holm, *Description of the Province of New Sweden: Now called by the English Pennsylvania in America,* ed. Peter S. Du Ponceau (Philadelphia: M'Carty & Davis, 1834), 49; William W. Newcomb Jr., "The Culture and Acculturation of the Delaware Indians," in *Michigan Museum of Anthropology: Anthropological Papers* 10 (Ann Arbor: University of Michigan, 1956), 13.

27. Howard, *Shawnee*, 49.

28. Howard, *Shawnee*, 50-53.

29. James Smith, *Scoouwa: James Smith's Indian Captivity Narrative*, ed. John J. Barsotti (Columbus: Ohio Historical Society, 1978), 60, original version published in 1799 under the title, *An Account of the Remarkable Occurrences in the Life and Travels of Col. James Smith*, ed. John Bradford of Lexington.

30. Clark, *Shawnee*, 40; Howard, *Shawnee*, 49.

31. Harvey, *History of the Shawnee,* 146.

32. Christopher Gist, *Christopher Gist's Journals*, ed. William M. Darlington (New York: Argonaut, 1966), 34.

33. David Zeisberger, *Diary of David Zeisberger*, 2 vols., ed. Eugene F. Bliss (Cincinnati: Robert Clarke, 1885, repr. 1972), 1:286, 321, and 2:375, 460; Smith, *Scoouwa,* 36, 46-47; Kraft, *Lenape,* 154.

34. White, *Middle Ground*, 133.

35. Harvey, *History of the Shawnee,* 148-149.

36. John Heckewelder, *History, Manners, and Customs of the Indian Nations Who Once Inhabited Pennsylvania and Neighboring States* (Philadelphia: Historical Society of Pennsylvania, 1876; repr., New York: Arno, 1971), 131; Clark, *Shawnee,* 39.

37. Henry Bouquet, *The Papers of Henry Bouquet*, ed. Donald H. Kent, Louis M. Waddell, and Autumn L. Leonard (Harrisburg: Pennsylvania Historical and Museum Commission, 1976), 3:47 (hereafter *PHB*).

38. Harvey, *History of the Shawnee,* 149.

39. Smith, *Scoouwa,* 53; Harvey, *History of the Shawnee,* 149.

40. Harvey, *History of the Shawnee,* 150.

41. Smith, *Scoouwa,* 52-53; Harvey, *History of the Shawnee,* 150.

42. Harvey, *History of the Shawnee,* 150.

43. White, *Middle Ground*, 132, 133.

44. Kraft, *Lenape,* 154-157.

45. C. C. Trowbridge, "Shawnese Traditions," in *Michigan University Museum of Anthropology*, ed. Vernon Kinietz and Erminie W. Voegelin (Ann Arbor: University of Michigan Press, 1939), 49.

46. Smith, *Scoouwa,* 46; Kraft, *Lenape,* 142.

47. Kraft, *Lenape,* 116.

48. Smith, *Scoouwa,* 51-52.
49. Alfred Kidder, *An Introduction to the Study of Southwestern Archaeology* (New Haven, CT: Yale University Press, 1924), 118.
50. George Woodcock, *Peoples of the Coast: The Indians of the Pacific Northwest* (Bloomington: Indiana University Press, 1977), 15.
51. Ibid.
52. Gabriel Franchere, *A Voyage to the Northwest Coast of America*, ed. Milo Milton Quaife (New York: Citadel Press, 1968), 179-180.
53. Alexander Ross, *Adventures of the First Settlers on the Oregon or Columbia River*, ed. Milo Milton Quaife (Chicago: Lakeside Press, 1923), 102 (hereafter *Adventures 1*).
54. George Simpson to Governor and Committee, 10 March 1825, Hudson Bay Company Archives, in Richard Mackie, *Trading beyond the Mountains* (Vancouver: UBC Press, 1997), 81.
55. Edward S. Curtis, *The North American Indian*, ed. Frederick Webb House (New York: Johnson Reprint, 1911), 85; Ross, *Adventures 1,* 95.
56. Gregory E. Dowd, *A Spirited Resistance* (Baltimore and London: Johns Hopkins University Press, 1992), 79; Cronon, *Changes,* 44. William Clark approximated the "Chinook nation as being about 400 souls . . . on the small rivers." Using Dowd's mode of estimation, the Chinook probably numbered between four hundred and ten thousand people. William Clark, *Original Journals of the Lewis and Clark Expedition, 1804–1806*, ed. Reuben Gold Thwaites (New York: Dodd, Mead, 1905), 3:230.
57. Ross, *Adventures 1,* 106.
58. Cronon, *Changes,* 42.

CHAPTER 2. THE SOCIOECONOMIC WORLD OF THE AMERICAN INDIAN FRONTIER

1. Sjoberg, *Preindustrial City*, 9, 11.
2. Gideon Sjoberg, "The Preindustrial City," *American Journal of Sociology* 60, no. 5 (1955): 439-441.
3. Sjoberg, *Preindustrial City*, 20-21.
4. Sjoberg, "Preindustrial City," 442.
5. Bronislaw Malinowski, "The Principle of Give and Take," in *The Gift: An Interdisciplinary Perspective*, ed. Aafke E. Komter (Amsterdam: Amsterdam University Press, 1996), 16.
6. Marshall Sahlins, *Stone Age Economics* (Chicago: Aldine-Atherton, 1972), 1-2.
7. Cronon, *Changes*, 79-81.
8. Dozier, *Pueblo Indians*, 133.
9. Ibid., 163, 168.
10. Frances Levine, *Our Prayers Are in This Place: Pecos Pueblo Identity over the Centuries* (Albuquerque: University of New Mexico Press, 1999), 73.
11. Ramon A. Gutierrez, *When Jesus Came, the Corn Mothers Went Away: Marriage, Sexuality, and Power in New Mexico, 1500–1846* (Stanford, CA: Stanford University Press, 1991), 8, 9.
12. Ibid., 9; Jane Collier, *Marriage and Inequality in Classless Societies* (Stanford, CA: Stanford University Press, 1988), 103-105.
13. Dozier, *Pueblo Indians*, 165; Gutierrez, *When Jesus Came*, 13.
14. Gutierrez, *When Jesus Came*, 12-13; Collier, *Marriage*, 76; Dozier, *Pueblo Indians*, 165.
15. Rasor, "Pecos Pueblo," 35. See also Don Francisco de Valverde, "Inquiry Concerning the New Provinces in the North, 1602," in *Don Juan de Oñate: Colonizer of New Mexico, 1595–1628*, ed. George P. Hammond and Agapito Rey (Albuquerque: University of New Mexico Press, 1953), 838.
16. Rasor, "Pecos Pueblo," 38.
17. Kessell, *Kiva*, 134.
18. Pedro de Castaneda, "The Narrative of the Expedition of Coronado," in *Original Narratives*

of Early American History: Spanish Explorers in the Southern United States, 1528–1543, ed. Frederick W. Hodge and T. H. Lewis (New York: Barnes and Noble, 1907; repr. 1970), 310.
19. Kessell, *Kiva*, 7.
20. Daniel K. Richter, *The Ordeal of the Longhouse: The Peoples of the Iroquois League in the Era of European Colonization* (Chapel Hill: University of North Carolina Press, 1992), 22.
21. Judith K. Brown, "Economic Organization and the Position of Women among the Iroquois," *Ethnohistory* 17, no. 3/4 (1970): 153-156.
22. Richter, *Ordeal*, 22-23.
23. Ibid., 40-44; Dean R. Snow, *The Iroquois* (Cambridge, MA: Blackwell, 1994), 64-65.
24. Cadwallader Colden, *The History of the Five Indian Nations: Depending on the Province of New-York in America* (Ithaca, NY: Great Seal Books, 1958, originally printed in 1727), xx; Richter, *Ordeal*, 44.
25. Richter, *Ordeal*, 22.
26. Paul A.W. Wallace, *Indians in Pennsylvania* (Harrisburg: Pennsylvania Historical and Museum Commission, 1964), 51.
27. Treaty Minutes, 12 July 1697, *New York Colonial Manuscripts*, vol. 41, New York State Archives, Albany, fol. 93, quoted in Richter, *Ordeal*, 44.
28. Aafke E. Komter, "Women, Gifts and Power," in *The Gift: An Interdisciplinary Perspective*, ed. Aafke E. Komter (Amsterdam: Amsterdam University Press, 1996), 119.
29. White, *Middle Ground*, 101.
30. Wallace, *Indians*, 17; Albert Cook Myers, ed., *Narratives of Early Pennsylvania, West New Jersey, and Delaware, 1630–1707* (New York, 1912), 230, 232-233.
31. Claude Levi-Strauss, "The Principle of Reciprocity," in Komter, *Gift*, 19.
32. David Cheal, "Moral Economy," in Komter, *Gift*, 90.
33. Bryce Walker and Jill Maynard, eds., *Through Indian Eyes: The Untold Story of Native American Peoples* (Pleasantville, NY: Reader's Digest Association, 1995), 28-29.
34. Carl Waldman, *Atlas of the North American Indian* (New York: Facts on File, the United States, 1985), 20-21; Alvin M. Josephy Jr., ed., *500 Nations* (New York: Alfred A. Knopf, 1994), 36-40; Jack Weatherford, *Native Roots* (New York: Fawcett Columbine, 1991), 13; Walker and Maynard, *Through Indian Eyes*, 28-29.
35. Olive P. Dickason, *Canada's First Nations* (Norman: University of Oklahoma Press, 1992), 70; Lisa A. Mills, "Mitochondrial DNA Analysis of the Ohio Hopewell of the Hopewell Mound Group," PhD diss., (Ohio State University, 2003), 84-109. For Indians and their relation with the environment, see Cronon, *Changes*, 39-41, 95-97, 101-103; for exchange of traditional Indian commodities see, ibid., 93.
36. Richter, *Ordeal*, 33.
37. Levi-Strauss, "Principle of Reciprocity," 18-19.
38. Snow, *Iroquois*, 134-136; Timothy J. Shannon, "Dressing for Success on the Mohawk Frontier: Hendrick, William Johnson, and the Indian Fashion," *William and Mary Quarterly* 53, no. 1, (1996): 26-27.
39. Shannon, "Dressing," 30-31.
40. Colden, *History*, xx.
41. Shannon, "Dressing," 31.
42. White, *Middle Ground*, x, 52.
43. Sahlins, *Stone Age*, 226.
44. White, *Middle Ground*, 100.
45. James Axtell, *The European and the Indian* (Oxford and New York: Oxford University Press, 1981), 256.
46. Neal Wood, *Foundations of Political Economy* (Berkeley: University of California Press, 1994), 217.
47. Karl Polanyi, *The Great Transformation* (Boston: Beacon Press, 1957), 46, cited in Wood, *Foundations*, 257.

48. Ian K. Steele, *Warpaths: Invasions of North America* (New York: Oxford University Press, 1994), 118; Snow, *Iroquois*, 110-111; Richter, *Ordeal*, 50-74; Francis Jennings, *The Ambiguous Iroquois Empire: The Covenant Chain Confederation of Indian Tribes with English Colonies from Its Beginnings to the Lancaster Treaty of 1744* (New York: W. W. Norton, 1984), 84-112.
49. Snow, *Iroquois,* 111.
50. Malinowski, "Principle," 16.
51. C. Hale Sipe, *The Indian Chiefs of Pennsylvania* (Baltimore: Wennawoods, 1995), 288.
52. "Council held at Philadelphia, 6 November 1747," in *Colonial Records of Pennsylvania*, ed. Samuel Hazard (Philadelphia: Joseph Severns, 1860), 5:138.
53. George Croghan, "Proceedings of George Croghan, Esquire, and Mr. Andrew Montour at Ohio, in the Execution of the Governor's Instructions to Deliver the Provincial Present to the Several Tribes of Indians Settled There," in *Early Western Journals, 1748–1765*, ed. Reuben Gold Thwaites (Lewisburg, PA: Wennawoods Publishing, 1998), 1:64. Also see George Croghan, "Proceedings of George Croghan, Esquire, and Mr. Andrew Montour at Ohio, in the Execution of the Governor's Instructions to Deliver the Provincial Present to the Several Tribes of Indians Settled There," in *Minutes of the Provincial Council of Pennsylvania, from the Organization to the Termination of the Proprietary Government* (Harrisburg, PA: Theo. Fenn, 1851), 5:533; also accessed April 21, 2020, https://babel.hathitrust.org/cgi/pt?id=wu.89066118753&view=1up&seq=562.
54. "Letter from John Mercer to Charlton Palmer, July 27, 1762," cited in Mulkearn, *Mercer Papers*, 62, 134, 280.
55. Shannon, "Dressing," 18. Jerry Clark, *The Shawnee* (Lexington: University Press of Kentucky, 1993), 58
56. White, *Middle Ground*, 136.
57. Levi-Strauss, "Principle of Reciprocity," 91.
58. Paul A. W. Wallace, "Indian Highways of Pennsylvania," *Pennsylvania Archaeologist* 23, no. 3-4 (December 1953): 111-122.
59. Clark, *Original Journals,* 294.
60. Edward S. Curtis, *The North American Indian*, ed. Frederick Webb House (New York and London: Johnson Reprint, 1911), 87.
61. Philip Drucker, *Indians of the Northwest Coast* (New York: McGraw-Hill, 1963), 55.
62. Woodcock, *Peoples*, 21; Drucker, *Indians*, 57; Robert H. Ruby and John A. Brown, *The Chinook Indians: Traders of the Lower Columbia* (Norman: University of Oklahoma Press, 1976), 9; Merwyn S. Garbarino and Robert F. Sasso, *Native American Heritage*, 3rd ed. (Prospect Heights, IL: Waveland Press, 1994), 161.
63. Rudy and Brown, *Chinook,* 10; Woodcock, *Peoples*, 17.
64. Drucker, *Indians*, 55; Verne F. Ray, "Lower Chinook Ethnographic Notes," *University of Washington Publications in Anthropology* 7, no. 2 (1938): 49, cited in Rudy and Brown, *Chinook*,11.
65. Woodcock, *Peoples*, 21; Rudy and Brown, *Chinook,* 9.
66. Curtis, *North American Indian*, 87.
67. Ruby and Brown, *Chinook*, 9.
68. Meriwether Lewis, *Original Journals of the Lewis and Clark Expedition, 1804–1806*, ed. Reuben Gold Thwaites (New York: Dodd, Mead, 1905), 3:360.
69. Gabriel Franchere, *Adventure at Astoria, 1810–1814*, ed. and trans. Hoyt C. Franchere (Norman: University of Oklahoma Press, 1967), 190.
70. Ruby and Brown, *Chinook,* 9.
71. Alexander Ross, *Adventures of the First Settlers on the Columbia River* (Ann Arbor, MI: University Microfilms, 1966), 95-96 (hereafter *Adventures 2*).
72. Garbarino and Sasso, *Native American Heritage,* 163.
73. Drucker, *Indians*, 58-60; Woodcock, *Peoples*, 16-19.

74. H. G. Barnett, "The Nature of the Potlatch," *American Anthropologist* 40 (1938): 349.
75. Garbarino and Sasso, *Native American Heritage*, 161-164; Woodcock, *Peoples*, 16-19.
76. Barnett, "Nature of the Potlatch," 351-354.
77. Drucker, *Indians*, 61; Rudy and Brown, *Chinook*, 11.
78. Garbarino and Sasso, *Native American Heritage*, 164.
79. Ross, *Adventures 1,* 106.
80. Franchere, *Adventure*, 187.
81. Rudy and Brown, *Chinook,* 16; Woodcock, *Peoples*, 134-136; Garbarino and Sasso, *Native American Heritage*, 158.
82. Ross, *Adventures 1,* 108.
83. Franchere, *Adventure*, 182.
84. Curtis, *North American Indian*, 87; Ruby and Brown, *Chinook,* 9.
85. Ross, *Adventures 1,* 83-85.
86. Robert Stuart, *On the Oregon Trail: Robert Stuart's Journey of Discovery*, ed. Kenneth A. Spaulding (Norman: University of Oklahoma Press, 1953), 29.
87. Mackie, *Trading*, 296.
88. Woodcock, *Peoples*, 15.
89. Ross, *Adventures 1,* 96.
90. Washington Irving, *Astoria: Or Anecdotes of an Enterprise beyond the Rocky Mountains*, ed. Edgeley W. Todd (Norman: University of Oklahoma Press, 1964), 337.
91. T. C. Elliot, "The Journal of the Ship Ruby," *Oregon Historical Quarterly* 28, no. 3 (September 1927): 262; Dorothy O. Johansen, *Empire of the Columbia: A History of the Pacific Northwest* (New York: Harper & Row, 1967), 60.
92. Cronon, *Changes*, 20.

CHAPTER 3. AMERICAN INDIAN POLITICAL SYSTEMS

1. Sjoberg, *Preindustrial*, 11.
2. Ibid., 220-222.
3. Ibid., 340.
4. Ibid., 12.
5. Ibid., 109.
6. Timothy Earle, *How Chiefs Come to Power: The Political Economy in Prehistory* (Stanford, CA: Stanford University Press, 1997), 3.
7. Ibid., 4-8.
8. Morton H. Fried, *The Evolution of Political Society: An Essay in Political Anthropology* (New York: Random House, 1967), 10-13.
9. Larry Nordby, "The Prehistory of the Pecos Indians," in *Pecos Ruins*, ed. David Grant Noble (Santa Fe, NM: Ancient City Press, 1993), 11.
10. Levine, *Our Prayers*, 83.
11. Gutierrez, *When Jesus Came*, 13.
12. Rasor, "Pecos Pueblo," 35; Garbarino and Sasso, *Native American Heritage*, 242; Dozier, *Pueblo Indians*, 188-189.
13. Gutierrez, *When Jesus Came*, 22.
14. Rasor, "Pecos Pueblo," 35; Garbarino and Sasso, *Native American Heritage,* 243-244; Dozier, *Pueblo Indians,* 188-189; Gutierrez, *When Jesus Came*, 22-23.
15. Gutierrez, *When Jesus Came*, 22.
16. Rasor, "Pecos Pueblo," 35.
17. Kessell, *Kiva,* 12.
18. Trudy Griffin-Pierce, *Native Peoples of the* Southwest (Albuquerque: University of New Mexico Press, 2000), 51. See also Gutierrez, *When Jesus Came*, 24.
19. Dozier, *Pueblo Indians,* 133.

20. Rasor, "Pecos Pueblo," 35.
21. Gutierrez, *When Jesus Came*, 25.
22. Castaneda, "Narrative of the Expedition of Coronado," 355-357.
23. Albert H. Schroeder, "Pecos Pueblo," in *Handbook of North American Indians*, ed. Alfonso Ortiz (Washington, DC: Smithsonian Institution, 1979), 9:435.
24. Dozier, *Pueblo Indians,* 188-189.
25. Garbarino and Sasso, *Native American Heritage,* 245.
26. Dozier, *Pueblo Indians,* 131.
27. Snow, *Iroquois*, 58-59; Walker and Maynard, *Through Indian Eyes*, 121-122.
28. Snow, *Iroquois*, 60-65; Lewis H. Morgan, *League of the Ho-de-no-sau-nee or Iroquois*, ed. Herbert M. Lloyd (New York: Dodd, Mead, 1966), 59-73; Richter, *Ordeal*, 42-45.
29. Richter, *Ordeal*, 23.
30. Snow, *Iroquois*, 60-61.
31. Snow, *Iroquois*, 59, 66; Richter, *Ordeal,* 44.
32. Snow, *Iroquois*, 74; Richter, *Ordeal*, 20; Walker and Maynard, *Through Indian Eyes*, 123.
33. Snow, *Iroquois*, 71-74.
34. Brown, "Economic Organization," 153, 155.
35. Earle, *How Chiefs*, 3-4.
36. Snow, *Iroquois*, 65; Brown, "Economic Organization," 155.
37. Quote from Richter, *Ordeal*, 43.
38. Snow, *Iroquois,* 65; Brown, "Economic Organization," 155-156; Richter, *Ordeal*, 43.
39. Snow, *Iroquois*, 65.
40. Morgan, *League*, 59-70; Richter, *Ordeal*, 43.
41. Morgan, *League*, 60; Snow, *Iroquois*, 61-65.
42. Richter, *Ordeal*, 40-41.
43. Morgan, *League*, 63-65.
44. Ibid., 99.
45. Steele, *Warpaths*, 110-118. Mourning wars were military actions taken to physically capture individuals from other Indian groups to replace the dwindling population of the Mohawk after disease and war reduced their numbers, or to be killed and tortured to death to complete the mourning process.
46. Richter, *Ordeal*, 42-43.
47. Ibid.
48. Earle, *Chiefs*, 5; Morton H. Fried, *The Notion of Tribe* (Menlo Park, CA: Cummings, 1975), 8.
49. Howard, *Shawnee*, 86.
50. Trowbridge, "Shawnese," 26.
51. Ibid., 17. Howard suggests that thirteen name groups existed as late as 1862. *Shawnee*, 88. The exact historical number is not fully known.
52. Clark, *Shawnee*, 29.
53. Thomas Wildcat Alford, *Civilization* (Norman: University of Oklahoma Press, 1936), 44-45. Found in Howard, 107-108.
54. Clark, *Shawnee,* 33; Howard, *Shawnee*,108.
55. Trowbridge, "Shawnese," 11.
56. Ibid., 11-12; Howard, *Shawnee*, 108.
57. Howard, *Shawnee*, 109; Trowbridge, "Shawnese," 12-13; Clark, *Shawnee*, 36.
58. Trowbridge, "Shawnese," 12.
59. Clark, *Shawnee*, 36.
60. Trowbridge, "Shawnese," 11; Clark, *Shawnee*, 33; Howard, *Shawnee*, 107-110.
61. Trowbridge, "Shawnese," 11.
62. Ibid., 13; Howard, *Shawnee*, 110; Clark, *Shawnee*, 36.
63. Alford, *Civilization*, 45; Howard, *Shawnee*, 110.

64. Howard, *Shawnee*, 110.
65. Trowbridge, "Shawnese," 13-14.
66. Ibid., 14; Howard, *Shawnee*, 111.
67. Howard, *Shawnee*, 110-112; Trowbridge, "Shawnese," 12-15; Alford, *Civilization*, 44-47; Clark, *Shawnee*, 36-37.
68. Wallace, *Indians in Pennsylvania*, 84.
69. C. A. Weslager, *The Delaware Indians* (New Brunswick, NJ: Rutgers University Press, 1972), 65; Kraft, *Lenape*, 121; C. A. Weslager, *The Delaware Indian Westward Migration* (Wallingford, PA: Middle Atlantic Press, 1978), 27.
70. William W. Newcomb Jr., "The Culture and Acculturation of the Delaware Indians," *Michigan Museum of Anthropology: Anthropological Papers* 10 (Ann Arbor: University Of Michigan, 1956), 31-58.
71. Weslager, *Delaware Indians*, 57.
72. Newcomb, "Culture and Acculturation," 49; Heckewelder, *History*, 51-52, 253.
73. Heckewelder, *History*, 51-2.
74. Anthony F. C. Wallace, *King of the Delawares: Teedyuschung 1700–1763* (Philadelphia: University of Pennsylvania Press, 1949), 8. Weslager, in *Delaware Indians,* states "the Delaware women did not take an active part in choosing a chief as did certain matrons in the Iroquois League of the Five Nations who were known as chiefmakers, although eligibility as a candidate for chieftaincy was determined by the succession in the female line" (64). Weslager is referring to the eighteenth and nineteenth centuries, after the Lenape began to organize more formally as a group, and not to their history before European contact.
75. Wallace, *King of the Delawares*, 8.
76. Wallace, *Indians*, 51.
77. Lewis H. Morgan, *Ancient Society* (Cambridge, MA: Belknap Press of Harvard University Press, 1964), 153.
78. Holm, *Description*, 133.
79. Weslager, *Delaware Indians,* 62.
80. Holm, *Description*,133.
81. Daniel Denton, *A Brief Description of New York Formerly Called New Netherlands* (New York: W. Gowans, 1845), 10. Also see Newcomb, "Culture and Acculturation," 52.
82. E. M. Ruttenber, *History of the Indian Tribes of Hudson's River* (Port Washington, NY: Kennikat Press, 1872), 48-49; Holm, *Description*, 136; Newcomb, "Culture and Acculturation," 53-54; Kraft, *Lenape*, 220-228.
83. Newcomb, "Culture and Acculturation," 53.
84. Ruttenber, *Indian Tribes*, 47; Archer Butler Hulbert and William Nathaniel Schwarze, eds., *David Zeisberger's History of Northern American Indians* (Columbus, OH: F. J. Heer Printing, 1910), 93, found in Newcomb, "Culture and Acculturation," 53.
85. Ruttenber, *Indian Tribes*, 47-48.
86. Frederick W. Hodge, ed., *Handbook of American Indians North of Mexico* (Washington, DC: Government Printing Office, 1912), citation found in Harry Forrest Lupold, *The Forgotten People* (Hicksville, NY: Exposition Press, 1975), 29.
87. Morgan, *Ancient Society*, 61.
88. Bruce G. Trigger, *The Huron: Farmers of the North*, 2d ed. (Chicago: Holt, Rinehart and Winston, 1990), 65; Morgan, *Ancient Society*, 66.
89. Morgan, *Ancient Society*, 67.
90. Elisabeth Tooker, "Northern Iroquoian Sociopolitical Organization," *American Anthropologist* 72 (1970): 90-97, found in Trigger, *Huron*, 66.
91. Morgan, *Ancient Society*, 67.
92. Trigger, *Children*, 45, 54-59; Trigger, *Huron*, 85-91; Morgan, *Ancient Society*, 93; Barry M. Pritzker, *A Native American Encyclopedia: History, Culture and Peoples* (New York: Oxford

University Press, 2000), 478-481; John Steckley, "The Clans and Phratries of the Huron," accessed April 9, 2020, https://www.ontarioarchaeology.org/Resources/Publications/oa37-3-steckley.pdf.

93. Morgan, *Ancient Society*, 101.

94. Schoolcraft, *Notes*, 496-497. For detailed information concerning the great council of the Iroquois Confederacy at Onondaga, several works exist. Some of the more notable are Francis Jennings, *The Ambiguous Iroquois Empire* (New York: W.W. Norton, 1984); Francis Jennings, William N. Fenton, Mary A. Druke, and David R. Miller, eds., *The History and Culture of Iroquois Diplomacy* (New York: Syracuse University Press, 1985); and Daniel K. Richter and James H. Merrell, eds., *Beyond the Covenant Chain* (New York: Syracuse University Press, 1987). For the Huron Confederacy see Trigger, *Children*.

95. Colden, *History*, xx.

96. Wallace, *Indians*, 86.

97. Morgan, *Ancient Society*, 105.

98. Trigger, *Huron*, 98.

99. Ruttenber, *Indian Tribes*, 257.

100. White, *Middle Ground*, 186.

101. Howard, *Shawnee*, 86; Weslager, *Delaware Indians*, 3-30.

102. Trigger, *Huron*, 66.

103. "Letter from Mercer to Palmer," in *Mercer Papers*, 62, 134, 280. George Mercer was a surveyor, officer in the 1st Virginia Regiment during the French and Indian War, and the Ohio Company agent in England following the war. Charlton Palmer was a solicitor the Ohio Company hired to represent it in front of the Board of Trade.

104. For an example, see "Letter to Pennsylvania Governor James Hamilton from Ohio Indian Commissioners Richard Peters, Isaac Norris and Benjamin Franklin, 1 November 1753," in *Colonial Records of Pennsylvania*, ed. Samuel Hazard (Philadelphia: Joseph Severns, 1860), 5:665-684. A conference occurred at Carlisle, Pennsylvania, between those commissioners and sachems from the Ohio Indians representing the Mingo (Five Nations), Delaware, Shawnee, Twightwee (Miami), and Wyandot. During the conference, the commissioners approached the delegation of Ohio Indians requesting that Scarouady not travel to Carolina to solicit the release of Shawnee prisoners taken by the colonial government.

105. Ibid., 674. "Belt" refers to a belt of wampum beads used in negotiations and ceremonies.

106. Michael N. McConnell, "Peoples 'In Between': The Iroquois and the Ohio Indians, 1720-1768," in Richter and Merrell, *Beyond*, 102.

107. William Trent, "William Trent's account of his proceedings with the Six Nations of Indians and their allies and the Distribution of a present amongst them," in *History of Colonel Henry Bouquet and the Western Frontiers of Pennsylvania, 1747–1764*, ed. Mary Carson Darlington (Privately printed, 1920), 19.

108. For Iroquois phratries see Morgan, *League of the Iroquois*, 91. The Logstonian clans derived from several sources based on clan affiliation of group leaders. The major leaders of Logstown were Kakowatcheky, the Shawnee leader of the Wolf clan; Shingas and his brother King Beaver (Tamaque), Delaware leaders of the Turkey clan, who replaced Olumpies (Sassoonan or Allumapees) "King of the Delawares," a leader of the Turtle clan who resided in eastern Pennsylvania; and Tanacharison, a Seneca born of a Catawba mother, and Scarouady, an Oneida, leaders of possibly the Turtle, Wolf, or Bear clans, who represented the Ohio Mingo and the Iroquois Confederacy in the Ohio Valley. Sipe, *Indian Chiefs*, vols. 2-7; Richter and Merrell, *Beyond*, 101; and Colden, *History*, xvii.

109. Monsieur de Celoron, "Journal of Celoron," in *Expedition of Celoron to the Ohio Country in 1749*, ed. C. B. Galbreath (Columbus, OH: F.J. Heer Printing, 1921), 34.

110. "Meeting of the Commissioners and Indians, 3 October 1753," in Samuel Hazard, ed., *Minuetes of the Provincial Council of Pennsylvania, from the Organization to the Termination*

of the Proprietary Government (Philadelphia: Joseph Severns, 1860), 5:676.
111. Ibid.
112. Timothy Earle, "The Evolution of Chiefdoms," in *Chiefdoms: Power, Economy and Ideology*, ed. Timothy Earle (Cambridge: Cambridge University Press, 1991), 1. In this anthology, Earle defines chiefdoms as "a polity that organizes centrally a regional population in the thousands . . . [with] some degree of heritable and social ranking and economic stratification." As is evident, Logstown existed as an urban settlement that attended to its own affairs while often working in conjunction with other Native Americans.
113. *Webster's II*, s.v. "oligarchy" and "oligarch."
114. White, *Middle Ground*, 186.
115. William R. Everdell, *The End of Kings: A History of Republics and Republicans* (New York: Free Press, 1983), 2-8.
116. Ibid., 8.
117. Philip Drucker, "Rank, Wealth, and Kinship in Northwest Coast Society," *American Anthropologist* 41 (1939): 58; Robert H. Ruby and John A. Brown, *The Chinook Indians: Traders of the Lower Columbia River* (Norman: University of Oklahoma Press, 1976), 9; Walker and Maynard, *Through Indian Eyes*, 236.
118. Ruby and Brown, *Chinook*, 11; Walker and Maynard, *Through Indian Eyes*, 236.
119. Lewis, *Original Journals*, 3:360.
120. Edward S. Curtis, *The North American Indian*, ed. Frederick Webb House (New York: Johnson Reprint, 1911), 8:87.
121. Ruby and Brown, *Chinook*, 9.
122. Franchere, *Adventure at Astoria*, 190.
123. Curtis, *North American Indian*, 87.
124. J. F. Santee, "Comcomly and the Chinooks," *Oregon Historical Quarterly* 33, no. 3 (September 1932): 271.
125. Franchere, *Adventure at Astoria*, 190.
126. Ross, *Adventures 1*, 95.
127. For an account of Chinook warfare see Franchere, *Adventure at Astoria*, 190-192.
128. Reverend Samuel Parker, *Journal of an Exploring Tour beyond the Rocky Mountains* (Minneapolis: Ross & Haines, 1967), 251.
129. Ibid., 250-251.

PART 2. RESETTLING THE AMERICAN FRONTIER

1. Turner, "Significance," 29.

CHAPTER 4. FOR GOD, GLORY, GOLD, AND PROTECTION

1. David J. Weber, *The Spanish Frontier in North America* (New Haven. CT: Yale University Press, 1992), 1-13. In 1585, New Spain comprised present-day Mexico, Central America north of what is now Panama, and Florida, Arizona, and New Mexico.
2. "*Entrada*" is a term used to describe a military conquest or occupation by Spanish forces that involved exploration into previously uncharted or unsettled regions in North America.
3. Álvar Núñez Cabeza de Vaca, "The Narrative of Cabeza de Vaca," in *Spanish Explorers in the Southern United States, 1528–1543: Original Narratives of Early American History*, ed. Frederick W. Hodge (New York: Barnes and Noble, 1971), 1-123; Weber, *Spanish Frontier*, 42-45; Álvar Núñez Cabeza de Vaca, "Álvar Núñez Cabeza de Vaca's Journey Across America, 1528–1536," in *Revealing America: Image and Imagination in the Exploration of North America*, ed. James P. Ronda (Lexington, MA: D. C. Heath, 1996), 47-54; Weber, *Spanish Frontier*, 45-46.
4. Weber, *Spanish Frontier*, 45-46; Fray Marcos de Niza, "The Narrative of Fray Marcos de Niza, 1539," in Ronda, *Revealing America*, 56.
5. Castaneda, "Narrative of the Expedition of Coronado," in Hodge, *Spanish Explorers*, 285-

384; Pedro de Castaneda, "Pedro de Castaneda Recalls the March to Cibola, 1540," in Ronda, *Revealing America*, 57-65; Weber, *Spanish Frontier*, 46-49, 78.

6. Weber, *Spanish Frontier*, 78-79.

7. George P. Hammond, ed., *The Rediscovery of New Mexico* (Albuquerque: University of New Mexico Press, 1966), 6-15; Ronda, *Revealing America*, 69-70; Weber, *Spanish Frontier*, 95.

8. Hammond, *Rediscovery*, 15-28; Kessell, *Kiva,* 41-45; Weber, *Spanish Frontier*, 79; Ronda, *Revealing America*, 69-70.

9. "Contract of Don Juan de Oñate for the Discovery and Conquest of New Mexico, September 21, 1595," in Hammond and Rey, *Don Juan de Oñate*, 1:42-57; Kessell, *Kiva,* 67-76; Andrew L. Knaut, *The Pueblo Revolt of 1680: Conquest Resistance in Seventeenth-Century New Mexico* (Norman: University of Oklahoma Press, 1995), 32; Levine, *Our Prayers*, 16.

10. Albert H. Schroeder and Dan S. Matson, *A Colony on the Move: Gaspar de Sosa's Journal, 1590–1591* (Salt Lake City: Alphabet Printing, 1965).

11. Don Francisco de Valverde, "Investigation of Conditions in New Mexico, 1601," in Hammond and Rey, *Don Juan de Oñate*, 2:656.

12. For quote see "Monterrey to the King, May 4, 1598," in ibid., 1:392; see also "Instructions to Don Juan de Oñate, October 21, 1595," in ibid., 65-66.

13. "Record of the Marches by the Army of New Spain to New Mexico, 1595–98," in ibid., 309-320; "Captain Velasco to the Viceroy, San Gabriel, March 22, 1601," in ibid., 609; Knaut, *Pueblo Revolt*, 122-124.

14. Hammond and Rey, *Don Juan de Oñate*, 17.

15. "Captain Velasco to the Viceroy, San Gabriel, March 22, 1601," in Hammond and Rey, *Don Juan de Oñate*, 2:609; "Instructions to Don Juan de Oñate, October 21, 1595," in ibid., 1:67-68; for "a community plot ... " see "Fray Juan de Escalona to the Viceroy, October 1, 1601," in ibid., 2:692-693; for encomienda and repartimiento systems see Weber, *Spanish Frontier*, 124-126.

16. "Don Juan de Oñate to the Viceroy of New Spain, March 2, 1599," in Hammond and Rey, *Don Juan de Oñate*, 1:483.

17. "Advantages and Disadvantages of the Modifications of the Contract," in ibid., 2:605.

18. "Don Juan de Oñate to the Viceroy of New Spain, March 2, 1599," in ibid., 1:480-486.

19. "Instructions to Don Juan de Oñate, October 21, 1595," in ibid., 65-68.

20. "Trial of the Indians of Acoma, 1598," in ibid., 1:455-456.

21. Fray Lope Izquierdo testimony, "Proceedings of the [Lieutenant] Governor of New Mexico with Regard to Breaking Camp, San Gabriel, September 7, 1601," in ibid., 2:678; Weber, *Spanish Frontier*, 124.

22. "Fray Juan de Escalona to the Viceroy, October 1, 1601," in Hammond and Rey, *Don Juan de Oñate*, 2:692.

23. "Captain Velasco to the Viceroy, San Gabriel, March 22, 1601," in ibid., 610.

24. Fray Francisco de San Miguel testimony, "Proceedings of the [Lieutenant] Governor of New Mexico with Regard to Breaking Camp, San Gabriel, September 7, 1601," in ibid., 674.

25. Captain Bernabe de las Casas testimony, "Proceedings of the [Lieutenant] Governor of New Mexico with Regard to Breaking Camp, San Gabriel, September 7, 1601," in ibid., 687; "Captain Velasco to the Viceroy, San Gabriel, March 22, 1601," in ibid., 608.

26. Gaspar Castaño de Sosa, "Castaño Reveals a Pueblo World of Plenty," in Ronda, *Revealing America*, 71.

27. Captain Velasco to the Viceroy, San Gabriel, March 22, 1601," in Hammond and Rey, *Don Juan de Oñate*, 2:610.

28. Fray Lope Izquierdo testimony, "Proceedings of the [Lieutenant] Governor of New Mexico with Regard to Breaking Camp, San Gabriel, September 7, 1601," in ibid., 680.

29. "Captain Velasco to the Viceroy, San Gabriel, March 22, 1601," in ibid., 610. See also, Captain Bernabe de las Casas, "Proceedings of the [Lieutenant] Governor of New Mexico with

Regard to Breaking Camp, San Gabriel, September 7, 1601," in ibid., 687.
30. "Fray Juan de Escalona to the Viceroy, October 1, 1601, in ibid., 693.
31. "Captain Velasco to the Viceroy, San Gabriel, March 22, 1601," in ibid., 610.
32. Benavides, *Harvest*, 56; Knaut, *Pueblo Revolt,* 129.
33. Fray Francisco de Zamora testimony, in Hammond and Rey, *Don Juan de Oñate*, 2:675; Fray Lope Izquierdo testimony, in ibid., 680.
34. "Captain Velasco to the Viceroy, San Gabriel, March 22, 1601," in ibid., 610.
35. Captain Diego de Zubia testimony, "Proceedings of the [Lieutenant] Governor of New Mexico with Regard to Breaking Camp, San Gabriel, September 7, 1601," in ibid., 686.
36. "True Report Based on Oñate's Letters, March 22, 1601," in ibid., 619-620.
37. Vicente de Zaldivar Mendoza, "Discovery of the Buffalo," in ibid., 1:398-405.
38. "Fray Juan de Escalona to the Viceroy, October 1, 1601," in ibid., 2:696.
39. Captain Diego de Zubia testimony, "Proceedings of the [Lieutenant] Governor of New Mexico with Regard to Breaking Camp, San Gabriel, September 7, 1601," in ibid., 686.
40. Captain Don Luis de Velasco, "Captain Velasco to the Viceroy, San Gabriel, March 22, 1601," in ibid., 608-618.
41. "Fray Juan de Escalona to the Viceroy, October 1, 1601," in ibid., 697; Kessell, *Kiva,* 90.
42. Alonso Varela, "Letter to the King from Some Conquerors of New Mexico, Asking Him to Aid don Juan de Oñate, January 1, 1602," in Hammond and Rey, *Don Juan de Oñate*, 2:761-762.
43. "Marquis of Montesclaros to the King," March 31, 1605, in ibid., 1001-1002; Hammond and Rey, *Don Juan de Oñate*, 1:30.
44. Frank V. Scholes, "Royal Treasury Records Relating to the Province of New Mexico, 1596–1683," *New Mexico Historical Review* 50, no.1 (1975): 11.
45. Council of the Indies, "Concerning the Excesses of Don Juan de Oñate and the Discovery of New Mexico, Valladolid, January 19, 1606," *Don Juan de Oñate*, 2:1034.
46. "Instructions to Don Pedro De Peralta, Who has been appointed Governor and Captain Genral of the Provinces of New Mexico, March 30, 1609," in ibid., 1087-1091.
47. Ibid., 2:1090.
48. Lansing B. Bloom, "When Was Santa Fe Founded?," *New Mexico Historical Review* 4, no. 2 (April 1929): 194; Marc Simmons, "Settlement Patterns and Village Plans in Colonial New Mexico, in *New Spain's Far Northern Frontier: Essays on Spain in the American West, 1540–1821*, ed. David J. Weber (Albuquerque: University of New Mexico Press, 1979), 102.
49. Kessell, *Kiva,* 124, 132.
50. "Marquis of Guadalcazar to the King, May 27, 1620," in Hammond and Rey, *Don Juan de Oñate*, 2:1140; Knaut, *Pueblo Revolt,* 132; Frank V. Scholes, "Royal Treasury Records Relating to the Province of New Mexico, 1596–1683," *New Mexico Historical Review* 50, no.2 (1975): 143; Simmons, "Settlement Patterns," 102. A real or reale was a silver monetary unit.
51. "Discussion and Proposal of the Points to His Majesty Concerning the Various Discoveries of New Mexico," in Hammond and Rey, *Don Juan de Oñate*, 2:914.
52. "Instructions to Don Pedro De Peralta, Who has been appointed Governor and Captain General of the Provinces of New Mexico, March 30, 1609," in ibid., 1088; Weber, *Spanish Frontier*, 125.
53. Benavides, *Harvest*, 26; Gutierrez, *When Jesus Came,* 102, 105; Levine, *Our Prayer,* 17.
54. "Petition and Report of Posadas to The Governor, Juan de Mirands, 1664," in *Historical Documents Relating to New Mexico, Nueva Vizcaya, and Approaches Thereto, to* 1773, ed. Charles Wilson Hackett (Washington, DC: Carnegie Institution of Washington, 1937), 3:255; "Declaration of Fray Gabriel de Torija, Santo Domingo, June 3, 1664," in ibid., 249; Kessell, *Kiva,* 186-190; Weber, *Spanish Frontier*, 124.
55. James H. Gunnerson, "Apaches at Pecos," in *Pecos: Gateway to Pueblos and Plains: The Anthology*, eds. John V. Bezy and Joseph P. Sanchez (Tucson, AZ: Southwest Parks and Monu-

ments Association, 1988), 42-43; Kessell, *Kiva,* 123.

56. Kessell, *Kiva,* 123.

57. Benavides, *Harvest,* 76; Kessell, *Kiva,* 129, 137.

58. Simmons, "Settlement Patterns," 103-105; Weber, *Spanish Frontier*, 124-126; Kessell, *Kiva,* 186-190; Gutierrez, *When Jesus Came,* 102, 105, 117.

59. Fray Francisco de San Miguel, "Proceedings of the [Lieutenant] Governor of New Mexico with Regard to Breaking Camp, San Gabriel, September 7, 1601," in Hammond and Rey, *Don Juan de Oñate,* 2:673; Weber, *Spanish Frontier*, 124-126; Kessell, *Kiva,* 186-190; Gutierrez, *When Jesus Came,* 102, 105, 117; Lansing B. Bloom, "A Glimpse of New Mexico in 1620," *New Mexico Historical Review* 3, no. 4 (October 1928): 365-369.

60. Weber, *Spanish Frontier*, 126-127; Gutierrez, *When Jesus Came,* 155.

61. Benavides, *Harvest,* 76.

62. Weber, *Spanish Frontier*, 127-129; "Trial of the Indians of Acoma, 1598," in Hammond and Rey, *Don Juan de Oñate*, eds. 1:477; Gutierrez, *When Jesus Came,* 149-156.

63. Fray Francisco de Zamora, "Proceedings of the [Lieutenant] Governor of New Mexico with Regard to Breaking Camp, San Gabriel, September 7, 1601," in Hammond and Rey, *Don Juan de Oñate*, 2:675.

64. "Marquis of Montesclaros to the King, March 31, 1605, in ibid., 1:1002; Hammond and Rey, *Don Juan de Oñate*, 1:30; France V. Scholes, *Church and State in New Mexico, 1610–1650* (Albuquerque: University of New Mexico Press, 1937), 12-16; Levine, *Our Prayer,* 18. Kessell, *Kiva,* 124-131.

65. Weber, *Spanish Frontier*, 106-108.

66. Scholes, "Church and State," 12-16; Weber, *Spanish Frontier*, 106-108.

67. Kessell, *Kiva,* 97-98, 124-131, 155, 199-203; Scholes, "Church and State," 12-16.

68. Knaut, *Pueblo Revolt,* 140. *Mestizos* were individuals with Spanish and Indian origins; *mulattos* were individuals with Spanish and African origins.

69. Knaut, *Pueblo Revolt,* 140-142; Gutierrez, *When Jesus Came,* 105-106; Weber, *Spanish Frontier*, 326-333.

70. Knaut, *Pueblo Revolt,* 144-150; Gutierrez, *When Jesus Came,* 131; Weber, *Spanish Frontier*, 316.

71. Levine, *Our Prayer,* 21; Weber, *Spanish Frontier*, 133-135; Gutierrez, *When Jesus Came,* 131-133; Nan A. Rothschild, *Colonial Encounters in a Native American Landscape: The Spanish and Dutch in North America* (Washington, DC: Smithsonian Books, 2003), 59-61.

72. Alvin M. Josephy Jr., *The Patriot Chiefs: A Chronicle of American Indian Leadership* (New York: Viking Press, 1961), 63-94.

73. Don Diego de Vargas, *First Expedition of Vargas into New Mexico, 1692,* ed. and trans. J. Manuel Espinosa (Albuquerque: University of New Mexico Press, 1940), 16-19; Weber, *Spanish Frontier*, 133-137; Gutierrez, *When Jesus Came,* 132-136; Knaut, *Pueblo Revolt,* 168-170.

74. Kessell, *Kiva,* 241; Gutierrez, *When Jesus Came,* 139; Oakah L. Jones Jr., *Pueblo Warriors and Spanish Conquest* (Norman: University of Oklahoma Press, 1966), 40; Knaut, *Pueblo Revolt,*175-176.

75. Knaut, *Pueblo Revolt,* 176-181; Vargas, *First Expedition*, 17-19; Weber, *Spanish Frontier*, 137.

76. John Francis Bannon, *The Spanish Borderlands Frontier, 1531–1821* (New York: Holt, Rinehart and Winston, 1970), 92-97.

77. Gutierrez, *When Jesus Came,*146; Knaut, *Pueblo Revolt,* 176-181; Vargas, *First Expedition*, 17-19; Weber, *Spanish Frontier*, 137.

78. Vargas, *First Expedition*, 19.

79. Vargas, *First Expedition*, 48-49; Gutierrez, *When Jesus Came,* 143.

80. Jones, *Pueblo Warriors,* 39-45; Vargas, *First Expedition*, 17, 30-32, 62, 68, 72-74, 115-116, 119, 162, 170, 182-183, 186, 207, 214, 245.

81. Jones, *Pueblo Warriors* 46; Vargas, *First Expedition*, 120-123, 129-130.
82. Reuben Gold Thwaites, *Early Western Travels, 1748–1846* (Cleveland: Arthur Clark, 1904), 19:269; Matthew Liebmann, Robert Preucel, and Joseph Aguilar, "The Pueblo World Transformed: Alliances, Factionalism, and Animosities in the Northern Rio Grande, 1680–1700," in *New Mexico and the Pimería Alta: The Colonial Period in the American Southwest*, ed. John G. Douglass and William M. Graves, 143-56 (Boulder: University Press of Colorado, 2017), accessed April 10, 2020, www.jstor.org/stable/j.ctt1mmftg6.12; Kessel, *Kiva*, 266.
83. Vargas, *First Expedition*, 120-133; Levine, *Our Prayer*, 22; Kessell, *Kiva*, 232-234, 249-250, 253, 256; Jones, *Pueblo Warriors*, 46-47.
84. Kessell, *Kiva*, 254; Don Diego de Vargas, *The Royal Crown Restored: The Journals of Don Diego Vargas, New Mexico, 1692–1694*, ed. John L. Kessell et al. (Albuquerque: University of New Mexico Press, 1995), 111-113.
85. Vargas, *Royal Crown*, 473.
86. Kessell, *Kiva*, 257.
87. Vargas, *Royal Crown*, 474.
88. Ibid., 474-476; Kessell, *Kiva*, 256-257.
89. Vargas, *Royal Crown*, 480.
90. Ibid., 416-417.
91. Kessell, *Kiva*, 258; Vargas, *Royal Crown*, 474-484; Elinore M. Barrett, *Conquest and Catastrophe: Changing Rio Grande Pueblo Settlement Patterns in the Sixteenth and Seventeenth Centuries* (Albuquerque: University of New Mexico Press, 2002), 86.
92. Vargas, *Royal Crown*, 495.
93. Ibid., 503-506.
94. Gutierrez, *When Jesus Came*, 145; Kessell, *Kiva*, 259.
95. Vargas, *Royal Crown*, 523-529; Kessell, *Kiva*, 260.
96. Vargas, *Royal Crown*, 529-530. "Santiago, Santiago" was a Christian battle cry that was adopted from the Spanish medieval period and called on St. James, the patron saint of Spain, to close off the country from all foreign invaders.
97. Ibid., 529-536; Kessell, *Kiva*, 260-262; Jones, *Pueblo Warriors*, 47-48.
98. Vargas, *Royal Crown*, 555.
99. Jones, *Pueblo Warriors*, 48.
100. Kessell, *Kiva*, 262-263.
101. Ibid., 262-266; Levine, *Our Prayer*, 23.
102. Jones, *Pueblo Warriors*, 48-50; Kessell, *Kiva*, 266-267.
103. Jones, *Pueblo Warriors*, 45.
104. Vargas, *First Expedition*, 176-177.
105. John L. Kessell, "The Ways and Words of the Other: Diego de Vargas and Cultural Brokers in Late Seventeenth-Century New Mexico," in *Between Indian and White Worlds: Cultural Brokers*, ed. Margaret Connell Szasz (Norman: University of Oklahoma Press, 1994), 25-34; Kessell, *Kiva*, 266; Jones, *Pueblo Warriors*, 39-47.
106. Kessell, *Kiva*, 270; Jones, *Pueblo Warriors*, 50;. Kessell, "Ways and Words," 37-39.
107. Jones, *Pueblo Warriors*, 50-53.
108. Bannon, *Spanish Borderlands*, 90.
109. Kessell, *Kiva*, 288-289; Kessell, "Ways and Words," 39-41.
110. Kessell, *Kiva*, 289-293; Don Diego de Vargas, *Blood on the Boulders: The Journals of Don Diego de Vargas, 1692–1694*, ed. John L. Kessell, et al. (Albuquerque: University of New Mexico Press, 1998), 677, 748-749, 809; Kessell, "Ways and Words," 39-41; Barrett, *Conquest*, 108; Jones, *Pueblo Warriors*, 59.
111. Jones, *Pueblo Warriors*, 58-59.
112. Kessell, *Kiva*, 270; Jones, *Pueblo Warriors*, 50; Kessell, "Ways and Words," 37-39.
113. Joseph P. Sanchez, "Pecos in the Eighteenth Century," in *Pecos: Gateway to Pueblos and*

Plains: The Anthology, ed. John V. Bezy and Joseph P. Sanchez (Tucson, AZ: Southwest Parks and Monuments Association, 1988), 71-73; Weber, *Spanish Frontier*, 141; Kessell, "Ways and Words," 41-43; Kessell, *Kiva*, 316-319.
114. Don Diego de Vargas, *The Disturbances Cease: The Journals of Don Diego de Vargas, 1697–1700*, ed. John L. Kessell et. al. (Albuquerque: University of New Mexico Press, 2000), 285-287; Josephy, *Patriot Chiefs*, 93-94; Jones, *Pueblo Warriors*, 65-67; Weber, *Spanish Frontier*, 141; Bannon, *Spanish Borderlands*, 168-171; Sanchez, "Pecos," 73.

CHAPTER 5. SETTLING NEW YORK'S FRONTIER

1.. Charles T. Gehring, "The Dutch among the People of the Long River," in *Annals of New Netherland* (2001): 5-7, accessed April 11, 2020, https://www.newnetherlandinstitute.org/files/8015/3816/0796/2001.pdf.
2. Robert Juet, "From 'The Third Voyage of Master Henry Hudson,' By Robert Juet, 1610," in Jameson, *NNN*, 21.
3. Ibid., 7.
4. De Laet, "From the 'New World,'" in Jameson, *NNN*, 38, 49; Van Cleaf Bachman, *Peltries or Plantations: The Economic Policies of the Dutch West India Company in New Netherland, 1623–1639* (Baltimore: Johns Hopkins University Press, 1969), 3; Emanuel van Meteren, "On Hudson's Voyage, 1610," in Jameson, *NNN*, 6-7.
5. Paul A. Otto, "New Netherland Frontier: Europeans and Native Americans along the Lower Hudson River, 1524–1664" (PhD diss., Indiana University, 1995), 85; John Heckewelder, "Indian Tradition of the First Arrival of the Dutch at Manhattan Island, Now New York," in *Collections of the New York Historical Society*, 2nd series (New York: New York Historical Society, 1841), 1:73-74.
6. Adriaen van der Donck, *A Description of New Netherland*, trans. Diederick William Goedhuys (Faerie Glen, South Africa: D. W. Goedhuys, 1992), 97; Isaack de Rasieres, "Letter of Issack de Rasieres to Samuel Blommaert, 1628 (?)," in Jameson, *NNN*, 106.
7. Meteren, "Hudson's Voyage," 6-7.
8. Otto, "New Netherland," 76-78; Bachman, *Peltries*, 3-9.
9. Simon Hart, *The Prehistory of the New Netherland Company: Amsterdam Notarial Records of the First Dutch Voyages to the Hudson* (Amsterdam, Netherlands: City of Amsterdam Press, 1959), 74; Bachman, *Peltries*, 6.
10. Paul R. Huey, "Aspects of Continuity and Change in Colonial Dutch Material Culture at Fort Orange, 1624–1664" (PhD diss., University of Pennsylvania, 1988), 17; Oliver A. Rink, *Holland on the Hudson: An Economic and Social History of Dutch New York* (Ithaca, NY: Cornell University Press, 1986), 34-35.
11. Otto, "New Netherland," 76-77.
12. Jonas Michaelius, "Letter of Reverend Jonas Michaelius, 1628," in Jameson, *NNN*, 128.
13. Otto, "New Netherland," 77.
14. Richter, *Ordeal*, 47.
15. Ibid., 85.
16. Trigger, *Children*, 247-261, 345; George T. Hunt, *Wars of the Iroquois: A Study in Intertribal Trade Relations* (Madison: University of Wisconsin Press, 1960), 24; Arthur James Weise, *The History of the City of Albany, New York: From the Discovery of the Great River in 1524 by Verrazzano, to the Present Time* (Albany: E. H. Bender, 1884), 10-12; Snow, *Iroquois*, 53, 77-82.
17. Thomas J. Condon, *New York Beginnings: The Commercial Origins of New Netherland* (New York: New York University Press, 1968), 30.
18. Rink, *Holland*, 34-35.
19. Snow, *Iroquois*, 80.
20. "General Charter for those who Discover any New Passages, Havens, Countries, or Places, 27th March 1614," in *Documents Relative to the Colonial History of the State of New York*, ed.

E. B. O'Callaghan (Albany: Weed, Parsons, 1856), 1:5 (hereafter *DCHNY*).

21. "Resolution of the States General on the Report of the Discovery of New Netherland, 11th October, 1614," in O'Callaghan, *DCHNY*, 1:10.

22. "General Charter for those who Discover any New Passages, Havens, Countries, or Places, 27th March 1614," in O'Callaghan, *DCHNY*, 1:5; "Grant of Exclusive Trade to New Netherland, 11th October 1614" in O'Callaghan, *DCHNY*, 1:11.

23. Weise, *City of Albany*, 10-14.

24. De Laet, in Jameson, *NNN*, 47-48; Nicolaes van Wassenaer, "From the 'Historish Verhael,' by Nicolaes van Wassenaer, 1624-1630," in Jameson, *NNN*, 68.

25. Shirley W. Dunn, *The Mohicans and Their Land, 1609–1730* (Fleischmanns, NY: Purple Mountain Press, 1994), 81.

26. Michaelius, in Jameson, *NNN*, 130.

27. Huey, "Aspects of Continuity," 34; Dunn, *Mohican*, 76-77.

28. Trigger, *Children*, 247-261, 345; Snow, *Iroquois*, 78-82; Hunt, *Wars*, 24; Weise, *City of Albany*, 10-12; E. B. O'Callaghan, *The Register of New Netherland, 1626–1674* (Albany: J. Munsell, 1865), xi.

29. "Narrative of a Journey into the Mohawk and Oneida Country, 1634–1635," in Jameson, *NNN*, 140; Harmen Meyndertsz van den Bogaert, *A Journey into Mohawk and Oneida Country, 1634–1635: The Journal of Harmen Meyndertsz van den Bogaert*, trans., and ed. Charles T. Gehring and William A. Strana (Syracuse, NY: Syracuse University Press, 1988), 1-4; Snow, *Iroquois*, 80.

30. Dunn, *Mohican*, 82.

31. O'Callaghan, *DCHNY*, 6: 881; Dunn, *Mohican*, 31-32.

32. Richter, *Ordeal*, 76.

33. Jennings, *Ambiguous*, 48; Dunn, *Mohican*, 81.

34. Allen W. Trelease, *Indian Affairs in Colonial New York: The Seventeenth Century* (Port Washington, NY: Kennikat Press, 1971), 33; Dunn, *Mohican*, 79-81.

35. Trigger, *Children*, 346; Trelease, *Indian*, 33.

36. Hart, *Prehistory*, 36-37.

37. Adrian van der Donck, *Description of the New Netherlands*, trans. Jeremiah Johnson (Wisconsin Historical Society Digital Library and Archives, 2003), 206, accessed April 11, 2020, American Journeys Collection, https://americanjourneys.org/aj-096/index.asp,.

38. Hart, *Prehistory*, 32; Dunn, *Mohican*, 68; Bachman, *Peltries*, 94.

39. Wassenaer, in Jameson, *NNN*, 70; A. J. F. van Laer, trans. and ed., "Instructions for Willem Verhulst Director of New Netherland, January 1625," in *Documents Relating to New Netherland, 1624–1626* (San Marino, CA: Henry E. Huntington Library and Art Gallery, 1924), 52-55; Jennings, *Ambiguous*, 48; Trigger, *Children*, 346; Richter, *Ordeal*, 84-85; Rink, *Holland*, 88-89.

40. Huey, "Aspects of Continuity," 16.

41. Paul R. Huey, "The Archeology of Fort Orange and Beverwijck," in *A Beautiful and Fruitful Place: Selected Rensselaerswijk Seminar Papers*, ed. Nancy Zeller (Albany: New Netherland Publishing, 1991), 327 (hereafter *ABFP*).

42. Ibid., 12-17.

43. "Resolution of the States General, on the Colonization of New Netherland," in O'-Callaghan, *DCHNY* 1:22; Condon, *New York*, 30-31.

44. "Charter of the West India Company, June 3, 1621," in *Van Rensselaer Bowier Manuscripts* (hereafter *VRBM*), trans. and ed. A. J. F. van Laer (Albany: University of the State of New York, 1908), 87-89; Condon, *New York*, 31-32; E. B. O'Callaghan, *History of New Netherland; or, New York Under the Dutch* (New York: D. Appleton, 1846), 1:85.

45. "Charter of the West India Company, June 3, 1621," in Laer, *VRBM*, 87-115; O'Callaghan, *History of New Netherland*, 1:91.

46. Bachman, *Peltrie*, 74; Charles T. Gehring, "Privatizing Colonization: The Patroonship of Renselaerswijck," in *Annals of New Netherland* (2000), 9, accessed April 11, 2020, https://www.newnetherlandinstitute.org/files/3713/5067/2997/2000.pdf.
47. Bachman, *Peltries*, 74-77; Condon, *New York*, 87-93.
48. Huey, "Aspects of Continuity," 26; Bachman, *Peltries*, 75.
49. Father Isaac Jogues, "Novum Belgium, 1646," in Jameson, *NNN*, 261; De Laet, in Jameson, *NNN*, 47-48.
50. Huey, "Archeology of Fort Orange," 327.
51. Jennings, *Ambiguous*, 78.
52. Huey, "Aspects of Continuity," 26; Trigger, *Children*, 346-347; Dunn, *Mohican*, 80-81, 84.
53. Laer, *VRBM*, 245.
54. Huey, "Aspects of Continuity," 25.
55. Catelyn Trico, "The First White Women in Albany: Catelyn Trico's Oath of Deposition to William Moores, 17 October 1688," in *Documentary History of the State of New York*, ed. E. B. O'Callaghan (Albany: Weed, Parsons, 1849–1851), 3:51; Dunn, *Mohican*, 88.
56. Wassenaer, in Jameson, *NNN*, 75-76, 78; Huey, "Aspects of Continuity," 27.
57. Jan Folkerts, "Kiliaen van Rensselaer and Agricultural Productivity in His Domain: A New Look at the First Patroon and Rensselaerswijck Before 1664," in Zeller, *ABFP*, 296, accessed April 11, 2020, https://www.newnetherlandinstitute.org/files/9513/5067/3660/9.1.pdf.
58. Samuel de Champlain, The *Works of Samuel de Champlain*, 6 vols., ed. H. P. Biggar (Toronto: Champlain Society, 1922–1936), 5:214-215; Bruce G. Trigger, "The Mohawk-Mahican War, 1624–1628: The Establishment of a Pattern," *Canadian Historical Review* 52 (1971): 279-280.
59. Trigger, "Mohawk-Mahican War," 277-279.
60. Champlain, *Works*, 5:73-80; Trigger, "Mohawk-Mahican War," 279.
61. Bogaert, *Journey*, 22; "Narrative of a Journey," in Jameson, *NNN*, 157.
62. Rasiere, in Jameson, *NNN*, 211; Trigger, *Children*, 463.
63. Condon, *New York*, 102-104; Rasiere, in Jameson, *NNN*, 251.
64. Rasiere, in Jameson, *NNN*, 216-219.
65. Wassenaer, in Jameson, *NNN*, 82n, 82-83; Huey, "Aspects of Continuity," 26; Bachman, *Peltries*, 94; Rasiere, in Jameson, *NNN*, 215.
66. Rasiere, in Jameson, *NNN*, 215.
67. Wasssenaer, 84-85; Trelease, *Indian*, 47-48; Trigger, "Mohawk-Mahican War," 282.
68. Steele, *Warpaths*, 115; Trigger, "Mohawk-Mahican War," 281-282.
69. Bachman, *Peltries*, 94; Wassenaer, in Jameson, *NNN*, 83.
70. Charles T. Gehring, "The Essays of A. J. F. van Laer," in *Annals of New Netherland* (1999), accessed April 11, 2020, https://www.newnetherlandinstitute.org/files/1213/5067/2997/1999.pdf, 10.
71. Rasiere, in Jameson, *NNN*, 207.
72. Wassenaer, in Jameson, *NNN*, 83-84; Gehring, "Essays of van Laer," 10; Folkerts, "Kiliaen," 296.
73. Gehring, "Dutch among the People," 15.
74. Laer, *VRBM*, 235-237; Rasiere, in Jameson, *NNN*, 203; O'Callaghan, *DCHNY*, 1:37-38, 181; Michaelius, in Jameson, *NNN*, 125.
75. Gehring, "Essays of van Laer," 10; Condon, *New York*, 105.
76. Rasiere, in Jameson, *NNN*, 232.
77. Rasiere, in Jameson, *NNN*, 104; Folkerts, "Kiliaen," 296.
78. Rasiere, in Jameson, *NNN*, 235-236.
79. O'Callaghan, *DCHNY*, 1:107.
80. Bachman, *Peltries*, 94.
81. Folkerts, "Kiliaen," 296; Condon, *New York*, 114-115; Bachman, *Peltries*, 96-99.

82. Michaelius, in Jameson, *NNN*, 127.
83. S.G. Nissenson, *The Patroon's Domain* (New York: Octagon, 1973), 13-15.
84. Laer, *VRBM*, 248.
85. Bachman, *Peltries*, 94.
86. Gehring, "Essays of van Laer," 1.
87. Gehring, "Dutch among the People," 15.
88. Laer, *VRBM*, 236.
89. Ibid., 212.
90. O'Callaghan, *DCHNY*, 1:415.
91. Snow, *Iroquois*, 88, 96-100; William A. Strana, "Seventeenth Century Dutch-Indian Trade: A Perspective from Iroquoia," in Zeller, *ABFP*, 246-247; Hunt, *Wars*, 23-37.
92. O'Callaghan, *DCHNY*, 13:175.
93. O'Callaghan, *DCHNY*, 13:205.
94. Trelease, *Indian*, 138.
95. Martin Kregier, "Journal of the Second Esopus War, 1663," in O'Callaghan, *Documentary History*, 4:42.
96. O'Callaghan, *DCHNY*, 13:49-50.
97. O'Callaghan, *DCHNY*, 13:18-19, 149-150, 179-184, 191-192; David de Vries, in Jameson, *NNN*, 217, 225-228; Megapolensis, in Jameson, *NNN*, 172; Trelease, *Indian*, 126-127, 153-154.
98. Megapolensis, in Jameson, *NNN*, 175; Laer, *VRBM*, 62, 72, 243, 266, 270, 304.
99. O'Callaghan, *DCHNY*, 1:150; Snow, *Iroquois*, 113.
100. *VRBM*, 302-304, 330; O'Callaghan, *DCHNY*, 13:109; A. J. F. van Laer, *Minutes of the Court of Fort Orange and Beverwyck, 1652-1656*, 2 vols. (Albany: University of the State of New York, 1920), 1:170-171, 175; Jennings, *Ambiguous*, 50, 71-72.
101. *VRBM*, 426, 565-566.
102. O'Callaghan, *DCHNY*, 13:35-36
103. Van Laer, *Minutes*, 175.
104. Jennings, *Ambiguous*, 80-83.
105. Trelease, *Indian*, 102.
106. Jennings, *Ambiguous*, 127-136.
107. Steele, *Warpaths*, 115.

CHAPTER 6. THE EMERGENCE OF PITTSBURGH

1. Marquis de la Jonquiere, "Instructions to be given to Marquis Dequence, April 1752," in O'Callaghan, *DCHNY*, 10:239-243.
2. "A country between" is from a speech the Half King delivered to the French commander at Fort Venango, in George Washington, *The Journal of Major George Washington*, ed. J. Christian Bay (Iowa: Torch, 1955), 7 (hereafter *JMGW*).
3. James Axtell, *The Invasion Within: The Contest of Cultures in Colonial North America* (New York: Oxford University Press, 1985), 3.
4. White, *Middle Ground*, 223.
5. Jennings, *Ambiguous*, 11, 199, 247.
6. "A Council held at Philadelphia, 18 June 1744," in *Minuetes of the Provincial Council of Pennsylvania, from the Organization to the Termination of the Proprietary Government*, ed. Samuel Hazard (Philadelphia: Joseph Severns, 1860), 4:697-736 (hereafter *MPC*); White, 235-6.
7. George P. Donehoo, *Indian Villages and Place Names in Pennsylvania* (Harrisburg, PA: Telegraph Press, 1928), 93; Witham Marshe, *Lancaster in 1744: Journal of the Treaty at Lancaster in 1744 with the Six Nations* (Lancaster, PA: New Era Steam and Book Print, 1884), 22, also at https://www.loc.gov/item/08009826/.

8. On the European continent, King George's War was known as the War of Austrian Succession. *American Military History*, Army Historical Series (Washington, DC: Government Printing Office, 1969), 31.
9. "A Council held at Philadelphia, 25 April 1745," in Hazard, *MPC*, 4:757-758; O'Callaghan, *DCHNY*, 10: 156, 1092; Michael N. McConnell, *A Country Between: The Upper Ohio Valley and Its Peoples, 1724-1774* (Lincoln: University of Nebraska Press, 1992), 65; White, 189-193.
10. "Memorandum to the Indians of Shamokin, 9 July 1747," in Hazard, *MPC*, 5:86-87.
11. "Council at Philadelphia, 13 November 1747," in Hazard, *MPC*, 5:145-151.
12. "Proclamation in Council at Philadelphia, 18 February 1747," in Hazard, *MPC*, 5:194. In the text of the conference, Logstown is not mentioned. However, one of the Indian delegates states that "[the] Indians on the Ohio had concluded to kindle a fire in their town, and had invited all the Indians to a considerable distance round about them to come to their Fire in the Spring, and that they had consented to it." But in his journal of 1748, Weiser noted that "the ensuring Council must be held at Logs Town, they had order'd it so last Spring." With this entry, it is confirmed that the delegation consisted of at least some influential members of the Logstonian council. Conrad Weiser, "The Journal of Conrad Weiser," in Hazard, *MPC*, 5:349.
13. "Journal of Conrad Weiser, 1748," in Hazard, *MPC*, 5:350. White, *Middle Ground*, 235-237; Sipe, *Indian Chiefs*, 106, 137-138.
14. Paul A. Wallace, *Conrad Weiser: Friend of Colonist and Mohawk* (Philadelphia: Oxford University Press, 1945), 262.
15. Hazard, *MPC*, 5:212-213.
16. *Pennsylvania Archives*, 1st ser., ed. Samuel Hazard (Philadelphia: Joseph Severns, 1852), 1:742 (hereafter *PA*).
17. "Letter from Richard Peters to Conrad Weiser, 31 March 1748," in Hazard, *MPC*, 5:214.
18. Ibid., 287-289.
19. "Minutes of the Lancaster Treaty, 20 July 1748," in Hazard, *MPC*, 5:308; R. David Edmunds, *American Indian Leaders: Studies in Diversity* (Lincoln: University of Nebraska Press, 1980), 6-7.
20. Ibid., 289.
21. Sipe, *Indian Chiefs*, 106.
22. White, *Middle Ground*, 227-235.
23. "Minutes of the Lancaster Treaty, July 1748," in Hazard, *MPC*, 5:307-310.
24. Sipe, *Indian Chiefs*, 118. For minutes of the Lancaster Treaty of 1748 see Hazard, *MPC*, 5:307-318.
25. "Journal of Conrad Weiser, 1748," in Hazard, *MPC*, 5:304; Reuben Gold Thwaites, *Early Western Travels, 1748–1846* (Cleveland: Arthur Clark, 1904), 1:20.
26. Hazard, *MPC*, 5:329-332. Establishment of a council fire was a recognition by the English colonies that they viewed the Ohio Indians as a separate autonomous political entity that was not under the domain or control of the Iroquois Confederacy.
27. McConnell, *Country Between*, 75-77.
28. Celoron, *Expedition*, 13.
29. Father Bonnecamps, "Account of the Voyage on the Beautiful River Made in 1749," in *The Jesuit Relations and Allied Documents*, ed. Reuben Gold Thwaites (Cleveland: Burrows Brothers, 1900), 69:175-177.
30. Celoron, 32, 35-36.
31. "Conference of Marquis de la Jonquiere with the Cayugas, May 15, 1750," in O'Callaghan, *DCHNY*, 10:208, 243-244.
32. Ibid., 242-243.
33. "Extract of a letter from Colonel Johnson to Governor Clinton, August 18, 1750," in O'-Callaghan, *DCHNY*, 6:289. George Croghan, "A Selection of Letters and Journals Relating to

Tours Into the Western Country," in *Early Western Travels, 1748–1846*, ed. Reuben Gold Thwaites (Lewisburg, PA: Wennawoods Publishing, 1998), 1:53-54.
34. "Letter from George Croghan to the Governor of Pennsylvania, Logstown, 16 December 1750," in Hazard, *MPC*, 5:496-498.
35. Ibid., 498.
36. Joseph S. Walton, *Conrad Weiser and the Indian Policy of Colonial Pennsylvania* (Philadelphia: George W. Jacobs, 1900), 195.
37. "Instructions given Mr. Christopher Gist by the Committee of the Ohio Company, September 11, 1750," in Gist, *Journals*, 31.
38. "A Message from Governor Hamilton to the Assembly, May 7, 1751," in Hazard, *MPC*, 5:525.
39. George Croghan, "An Account of the Proceedings of George Croghan, Esquire, and Mr. Andrew Montour at Ohio, 1751," in *Minuetes of the Provincial Council of Pennsylvania, from the Organization to the Termination of the Proprietary Government* (Harrisburg: Theo. Fenn, 1851) 5:530-531, accessed April 21, 2020, https://babel.hathitrust.org/cgi/pt?id=wu.8906 6118753 &view=1up&seq=562.
40. Gist, *Journals*, 163.
41. "An Account of the Proceedings of George Croghan, Esquire, and Mr. Andrew Montour at Ohio, May 21, 1751," in Hazard, *MPC*, 5:538. For general information on the role of the sachem Beaver, also known as King Beaver, see Sipe, *Indian Chiefs*, 305-309.
42. White, *Middle Ground*, 188.
43. "Letter from Governor Dinwiddie to Joshua Fry, 12 December 1751," in *The Official Records of Robert Dinwiddie*, ed. R.A. Brock (Richmond: Virginia Historical Society, 1883), 1:8 (hereafter *ORRD*).
44. "Instructions Given to Christopher Gist, April 28, 1752," in Mercer, *Papers*, 52-54. See also "The Treaty of Logg's Town, 1752. Commission, Instructions, &c., Journal of Virginia Commissioners, and Text of Treaty," accessed April 12, 2020, https://www.jstor.org/stable/4242735?seq=1#metadata_info_tab_contents.
45. "Instructions Given to Mr. Christopher Gist by the Committee of the Ohio Company, July 16, 1751," in Gist, *Journals*, 67-68.
46. "A Treaty Held at the Town of Lancaster . . . With the Indians of the Six Nations, June 1744," in Hazard, *MPC*, 4:698-736.
47. Mary A. Druke, "Iroquois Treaties: Common Forms, Varying Interpretations," in *The History and Culture of Iroquois Diplomacy*, ed. Francis Jennings, et al. (New York: Syracuse University Press, 1985), 85-98.
48. "Extracts from the Treaty with the Indians at Loggs Town in the year 1752," in Mercer, *Papers*, 57.
49. Ibid., 54-61.
50. "A Journal of Christopher Gist's Journey," in Mercer, *Papers*, 135.
51. Ibid., 136; James H. Merrell, *Into the American Woods: Negotiators on the Pennsylvania Frontier* (New York: W.W. Norton, 1999), 208-209.
52. Ibid., 137-138.
53. "Extract of a letter from M. Duquesne to M. de Machault, October 28, 1754," in O'-Callaghan, *DCHNY*, 10:264.
54. "Extract of a letter from Francois Bigot to the Minister, October 26, 1752," in *Wilderness Chronicles of Northwestern Pennsylvania*, ed. S. K. Stevens and Donald H. Kent (Harrisburg, PA: Commonwealth of Pennsylvania, Dept. of Public Instruction, Pennsylvania Historical Commission, 1941), 40, found in Donald H. Hunt, *The French Invasion of Western Pennsylvania, 1753* (Harrisburg, PA: Pennsylvania Historical and Museum Commission, 1954), 12.
55. Ibid.

56. "Minute of Instructions to be given to M. Duquesne, April 1752," in O'Callaghan, *DCHNY*, 10:242-245.
57. Carl Waldman, *Atlas of the North American Indian* (New York: Facts on File, 1985), 102.
58. Hunt, *French Invasion*, 43.
59. "Message of Governor Dinwiddie to the House of Burgesses, November 1, 1753," in *ORRD*, 1:39-40.
60. "Letter to the Honorable Robert Dinwiddie from William Trent, 17 November 1753," in *History of Colonel Henry Bouquet and the Western Frontiers of Pennsylvania, 1747–1764*, ed. Mary Carson Darlington (Privately published, 1920), 17.
61. The Logstonian leaders consisted of Tanacharison and Scarouady, the Mingo sachems; Shingas and King Beaver, the Delaware sachems; Neucheconneh, the Shawnee sachem; The Turtle, the Twightwee sachem; and the Wyandot Chief, the Wyandot sachem. William Trent's journal, in Carson, *Bouquet*, 27.
62. "Account of William Trent's meeting with the Ohio Indians, December 7 to December 24, 1753," in Carson, *Bouquet*, 27-40.
63. Randolph C. Downes, *Council Fires of the Upper Ohio* (Pittsburgh: University of Pittsburgh Press, 1940), 62.
64. "Copy of his Honour the Governor's Letter to the Commandant of the French Forces on the Ohio, sent by Major Washington" in *JMGW*, 25.
65. Speech related to George Washington by Tanacharison, in ibid., 7.
66. Ibid., 8.
67. Ibid., 12.
68. "Governor Dinwiddie to the Right Honorable Lord Fairfax, January, 1754," in *ORRD*, 48-49; see also, Hazard, *MPC*, 5:689; George Washington, *The Writings of George Washington, 1745–1756*, ed. John C. Fitzpatrick (Washington, DC: Government Printing Office, 1931), 1:37-38 (hereafter *WGW*); Downes, *Council Fires*, 64.
69. Edmunds, *American Indian*, 17.
70. Downes, *Council Fires*, 65.
71. Ibid., 731-735.
72. "George Croghan's Journal, 1754," in Hazard, *MPC*, 5:734.
73. For quote and explanation of Captain Trent's actions see E. Ward's Deposition, 13 June 1756, in Carson, *History of Colonel Henry Bouquet*, 42.
74. Ibid., 44.
75. "Detail of Indian Affairs, 1752-54," in Hazard, *PA*, 2:237.
76. White, *Middle Ground*, 241; see also *ORRD*, 148n.
77. Fitzpatrick, *WGW*, 1:63-67.
78. Frank W. Brecher, *Losing a Continent: France's North American Policy, 1753–1763* (Westport, CT: Greenwood, 1998), 47-64.
79. "Journal of Conrad Weiser at Aucquick, August and September 1754," in Hazard, *MPC*, 6:158.
80. Ibid., 154.
81. "A Council held at Carlisle, 16 January 1756," in ibid., 7:5.
82. Charles Frederick Post, "Two journals of Western Tours, October 25, 1758–January 10, 1759," in Thwaites, *Early Western Travels*, 1:281; Hazard, *MPC*, 8:469-491; Charles A. Hanna, *The Wilderness Trail: The Ventures and Adventures of the Pennsylvania Traders on the Allegheny Path* (New York and London: G. P. Putnam's Sons, Knickerbocker Press, 1911), 1:377.
83. Donehoo, *Indian Villages*, 96.
84. "Reverend Claude Godfroy Cocquard to his Brother, March 1757," in ibid., 528.
85. "Letter from M. de Vaudreuil to M. de Moras, Montreal, 12 July 1757," in O'Callaghan, *DCHNY*, 10:583.
86. "Letter from M. de Vaudreuil to M. de Machault, Montreal, 24 July 1755," in ibid., 307, and Abstract of Despatches received from Canada, 4 June 1756, in ibid., 408.

87. "Letter from M. de Vaudreuil to M. de Moras, Montreal, 12 July 1757," in ibid., 583.
88. "Letter from M. Duquesne to M. de Vaudreuil, Quebec, 6 July 1755," in ibid., 300.
89. White, *Middle Ground*, 250.
90. Charles de Raymonds, *On the Eave of the Conquest: The Chevalier De Raymonds Critique of New France in 1754*, ed. and trans. Joseph L. Peyser (East Lansing: Michigan State University Press, 1997), 91.
91. Charles W. Dahlinger, *The Marquis Duquesne Sieur de Menneville: Founder of the City of Pittsburgh* (Pittsburgh: Historical Society of Western Pennsylvania, 1932), 60. For measurement of *minot* see footnotes in John Richardson, "Deed of Concession, 28 December 1822," in "Seigneurie de Beauharnois," transcribed by Burton Lang, accessed April 12, 2020, http://www.rootsweb.com/~qcchatea/sarault/sample.htm.
92. "Letter from M. Duquesne to M. de Vaudreuil, Quebec, 6 July 1755," in O'Callaghan, *DCHNY*, 10:300.
93. "Letter from La Chauvignerie to Jacques Legardeur De Saint-Pierre, Chiningué, 10 February 1754," in Jacques de Saint-Pierre, *Jacques Legardeur De Saint-Pierre: Officer, Gentleman, Entrepreneur*, ed. and trans. Joseph L. Peyser (East Lansing: Michigan State University Press, 1996), 215.
94. "Letter from Joncaire to Jacques Legardeur De Saint-Pierre, Chiningué, 20 February 1754," in ibid., 218.
95. William A. Hunter, *Forts on the Pennsylvania Frontier, 1753–1758* (Harrisburg, PA: Pennsylvania Historical and Museum Commission, 1960), 106-115.
96. Thomas A. Lewis, *For King and Country: George Washington, the Early Years* (New York: John Wiley & Sons, 1993), 176.
97. For "yelping and screaming" and an account of Braddock's defeat see Fred Anderson, *Crucible of War: The Seven Years' War and the Fate of Empire in British North America, 1754–1766* (New York: Alfred A. Knopf, 2000), 102; for "coming very swift" see Thomas Gist, "Thomas Gist's Indian Captivity," ed. Howard H. Peckham, *Pennsylvania Magazine of History and Biography* 80, no. 3 (July 1956): 285-311, accessed April 20, 2020, https://eps.cc.ysu.edu:2251/stable/pdf/20088873.pdf?ab_segments=0%252Fbasic_SYC-5152%252Fcontrol&refreqid=excelsior%3A151f83c851f996e4f77e2f867cecae6f; for "the small British parties" see Lewis, *King*, 182.
98. Fitzpatrick, *WGW*, 151.
99. O'Callaghan, *DCHNY*, 10:390.
100. "An Account of the Battle of the Monongahela, 1755, 1756," in ibid., 396; Timothy J. Todish, *America's First First World War* (Grand Rapids, MI: Suagothel Productions, 1982), 7; Lewis, *King*,188; Fitzpatrick, *WGW*, 150-152.
101. "Abstract of Occurrences in Canada, 6 July 1755," in O'Callaghan, *DCHNY*, 10:300.
102. Anderson, *Crucible*, 99-107. For a brief explanation of the historical interpretations of Braddock's defeat see Louis M. Waddell and Bruce D. Bomberger, *The French and Indian War in Pennsylvania, 1753–1754: Fortification and Struggle during the War for Empire* (Harrisburg, PA: Pennsylvania Historical and Museum Commission, 1996), 14-15.
103. Lewis, *King*, 177.
104. O'Callaghan, *DCHNY*, 10:408, 469, 479-480, 528.
105. "Letter from M. de Vaudreuil to M. de Machault, Montreal, 8 August, 1756," in O'-Callaghan, *DCHNY*, 10:437, 438.
106. "Letter from M. de Vaudreuil to M. de Machault, Montreal, 10 July, 1755," in O'Callaghan, *DCHNY*, 10:305.
107. Lewis, *King*, 176; Todish, *America's*, 6.
108. For instances of Ohio Indian informational support at Fort Duquesne see George T. Fleming, *History of Pittsburgh and Environs* (New York: American Historical Society, 1922); Charles M. Stotz, *Outposts of the War for Empire* (Pittsburgh: University of Pittsburgh Press,

1985); Frank C. Harper, *Pittsburgh: Forge of the Universe* (New York: Comet Press Books, 1957); Walter O'Meara, *Guns at the Forks* (Englewood Cliffs, NJ: Prentice-Hall, 1965); C. Hale Sipe, *Fort Ligonier and Its Times* (Harrisburg, PA: Telegraph Press, 1932).

109. "Letter from M. de Montcalm to M. de Paulmy, Montreal, 10 April, 1758," in O'Callaghan, *DCHNY*, 10:693.

110. Post, "Two journals," in Thwaites, *Early Western Travels*, 1:281.

111. Louis Antoine de Bougainville, *Adventures in the Wilderness: The American Journals of Louis Antoine de Bougainville, 1756–1760*, ed. and trans. Edward P. Hamilton (Norman: University of Oklahoma Press, 1964), 294-295.

112. "Letter from M. de Bougainville to M. de Cremille, Quebec, 8 November, 1758," in O'-Callaghan, *DCHNY*, 10:886.

113. Bougainville, *Adventures*, 294.

114. "Letter from M. de Montcalm to M. de Cremille, Montreal, 12 April, 1759," in O'-Callaghan, *DCHNY*, 10:958.

115. Albert T. Volwiler, *George Croghan and the Westward Movement, 1741–1782* (Cleveland: Arthur H. Clark, 1926), 139.

116. Lewis, *King*, 271.

117. Harper, *Pittsburgh*, 3-4; O'Meara, *Guns*, 224.

118. McConnell, *Country Between*, 129-132.

119. "Examination of a Delaware Prisoner, 1757," in Hazard, *PA*, 3:147-148.

120. John Forbes, *Writings of General John Forbes*, ed. Alfred Proctor James (Menasha, WI: Collegiate Press, 1938), 253 (hereafter *WGJF*).

121. For Shingas's role in French and Indian attacks see "Intelligence from Benjamin Chambers to the Pennsylvania Assembly, 2 November 1755," in Hazard, *MPC*, 6:675-678; Sipe, *Indian Chiefs*, 289-295, 306.

122. Sipe, *Indian Chiefs*, 295-297, 306.

123. Forbes, *WGJF*, 116. See also "Letter from Forbes to Bouquet, 16 June 1758," in Bouquet, *PHB*, 2:104; McConnell, *Country Between*, 128.

124. Charles Frederick Post, "Two Journals of Western Tours, October 25, 1758–January 10, 1759," in *Early Western Travels*, ed. Reuben Gold Thwaites (Lewisburg, PA: Wennawoods Publishing, 1998), 1:193-223.

125. "Letter from Bouquet to Anne Willing, 28 November 1758," in Bouquet, *PHB*, 2:608.

126. McConnell, *Country Between*, 139.

127. "Letter from Bouquet to the Duke of Portland, Fort DuQuesne, 3 December 1758," in Bouquet, *PHB*, 2:620.

128. "Croghan to Johnson, January 25, 1760," in Sir William Johnson, *The Papers of Sir William Johnson*, ed. James Sullivan (Albany: University of the State of New York, 1921-1965), 10:134. See also, White, *Middle Ground*, 257

129. Forbes, *WGJF*, 265; see also "Letter from Forbes to Governor Denny," Hazard, *MPC*, 8:232; Fleming, *History*, 413-415; Harper, *Pittsburgh*, 86.

130. Forbes, *WGJF*, 265.

131. "Letter from Bouquet to Amherst, 13 March 1759," in Bouquet, *PHB*, 3:193.

132. Ibid., 275, 289-290.

133. "A Letter to Governor Denny from Colonel Mercer, Pittsburgh, 8 January, 1759," in Hazard, *MPC*, 8:292-293. For Mercer's order to abandon see "Letter from Bouquet to Amherst, 13 March 1759," in Bouquet, *PHB*, 3:193.

134. McConnell, *Country Between*, 139; White, *Middle Ground*, 255-256; Fleming, *History*, 449-450.

135. Volwiler, 144.

136. "Letter from Bouquet to Mercer, 8 May 1759," in Bouquet, *PHB*, 3:273.

137. "Minutes of Conferences held at Pittsburgh with the Indians," in Hazard, *MPC*, 8:293-297.

138. White, *Middle Ground,* 252.
139. Post, "Journal of July 15-September 22, 1758," in Thwaites, *Early Western Travels,* 1:240.
140. "Letter to Governor Denny from Colonel Mercer, Pittsburgh, 8 January, 1759, in Hazard, *MPC,* 8:292; Neville B. Craig, ed. *The Olden Time* (Pittsburgh: Dumars, 1846), 1:193-195; White, *Middle Ground,* 255; Fleming, *History,* 451-452.
141. Post, "Journal of July 15-September 22, 1758," in Thwaites, *Early Western Travels,* 1:274, 278, 283-285; Merrell, *Into,* 209-212.
142. Post, "Journal of July 15-September 22, 1758," in Thwaites, *Early Western Travels,* 1:278.
143. For quote see. Post, "Journal of July 15-September 22, 1758," in Thwaites, *Early Western Travels,* 1:278; "Minutes of Conferences held at Pittsburgh with the Indians," in Hazard, *MPC,* 8:296.
144. "Minutes of Conferences held at Pittsburgh, July, 1759," in Hazard, *MPC,* 8:390.
145. Ibid., 382-393.
146. Ibid., 390, 392.
147. "Minutes of Conference Held by Croghan, 7 August 1759," in Bouquet, *PHB,* 3:510; McConnell, *Country Between,* 143.
148. "Letter from Mercer to Bouquet, Pittsburgh, 22 July 1759," in Bouquet, *PHB,* 3:437.
149. White, *Middle Ground,* 255.
150. "Another Letter to Governor Denny from Colonel Mercer, 12 August, 1759," in Hazard, *MPC,* 8:394.
151. "General Stanwix's Letter to Governor Denny, 18 October, 1759," in ibid., 427.
152. "At a Conference by The Honourable Brigadier General Moncton with the Western Nation of Indians, Pittsburgh, 12 August 1760," in Hazard, *PA,* 3:744-745. The Ohio Indian population consisted of 362 warriors, 262 women, and 295 children from the Mingo, Twightwee, Lenape, Ottawa, Shawnee, Wyandot, and Potawatomis. Of these nations, the Lenape made up the largest contingent with 561: 202 warriors, 168 women, and 191 children.
153. Ibid., 744-752.
154. "Letter from Bouquet to Mercer, Philadelphia, 1 June 1759," in Bouquet, *PHB,* 3:358.
155. "Certificate for Callender and Hughes, 1 May 1760," in ibid., 4:546. See also, George Croghan, "George Croghan's Journal, April 3, 1759 to April 30, 1763," in *Pennsylvania Magazine of History and Biography* 71 (1947): 325-326.
156. Bouquet, *PHB,* 5:15-16, 70-71, 89, 266-267, 443, 546-547.
157. "Letter from Burd to Mercer, Camp at Monongahela, 28 October, 1759," in ibid., 4:268-269. See also Sipe, *Fort Ligonier,* 36, 130-134.
158. James Kenny, "Journal of James Kenny, 1759," in *Pen Pictures of Early Western Pennsylvania,* ed. John W. Harpster (Pittsburgh: University of Pittsburgh Press, 1938), 81. See also James Kenny, "Journal to ye Westward, 1758–1759," ed. John W. Jordan, *Pennsylvania Magazine of History and Biography* 37, no. 4 (1913): 420.
159. "Letter from Bouquet to Monckton, Fort Littleton, 7 June 1760," in Bouquet, *PHB,* 4:585. For Monckton's offer see ibid., 578.
160. "Letter from Mercer to Bouquet, Pittsburgh, 11 July 1759," in ibid., 400; McConnell, *Country Between,* 153-157.
161. "Letter from Bouquet to Croghan, Lancaster, 13 July 1759," in *PHB,* 4:409.
162. "Letter from Mercer to Bouquet, Pittsburgh, 16 July 1759," in ibid., 420.
163. "Letter from Bouquet to Croghan, Fort Bedford, 10 August 1759," in ibid., 3:531.
164. "General Stanwix's Letter to Governor Denny, Pittsburgh, October 18, 1759," in Hazard, *MPC,* 8:427.
165. "Letter from Bouquet to the Duke of Portland, Fort DuQuesne, 3 December 1758," in Bouquet, *PHB,* 2:620.
166. For garrison size see Forbes, *WGJF,* 265; "Letter from Forbes to Governor Denny," Hazard, *MPC,* 8:232; Fleming, *History,* 413-415; and Harper, *Pittsburgh,* 86. For garrison size due

to supply problems see Bouquet, *PHB*, 2:610. For French threat see ibid., 292; Donehoo, *Indian Villages*, 244.
167. "Letter from Bouquet to Forbes, Bedford, 13 January 1759," in Bouquet, *PHB*, 3:40, 43.
168. "Letter from Stanwix to Bouquet, Pittsburgh, 8 September 1759," in ibid., 4:58.
169. "Letter from Bouquet to Forbes, Bedford, 15 January 1759," in ibid., 50, 53.
170. "Letter from Bouquet to Mercer, Fort Ligonier, 26 December, 1758" in ibid., 2:642.
171. McConnell, *Country Between*, 154.
172. Bouquet, *PHB*, 4:15-16, 70-71, 89, 266-267.
173. "Letter from Bouquet to Monckton, Fort Littleton, 7 June 1760," in Bouquet, *PHB*, 4:585.
174. "Letter from Bouquet to Croghan, Fort Bedford, 10 August 1759," in ibid., 3:531.
175. "Letter from Bouquet to Pemberton, Fort Bedford, 1 September 1759," in ibid., 4:7. See also "Letter from Tulleken to Bouquet, Fort Pitt, 2 April, 1760," in ibid., 506.
176. James Kenny, "Journal of James Kenny, 1761-63," ed. John W. Jordan, *Pennsylvania Magazine of History and Biography* 37, no. 1 (1913): 17, accessed April 22, 2020, https://ia801700.us.archive.org/11/items/jstor-20085624/20085624.pdf.
177. For 51 percent of the foodstuffs from venison see "Extract from Hutchins to Hoops, Lancaster, 23 January 1759," in Bouquet, *PHB*, 3:79. For sale of goods for black wampum see "Letter from Bouquet to Forbes, Bedford, 13 January 1759," in ibid., 44. For trade goods see "List of Indian Goods, 13 January 1759," in ibid., 47; McConnell, *Country Between*, 154-155.
178. For harvest of Logstown cornfield see "Letter from Mercer to Bouquet, Pittsburgh, 19 December 1758," in *PHB*, 2:635-636. For purchase of corn see ibid., 642.
179. Kenny, "Journal of James Kenny, 1761-63," 94.
180. "Letter from Meyer to Bouquet, 22 October, 1761," in ibid., 5:833.
181. "Letter from Forbes to Amherst, Philadelphia, January 26, 1759," in *WGJF*, 285. By March 17, 1759, Fort Pitt's garrison comprised 459 men: 10 officers, 18 noncommissioned officers, 346 rank and file, 3 drummers, 79 sick, 3 unaccounted. Of these, 320 were provincial troops. For force composition see Fleming, *History*, 452, and Craig, *Olden Time*, 1:195.
182. "Letter from Mercer to Bouquet, Pittsburgh, 1 August 1759," *PHB*, 3:478.
183. Stotz, 131.
184. "Extract of a Letter from Pittsburgh, September 24, 1759," in Craig, *Olden Time*, 197-198.
185. "Fort at Pittsburgh, March 21, 1760," in ibid., 198.
186. Stotz, *Outposts*, 131. See also Harper, *Pittsburgh*, 88; O'Meara, *Guns*, 227; Lois Mulkearn and Edwin V. Pugh, *The Traveler's Guide to Historic Western Pennsylvania* (Pittsburgh: University of Pittsburgh Press, 1954), 4.
187. "Letter from Bouquet to Hugh Mercer, Fort Ligonier, 26 December, 1758," in *PHB*, 2:642-643; "Extract of a Letter From Colonel Hugh Mercer, Pittsburgh January 8, 1759," in *Olden Time*, 194; Hunter *Forts*, 94-97; Fleming, *History*, 451, 452.
188. "Intelligence received the 17th of March, 1759, at Pittsburgh," in Hazard, *MPC*, 8:311-313; "Mercer: Indian Intelligence, 17 March, at Pittsburgh, 1759," *PHB*, 3:204; Hunter, *Forts*, 95.
189. "Mercer: Indian Intelligence, April, at Pittsburgh, 1759," in *PHB*, 3:278-280; "Colonel Mercer, Pittsburgh, 25 April 1759," in Hazard, *PA*, 3:624-626.
190. "Letter from Stanwix to Mercer, Fort Bedford, 2 August 1759," in *PHB*, 3:484-486.
191. "Intelligence received from Pittsburgh, 16 August 1759," in Hazard, *MPC*, 8:38; Donehoo, *Indian Villages*, 244.
192. Croghan, "George Croghan's Journal," 317-321.
193. Ibid., 320.
194. Kenny, "Journal of James Kenny," 10; McConnell, *Country Between*, 156; "Letter from Bouquet to Monckton, Presqu'Isle, 11 August 1760," in *PHB*, 4:687.
195. Croghan, "George Croghan's Journal," 323-324.

196. Darlington, *History of Colonel Henry Bouquet*, 107.
197. Stotz, *Outposts*, 127-136.
198. Harper, *Pittsburgh*, 88.
199. O'Meara, *Guns*, 213-222; Stotz, *Outposts*, 127.
200. O'Meara, *Guns*, 218-219.

CHAPTER 7. THE BUILDING OF ASTORIA

1. Franchere, *Adventure*, 11-12; Mackie, *Trading*, 14.
2. Alexander Ross, *The Fur Hunters of the Far West*, ed. Kenneth A. Spaulding (Norman: University of Oklahoma Press, 1956), 3.
3. James P. Ronda, *Astoria and Empire* (Lincoln: University of Nebraska Press, 1990), 221; William A. Bowen, *The Willamette Valley: Migration and Settlement on the Oregon Frontier* (Seattle: University of Washington Press, 1978), xii.
4. Ronda, *Astoria*, 7.
5. Ross, *Adventures 1*, 73.
6. Ibid., 74.
7. Ross, *Adventures 2*, 69, 70.
8. Stuart, *On the Oregon Trail*, 30-31; Ross, *Adventures 2*, 72.
9. Ross, *Adventures 2*, 73-74.
10. Stuart, *On the Oregon Trail*, 28-29; Ruby and Brown, *Chinook Indians*, 133.
11. Franchere, *Adventure*, 35; Ronda, *Astoria*, 204.
12. Ross, *Adventures 2*, 74-75; David Thompson, *David Thompson's Narrative of his Explorations in Western America, 1784–1812*, ed. J. B. Tyrrell (Toronto: Champlain Society, 1916), 501-502.
13. Ronda, *Astoria*, 209-210; Ross, *Adventures 2*, 70-76.
14. Ross, *Adventures 2*, 75-76.
15. Ronda, *Astoria*, 204.
16. Ibid., 207.
17. Ibid.; Duncan McDougall, "Journal: Commencing Septr. 6th 1810, Ending 18th April 1812," in *Annals of Astoria: The Headquarters Log of the Pacific Fur Company on the Columbia River, 1811–1813*, ed. Robert F. Jones (New York: Fordham University Press, 1999), 6.
18. Ross, *Adventures 2*, 80; Ronda, *Astoria*, 204-206.
19. Stuart, *On the Oregon Trail*, 30; Ronda, *Astoria*, 206.
20. John A. Hussey, *The History of Fort Vancouver and Its Physical Structure* (Tacoma, WA: Washington State Historical Society, 1957), 37.
21. Stuart, *On the Oregon Trail*, 29; Elliot Coues, ed., *New Light on the Early History of the Greater Northwest: The Manuscript Journals of Alexander Henry and of David Thompson* (Minneapolis: Ross and Haines, 1965), 2:875; Ronda, *Astoria*, 213.
22. Franchere, *Adventure*, 64; Ronda, *Astoria*, 208.
23. Franchere, *Adventure*, 73.
24. Ronda, *Astoria*, 208, 221.
25. For description of the *Tonquin*'s destruction see Ross, *Adventures 2*, 159-165; Franchere, *Adventure*, 80-84; for Astor's Russian designs see Ronda, *Astoria*, 71-86; Thompson, 502; for quote see Ross, *Adventures 2*, 81.
26. Franchere, *Voyage*, 87; Ronda, *Astoria*, 204; Ross, *Adventures 2*, 74.
27. Ross, *Adventures 2*, 97; McDougall, "Journal," 21; Ronda, *Astoria*, 220-221.
28. Franchere, *Adventure*, 59.
29. Ronda, *Astoria*, 208.
30. Franchere, *Adventure*, 68; Ronda, *Astoria*, 208.
31. Ross, *Adventures 2*, 187-194; Franchere, *Adventure*, 64-68.
32. Ross, *Adventures 2*, 139.

33. Mackie, *Trading*, 153; John McLoughlin, *Dr. John McLoughlin: Master of Vancouver Father of Oregon*, ed. Nancy Wilson and Bert Webber (Medford, OR: Webb Research Group, 1994), 25; Frederick V. Holman, *Dr. John McLoughlin: The Father of Oregon* (Cleveland: Arthur H. Clark, 1907), 27-29.
34. Ronda, *Astoria*, 221.
35. Ross, *Adventures 2*, 95-96, 118.
36. Stuart, *On the Oregon Trail*, 32.
37. Ross, *Adventures 2*, 77-78.
38. Ruby and Brown, *Chinook Indians*, 133.
39. Ronda, *Astoria*, 222.
40. Ross, *Adventures 2*, 72.
41. Ibid., 78, 90; Franchere, *Adventure*, 47.
42. Stuart, *On the Oregon Trail*, 41.
43. Franchere, *Adventure*, 66; Cecil W. MacKenzie, *Donald MacKenzie: King of the Northwest* (Los Angeles: Ivan Beach Jr., 1937), 46; Ross, *Adventures 2*, 199.
44. Ross, *Adventures 2*, 91-93; Stuart, *On the Oregon Trail*, 35.
45. Lewis and Clark, *Journals*, 281-282, 294-295; Coues, *New Light*, 2:868, 871-875; Ronda, *Astoria*, 227-228.
46. Ronda, *Astoria*, 163-164; James P. Ronda, *Lewis and Clark among the Indians* (Lincoln: University of Nebraska Press, 1984), 64.
47. Ross, *Adventures 2*, 77; Franchere, *Adventure*, 58; Ronda, *Astoria*, 223.
48. Ross, *Adventures 2*, 89.
49. Ross, *Adventures 1*, 78.
50. Ross, *Adventures 2*, 89; Stuart, *On the Oregon Trail*, 28-29; Ruby and Brown, *Chinook Indians*, 133.
51. Ross, *Adventures 2*, 89.
52. Ibid., 90, 91.
53. Ruby and Brown, *Chinook Indians*, 157.
54. Ross, *Adventures 2*, 115-116.
55. Ibid., 80.
56. Ibid., 112-113, 185; Franchere, *Adventure*, 69.
57. Santee, "Comcomly," 275; Ruby and Brown, *Chinook Indians*, 169. "Nor'westers" refers to members of the North West Company.
58. Ruby and Brown, *Chinook Indians*, 143-145.
59. Ruby and Brown, *Chinook Indians*, 109-114, 150; Woodcock, *Peoples*, 7, 44-45.
60. Ronda, *Astoria*, 249.
61. McDougall, "Journal," 14, 21.
62. Ross, *Adventures 2*, 79-80.
63. Franchere, *Voyage*, 48-50; Ross, *Adventures 2*, 80.
64. Franchere, *Voyage*, 70; Ronda, *Astoria*, 202-203.
65. Ross, *Adventures 1*, 169.
66. Ross, *Adventures 2*, 156-165.
67. Ruby and Brown, *Chinook Indians*, 109-122.
68. Ross Cox, *Adventures on the Columbia River* (New York: J&J Harper, 1832), 132-133. This same account is given in Ross, *Adventures 1*, 275-276.
69. Cox, *Adventures*, 132-133.
70. Ronda, *Astoria*, 265-266, 295-297; Ruby and Brown, *Chinook Indians*, 147-150.
71. Ronda, *Astoria*, 290-291; Ruby and Brown, *Chinook Indians*, 147n.
72. For a detailed account of Fort Vancouver's construction see Ross Cox, *The Columbia River*, ed. Edgar I. Stewert and Jane R. Stewert (Norman: University of Oklahoma Press, 1957).
73. Leonard A. Wrinch, "The Formation of the Puget's Sound Agricultural Company," *Washington Historical Quarterly* 24 (1933): 3-8.

74. Major John S. Hatheway, *Frontier Soldier: The Letters of Maj. John S. Hatheway, 1833–1853*, ed. Ted Van Arsdol (Vancouver, WA: Vancouver National Historic Reserve Trust, 1999), 118.
75. Nathaniel J. Wyeth, "The First American Invaders: Nathaniel J. Wyeth's Journal, October 29, 1832," in *America's Frontier Story: A Documentary History of Westward Expansion*, ed. Martin Ridge and Ray Allen Billington (New York: Holt, Rinehart and Winston, 1969), 445; McLoughlin, *Dr. John McLoughlin*, 47-48.
76. Ross, *Adventures 2*, 168.

CONCLUSION

1. Robert Griffing, *The Artwork of Robert Griffing: His Journey into the Eastern Frontier* (Stow, NY: Paramount Press, 2003).
2. Red Jacket, "Red Jacket Lectures a Missionary, 1828," in *Major Problems in American Indian History*, ed. Albert L. Hurtado and Peter Iverson (Lexington, MA: D. C. Heath, 1994), 94.

Bibliography

PRIMARY SOURCES

Benavides, Fray Alonso de. *A Harvest of Reluctant Souls: The Memorial of Fray Alonso de Benavides, 1630*. Translated and edited by Baker H. Morrow. Niwot: University of Colorado Press, 1996.

———. *The Memorial of Fray Alonso De Benavides, 1630*. Translated by Edward E. Ayer. Chicago: privately printed, 1916.

Bogaert, Harmen Meyndertsz van den. *A Journey into Mohawk and Oneida Country, 1634–1635: The Journal of Harmen Meyndertsz van den Bogaert*. Edited and translated by Charles T. Gehring and William A. Strana. Syracuse, NY: Syracuse University Press, 1988.

Bonnecamps, Father. "Account of the Voyage on the Beautiful River Made in 1749." In *The Jesuit Relations and Allied Documents*. Vol. 69. Edited by Reuben Gold Thwaites. Cleveland: Burrows Brothers, 1900.

———. "Bonnecamps' Journal." In *The Jesuit Relations and Allied Documents*. Vol. 69. Edited by Reuben Gold Thwaites. Cleveland: Burrows Brothers, 1900.

Bougainville, Louis Antoine de. *Adventures in the Wilderness: The American Journals of Louis Antoine de Bougainville, 1756–1760*. Edited and translated by Edward P. Hamilton. Norman: University of Oklahoma Press, 1964.

Bouquet, Henry. *The Papers of Henry Bouquet*. Vols. 1-5. Edited by Donald H. Kent, Louis M. Waddell, and Autumn L. Leonard. Harrisburg, PA: Pennsylvania Historical and Museum Commission, 1976.

Castaneda, Pedro de. "The Narrative of the Expedition of Coronado." In *Original Narratives of Early American History: Spanish Explorers in the Southern United States, 1528–1543*. Edited by Frederick W. Hodge and T. H. Lewis, 285-384. New York: Barnes and Noble, 1907; repr. 1970.

———. "Pedro de Castaneda Recalls the March to Cibola, 1540." In *Revealing America: Image and Imagination in the Exploration of North America*. Edited by James P. Ronda. Lexington, MA: D. C. Heath, 1996.

———. "Relacion de la jornada de Cibola." In "The Coronado Expedition," *Fourteenth Annual Report*, Bureau of Ethnology, Smithsonian Institution, 1892–1893. Vol. 1. Washington, DC: Government Printing Office, 1896: 329-613.

Celoron, Monsieur de. *Expedition of Celoron to the Ohio Country in 1749.* Edited by C. B. Galbreath. Columbus. OH: F. J. Heer Printing, 1921.

Champlain, Samuel de. *The Works of Samuel de Champlain.* Vols. 1-6. Edited by H. P. Biggar. Toronto: Champlain Society, 1922–1936.

"Charter of the West India Company, June 3, 1621." In *Van Rensselaer Bowier Manuscripts.* Translated and edited by A. J. F. van Laer. Albany: University of the State of New York, 1908: 87-116.

Clark, William. *Original Journals of the Lewis and Clark Expedition, 1804–1806.* Vol. 3. Edited by Reuben Gold Thwaites. New York: Dodd, Mead, 1905.

Colden, Cadwallader. *The History of the Five Indian Nations: Depending on the Province of New York in America.* Ithaca, NY: Great Seal Books, 1958, originally printed in 1727.

Coues, Elliot, ed. *New Light on the Early History of the Greater Northwest: The Manuscript Journals of Alexander Henry and of David Thompson.* Vols. 1-2. Minneapolis: Ross and Haines, 1965.

Cox, Ross. *Adventures on the Columbia River.* New York: J&J Harper, 1832.

———. *The Columbia River.* Edited by Edgar I. Stewert and Jane R. Stewert. Norman: University of Oklahoma Press, 1957.

Croghan, George. "An Account of the Proceedings of George Croghan, Esquire, and Mr. Andrew Montour at Ohio, 1751." In *Minuetes of the Provincial Council of Pennsylvania, from the Organization to the Termination of the Proprietary Government.* Vol. 5, 530-540. Harrisburg: Theo. Fenn, 1851. Accessed April 21, 2020. https://babel.hathitrust.org/cgi/pt?id=wu.89066118753&view=1up&seq=562.

———. "George Croghan's Journal, April 3, 1759 to April 30, 1763." *Pennsylvania Magazine of History and Biography* 71 (1947): 313-444.

———. "Proceedings of George Croghan, Esquire, and Mr. Andrew Montour at Ohio, in the Execution of the Governor's Instructions to Deliver the Provincial Present to the Several Tribes of Indians Settled There." In *Early Western Journals, 1748–1765.* Vol. 1. Edited by Reuben Gold Thwaites, 58-69. Lewisburg, PA: Wennawoods Publishing, 1998.

———. "A Selection of Letters and Journals Relating to Tours Into the Western Country." In *Early Western Travels, 1748–1846.* Vol. 1. Edited by Reuben Gold Thwaites, 53-57. Lewisburg, PA: Wennawoods Publishing, 1998.

Dahlinger, Charles W. *The Marquis Duquesne Sieur de Menneville: Founder of the City of Pittsburgh.* Pittsburgh: Historical Society of Western Pennsylvania, 1932.

Denton, Daniel. *A Brief Description of New York Formerly Called New Netherlands.* New York: W. Gowans, 1845.

Dinwiddie, Robert. *The Official Records of Robert Dinwiddie.* 2 vols. Edited by R. A. Brock. Richmond: Virginia Historical Society, 1883.

Documents Relating to New Netherland, 1624–1626. San Marino, CA: Henry E. Huntington Library and Art Gallery, 1924.

Donck, Adriaen van der. *A Description of New Netherland.* Translated by Diederick William Goedhuys. Faerie Glen, South Africa: D.W. Goedhuys, 1992.

———. *Description of the New Netherlands*. Translated by Jeremiah Johnson. Wisconsin Historical Society Digital Library and Archives, 2003. American Journeys Collection. Accessed April 11, 2020. https://americanjourneys.org/aj-096/index.asp.

Forbes, John. *Writings of General John Forbes*. Edited by Alfred Proctor James. Menasha, WI: Collegiate Press, 1938.

Franchere, Gabriel. *Adventure at Astoria, 1810–1814*. Edited and translated by Hoyt C. Franchere. Norman: University of Oklahoma Press, 1967.

———. *A Voyage to the Northwest Coast of America*. Edited by Milo Milton Quaife. New York: Citadel Press, 1968.

Gallegos, Hernan. "Relation of the Chamuscado-Rodriguez Expedition." In *The Rediscovery of New Mexico*. Edited by George P. Hammond. Albuquerque: University of New Mexico Press, 1966.

Garbarino, Merwyn S., and Robert F. Sasso. *Native American Heritage*. 3rd ed. Prospect Heights, IL: Waveland Press, 1994.

Gist, Christopher. *Christopher Gist's Journals*. Edited by William M. Darlington. New York: Argonaut, 1966.

———. "A Journal of Christopher Gist's Journey." In *George Mercer Papers*. Edited by Lois Mulkearn, 97-139. Pittsburgh: University of Pittsburgh Press, 1954.

Gist, Thomas. "Thomas Gist's Indian Captivity." Edited by Howard H. Peckham. *Pennsylvania Magazine of History and Biography* 80, no. 3 (July 1956): 285-311. Accessed April 20, 2020. https://eps.cc.ysu.edu:2251/stable/pdf/20088873.pdf?ab_segments=0%252Fbasic_SYC-5152%252Fcontrol&refreqid=excelsior%3A151f83c851f996e4f77e2f867cecae6f.

Hackett, Charles Wilson, ed. and trans. *Historical Documents Relating to New Mexico, Nueva Vizcaya, and Approaches Thereto, to 1773*. Vol. 3. Washington, DC: Carnegie Institution of Washington, 1937.

Hammond, George P., ed. *The Rediscovery of New Mexico*. Albuquerque: University of New Mexico Press, 1966.

Hammond, George P., and Agapito Rey, eds. *Don Juan de Oñate: Colonizer of New Mexico, 1595–1628*. 2 vols. Albuquerque: University of New Mexico Press, 1953.

Harvey, Henry. *History of the Shawnee Indians*. Cincinnati: Ephraim Morgan & Sons, 1855.

Hatheway, Major John S. *Frontier Soldier: The Letters of Maj. John S. Hatheway, 1833–1853*. Edited by Ted Van Arsdol. Vancouver, WA: Vancouver National Historic Reserve Trust, 1999.

Hazard, Samuel, ed. *Colonial Records of Pennsylvania*. Vol. 5. Philadelphia: Joseph Severns, 1860.

———. *Minuetes of the Provincial Council of Pennsylvania, from the Organization to the Termination of the Proprietary Government*. Vols. 3-8. Philadelphia: Joseph Severns, 1860.

———. *Pennsylvania Archives*. 1st ser. Vols. 1-4. Philadelphia: Joseph Severns, 1852.

Holm, Thomas Campanius. *Description of the Province of New Sweden: Now called by the English Pennsylvania in America*. Edited by Peter S. Du Ponceau. Philadelphia: M'Carty & Davis, 1834.

Huey, Paul R. "Aspects of Continuity and Change in Colonial Dutch Material Culture at Fort Orange, 1624–1664." PhD diss., University of Pennsylvania, 1988.

Irving, Washington. *Astoria: Or Anecdotes of an Enterprise beyond the Rocky Mountains*. Edited by Edgeley W. Todd. Norman: University of Oklahoma Press, 1964.

Jameson, J. Franklin, ed. *Narratives of New Netherland, 1609–1664*. Washington, DC: Scribner & Sons, 1909; New York: Barnes and Noble, 1937.

Jogues, Father Isaac. "Novum Belgium, By Father Issac Jogues 1646." In *Narratives of New Netherland, 1609–1664*. Edited by J. Franklin Jameson, 259-263. Washington, DC: Scribner & Sons, 1909; New York: Barnes and Noble, 1937.

Johansen, Dorothy O. *Empire of the Columbia: A History of the Pacific Northwest*. New York: Harper & Row, 1967.

Johnson, Sir William. *The Papers of Sir William Johnson*. Vol. 10. Edited by James Sullivan. Albany: University of the State of New York, 1921–1965.

Juet, Robert. "From 'The Third Voyage of Master Henry Hudson,' By Robert Juet, 1610." In *Narratives of New Netherland, 1609–1664*. Edited by J. Franklin Jameson, 29-58. Washington, DC: Scribner & Sons, 1909; New York: Barnes and Noble, 1937.

Kenny, James. "Journal of James Kenny, 1759." In *Pen Pictures of Early Western Pennsylvania*. Edited by John W. Harpster. Pittsburgh: University of Pittsburgh Press, 1938.

———. "Journal of James Kenny, 1761–1763." Edited by John W. Jordan. *Pennsylvania Magazine of History and Biography* 37, no. 1 (1913): 1-47. Accessed April 22, 2020. https://ia801700.us.archive.org/11/items/jstor-20085624/20085624.pdf.

———. "Journal to ye Westward, 1758–1759." Edited by John W. Jordan. *Pennsylvania Magazine of History and Biography* 37, no. 4 (1913): 395-449.

Knaut, Andrew L. *The Pueblo Revolt of 1680: Conquest Resistance in Seventeenth Century New Mexico*. Norman: University of Oklahoma Press, 1995.

Laer, A. J. F. van, trans. and ed. *Minutes of the Court of Fort Orange and Beverwyck, 1652–1656*. Vols. 1-2. Albany: University of the State of New York, 1920.

———. *Van Rensselaer Bowier Manuscripts*. Albany: University of the State of New York, 1908.

Laet, Johan de. "From the 'New World,' 1625, 1630, 1633, 1640." In *Narratives of New Netherland, 1609–1664*. Edited by J. Franklin Jameson, 29-58. Washington, DC: Scribner & Sons, 1909; New York: Barnes and Noble, 1937.

Lewis, Meriwether. *Original Journals of the Lewis and Clark Expedition, 1804–1806*. Vol. 3. Edited by Reuben Gold Thwaites. New York: Dodd, Mead, 1905.

Lewis, Meriwether, and William Clark. *The Journals of Lewis and Clark*. Edited by John Bakeless. New York: Mentor, 1964.

McDougall, Duncan. "Journal: Commencing Septr. 6th 1810, Ending 18th April 1812." In *Annals of Astoria: The Headquarters Log of the Pacific Fur Company on the Columbia River, 1811–1813*. Edited by Robert F. Jones. New York: Fordham University Press, 1999.

McLoughlin, John. *Dr. John McLoughlin: Master of Vancouver Father of Oregon*. Edited by Nancy Wilson and Bert Webber. Medford, OR: Webb Research Group, 1994.

Mercer, George. *George Mercer Papers*. Edited by Lois Mulkearn. Pittsburgh: University of Pittsburgh Press, 1954.

Merrell, James H. *Into the American Woods: Negotiators on the Pennsylvania Frontier*. New York: W. W. Norton, 1999.

Meteren, Emanuel van. "On Hudson's Voyage, 1610." In *Narratives of New Netherland, 1609–1664*. Edited by J. Franklin Jameson, 6-9. Washington, DC: Scribner & Sons, 1909; New York: Barnes and Noble, 1937.

Michaelius, Jonas. "Letter of Reverend Jonas Michaelius, 1628." In *Narratives of New Netherland, 1609–1664*. Edited by J. Franklin Jameson, 122-133. Washington, DC: Scribner & Sons, 1909; New York: Barnes and Noble, 1937.

"Narrative of a Journey into the Mohawk and Oneida Country, 1634–1635." In *Narratives of New Netherland, 1609–1664*. Edited by J. Franklin Jameson, 135-180. Washington, DC: Scribner & Sons, 1909; New York: Barnes and Noble, 1937.

O'Callaghan, E. B., ed. *Documentary History of the State of New York*. Vols. 1-4. Albany: Weed, Parsons, 1849–1851.

———. *Documents Relative to the Colonial History of the State of New York*. Vols. 1-15. Albany: Weed, Parsons, 1853-1887.

———. *The Register of New Netherland, 1626–1674*. Albany: J. Munsell, 1865. Office of the Secretary of State. *First Census of the United States*. Philadelphia: Childs and Swaine, 1791.

Oñate, Juan de. *Juan de Oñate Recounts His Journey to the Great Plains, 1601*. In *Revealing America: Image and Imagination in the Exploration of North America*. Edited by James P. Ronda. Lexington, MA: D. C. Heath, 1996.

Parker, Reverend Samuel. *Journal of an Exploring Tour beyond the Rocky Mountains*. Minneapolis: Ross & Haines, 1967.

Post, Charles Frederick. "Two Journals of Western Tours, October 25, 1758–January 10, 1759." In *Early Western Travels*. Vol. 1. Edited by Reuben Gold Thwaites. Lewisburg, PA: Wennawoods Publishing, 1998.

Rasieres, Isaack de. "Letter of Issack de Rasieres to Samuel Blommaert, 1628 (?)." In *Narratives of New Netherland, 1609–1664*. Edited by J. Franklin Jameson, 99-115. Washington, DC: Scribner & Sons, 1909; New York: Barnes and Noble, 1937.

Raymonds, Charles de. *On the Eave of the Conquest: The Chevalier De Raymonds Critique of New France in 1754*. Edited and translated by Joseph L. Peyser. East Lansing: Michigan State University Press, 1997.

Rink, Oliver A. *Holland on the Hudson: An Economic and Social History of Dutch New York*. Ithaca, NY: Cornell University Press, 1986.

Ross, Alexander. *Adventures of the First Settlers on the Columbia River*. Ann Arbor, MI: University Microfilms, 1966.

———. *Adventures of the First Settlers on the Oregon or Columbia River*. Edited by Milo Milton Quaife. Chicago: Lakeside Press, 1923.

———. *The Fur Hunters of the Far West*. Edited by Kenneth A. Spaulding. Norman: University of Oklahoma Press, 1956.

Saint-Pierre, Jacques de. *Jacques Legardeur De Saint-Pierre: Officer, Gentleman, Entrepreneur*. Edited and translated by Joseph L. Peyser. East Lansing: Michigan State University Press, 1996.

Scholes, Frank V. "Royal Treasury Records Relating to the Province of New Mexico, 1596-1683." *New Mexico Historical Review* 50, nos. 1 and 2 (1975): 5-23, 139-165.

Schroeder, Albert H., and Dan S. Matson. *A Colony on the Move: Gaspar de Sosa's Journal, 1590–1591*. Salt Lake City: Alphabet Printing, 1965.

Smith, James. *Scoouwa: James Smith's Indian Captivity Narrative*. Edited by John J. Barsotti. Columbus: Ohio Historical Society, 1978.

Sosa, Gaspar Castaño de. "Castaño de Sosa's 'Memoria.'" In *The Rediscovery of New Mexico*. Edited by George Hammond. Albuquerque: University of New Mexico Press, 1966.

Spencer, Oliver. *The Indian Captivity of O. M. Spencer*. Edited by Milo Milton Quaife. Chicago: Lakeside Press, 1917.

Stuart, Robert. *On the Oregon Trail: Robert Stuart's Journey of Discovery*. Edited by Kenneth A. Spaulding. Norman: University of Oklahoma Press, 1953.

Thompson, David. *David Thompson's Narrative of his Explorations in Western America, 1784–1812*. Edited by J. B. Tyrrell. Toronto: Champlain Society, 1916.

"The Treaty of Logg's Town, 1752. Commission, Instructions, &c., Journal of Virginia Commissioners, and Text of Treaty." Accessed April 12, 2020. https://www.jstor.org/stable/4242735?seq=1#metadata_info_tab_contents.

Trent, William. "Trent's Journal." In *History of Colonel Henry Bouquet and the Western Frontiers of Pennsylvania, 1747–1764*. Edited by Mary Carson Darlington. Privately published, 1920.

Trowbridge, C. C. "Shawnese Traditions." In *Michigan University Museum of Anthropology*. Edited by Vernon Kinietz and Erminie W. Voegelin. Ann Arbor: University of Michigan Press, 1939.

Vaca, Álvar Núñez Cabeza de. "Álvar Núñez Cabeza de Vaca's Journey across America, 1528–1536." In *Revealing America: Image and Imagination in the Exploration of North America.* Edited by James P. Ronda, 47-54. Lexington, MA: D. C. Heath, 1996.

———. "The Narrative of Cabeza de Vaca." In *Spanish Explorers in the Southern United States, 1528–1543: Original Narratives of Early American History*. Edited by Frederick W. Hodge, 1-123. New York: Barnes and Noble, 1971.

Valverde, Don Francisco de. "Inquiry Concerning the New Provinces in the North, 1602." In *Don Juan de Oñate: Colonizer of New Mexico, 1595–1628*. Edited by George P. Hammond and Agapito Rey. Albuquerque: University of New Mexico Press, 1953.

———. "Investigation of Conditions in New Mexico, 1601." In *Don Juan de Oñate: Colonizer of New Mexico, 1595–1628.* Edited by George P. Hammond and Agapito Rey, vol. 6, 623-669. Albuquerque: University of New Mexico Press, 1953.

Vargas, Don Diego de. *Blood on the Boulders: The Journals of Don Diego de Vargas, 1692–1694*. Edited by John L. Kessell, Rick Hendricks, and Meredith Dodge. Albuquerque: University of New Mexico Press, 1998.

———. *The Disturbances Cease: The Journals of Don Diego de Vargas, 1697–1700*. Edited by John L. Kessell, Rick Hendricks, and Meredith Dodge. Albuquerque: University of New Mexico Press, 2000.

———. *First Expedition of Vargas into New Mexico, 1692*. Edited and translated by J. Manuel Espinosa. Albuquerque: University of New Mexico Press, 1940.

———. *The Royal Crown Restored: The Journals of Don Diego Vargas, New Mexico, 1692–1694*. Edited by John L. Kessell, Rick Hendricks, and Meredith Dodge. Albuquerque: University of New Mexico Press, 1995.

Vries, David de. "From the 'Korte Historiael ende Journaels Aenteyckeninge,' 1633–1643 (1655). In *Narratives of New Netherland, 1609–1664*. Edited by J. Franklin Jameson, 181-234. Washington, DC: Scribner & Sons, 1909; New York: Barnes and Noble, 1937.

Washington, George. *The Journal of Major George Washington*. Edited by. J. Christian Bay. Iowa: Torch, 1955.

———. *The Writings of George Washington*. Vol. 1, 1745–1756. Edited by John C. Fitzpatrick. Washington, DC: Government Printing Office, 1931.

Wassenaer, Nicolaes van. "From the 'Historish Verhael,' by Nicolaes van Wassenaer, 1624-1630." In *Narratives of New Netherland, 1609–1664*. Edited by J. Franklin Jameson, 67-96. Washington, DC: Scribner & Sons, 1909; New York: Barnes and Noble, 1937.

Weise, Arthur James. *The History of the City of Albany, New York: From the Discovery of the Great River in 1524 by Verrazzano, to the Present Time*. Albany: E. H. Bender, 1884.

Weiser, Conrad. "The Journal of Conrad Weiser." In *Minuetes of the Provincial Council of Pennsylvania, from the Organization to the Termination of the Proprietary Government*. Vol. 5. Edited by Samuel Hazard. Philadelphia: Joseph Severns, 1860.

Wyeth, Nathaniel J. "The First American Invaders: Nathaniel J. Wyeth's Journal, October 29, 1832." In *America's Frontier Story: A Documentary History of Westward Expansion*. Edited by Martin Ridge and Ray Allen Billington. New York: Holt, Rinehart and Winston, 1969.

Zeisberger, David. *Diary of David Zeisberger*. Vols. 1-2. Edited by Eugene F. Bliss. Cincinnati: Robert Clarke, 1885, repr. 1972.

SECONDARY SOURCES

Adelman, Jeremy, and Stephen Aron, eds. "From Borderlands to Borders: Empires, Nation-States, and the Peoples in Between in North American History." *American Historical Review* 104, no. 3 (1999): 814-841.

Alford, Thomas Wildcat. *Civilization*. Norman: University of Oklahoma Press, 1936.

American Military History. Army Historical Series. Washington, DC: Government Printing Office, 1969.

Anderson, Fred. *Crucible of War: The Seven Years' War and the Fate of Empire in British North America, 1754–1766*. New York: Alfred A. Knopf, 2000.

Aquila, Richard. *The Iroquois Restoration*. Detroit: Wayne State University Press, 1983.

Axtell, James. *The European and the Indian*. Oxford and New York: Oxford University Press, 1981.

———. *The Invasion Within: The Contest of Cultures in Colonial North America*. New York: Oxford University Press, 1985.

Bachman, Van Cleaf. *Peltries or Plantations: The Economic Policies of the Dutch West India Company in New Netherland, 1623–1639*. Baltimore: Johns Hopkins University Press, 1969.

Bannon, John Francis. *The Spanish Borderlands Frontier, 1531–1821*. New York: Holt, Rinehart and Winston, 1970.

Barnett, H. G. "The Nature of the Potlatch." *American Anthropologist* 40, no. 3 (1938): 349-358.

Barrett, Elinore M. *Conquest and Catastrophe: Changing Rio Grande Pueblo Settlement Patterns in the Sixteenth and Seventeenth Centuries*. Albuquerque: University of New Mexico Press, 2002.

Bloom, Lansing B. "A Glimpse of New Mexico in 1620." *New Mexico Historical Review* 3, no. 4 (October 1928).

———. "When Was Santa Fe Founded?" *New Mexico Historical Review* 4, no. 2 (April 1929).

Bowen, William A. *The Willamette Valley: Migration and Settlement on the Oregon Frontier*. Seattle: University of Washington Press, 1978.

Brecher, Frank W. *Losing a Continent: France's North American Policy, 1753–1763*. Westport, CT: Greenwood, 1998.

Brown, Judith K. "Economic Organization and the Position of Women among the Iroquois." *Ethnohistory* 17, no. 3/4 (1970): 151-167.

Cayton, Andrew R. L., and Fredrika J. Teute. *Contact Points: American Frontiers from the Mohawk Valley to the Mississippi, 1750–1830*. Chapel Hill: University of North Carolina Press, 1998.

Cheal, David, "Moral Economy." In *The Gift: An Interdisciplinary Perspective*. Edited by Aafke E. Komter. Amsterdam: Amsterdam University Press, 1996.

Clark, Jerry E. *The Shawnee*. Lexington: University Press of Kentucky, 1993.

Collier, Jane. *Marriage and Inequality in Classless Societies*. Stanford, CA: Stanford University Press, 1988.

Condon, Thomas J. *New York Beginnings: The Commercial Origins of New Netherland*. New York: New York University Press, 1968.

Craig, Neville B., ed. *The Olden Time*. Vols. 1-2. Pittsburgh: Dumars, 1846.

Cronon, William. *Changes in the Land*. New York: Hill and Wang, 1983.

Curtis, Edward S. *The North American Indian*. Edited by Frederick Webb House. Vol. 8. New York: Johnson Reprint. 1911.

Darlington, Mary Carson, ed. *History of Colonel Henry Bouquet and the Western Frontiers of Pennsylvania, 1747–1764*. Privately printed, 1920.

Diamond, Jared. *Guns, Germs, and Steel: The Fates of Human Societies*. New York: W. W. Norton, 1999.

Dickason, Olive P. *Canada's First Nations*. Norman: University of Oklahoma Press, 1992.

Donehoo, George P. *Indian Villages and Place Names in Pennsylvania*. Harrisburg, PA: Telegraph Press, 1928.

Dowd, Gregory E. *A Spirited Resistance*. Baltimore: Johns Hopkins University Press, 1992.

Downes, Randolph C. *Council Fires of the Upper Ohio*. Pittsburgh: University of Pittsburgh Press, 1940.

Dozier, Edward P. *The Pueblo Indians of North America*. New York: Holt, Rinehart and Winston, 1970.

Drucker, Philip. *Indians of the Northwest Coast*. New York: McGraw-Hill, 1963.

———. "Rank, Wealth, and Kinship in Northwest Coast Society." *American Anthropologist* 41, no. 1 (January-March 1939): 55-65.

Druke, Mary A. "Iroquois Treaties: Common Forms, Varying Interpretations." In *The History and Culture of Iroquois Diplomacy*. Edited by Francis Jennings. New York: Syracuse University Press, 1985.

Dunn, Shirley W. *The Mohicans and Their Land, 1609–1730*. Fleischmanns, NY: Purple Mountain Press, 1994.

Earle, Timothy. "The Evolution of Chiefdoms." In *Chiefdoms: Power, Economy and Ideology*. Edited by Timothy Earle. Cambridge: Cambridge University Press, 1991.

———. *How Chiefs Come to Power: The Political Economy in Prehistory*. Stanford, CA: Stanford University Press, 1997.

Edmunds, R. David. *American Indian Leaders: Studies in Diversity*. Lincoln: University of Nebraska Press, 1980.

Elliot, T. C. "The Journal of the Ship Ruby." *Oregon Historical Quarterly* 28, no. 3, (September 1927): 258-280.

Everdell, William R. *The End of Kings: A History of Republics and Republicans*. New York: Free Press, 1983.

Fixico, Donald L. "Methodologies in Reconstructing Native American History." In *Rethinking American Indian History*. Albuquerque: University of New Mexico Press, 1997.

———, ed. *Rethinking American Indian History*. Albuquerque: University of New Mexico Press, 1997.

Fleming, George T. *History of Pittsburgh and Environs*. New York: American Historical Society, 1922.

Folkerts, Jan. "Kiliaen van Rensselaer and Agricultural Productivity in His Domain: A New Look at the First Patroon and Rensselaerswijk Before 1664." In *A Beautiful and Fruitful Place: Selected Rensselaerswijk Seminar Papers*. Edited by Nancy Zeller, 295-308. Albany: New Netherland Publishing, 1991. Accessed April 11, 2020. https://www.newnetherlandinstitute.org/files/9513/5067/3660/9.1.pdf.

Forbes, Jack D. *Frontiers in American History and the Role of the Frontier Historian*. Desert Research Institute, 21. Reno: University of Nevada, 1966.

Fried, Morton H. *The Evolution of Political Society: An Essay in Political Anthropology*. New York: Random House, 1967.

———. *The Notion of Tribe*. Menlo Park, CA: Cummings, 1975.

Gannett, Henry. *Statistical Atlas of the United States 1900*. Washington: US Census Office, 1903.

Gehring, Charles T. "The Dutch among the People of the Long River." In *Annals of New Netherland* (2001). Accessed April 11, 2020. https://www.newnetherlandinstitute.org/files/8015/3816/0796/2001.pdf.

———. "The Essays of A. J. F. van Laer." In *Annals of New Netherland* (1999). Accessed April 11, 2020. https://www.newnetherlandinstitute.org/files/ 1213/5067/2997/1999.pdf.

———. "Privatizing Colonization: The Patroonship of Renselaerswijck." In *Annals of New Netherland* (2000). Accessed April 11, 2020. https://www.newnetherlandinstitute.org/files/3713/5067/2997/2000.pdf.

Genovese, Eugene D. "Scholar Spearheads New Historical Society to Reshape the Profession." Interview by Courtney Leatherman. *Chronicle of Higher Education* (March 20, 1998): A12-A13.

Griffin-Pierce, Trudy. *Native Peoples of the Southwest.* Albuquerque: University of New Mexico Press, 2000.

Griffing, Robert. *The Artwork of Robert Griffing: His Journey into the Eastern Frontier.* Stow, NY: Paramount Press, 2003.

Gunnerson, James H. "Apaches at Pecos." In *Pecos: Gateway to Pueblos and Plains: The Anthology.* Edited by John V. Bezy and Joseph P. Sanchez, 40-44. Tucson, AZ: Southwest Parks and Monuments Association, 1988.

Gutierrez, Ramon A. *When Jesus Came, the Corn Mothers Went Away: Marriage, Sexuality, and Power in New Mexico, 1500–1846.* Stanford, CA: Stanford University Press, 1991.

Hamalainen, Pekka. "The Shapes of Power: Indians, Europeans, and North American Worlds from the Seventeenth to the Nineteenth Century." In *Contested Spaces of Early America.* Edited by Juliana Barr and Edward Countryman. Philadelphia: University of Pennsylvania Press, 2014.

Hanna, Charles A. *The Wilderness Trail: The Ventures and Adventures of the Pennsylvania Traders on the Allegheny Path.* 2 vols. New York and London: G. P. Putnam's Sons, Knickerbocker Press, 1911.

Harper, Frank C. *Pittsburgh: Forge of the Universe.* New York: Comet Press Books, 1957.

Harper, Rob. "The Politics of Coalition Building in the Ohio Valley, 1765–1774." In *Borderland Narrratives: Negation and Accommodation in North America's Contested Spaces, 1500–1850.* Edited by Andrew K. Frank and A. Glenn Crothers. Gainesville: University Press of Florida, 2017.

Hart, Simon. *The Prehistory of the New Netherland Company: Amsterdam Notarial Records of the First Dutch Voyages to the Hudson.* Amsterdam, Netherlands: City of Amsterdam Press, 1959.

Heckewelder, John. *History, Manners, and Customs of the Indian Nations Who Once Inhabited Pennsylvania and Neighboring States.* Philadelphia: Historical Society of Pennsylvania, 1876; repr., New York: Arno, 1971.

———. "Indian Tradition of the First Arrival of the Dutch at Manhattan Island, Now New York." *Collections of the New York Historical Society.* 2nd ser. Vol. 1. New York: New York Historical Society, 1841.

Hodge, Frederick W., ed. *Handbook of American Indians North of Mexico.* Washington, DC: Government Printing Office, 1912.

Holman, Frederick V. *Dr. John McLoughlin: The Father of Oregon*. Cleveland: Arthur H. Clark, 1907.

Holmberg, Allan R. *Nomads of the Long Bow: The Siriono of Eastern Bolivia*. Washington, DC: Smithsonian Institution Press, 1950.

Howard, James H. *Shawnee*. Athens: Ohio University Press, 1981.

Huey, Paul R. "The Archeology of Fort Orange and Beverwijck." In *A Beautiful and Fruitful Place: Selected Rensselaerswijk Seminar Papers*. Edited by Nancy Zeller. Albany: New Netherland Publishing, 1991.

———. "Aspects of Continuity and Change in Colonial Dutch Material Culture at Fort Orange, 1624–1664." PhD diss., University of Pennsylvania, 1988.

Hulbert, Archer Butler, and William Nathaniel Schwarze, eds. *David Zeisberger's History of Northern American Indians*. Columbus, OH: F. J. Heer Printing, 1910.

Hunt, Donald H. *The French Invasion of Western Pennsylvania, 1753*. Harrisburg, PA: Pennsylvania Historical and Museum Commission, 1954.

Hunt, George T. *Wars of the Iroquois: A Study in Intertribal Trade Relations*. Madison: University of Wisconsin Press, 1960.

Hunter, William A. *Forts on the Pennsylvania Frontier, 1753–1758*. Harrisburg, PA: Pennsylvania Historical and Museum Commission, 1960.

Hussey, John A. *The History of Fort Vancouver and Its Physical Structure*. Tacoma, WA: Washington State Historical Society, 1957.

Jennings, Francis. *The Ambiguous Iroquois Empire: The Covenant Chain Confederation of Indian Tribes with English Colonies from Its Beginnings to the Lancaster Treaty of 1744*. New York: W. W. Norton, 1984.

———. *The History and Culture of Iroquois Diplomacy*. New York: Syracuse University Press, 1985.

———. *The Invasion of America: Indians, Colonialism, and the Cant of Conquest*. New York: W. W. Norton, 1976.

Jones, Oakah L., Jr. *Pueblo Warriors and Spanish Conquest*. Norman: University of Oklahoma Press, 1966.

Josephy, Alvin M., Jr. *The Patriot Chiefs: A Chronicle of American Indian Leadership*. New York: Viking Press, 1961.

Kehoe, Alice Beck. *America before the European Invasions*. New York: Longman, 2002.

Kessell, John L. *Kiva, Cross, and Crown: The Pecos Indians and New Mexico, 1540–1840*. Tucson, AZ: Western National Parks Association, courtesy University of New Mexico Press, 1987.

———. "The Ways and Words of the Other: Diego de Vargas and Cultural Brokers in Late Seventeenth-Century New Mexico." In *Between Indian and White Worlds: Cultural Brokers*. Edited by Margaret Connell Szasz, 25-34. Norman: University of Oklahoma Press, 1994.

Kidder, Alfred. *An Introduction to the Study of Southwestern Archaeology*. New Haven, CT: Yale University Press, 1924.

Komter, Aafke E. "Women, Gifts and Power." In *The Gift: An Interdisciplinary Perspective*. Edited by Aafke E. Komter. Amsterdam: Amsterdam University Press, 1996.

———, ed. *The Gift: An Interdisciplinary Perspective.* Amsterdam: Amsterdam University Press, 1996.

Kraft, Herbert C. *The Lenape.* Newark: New Jersey Historical Society, 1986.

Laramie, Michael G. *King William's War: The First Contest for North America, 1689–1697.* Yardley, PA: Westholme Publishing, 2017.

Levine, Frances. *Our Prayers Are in This Place: Pecos Pueblo Identity over the Centuries.* Albuquerque: University of New Mexico Press, 1999.

Levi-Strauss, Claude. "The Principle of Reciprocity." In *The Gift: An Interdisciplinary Perspective.* Edited by Aafke E. Komter. Amsterdam: Amsterdam University Press, 1996.

Lewis, Kenneth. *The American Frontier: An Archaeological Study of Settlement Pattern and Process.* Orlando, FL: Academic Press, 1984.

Lewis, Thomas A. *For King and Country: George Washington, the Early Years.* New York: John Wiley & Sons, 1993.

Liebmann, Matthew, Robert Preucel, and Joseph Aguilar. "The Pueblo World Transformed: Alliances, Factionalism, and Animosities in the Northern Rio Grande, 1680–1700." In *New Mexico and the Pimería Alta: The Colonial Period in the American Southwest.* Edited by John G. Douglass and William M. Graves, 143-56. Boulder: University Press of Colorado, 2017. Accessed April 10, 2020. www.jstor.org/stable/j.ctt1mmftg6.12.

Lupold, Harry Forrest. *The Forgotten People.* Hicksville, NY: Exposition Press, 1975.

MacKenzie, Cecil W. *Donald MacKenzie: King of the Northwest.* Los Angeles: Ivan Beach Jr., 1937.

Mackie, Richard. *Trading beyond the Mountains.* Vancouver: UBC Press, 1997.

Malinowski, Bronislaw. "The Principle of Give and Take." In *The Gift: An Interdisciplinary Perspective.* Edited by Aafke E. Komter. Amsterdam: Amsterdam University Press, 1996.

Marshe, Witham. *Lancaster in 1744: Journal of the Treaty at Lancaster in 1744 with the Six Nations.* Lancaster, PA: New Era Steam and Book Print, 1884.

McConnell, Michael N. *A Country Between: The Upper Ohio Valley and Its Peoples, 1724–1774.* Lincoln: University of Nebraska Press, 1992.

———. "Peoples 'In Between': The Iroquois and the Ohio Indians, 1720–1768." In *Beyond the Covenant Chain: The Iroquois and Their Neighbors in Indian North America, 1600–1800.* Edited by Daniel K. Richter and James H. Merrell, 93-112. New York: Syracuse University Press, 1987.

Miller, J. "Old Religion among the Delawares: The Gamwing (Big House Rite)." *Ethnohistory* 44, no. 1 (Winter 1997): 113-134.

Mills, Lisa A. "Mitochondrial DNA Analysis of the Ohio Hopewell of the Hopewell Mound Group." PhD diss., Ohio State University, 2003.

Morgan, Lewis H. *Ancient Society.* Cambridge, MA: Belknap Press of Harvard University Press, 1964.

———. *League of the Ho-de-no-sau-nee or Iroquois.* Edited by Herbert M. Lloyd. New York: Dodd, Mead, 1966.

Mulkearn, Lois, and Edwin V. Pugh. *The Traveler's Guide to Historic Western Pennsylvania*. Pittsburgh: University of Pittsburgh Press, 1954.
Myers, Albert Cook, ed. *Narratives of Early Pennsylvania, West New Jersey, and Delaware, 1630–1707*. New York, 1912.
Nash, Roderick. *Wilderness and the American Mind*. 3rd ed. New Haven, CT: Yale University Press, 1982.
Newcomb, William W., Jr. "The Culture and Acculturation of the Delaware Indians." *Michigan Museum of Anthropology: Anthropological Papers* 10. Ann Arbor: University of Michigan, 1956.
Nissenson, S. G. *The Patroon's Domain*. New York: Octagon, 1973.
Nordby, Larry. "The Prehistory of the Pecos Indians." In *Pecos Ruins*. Edited by David Grant Noble. Santa Fe, NM: Ancient City Press, 1993.
O'Callaghan, E. B. *History of New Netherland; or, New York Under the Dutch*. Vols. 1–2. New York: D. Appleton, 1846.
O'Meara, Walter. *Guns at the Forks*. Englewood Cliffs, NJ: Prentice-Hall, 1965.
Otto, Paul A. "New Netherland Frontier: Europeans and Native Americans along the Lower Hudson River, 1524–1664." PhD diss., Indiana University, 1995.
Polanyi, Karl. *The Great Transformation*. Boston: Beacon Press, 1957.
Prescott, J. R. V. *The Geography of Frontiers and Boundaries*. Chicago: Aldine, Price, 1965.
Pritzker, Barry M. *A Native American Encyclopedia: History, Culture and Peoples*. New York: Oxford University Press, 2000.
Radford, John P. "Testing the Model of the Pre-industrial City: The Case of Ante-Bellum Charleston, South Carolina." *Transactions of the Institute of British Geographers*, New Series 41, no. 3 (1979): 392-410.
Rasor, Ann. "Pecos Pueblo." In *Pecos: Gateway to Pueblos & Plains*. Edited by John V. Bezy and Joseph P. Sanchez, 32-39. Tucson, AZ: Southwest Parks and Monuments Association, 1988.
Red Jacket. "Red Jacket Lectures a Missionary, 1828." In *Major Problems in American Indian History*. Edited by Albert L. Hurtado and Peter Iverson, 93-95. Lexington, MA: D. C. Heath, 1994.
Richardson, John. "Deed of Concession, 28 December 1822." In "Seigneurie de Beauharnois." Transcribed by Burton Lang. Accessed April 12, 2020. http://www.rootsweb.com/~qcchatea/sarault/sample.htm.
Richter, Daniel K. *Facing East from Indian Country: A Native History of Early America*. Cambridge, MA: Harvard University Press, 2001.
———. *The Ordeal of the Longhouse: The Peoples of the Iroquois League in the Era of European Colonization*. Chapel Hill: University of North Carolina Press, 1992.
Richter, Daniel K., and James H. Merrell, eds. *Beyond the Covenant Chain*. New York: Syracuse University Press, 1987.
Ronda, James P. *Astoria and Empire*. Lincoln: University of Nebraska Press, 1990.
———. *Lewis and Clark among the Indians*. Lincoln: University of Nebraska Press, 1984.

———. *Revealing America: Image and Imagination in the Exploration of North America*. Edited by James P. Ronda. Lexington, MA: D. C. Heath, 1996.

Rothschild, Nan A. *Colonial Encounters in a Native American Landscape: The Spanish and Dutch in North America*. Washington, DC: Smithsonian Books, 2003.

Ruby, Robert H., and John A. Brown. *The Chinook Indians: Traders of the Lower Columbia*. Norman: University of Oklahoma Press, 1976.

Ruttenber, E. M. *History of the Indian Tribes of Hudson's Bay*. Port Washington, NY: Kennikat Press, 1872.

Sahlins, Marshall. *Stone Age Economics*. Chicago: Aldine-Atherton, 1972.

Sanchez, Joseph P. "Pecos in the Eighteenth Century." In *Pecos: Gateway to Pueblos and Plains: The Anthology*. Edited by John V. Bezy and Joseph P. Sanchez, 68-75. Tucson, AZ: Southwest Parks and Monuments Association, 1988.

Santee, J. F. "Comcomly and the Chinooks." *Oregon Historical Quarterly* 33, no. 3 (September 1932): 271-278.

Scholes, France V. *Church and State in New Mexico, 1610–1650*. Albuquerque: University of New Mexico Press, 1937.

Schoolcraft, Henry R. *Notes on the Iroquois*. Albany: Erastus H. Pease, 1847.

Schroeder, Albert H. "Pecos Pueblo." In *Handbook of North American Indians*. Vol. 9. Edited by Alfonso Ortiz. Washington, DC: Smithsonian Institution, 1979.

Shannon, Timothy J. "Dressing for Success on the Mohawk Frontier: Hendrick, William Johnson, and the Indian Fashion." *William and Mary Quarterly* 53, no. 1 (1996): 13-42.

Simmons, Marc. "Settlement Patterns and Village Plans in Colonial New Mexico." In *New Spain's Far Northern Frontier: Essays on Spain in the American West, 1540–1821*. Edited by David J. Weber. Albuquerque: University of New Mexico Press, 1979.

Sipe, C. Hale. *Fort Ligonier and Its Times*. Harrisburg, PA: Telegraph Press, 1932.

———. *The Indian Chiefs of Pennsylvania*. Baltimore: Wennawoods Publishing, 1995.

———. *The Indian Wars of Pennsylvania*. Harrisburg, PA: Telegraph Press, 1929.

Sjoberg, Gideon. "The Preindustrial City." *American Journal of Sociology* 60, no. 5 (1955): 439-441.

———. *The Preindustrial City: Past and Present*. Glencoe, IL: Free Press, 1960.

Snow, Dean R. *The Iroquois*. Cambridge, MA: Blackwell, 1994.

Steckley, John. "The Clans and Phratries of the Huron." Accessed April 9, 2020. https://www.ontarioarchaeology.org/Resources/Publications/oa37-3-steckley.pdf.

Steele, Ian K. *Warpaths: Invasions of North America*. New York: Oxford University Press, 1994.

Stevens, S. K., and Donald H. Kent, eds. *Wilderness Chronicles of Northwestern Pennsylvania*. Harrisburg, PA: Commonwealth of Pennsylvania, Dept. of Public Instruction, Pennsylvania Historical Commission, 1941.

Stotz, Charles M. *Outposts of the War for Empire*. Pittsburgh: University of Pittsburgh Press, 1985.

Strana, William A. "Seventeenth Century Dutch-Indian Trade: A Perspective from Iroquoia." In *A Beautiful and Fruitful Place: Selected Rensselaerswijk Seminar Papers.* Edited by Nancy Zeller, 243-249. Albany: New Netherland Publishing, 1991.

Todish, Timothy J. *America's First First World War.* Grand Rapids, MI: Suagothel Productions, 1982.

Tooker, Elisabeth. "Northern Iroquoian Sociopolitical Organization." *American Anthropologist* 72, no. 1 (February1970): 90-97.

Trelease, Allen W. *Indian Affairs in Colonial New York: The Seventeenth Century.* Port Washington, NY: Kennikat Press, 1971.

Trigger, Bruce G. *The Children of Aataentsic: A History of the Huron People to 1660.* Quebec: MGill-Queen's University Press, 1987.

———. *The Huron: Farmers of the North.* 2nd ed. Chicago: Holt, Rinehart and Winston, 1990.

———. "The Mohawk-Mahican War, 1624–1628: The Establishment of a Pattern." *Canadian Historical Review* 52, no. 3 (September1971): 276-286.

Turner, Frederick Jackson. *The Frontier in American History.* New York: Holt, 1920.

———. "The Significance of the Frontier in American History." In *Does the Frontier Experience Make America Exceptional?* Edited by Richard W. Etulain. Boston and New York: Bedford/St. Martin's, 1999.

Thwaites, Reuben Gold. *Early Western Travels, 1748–1846.* Vols. 1-2 and 19. Cleveland: Arthur Clark, 1904.

———. *Early Western Travels, 1748–1846.* Vol. 1. Lewisburg, PA: Wennawoods Publishing, 1998.

Volwiler, Albert T. *George Croghan and the Westward Movement, 1741–1782.* Cleveland: Arthur H. Clark, 1926.

Waddell, Louis M., and Bruce D. Bomberger. *The French and Indian War in Pennsylvania, 1753–1754: Fortification and Struggle during the War for Empire.* Harrisburg, PA: Pennsylvania Historical and Museum Commission, 1996.

Wade, Richard C. *The Urban Frontier: Pioneer Life in Early Pittsburgh, Cincinnati, Lexington, Louisville, and St. Louis.* Cambridge, MA: Harvard University Press, 1959.

Waldman, Carl. *Atlas of the North American Indian.* New York: Facts on File, 1985.

Walker, Bryce, and Jill Maynard, eds. *Through Indian Eyes: The Untold Story of Native American Peoples.* Pleasantville, NY: Reader's Digest Association, 1995.

Wallace, Anthony F. C. *King of the Delawares: Teedyuschung 1700–1763.* Philadelphia: University of Pennsylvania Press, 1949.

Wallace, Paul A. *Conrad Weiser: Friend of Colonist and Mohawk.* Philadelphia: Oxford University Press, 1945.

———. "Indian Highways of Pennsylvania." *Pennsylvania Archaeologist* 23, nos. 3-4 (December 1953): 111-122.

———. *Indians in Pennsylvania.* Harrisburg, PA: Pennsylvania Historical and Museum Commission, 1964.

Walton, Joseph S. *Conrad Weiser and the Indian Policy of Colonial Pennsylvania.* Philadelphia: George W. Jacobs, 1900.

Weatherford, Jack. *Native Roots*. New York: Fawcett Columbine, 1991.

Weber, David J. *The Spanish Frontier in North America*. New Haven, CT: Yale University Press, 1992.

Weslager, C. A. *The Delaware Indians*. New Brunswick, NJ: Rutgers University Press, 1972.

———. *The Delaware Indian Westward Migration*. Wallingford, PA: Middle Atlantic Press, 1978.

White, Richard. *It's Your Misfortune and None of My Own: A New History of the American West*. Norman: University of Oklahoma Press, 1991.

———. *The Middle Ground: Indians, Empires, and Republics in the Great Lakes Region, 1650–1815*. Cambridge: Cambridge University Press, 1991.

Wood, Neal. *Foundations of Political Economy*. Berkeley: University of California Press, 1994.

Woodcock, George. *Peoples of the Coast: The Indians of the Pacific Northwest*. Bloomington: Indiana University Press, 1977.

Wrinch, Leonard A. "The Formation of the Puget's Sound Agricultural Company." *Washington Historical Quarterly* 24, no. 1 (January1933): 3-8.

Zeller, Nancy, ed. *A Beautiful and Fruitful Place: Selected Rensselaerswijk Seminar Papers*. Albany: New Netherland Publishing, 1991.

Acknowledgments

No individual is solely responsible for the successes and accomplishments of their life. They are the sum of all the experiences and people who shape them and support them. In my fifty-three years of life, I have many people to thank for the shaping of my personality, character, and values, which have led me to the successful completion of this work.

First off, I must thank the people who are the center of my universe and the foundation of rock for this straw man: my wife and our three sons Joseph, Nathan, and Joshua. Without their constant support, sacrifice, and devotion, this project would never have been completed. Second, I must thank my parents and siblings and cousin Ray "Tiger" Moore. No words could express the amount of gratitude that I feel for this wonderful group of people who have guided me throughout my life. Third, I must thank my mentors who never lost faith in me, supported me when others doubted, and who provided me with the guidance and insight to shape the thesis of this work—Don Critchlow, Tom Curran, Saul Friedman, Martha Pallante, Michal Rozbicki, Fred Viehe, and John White. Lastly, I would like to thank those who supported this project in other ways—Col. Robert Doughty, Lt. Col. Stephen Arata, Heather Bishof, and my colleagues in the Department of History at the United States Military Academy, as well as all of the fine soldiers I served with in over twenty years of service, my dearest friends Shawn, Kenny, Dave, and my buckskinning brothers and sisters who fostered my love of history.

Index